ANTIQUES
& COLLECTIBLES

ELTING MEMORIAL LIBRARY ··· NEW PALTZ, N.Y.

Ex Libris

GIVEN BY

WILLIAM HEIDGERD

IN MEMORY OF HIS MOTHER

THE
OFFICIAL®
1989 PRICE GUIDE
TO ANTIQUES
& COLLECTIBLES

FROM THE EDITORS OF THE HOUSE OF COLLECTIBLES

Consulting Editors
Charles and Donna Jordan

54,836

NINTH EDITION

The House of Collectibles
New York, New York 10022

Important Notice. The format of *The Official Price Guide Series,* published by the *House of Collectibles,* is based on the following proprietary features: *All facts and prices are compiled through a nationwide sampling of information* obtained from noteworthy experts, auction houses, and specialized dealers. *Detailed "indexed" format* enables quick retrieval of information for positive identification. *Encapsulated histories* precede each category to acquaint the collector with the specific traits that are peculiar to that area of collecting.

All of the information, including valuations, in this book has been compiled from the most reliable sources, and every effort has been made to eliminate errors and questionable data. Nevertheless, the possibility of error, in a work of such immense scope, always exists. The publisher will not be held responsible for losses which may occur in the purchase, sale, or other transaction of items because of information contained herein. Readers who feel they have discovered errors are invited to *write* and inform us, so they may be corrected in subsequent editions. Those seeking further information on the topics covered in this book are advised to refer to the complete line of *Official Price Guides* published by the House of Collectibles.

Published by: The House of Collectibles
201 East 50th Street
New York, New York 10022

Distributed by Ballantine Books, a division of Random House, Inc., New York and simultaneously in Canada by Random House of Canada Limited, Toronto.

Manufactured in the United States of America

Library of Congress Catalog Card Number: 84-642991

ISBN: 0-876-37755-X

10 9 8 7 6 5 4 3 2 1

Contents

Acknowledgments

The editors would like to thank the many dealers, organizations, and auction houses that have provided the listings, photographs, and general information that serve as the foundation for this year's annual. Without them, our task would indeed have been impossible.

Frank H. Boos Gallery, Bloomfield Hills, Michigan
Butterfield & Butterfield, San Francisco
Christie, Manson & Woods, New York
Christie's East, New York
Bowers and Merena, Wolfeboro, New Hampshire
Robert W. Skinner, Inc., Bolton, Massachusetts
Collector's Bookstore, Hollywood, California
Sotheby's, New York
Phillips Son & Neale, New York
The Classic Car Club of America, Chicago
Buttonwood Galleries
National Association of Brewiana Collectors
Stein's Antiques
Old Newspaper and Map Mail Auction
Pen Fancier's Club

We would also like to extend our deepest appreciation to our contributors, whose interest and affection for their hobbies have inspired countless collectors across the country. (See "Credits" at the back of this book.)

Finally, we would like to thank Galina Kolev and Scotia Jordan for their help in the preparation of the final manuscript.

Market Review

Record-breaking sales galore: That's how one can best sum up 1987. With money flowing freely and collectors and personal property owners seeing the time as ideal to move prospective hot items into the marketplace, the late 1980s are seeing a dizzying series of records that have become almost routine.

This was the year that a painting fetched the incredible sum of $39.85 million.* This was also the year that records were established in such diverse fields as early needlework, carousel animals, animation celluloids, and American furniture. Meanwhile, an unpublished series of photos of Marilyn Monroe at the start of her career sold for $23,120.

The Official 1989 Price Guide to Antiques and Collectibles begins by taking readers on a walk through some of the most memorable sales of the year, against a backdrop of some of the world's most prestigious auction galleries. It is ironic to remember that the items detailed were never designed to fetch the remarkable prices they have achieved. For the vast majority of collectors, however, these sorts of sales are auxiliary to the key reason people collect: for the

*After we went to press, Van Gogh's *Irises* surpassed all expectations by selling at Sotheby's for over $50 million—clear evidence that the stock market crash of October did not hurt the buying power of some people.

1

fun of it. And as this year's edition shows, what we collect "for the fun of it" has grown to include more categories of interest than ever before.

AMERICANA

Americana has long been a staple in the world of collecting. Diversity is the key word when it comes to this ever-growing field, which runs the gamut from handcrafted quilts to wooden tools. In nearly every major general auction held in this country one can expect to find lots representing one form of Americana or another. And in most cases this year the articles were snapped up as soon as the bidding began.

Americana sales have garnered their share of the headlines lately. A Hampton Falls, New Hampshire, resident made collecting headlines in January 1986 by becoming the first person in collecting history to pay over $1 million for a piece of American furniture. The same collector was back in the news one year later when he topped all previous records in American textile collecting by paying $187,000 for a piece of needlework. (The previous record in this field, $121,000, was paid at a Sotheby's auction for a sampler done in 1791 and signed by twelve-year-old Mary Russell of Marblehead, Massachusetts.)

The new record-breaking needlework picture was sold at a Christie's auction in January 1987. It depicts a hunt set against a pastoral landscape of farmhouses and grazing cattle. The needlework was signed "Mary Flower, 1768" in cross-stitch on its lower border. Christie's had set the pre-sale value on this piece at $10,000 to $15,000 in their auction catalog.

Other notable records were set at the same auction, particularly in the area of early American furniture. A Philadelphia Chippendale side chair of carved mahogany brought $341,000. The chair, made for Charles Thompson, secretary of the Continental Congress during the American Revolution, dates from the 1765–1780 period. A Queen Anne side chair that sold at Christie's in 1983 held the previous record price, selling for $275,000.

CAROUSELS AND CIRCUS MEMORABILIA

Giant leaps were made in the world of circus memorabilia over the past year. As has often been the case in this decade, the Big Show and all of the romance associated with its place in American history captured the imagination and pocketbooks of serious collectors looking for something flamboyant to add to their collections. Traditional circus memorabilia (posters, toys, programs, and other small souvenirs) are suddenly sharing the spotlight increasingly with the hardware and actual trappings of the circus. Carousel figures, fairground displays, and booths are turning in remarkable figures when brought up for auction, with the largest area of growth mainly in the field of carved circus figures.

The May 2, 1987, carousel extravaganza auction by Phillips provided several new world's records. A rare Charles Looff greyhound carousel figure, retaining its original paint, sold for $59,400. The figure, carved around 1895, featured the original rosettes and etched, star-mirrored jewels. The seventy-seven lots of Looff animals on the bill turned out to be the big attractions at the auction. A Looff stander horse (circa 1895) realized $22,000, and an outsider jumper (from 1900) went for $17,600.

Other American carousel carvers also fared well at the auction. One of the rarest Charles Dare carvings, a sea horse circa the 1890s, went for $22,000. A zebra carved by Gustav Dentzel (circa 1895) sold for $25,300. A rare camel jumper fetched $16,500, and a Dentzel prancing goat (an outside-row jumper circa 1890, 66 inches long and 68 inches high, with a fur face and double eagle back saddle) sold for $15,000.

The Phillips auction proved to be a showcase not only for American carvers; European artists fared equally well. A Bayol donkey that featured a nodding head and was made about 1905 in France went for $8,300. A Bayol rabbit, also French and of 1900 vintage, went for the same amount. A German Heyn figure, a rare carved elephant (circa 1911), went over the block for $14,300.

With prices in the carousel collectors' market continuing to rise, as vividly indicated by these prices, carousel figures have proved themselves to be permanent investments and a strong fixture in the collecting world.

DECOYS

Decoy collecting has become so popular over the past two years that decoy prices have soared to almost ten times what they were in the previous decade.

The James D. Julia–Gary Guyette, Inc., auction, held on April 23 and 24, 1987, in conjunction with the National Antique Decoy Show in St. Charles, Illinois, stands as one of the biggest decoy events of the year. Carvings by Elmer Crowell made significantly strong showings. A black-breasted plover brought $49,500, a running yellowleg went for $20,350, and two golden plovers brought in $9,000 each.

Bidding was heavy for an extremely rare Canadian goose. The decoy by Sam Soper went for $34,100. A black duck decoy by Ben Holmes of Stratford, Connecticut, sold for $25,850. Canadian decoys sold for high prices this year as well. A decoy by Ken Anger of Ontario went for $4,100. The mallard hen carved figure set a new world record for Anger decoys. A Quebec wood duck drake sold for $2,600, and a pair of decoys by Tom Chambers of Toronto went for $2,925.

With figures such as the $25,300 paid for a pair of "Shang" Wheeler redheads occurring more commonly, collectors are becoming aware of the serious investments to be made in the world of decoy collecting.

DOLLS

Of the thousands of collecting fields in the world today, few can rival the tremendous popularity of the doll market. There are numerous periodicals available that are dedicated to doll collecting, many organizations and fan clubs, and an abundance of auctions at any given time.

The September 1987 Theriault auction held in Los Angeles brought in top dollars in the doll field, proving once and for all that there is a healthy doll market in America today.

Mad Hatter, the Duchess, and the Frogman from the "Alice In Wonderland" set, made by Martha Chase around the turn of the century, sold for $20,000, thus establishing a new world's record for Chase dolls. It is interesting to note that the fee was more than four times the scale the consignor had received before the actual sale.

In London, in September 1987, a rare English William and Mary doll was whisked off for the amazing price of $43,500. Even though the wooden doll was missing all of its toes and two fingers from each hand, it went for that sum simply because its head turns—a rare feature among the dolls of that period.

The antique doll market is not the only aspect of this field to continue to bring in hefty prices and sound investments. Limited editions are continually being made, and they sell at a rapid rate. Offerings in 1987 included one that brought back Charles Dana Gibson's Gibson Girl, a doll based on the celebrated illustrator's turn-of-the-century creation. It is offered by Franklin Heirloom Dolls and retails for $195. This figure will most certainly escalate in value because these are the first authorized Gibson dolls made, and there is considerable collector interest in Gibson's work.

Jacqueline Beaulieu Creations of Stamford, Connecticut, offered the Art Deco–style doll of the year. Entitled "Melodie" and selling for $495, only five hundred of these dolls (clad in a remarkable costume consisting of thirty thousand beads) were made. These are but two of the hundreds of limited-edition dolls that have joined their antique ancestors in the collecting ranks during the past year. These additions spell a healthy outlook for doll collecting in the years ahead.

MOTION PICTURE MEMORABILIA

America's love affair with the silver screen shows no sign of abating. For over seventy-five years America has supported and adored the stars, the producers, the studios, the movies, the awards, the glamour, and the tragedy that have been a part of the celluloid kingdom. Film buffs worldwide continue to collect the artifacts of cinematography—posters, stills, promotional items, and thousands of other products associated with the movie industry. Prices have yet to stabilize in this incredibly volatile field, as the figures achieved for cinemabilia in 1987 bear witness.

The reigning goddess of the 1950s, Marilyn Monroe, was once again under the floodlights, when articles of her clothing sold for high, high prices. The jumpsuit, made of sapphire-blue velvet with a plunging V-neckline, worn by Miss Monroe in the 1953 classic film *Gentlemen Prefer Blondes* was sold to a Swedish collector by Christie's East of New York for $1,980. (A beautiful beaded ivory gown worn by Jeannette MacDonald in the 1937 film *Firefly* went for the same price.)

Monroe made the headlines again when a series of twenty-five images of the late actress were sold for $23,130. The pictures, all but two of them transparencies, were taken by an army photographer in 1945. David Conover, the photographer, had been under the command of one Ronald Reagan, who wanted promotional pictures of women involved in war work. Miss Monroe was at the time working for the Radiophone Corporation under the name of Norma Jean Dogherty. What was unusual about the prints was that some fifteen of them had never before been published. All twenty-five were sold, along with their copyright.

Animation was another area where the auction world again reflected collector interest. At a Guernsey's auction held May 29–31, 1987, animated Disney cels caused heavy bidding. Two cels from *Snow White and the Seven Dwarfs* went for $5,500 and $3,850, respectively.

A Phillips auction on April 11, 1987, drew enthusiastic bids from art and movie collectors alike. Outstanding prices were realized for just about every lot up for bid. A key cel gouache to a watercolored master background cel of "Captain Hook Aboard His Ship with Full Crew" (taken from the 1953 movie *Peter Pan*) went for an astonishing $17,000 (with a buyer's premium added on). A scene from *Pinocchio* entitled "Figaro the Cat Goes Fishing in the Belly of the Whale" sold for $14,300. Items from the film *Alice in Wonderland* sold for $17,600.

Posters also did well at the Guernsey auction, where a six-sheet poster for the Humphrey Bogart classic *Casablanca* sold for $17,600. This shattered the previous Guernsey record of over $13,000 paid for a *King Kong* poster. A six-sheet poster for the classic James Cagney film *Yankee Doodle Dandy* sold for $3,300. Substantial prices on all movie memorabilia fronts reveal that the power and the magic that is Hollywood seemingly never dim.

NEWS HIGHLIGHTS

A tale of big money and deception involved stamp collecting—combined with political intrigue. Eighty-six rare and misprinted stamps, allegedly sold illegally by CIA employees, are reputed to be worth millions of dollars. The story involves some four hundred stamps with a face value of $1 that had been printed upside down by the U.S. Post Office. The stamps depict a candleholder and a lighted candle. The silhouette of the candle and the halo of its flame were printed upside down, thus creating a million-dollar error. The search for the remaining stamps became one of the most intensified stamp hunts in America. An investigation, launched by the Bureau of Engraving and Printing, discovered that nine CIA employees, realizing the worth of these stamps, had sold eighty-five of them, given away one torn one, and kept nine for themselves. One Connecticut stamp dealer claims to have paid nearly $1 million for the rare stamps. If they were sold in one bulk, each stamp would be worth between $25,000 and $30,000 apiece, spelling a net worth of $10 million to $12 million for the entire group.

With news like this, it is little wonder that stamp collecting interest is riding a crest. The average price of stamps, based on the stamp collector's index for the top fifty stamps, has increased by roughly 7.5 percent over a year's time.

Not all of the news in the collecting world concerned theft and forgery. The auction world continued to bring in astonishing profits and set the trend for a variety of collecting fields. Perhaps no report received more coverage in the press than the amazing prices paid for paintings by the Impressionist artist Vincent Van Gogh. The prices realized by these paintings sent waves of shock through the art community.

The first painting, entitled *Sunflowers* and completed in 1888, was sold to a Japanese insurance company. The event brought the world's record for any painting ever sold, the nearly unimaginable sum of $39.85 million, at Christie's auction house in London. Estimated at $15 million, the actual bidding took less than five minutes, with the sales price including more than $3 million in commission fees. This is all made ironic when one considers that Van Gogh had originally hoped to receive $125 for the painting.

On June 29, 1987, yet another Van Gogh, entitled *The*

Bridge at Trinquetaille, went for the second-highest price ever paid for a painting when the gavel came down at $20.2 million. (The final bid for the painting was $18.4 million, with a 10 percent commission fee charged to the buyer.) The painting, completed in 1888, was sold in a little over a minute.

The star among the bevy of record prices, Van Gogh, was born in 1853 and lived on the handouts of his brother Theo, an art dealer. Upon discovering stacks of his unsold paintings safely hidden at his brother's house, Van Gogh (realizing he was existing on his brother's charity and not his own artistic merit) shot himself to death at the age of 37.

On May 29, 1987, Christie's set further records with the sale of a bust of Thomas Jefferson sculpted by Jean Antoine Houdon in 1789. The image, considered to be the definitive likeness of the third president, was used as a model for Jefferson's profile on the American nickel. It went for the staggering price of $2.86 million.

And the Royal Family was back in the swing of it all this year during the auctioning of the Duchess of Windsor's jewels. The collection, sold by Sotheby's in Geneva, went for a total value of $50.3 million, almost seven times more than its estimated presale value.

Butterfield and Butterfield, the San Francisco–based auction house, saw unexpected high prices in its June 1987 auction. Tiffany glassware fared particularly well. A rare bronze ball lamp went for $37,000. The forty-six lots of Flora Danica all sold, many far outselling their presale estimates. One lot, comprising twelve dinner plates, fetched $8,250.

Among the more unusual sale items that did well at the Butterfield and Butterfield auction were gentlemen's vintage wristwatches. A Rolex Prince watch sold for $4,950; a rectangular watch by Patek Philippe and a Rolex Oyster perpetual each commanded $4,675. An enameled pendant manufactured by Cartier sold for $7,700; and big sales in ladies' antique jewelry rounded out the sale, which saw a convertible cultured pearl necklace land $16,500.

Joining the ranks of unusual items brought before auction-goers were the curios sold by Onslow's Auctioneers pertaining to the *Titanic.* The 46,000-ton luxury liner struck an iceberg and sank on April 15, 1912, claiming more than fifteen hundred lives. The recent discovery and controversial salvage of the ship off the shores of Newfoundland have rejuvenated interest in the liner. None of the items sold was part of the salvage but rather items associated with the famous liner, as well as a few previous items saved by passengers fleeing the ship.

The Ulster Folk and Transport Museum of Belfast, Northern Ireland, where the ship was built, paid $5,280 for a collection of carbon copies, on official forms, of radio messages sent out and received by the ocean liner *Olympic* in the vicinity of the disaster. Among these were the papers with the first words of the impending disaster, a message sent at 11 P.M., New York time, that read: "We have struck an iceberg."

The total sum of the sale items was $198,320. The French and American crew that retrieved items from the ocean bottom in 1987, by the way, have vowed not to sell any of the memorabilia but will, rather, exhibit them at select museums around the globe.

The world of teddy bear collecting continued on its upward climb, with the biggest demand centering on German bears, circa early twentieth century. A plush white German Steiff bear now holds the record by selling for approximately $15,000 at a Sotheby's auction in 1987. The bear, circa 1913, beat out the former record set only a mere three months earlier. (The previous record had been $8,560 for a 1904 Steiff bear.) A bear similar to the record breaker went for $9,860.

With high-priced auctions combined with the dream of making the great find, one thing is sure about the year ahead: With all those collectors around, records will continue to be broken.

Building a Collection

Virtually every type of item offers the possibility of being the first of a collection and landing to a hobby that can last a lifetime. All of those listed in this book, as obscure or remote as some may appear, have had just that effect on many people. And there are numerous others—hundreds, in fact—that space limitations prevent us from covering.

Collecting need not be expensive. And it need not be time-consuming if you don't want it to be. This depends on you and on what you want from your hobby. The goals and motives of collectors are diverse. Some collectors receive most of their pleasure and satisfaction from seeing their collection grow. Others enjoy the hunt—tracking down hard-to-find items and following their trail wherever it leads. To them, browsing for three hours in a crowded antique shop and leaving with dust-laden hands and clothing is exhilarating. Still others enjoy collecting because it leads to meeting other collectors and widening their circle of friends and social activities.

Your selection of a collecting interest depends on finances, space, and other considerations but mainly on your own personal tastes and inclinations. It's largely a matter of what you'll be most comfortable with. Looking through this book will provide a kaleidoscope of suggestions. While you're pondering what to collect, here are some points to consider. Most areas of collecting can be pursued inexpensively and adapted to fit just about any budget. But this is not, unfortunately, true of *every* type of collectible. You cannot collect Tiffany lamps or Currier & Ives lithographs without spending rather substantial amounts of money. This has nothing to do with the size or scope of the particular hobby. Competition is a factor in price, but so is availability. There are millions of coin and stamp collectors, yet the vast majority of stamps and coins are inexpensive. These are hobbies in which great rarities exist alongside pieces that can be bought for a few pennies. Book collecting is another pursuit in which prices run from zero to lofty heights. Original art, antique furniture, and porcelain are others in that category (with plenty to choose from, pricewise). And there are some collecting areas in which the *most* valuable existing items are not expensive at all.

One thing you may want to consider is whether you'd like to collect objects that have a direct relationship to each other, such as sets. Set collecting can be done with material that was originally issued as a set (as in silverware) or that carries dates or numbers that permit set assembly (such as comic books or coins). A typical example of a set collection is a run of Lincoln cents, beginning with the earliest one, for 1909, and continuing up to the present. With this sort of collection, you always have a clear direction, and you will not lose sight of your purpose.

Another point to consider is whether you'd like to participate in a well-established hobby that is amply supplied with reference literature, clubs, and periodicals or would rather get in on the "ground floor" of a hobby that's just in the process of developing. There are pros and cons on both sides of the fence, so it becomes a matter of personal preference. With a well-established hobby, you receive the benefit of all of the work already done by the experts in terms of research, classification, and inquiry into fakes and counterfeits. On the other hand, items in such a group all carry an equally well established market value. Consequently, there is less chance of finding bargains or making any discoveries on your own. In a hobby that has not yet been well developed, you can make some really excellent buys (items that might be soaring skyward in value next year or five years from now), but they'll be somewhat harder to find and possibly more difficult to authenticate. If the hobby is really new, the dealers may not have had the chance to accumulate much knowledge and will hesitate to proclaim an item as "genuine" or "fake."

What it finally boils down to is this: What do you like? What do you enjoy owning, looking at, handling, and thinking about? For example, do you like detective shows on TV? You might be at home collecting first editions of detective novels or police memorabilia or old "wanted" posters.

Do you like pets? Many collections have been made of animal-motif items, such as porcelain dogs and cats or mechanical banks in the shape of animals.

Are you a travel enthusiast? Stamps, foreign bank notes, and coins can take you to faraway places.

Are you interested in cooking? There are old and scarce cookbooks to be collected, as well as the implements used by our forebears in cooking and eating.

In other words, just about anything that interests you can be turned into a hobby, even if you never thought about it from the standpoint of collecting. For sports fans, there are baseball and football cards, autographs, team equipment, yearbooks, and plenty of other collectibles. For the car buff, there are antique components (automobilia) rescued from vintage autos, as well as all kinds of automotive ephemera.

And what about your job? Are you ever curious about the way predecessors in your type of job worked fifty to a hundred years ago and the implements they used? Quite a few collectors are curious enough to become historians of their professions.

More doctors and dentists build collections around their profession than anyone else. In the hobbyist publications you will encounter many ads placed by doctors and dentists seeking to buy medical or dental memorabilia of yesteryear. These are ideal fields for collecting because the professions are very old, have well-documented histories, and have produced vast quantities of collectible items of every description. But these are by no means the only ones.

Condition

The condition of collector's items has become an important factor today, with collectors being more demanding regarding condition. For investors, condition is of great importance, since it has been shown that collector's items in the best grades of condition rise the most quickly in value.

Nearly all collector's items in well-preserved condition are rarer (and more expensive) than the *very same items* in lesser degrees of condition. This is because the majority of existing specimens are, almost invariably, in less than outstanding condition. With some items there may be one "mint" specimen in circulation for every ten showing signs of wear, use, or abuse. With others the ratio could be one to one hundred or even one thousand. It varies, of course, with the type of collectible and the age.

As a result, condition is a prime influence in buying or selling collector's items. Whether the beginning collector is really concerned about condition or not, he needs to learn something about it and its effect on prices. Otherwise he is likely to see bargains where they do not exist or accuse a seller of overpricing when a premium is being charged because of noteworthy condition. If you're bidding at auction sales, you must be even more alert to condition and the difference it makes in values.

No grading system fits all varieties of collector's items.

Each item has to be judged in terms of its material, age, the use for which it was intended, and other considerations. Something made as a household decoration to be hung on a wall and admired is in a much different category from that of a tool or cooking utensil. You would not expect a nineteenth-century sledgehammer to be free of any nicks and scratches.

Don't expect the impossible. But also don't settle for slipshod specimens of items that could have been much better preserved.

Fakes

In nearly all cases, fakes fall into one of the following categories:

1. *The outright fake.* This is what most people think of as fake, being unaware that other kinds exist. An outright fake is made wholly by the faker "from scratch." He obtains materials and uses his own processes to create the object, his goal being to defraud the eventual buyer.

2. *The honest reproduction.* These are multiplying in number. An honest reproduction is a facsimile of a collector's item made as a decoration, souvenir, curio, or for some other legitimate purpose without the intent to defraud. It is, however, sometimes mistaken for an original.

3. *The doctored item.* This is a genuine collector's item that has been changed in some way to make it appear more valuable, such as a coin on which a mintmark is removed or a silver porringer to which an inscription and date are added.

4. *The hybrid.* This is an object made from components of two or more collectors' items. Hybrids occur most frequently in furniture. To achieve this, someone will, for example, take two tables, one with good legs and

the other with a good top, and meld the well-preserved components.

Of these four categories of fakes, objects falling into the first (outright fakes) are automatically worthless, except for intrinsic value if they happen to contain precious metal.

Honest reproductions can, and usually do, have some value, but the value is considerably less than that of the model. There are occasional exceptions to this rule. When a reproduction is made in a deluxe manner, using the best materials and workmanship, it can be a desirable collector's item in itself, *possibly* of even greater value than the original. Some reproductions of antique firearms, for example, attain very high collector value.

Doctored items tend to be considered "spoiled" by collectors, even if they had substantial value originally. As for hybrids, these are very commonplace on the antiques market and are sold regularly. While the collector value or historical value of any hybrid is open to debate, there is definitely a good demand for them. They have the look of antiques and have utilitarian value if they are pieces of furniture; many noncollecting buyers will ask no further questions about them.

One of your chief weapons against buying fakes is to buy only from the more respected sources of supply. This advice makes obvious sense. Specialist dealers who handle just one type of collectible are likely to be knowledgeable on that type of collector's item. Because of their reputation for knowing their subject, specialist dealers are very seldom offered fakes for sale. Anyone who knowingly wants to sell a fake will, nine times in ten, take it to a general antiques dealer. This may mean a lower price, but the danger of detection is lower also, and that is what counts in such situations. The less careful and less knowledgeable the dealer is, the more careful and expert his customers must be.

Buying Tips

BUYING FROM DEALERS

There may be occasional problems or drawbacks in buying from dealers, but generally they serve a vital purpose. Most of the collecting hobbies covered in this book could not exist without professional dealers. They do the legwork for you in finding the material and bringing a large selection of it together for your perusal. They serve as a kind of buffer between you and the counterfeiters who manufacture bogus collectibles. Occasionally, fakes find their way onto dealer shelves; but without the dealers as a line of defense, things would be far worse. Dealers can be helpful to you in many ways. They have contacts within the trade that would be hard for a private hobbyist to duplicate. If they know exactly what type of item you're looking for, even if it's something very offbeat or scarce, they can usually find it for you.

There are basically two types of dealers in collector's items. The first is the general dealer. Most antiques dealers fall into that category. They offer a broad variety of collector's items as well as objects that could not be called collector's items but are decorative and interesting. The second type is the specialist dealer. He sells, primarily or exclusively, collector's items of a specific kind, such as stamps, comic books, or prints. Today there are specialist dealers for nearly every type of collectible. Naturally, the bigger hobbies have the most specialist dealers; thousands of dealers specialize in coins, for example, while only a handful restrict themselves to something like firefighting memorabilia. This is governed strictly by the degree of hobbyist activity and the amount of money being spent in each field. What are the basic differences in buying from a general dealer as opposed to buying from a specialist?

In general antiques dealers' shops, you will find many of the identical items offered by specialist dealers. There *is* a difference, however. The prices are usually a bit lower. When you buy from a general dealer, you will usually pay a lower price for the same item than if you acquired it from a specialist. The savings might be only 5 or 10 percent but could be as much as 50 percent.

The general dealer does not have as large a selection of specialist items. If you collect Depression glass, for example, the general dealer might have a dozen pieces—or perhaps none at all. A specialist dealer in glassware will be displaying hundreds of examples of Depression glass. The general antiques dealer does not, in most instances, profess to be an expert on everything in his stock. His wares represent a conglomeration of purchases from many different sources, and he offers them "as they come." Not all general antiques dealers fall into that category, as some deal in a higher grade of merchandise and have experts on their staff to appraise and identify incoming stock. In return for the opportunity to get a bargain, the responsibility falls on you, the customer, to decide whether an item is exactly what it appears to be.

The specialist dealer goes to great lengths and he inspects his merchandise more carefully. He has expert knowledge of his pet subject and a reputation within the field. There is very little likelihood that fakes, counterfeits, or restorations can slip by him.

Price Variations

These are the questions most often asked by beginners about buying in antique shops: How firm are the prices? What will happen if I make a counteroffer? Will the dealer be offended? Do I stand much chance of getting an item for less than the named price?

The situation is generally this: The dealer has a price in mind that he would *like* to get—a price that would cover his cost and leave a favorable margin of profit. It may be double the sum or even triple; this varies depending on the item and its nature and also his style and volume of business. A dealer will be more apt to show flexibility on a price if the item has been in stock for a considerable length of time. When stock is relatively new, the dealer holds out, hoping that it will sell for the full price he wishes to get. As time passes and it fails to sell, it becomes evident that the price may need to be adjusted. The waiting period before the price adjustment may be very short, as some dealers like to turn over their stock rapidly.

The term "reducing the price" is apt to be misleading. To determine whether the reduction results in a favorable buy, you would need to know if the *original* price was in line with the true market value. If a dealer prices something at $300, when the average market price is $200, he can reduce it by 20 percent and still be charging more than most of his competitors.

Dickering brings mixed reactions among dealers. Some dealers are insulted; some pretend to be insulted but aren't. Some welcome a no-holds-barred discussion about price because it gets the customer talking, and a talking customer is likely to end up buying. You're apt to get a more favorable reception by not drawing attention to flaws or taking an overly casual approach. The skilled bargainer always takes a positive attitude about the item under discussion. He never asks for a discount because the item isn't *exactly* what he wants. Rather, he acknowledges his interest in it and says something like: "If I could get this for fifty dollars, I wouldn't hesitate for a minute," or words to that effect. If you have experience at all with antique shops and their proprietors, you can usually tell when dickering will be successful and when it won't. If you and the owner are too far apart in price, it's just a waste of your time to get into believing that you can work the price down to half of the original sum. In most cases, a discount of 10 or 15 percent is the most you're going to get—because 10 percent off the price means at least 20 percent off the profit in most cases. There are many possible variations on approaches to bargaining. One novel method involves a collector who would browse around an antique shop until he found something he wanted, say a tin pelican priced at $30. He would pretend he hadn't seen the item, then casually ask the dealer, "Do you happen to have any tin pelicans at around twenty dollars?" This is a very effective approach because it establishes your price range before the dealer has a chance to establish his price range. It's a way of bargaining without appearing to be bargaining.

BUYING AT AUCTIONS

Auction buying is exciting and offers more opportunities for bargains than does buying from dealers. But it also carries somewhat greater risks. As a rule, auction buying is more suitable for the experienced collector. But there is no reason why a beginner, using caution and common sense, cannot attend auctions and try his luck in the competition.

If you buy at an auction, you are apt to be involved in bidding under a broad variety of circumstances. You will sometimes be bidding on a lot for which your maximum bid represents one-tenth of the sum another bidder is ready, willing, and able to pay. And you will frequently (or perhaps more so) come prepared to give a small fortune for an item that not a single other bidder wants. The price that something brings at an auction is not, therefore, an indication of its value but rather only of its value to the bidders in that particular sale. If sold again the next day, with different bidders on the floor, it could go considerably higher or lower.

If it sounds as though auction buying involves a substantial measure of uncertainty, it does indeed. But if you know the mechanics of auctions and have a relatively cool head and sound judgment about collector's items, you can do very well in the auction arena. The important thing is to keep a rein on your emotions and not overpay unless the item is something very special. Also important is to know what you're bidding on: if it's authentic, if it's in good condition, and whether it truly merits the size of the bid you intend to place.

If you're going to attend the sale, don't fail to attend the presale exhibition also. You can wander around the presale exhibit and see what catches your fancy. This is often time-consuming, and a better approach is to check off lots that appeal to you. Then at the presale exhibit you can go directly to them and spend your time giving each a thorough examination.

As you make your inspections, mark your bid limit for each item in the catalog. This is the time to think about price, not during the heat of the competition. At the presale exhibit you're not being influenced by the prices other bidders are willing to pay. You can make a much sounder judgment of how much you want the item and how much it's worth to you in dollars and cents.

Selling Tips

Many factors enter into the price you receive or the price you're offered when selling collectibles. Let's take a look at some of them:

1. Dealer's stock on hand. This, of course, varies from dealer to dealer and even among the same dealers at different times of the year. You are not in a position to know what kind of stock the dealer has on hand or what he has coming in, yet this does play a role in determining whether he'll be interested in purchasing your antiques and the extent of investment he cares to make in them. When a dealer says he's overstocked, this is not necessarily a ploy to induce you to accept a low price. All dealers do become overstocked periodically—and they become *understocked*, too. It all hinges on the pace at which material moves in and out, and that's governed largely by circumstances over which the dealer has only partial control. Sometimes he'll go for weeks without anyone offering to sell him anything. Then armies of sellers all arrive at the same time. This works fine if the volume and flow of buying is comparable to that of selling. But if the dealer has been buying more than he's been selling, he has no choice but to slow down for a while. No dealer likes to bypass the opportunity to buy worthwhile

22

merchandise, but he can't have more cash going out than coming in.

2. The dealer's clientele. Every dealer—whether he sells antiques, militaria, dolls, or whatever—has his own special group of customers who are the lifeblood of his business. Some of these customers are sure to be general collectors, but others are specialists, and the specialties of these clients can be very exclusive in some cases. An antiques dealer may have a customer who wants nothing but augers (old tools used to bore holes in wood). You could survey ninety-nine other antiques dealers and find no one who has customers for augers, but this particular dealer has one—and an avid one to boot. The customer possibly has one of the largest collections in the country. He wants to buy any and all specimens that he can find, regardless of size, shape, or color. Consequently, the dealer knows he can sell any augers that come into his stock. When an auger is offered to him, he automatically buys it, so his degree of risk is just about zero.

The type of item that a dealer displays in his shop may be a clue to those he's most interested in buying. Certainly, if you find an antiques shop whose stock consists mainly of glass, this would be a more likely place to sell a glassware collection than a general antique shop would be. But it does not always work that way. In the example given above, you would not find a single auger in the shop, even though its proprietor would rather buy them than anything else. Why? Because every one he purchases is sold immediately to his special customer without ever going on display in the shop. This is the situation with many kinds of merchandise in many collectors' shops. What you see displayed to the public is the general stock. Articles that have been bought for special clients aren't around any longer.

3. Geographical location. With some types of collector's items, the place of sale can be a factor in the price. Values given in this book are averages for the country as a whole. If an item has definite regional interest, it can be counted on to sell somewhat higher in that locality and usually a bit lower than the average elsewhere. More collector's items have regional interest than you might imagine, although it is not usually strong enough to influence the value by more than 10 percent or, at the most, 15 percent.

Certain collecting hobbies thrive a bit better in some parts of the country than in others for no explicable reason. This has been the case with knife collecting, to name one; it has been more popular in the southern states than elsewhere. In the earlier days of rock 'n' roll record collecting, nearly all collecting activity was confined to New York and California. Comic book collecting was a big hobby in New York long before it surfaced anywhere else.

4. Condition. It is an inescapable fact that when an item is worn, damaged, or otherwise not in the best of condition, it is not worth the full retail value. It may still be collectible and salable to a dealer, but it represents a kind of question mark for him. If the item is not in mint condition, he will automatically wonder how long it will take to sell and whether it will sell at all. Some dealers do not care to stock damaged or defective items. Others will do so in certain cases, but their buying offer will be considerably less than their offer for a mint or near-mint specimen—maybe just 10 percent of the retail value of a mint specimen or even less. If that seems unfair, you should stop to consider that the dealer is in a bind when he handles merchandise of this kind. He has to offer his customers a very healthy discount on it, possibly selling it for a third as much as a mint specimen. Therefore he can put very little money into it.

If you have a collection that is mostly in good condition but contains some defective items, it may be best to remove the defective items before offering it for sale. These sub-par components in a collection will always catch the dealer's eye and may give him a negative feeling toward the collection as a whole. When you then discuss price, the dealer is sure to point out the inferior condition of such items. Just like your garden, your collection may need weeding out before you can sell it. Put it in the best shape you can, and you'll stand an excellent chance of getting a satisfactory price for it.

SELLING BY AUCTION

Maybe you enjoy buying at an auction. Have you considered the possibility of selling your collection in the same fashion when the time comes?

Auction sales have become a much more popular method for selling all types of collector's items. The chief attraction of selling by auction is that you have the chance, with a little luck, of realizing more than a dealer would pay for your collection. A dealer has to resell the material, so of course he takes a deduction from its retail market value in figuring his purchase price. At auctions, the sky is the limit. If two or three determined bidders lock horns on something you own, they could drive the price up far beyond the retail market value. Even after the auctioneer's "house commission" is deducted from the selling price, you would end up doing better than selling outright to a dealer.

Of course, it doesn't always work that way. Auctions are unpredictable. Just as you have the opportunity at auction of realizing more than a dealer would pay, the possibility also exists that your collection will bring *less* than a dealer would have given. Those are the chances one takes in the auction game.

The best types of collections to sell by auction are those that are highly specialized and those containing a large proportion of investment items. But as you will see by attending auctions or just reading the reports of them, many collections are sold—thousands of them annually—that do not fall into either of these categories. Their owners chose the auction route when they could have sold to a dealer and received quicker payment.

There are all types of auctions, including posh sales of art and jewels, accompanied by lavish catalogs that serve as reference books in themselves. At such sales, bids totaling more than a million dollars might be recorded in less than an hour. At the other end of the scale are country auctions and estate sales, at which anything under the sun is apt to turn up and where lots can go for as low as $1 each. (But don't underestimate the country or estate sale, either; when desirable collector's items are included, dealers and collectors flock to them, and the prices can get very strong.)

Some auctioneers are specialists; others handle whatever

comes along, if it falls in the category of secondhand property. The biggest groups of specialist auctioneers are those handling coins and stamps. Material of this nature requires specialist knowledge to appraise and classify, so it is very seldom sold by the general art or antiques auctioneers. If you have a specialized collection, it is advisable (when selling by auction) to seek out an auctioneer whose sales are geared to that type of merchandise. Such an auctioneer has an established mailing list of active buyers for that particular type of collectible, and you're sure to do much better pricewise than if you select a local auctioneer just because of convenience.

The procedures vary among auction houses in terms of the arrangement made with dealers and also the actual rules and regulations of their sales. The amount of their commission varies, too, but this usually proves to be a rather minor detail. You should not automatically choose the auctioneer who offers the lowest commission rate (i.e., the percentage rate he deducts from the sale price of each lot before settling with the owner). When one house is operating on a 10 percent commission and another on a 15 percent commission, it might seem as though the one at 10 percent is the obvious choice. This just isn't so. Usually, when the auctioneer is charging slightly higher commission rates than the competition, it's because he spends a great deal more in advertising and promoting his sales and on the preparation of his catalogs. Therefore, prices realized at his sales are likely to be *much* higher, so you would do better selling through him even though his commission rate might seem discouraging. A low commission rate is often an indication that the house has a hard time attracting property for sale. When an auction house has an established record of successful sales and satisfied clients, it has no problem getting material to sell. So do not allow yourself to be influenced by differences in commission rates.

When you put material up for sale by auction, it is never sold immediately. It has to be lotted and cataloged, and the catalogs have to be distributed. All of this takes time. It may be two or three months between placing the merchandise in the auctioneer's hands and the actual date of the sale. It might be another thirty days before you receive settlement. Settlement is seldom made quickly. Each auction house works by contract. You and the auctioneer sign a sales contract at the time of placing the material in the auctioneer's care. The contract spells out all of these details: the rate of commission, the sale date, and the length of waiting time between the sale date and receiving your payment.

Periodicals
of Interest

AB Bookman's Weekly, P.O. Box AB, Clifton, NJ 07015.
American Philatelist, P.O. Box 8000, State College, PA 16803.
American Rifleman, c/o National Rifle Association, 600 Rhode Island Avenue NW, Washington, DC 20036.
Americana Magazine, 205 West Center Street, Marion, OH 43302.
Antique & Collecting Hobbies, c/o Lightner Publishing Co., 1006 S. Michigan Avenue, Chicago, IL 60605.
Antique Collecting, P.O. Box 327, Ephrata, PA 17522.
Antique Market Report, P.O. Box 12830, Wichita, KS 67277.
Antique Monthly, c/o Boone, Inc., P.O. Drawer 2, Tuscaloosa, AL 35401.
Antique Press, 12403 N. Florida Avenue, Tampa, FL 33612.
Antique Toy World, 3941 Belle Plaine, Chicago, IL 60618.
Antique Trader Weekly, P.O. Box 1050, Dubuque, IA 52001.
Antiques, The Magazine, 551 Fifth Avenue, New York, NY 10017.
Antiques & Auction News, Joel Sater's, P.O. Box 500, Mount Joy, PA 17552.

Antiques and the Arts Weekly, c/o *The Newtown Bee,* Newtown, CT 06470.

Antiques & Collectibles, P.O. Box 268, Greenvale, NY 11548.

Antiques Dealer, The, P.O. Box 2147, Clifton, NJ 07015.

Antiques Journal, P.O.Box 1046, Dubuque, IA 52001.

Art & Antiques, 89 Fifth Avenue, New York, NY 10003.

Art & Auction, 250 West 57th Street, New York, NY 10019.

Beckett's Baseball Card Monthly, 3410 Mid Court Road, Suite 100, Carrollton, TX 75006.

Buckeye Marketeer, The, 2256½ East Main Street, Columbus, OH 43209.

Carnival Glass News & Views, P.O. Box 5421, Kansas City, MO 64131.

Clarion, The, 49 West 53rd Street, New York, NY 10019.

Coin Age, 16001 Ventura Boulevard, Encino, CA 91316.

Coin World, P.O.Box 150, Sydney, OH 45367.

Collector, 467 North Main Street, Pomona, CA 91768.

Collectors Journal, P.O. Box 601, Vinton, IA 52349-0601.

Collector's Showcase, P.O. Box 27948, San Diego, CA 92128.

Comics Buyers Guide, The, 700 East State Street, Iola, WI 54990.

Country Living Magazine, 224 West 57th Street, New York, NY 10019.

Daze, The, P.O. Box 57, Otisville, MI 48463 (Depression glass).

Doll Reader, c/o Hobby House Press, Inc., 900 Frederick Street, Cumberland, MD 21502.

Dolls—The Collector Magazine, c/o Collector Communications, 170 Fifth Avenue, New York, NY 10010.

Glass Review, P.O. Box 542, Marietta, OH 45750.

Goldmine, 700 East State Street, Iola, WI 54990 (records).

Heisey News, P.O. Box 27, Newark, OH 43055.

Hemmings Motor News, P.O. Box 380, Route 9W, Bennington, VT 05201.

Jersey Devil, The, P.O. Box 202, Lambertville, NJ 08530.

Jukebox Trader, P.O. Box 1081, Des Moines, IA 50311.

Linn's Stamp News, P.O. Box 29, Sidney, OH 45365.

Loose Change, c/o Mead Publishing Co., 21176 South Alameda Street, Long Beach, CA 90810 (coin-operated machines).

Maine Antiques Digest, P.O. Box 645, Waldoboro, ME 04572.

Midatlantic Antiques Magazine, P.O. Box 908, Henderson, NC 27536.

New England Antiques Journal, 4 Church Street, Ware, MA 01082 (formerly *New England Country Antiques*).

New York Antique Almanac, P.O. Box 335, Lawrence, NY 11559.

New York–Pennsylvania Collector, The, P.O. Drawer C, Fishers, NY 14453.

Numismatic News, 700 East State Street, Iola, WI 54990.

Ohio Antique Review, 72 North Street, Worthington, OH 43085.

Old Bottles Magazine, P.O. Box 243, Bend, OR 97701.

Old Cars Weekly, 700 East State Street, Iola, WI 54990.

Orientalia Journal, P.O. Box 94, Dept.T, Little Neck, NY 11363.

Paper & Advertising Collector, P.O. Box 500, Mount Joy, PA 17552.

Paper Collectors' Marketplace, 700 East State Street, Iola, WI 54990.

Political Collector, 503 Madison Avenue, York, PA 17404.

Postcard Collector, 700 East State Street, Iola, WI 54990.

Prints Magazine, P.O. Box 1468, Alton, IL 62002.

Renninger's Antique Guide, P.O. Box 495, Lafayette Hill, PA 19444.

Scott's Stamp Monthly, P.O. Box 828, Sidney, OH 45365.

Shotgun News, P.O. Box 669, Hastings, NE 68901.

Silver Magazine, P.O. Box 1243, Whittier, CA 90609.

Smithsonian Magazine, 900 Jefferson Drive SW, Washington, DC 20560.

Tri-State Trader, 27 N. Jefferson, P.O. Box 90, Knightstown, IN 46148.

Vintage Collectibles, P.O. Box 5072, Chattanooga, TN 37406.

Yesteryear, P.O. Box 2, Princeton, WI 54968.

Index to Specialists and Clubs

Note: Please remember when writing to any of these addresses to be certain to include a self-addressed, stamped envelope. The editors of this book cannot guarantee that everyone will respond to letters.

Animal Collectibles
Cat Collectors Club, c/o Marilyn Dipboye, 31311 Blair Drive, Warren, MI 48092; National Elephant Collectors Society, c/o Richard W. Massiglia, 89 Massachusetts Avenue, Box 7, Boston, MA 02115.

Autographs
Jack B. Good Autographs, P.O. Box 4462, Ft. Lauderdale, FL 33338.

Aviation
John Wm. Aldrich, Pine Mountain Lake Airport, P.O. Box 706, Groveland, CA 95321.

Bookplates
American Society of Bookplate Collectors and Designers, 605 No. Stoneman Avenue, #F, Alhambra, CA 91801.

Bottles
Avon—Western World Publishing, Box 23785, Pleasant Hill, CA 94523.

Jim Beam—International Association of Jim Beam and Specialties Club, 5210 Belmont Road, Suite D, Downers Grove, IL 60515.

Breweriana
National Association of Breweriana Advertising, c/o Robert Jaeger, 2343 Met-To-Wee Lane, Wauwatosa, WI 53226.

Buttons
The National Button Society, 2733 Juno Place, Akron, OH 44313.

Circus
Circus Historical Society, c/o Fred Pfening, Jr., 2515 Dorset Road, Columbus, OH 43221.

Coins
Herbert J. Kwart, P.O. Box 2172, Ridgecrest, CA 93555.

Decoys
James D. Julia Auctions, RFD #1, Box 91, Fairfield, ME 04937.

Fans
Mechanical fans—The Fan Man, Kurt House, 4606 Travis, Dallas, TX 75205.

Fishing Tackle
National Fishing Lure Collectors Club, 3907 Wedgewood Drive, Portage, MI 49081.

Glass, Carnival
International Carnival Glass Association, Lee Markley, RR #1, Box 14, Mentone, IN 46539.

Graniteware
National Graniteware Society, Jacki Rozek, 4818 Reamer Road, Center Point, IA 52213.

Inkwells and Inkstands
Society of Inkwell Collectors, 5136 Thomas Avenue South, Minneapolis, MN 55410.

Insulators
Carol MacDougall, P.O. Box 99250, Cleveland, OH 44101.

Marbles
Marble Collectors Society, P.O. Box 222, Trumbull, CT 06611.

Movies
Collectors Bookstore, Malcolm Willits, 1708 N. Vine St., Hollywood, CA 90028.

Newspapers
Phil Barber Newspaper Auctions, P.O. Box 8694, Boston, MA 02114.

Nippon
National Nippon Collectors Club, Joan F. Van Patten, P.O. Box 102, Rexford, NY 12148.

Occupied Japan
Occupied Japan Collectors Club, Robert W. Gee, Sr., 18309 Faysmith Avenue, Torrance, CA 90504.

Ocean Liner Memorabilia
Oceanic Navigational Society, Charles Ira Sachs, P.O. Box 8005, Universal City, CA 91608.

Paper Money
Herbert J. Kwart, P.O. Box 2172, Ridgecrest, CA 93555.

Pens
Pen Fanciers Club, 1169 Overcash Drive, Dunedin, FL 33528.

Political Memorabilia
American Political Items Collectors, Norman Loewenstern, 5731 Jackwood, Houston, TX 77096.

Radios
Gary B. Schneider, 9511 Sunrise Blvd., #J-23, North Royalton, OH 44133.

Railroadiana
Railroadiana Collectors Association, Inc., Joseph C. Mazanek, P.O. Box 58, Prairie View, IL 60069.

Scouting
The Carolina Trader, Richard E. Shields, Jr., P.O. Box 26986, Charlotte, NC 28221.

Scripophily
Buttonwood Galleries, P.O. Box 1006, Throggs Neck Station, New York, NY 10465.

Steins
Stein Collectors International, Jack G. Lowenstein, P.O. Box 463, Kingston, NJ 08528.

Stoves
Midwest Antique Stove Information Clearinghouse and Parts Registry, Clifford Boram, 417 North Main Street, Monticello, IN 47960.

Tobacco
Cigarette Pack Collectors Association, Dick Elliot, 61 Searle Street, Georgetown, MA 01833.

Toys and Games
Toys—Richard Friz, P.O. Box 155, RFD 2, Peterborough, NH 03548.
Games—Lee Dennis, 110 Spring Road, Peterborough, NH 03458.

Advertising

TOPIC: Advertising collectibles are considered to be any items with a company's name or logo on them.

TYPES: Advertising collectibles can be found in any form. Common items used for advertising range from ashtrays to posters to yo-yos.

PERIOD: Advertising has been around almost since humanity became literate, but advertising collectibles of interest to the modern enthusiast began around 1800. Pre-1900 items are scarce and valuable.

MATERIALS: These items are usually made of ceramics, glass, paper, or tin, although the material depends on the item.

COMMENTS: Many large companies (such as Coca-Cola) put much effort into producing promotional items that are now very collectible. Because of this, a collector may focus on procuring items that pertain to a particular company. Other enthusiasts, however, collect a certain item (mirrors, for example) regardless of the company or product that is advertised.

ADDITIONAL TIPS: The listings in this section are arranged in the following order: item, company or product advertised, title, description, what it was used for, material, shape, size, and date manufactured. Other information is included where relevant.

Price Range

☐ **Ashtray,** Armstrong tire, clear, red decal, round, 5⅞″ diameter — 9.00 / 12.00

☐ **Ashtray,** Bacardi rum, white china, round, 4½″ diameter ...... — 3.50 / 7.00

☐ **Ashtray,** Budweiser, glass, round, 5″ diameter .... — 3.00 / 5.00

☐ **Ashtray,** Camel cigarettes, Camel logo in center, tin, round, 3½″ diameter .... — 1.50 / 2.50

☐ **Ashtray,** Chivas Regal, Wade china, triangular with rounded sides, 11½″ .... — 5.00 / 9.00

☐ **Ashtray,** Firestone Tire, 1936 Texas Central Expo .... — 13.00 / 18.00

☐ **Ashtray,** Goodrich, for Silvertown Heavy Duty Cord, round, 6⅜″ diameter .... — 6.00 / 12.00

☐ **Ashtray,** Goodrich, for Silvertown Cord tires, 1776 decal, round, 6¼″ diameter .... — 10.00 / 16.00

☐ **Ashtray,** Labatt's Stout-Lager-Ales, cream-colored porcelain, round, 6½″ diameter .... — 3.00 / 7.00

☐ **Ashtray,** Michelob beer, round, 5½″ diameter .... — 3.00 / 7.00

☐ **Ashtray,** Pennsylvania, for Balloon Cord tires, round, 6⅛″ diameter .... — 8.00 / 12.00

☐ **Bank,** Pepsi Cola, 75 Year Commemorative, red, tin can style, 1973 .... — 2.00 / 5.00

☐ **Bank,** R.C.A. dog, ''Nipper,'' ceramic, 6½″ tall .... — 8.00 / 12.00

☐ **Bank,** Texaco oil can, 1 quart, 1970s .... — 1.00 / 3.50

☐ **Banner,** De Soto auto, red, gold, and black fringed silk, 38″ × 66″, 1951 .... — 55.00 / 65.00

☐ **Booklet,** for Thall's Home Remedies, 1920s, 20 pp, excellent condition .... — 4.00 / 6.00

Cigar store Indian, carved and poly-chromed, painted overall in tones of reds, yellows, and blues, 6'6" high, $1430. (*Photo courtesy of Butterfield & Butterfield, San Francisco*)

	Price Range	
☐ **Card,** business of M. Garfinkel, Eyesight Specialist, Middletown, NY, his picture on front, 3" × 5", c. 1910s	5.00	7.00
☐ **Chessie Cat ad,** color, with sleeping "Chessie," 1938	5.00	7.50
☐ **Cigar store Indian,** carved and polychromed, painted overall in tones of red, yellow, and blue, 6'6" high		1430.00

	Price Range	
☐ **Cigarette ad, Chesterfield,** with Ronald Reagan, from 1948 *Life* magazine, full page, full color, excellent condition	20.00	30.00
☐ **Cigarette ad,** color, 1946 Chesterfield ad, red-white-blue motif, "With the Fans at Yankee Stadium and Polo Grounds," 10″ × 14″ ..	15.00	20.00
☐ **Cigarette ad,** reads "Naturally incessant smokers say Keep 'Mouth Happy' "; bottom in small print, "Spud is the cigarette of the heaviest smokers who smoke 3 packs a day"; 7″ × 11″	18.00	20.00
☐ **Cigarette ad,** 9″ × 12″, fat man in athletic gear in a shadow effect in back of young trim man with ad caption, "Don't Surrender when tempted to over-indulge. 'Reach for a Lucky instead,' " 1930	35.00	40.00
☐ **Coffee ad,** "Santa," by J. C. Leyendecker, 14″ × 10½″, color, matted, 1940	8.00	10.00
☐ **Coffee ad,** by J. C. Leyendecker, showing woman and child measuring coffee, matted, 1940	8.00	10.00
☐ **Dole Pineapple ad,** by Millard Sheets, color, 14″ × 10″, 1939 .	12.50	15.00
☐ **Front envelope,** advertising for "Ulmer's Heavy Powders" and listing four other medicines from this company in West Valley, NY, c. 1890s	2.00	4.00
☐ **General Motors** installment plan ad, featuring an elderly gentleman, "Just a Minute, young feller!"	12.50	15.00
☐ **General Motors,** installment plan ad with farmer, "Makes Good Sense To Me."	15.00	17.50

Price Range

☐ **Indianapolis Speedway ad,** black-and-white ad for Ethyl, shows cars/stands, has the NRA symbol in upper left, 12″ × 8⅕″, 1934 .... 10.00   12.00

☐ **Ink blotter,** for Mutual Life Insurance of NY, 4″ × 9½″, 1893 .... 3.00   5.00

☐ **Ivory Soap ad,** 1930s, color, 11″ × 22″ 2.00   4.00

☐ **Maxfield Parrish ad,** Swift's Premium ham, 1921, excellent condition, full color 25.00   35.00

☐ **Medicine flyer,** for T's Morbus Pills, 7½″ × 6″, c. 1890s 3.00   5.00

☐ **Mickey Mouse,** double-page Ingersoll ad, in color, mint condition 16.00   20.00

☐ **Milk cans,** advertising flyer, 4 pp., 8½″ × 11″, illustrated, for Shepard Co., c. 1900 .... 8.00   10.00

☐ **Norman Rockwell,** rare movie ad for *The Song of Bernadette,* 10″ × 14″ plus 3″ mat, 1943 ... 15.00   20.00

☐ **Papers,** sample envelope, 3″ × 5″, from Hammermill, c. 1928 ... 2.00   4.00

☐ **Pabst Blue Ribbon Beer ad,** color, ''Here's Your Blue Ribbon,'' 12″ × 8″, 1934 .... 18.00   20.00

☐ **Peter, Paul and Mary,** full-color photo ad, autograph 20.00   30.00

☐ **Sign,** American Agriculturist, tin, embossed, 6½″ × 13½″, 1920s 7.00   10.00

☐ **Sign,** Arrow Trailer Rentals, picture of U.S. map, embossed, 14″ × 18″, 1940s 12.00   16.00

☐ **Sign,** Barnum's Animal Crackers, commemorative, tin, 4″ diameter, 6″ tall, 1979 .... 3.00   5.00

☐ **Sign,** Bayer Aspirin, tin, 15″ × 18″ 25.00   35.00

Price Range

☐ **Sign,** Beechnut Tobacco, rectangular 12.00 17.00

☐ **Sign,** Borden, glass, 12″ × 20″ 62.00 72.00

☐ **Sign,** Budweiser, plastic, with bottle, lighted, 5″ × 12″ 12.00 18.00

☐ **Sign,** Bull Durham, cardboard, 14″ × 22″ 35.00 45.00

☐ **Sign,** Bunny Bread, red and white, tin, embossed, 3½″ × 28″, 1930s 8.00 12.00

☐ **Sign,** Burma Shave, wooden, 10″ × 3½″ 1.50 2.50

☐ **Sign,** Busch Ginger Ale, picture of eagle, porcelain, 10″ × 20″, 1920s 75.00 85.00

☐ **Sign,** Camel Cigarettes, picture of blond woman, cardboard, 20″ × 11″, c. 1941 .... 13.00 18.00

☐ **Sign,** Coca-Cola, "Join the Friendly Circle," c. 1954 .... 25.00 35.00

☐ **Sign,** Coors Beer, picture of lake and mountain, lighted 25.00 35.00

☐ **Sign,** Dr. Meyer's Foot Soap, picture of hands holding soap, cardboard, 7″ × 10″ 4.00 6.00

☐ **Sign,** Dr. Nutt Soda, tin, embossed, 10″ × 13″, 1920s 25.00 32.00

☐ **Sign,** Dr. Pepper, red and white, tin, 6″ × 18″, 1950s 7.00 11.00

☐ **Sign,** DuBois Budweiser, tin, 21″ × 13″ 18.00 22.00

☐ **Sign,** Dutch Boy, "wet paint," picture of boy, cardboard, 6″ × 9″, 1930s 2.00 5.00

☐ **Sign,** Fairy Soap, 5¢, for a trolley car, rectangular 85.00 115.00

☐ **Sign,** Ford Tractor, masonite, 11″ × 21″, 1942 .... 20.00 25.00

☐ **Sign,** Free Lance Cigar, cardboard, embossed, 8″ × 10″, c. 1910 .... 8.00 12.00

	Price Range	
☐ **Sign,** Goodyear Tires, oval	22.00	26.00
☐ **Sign,** Hires Root Beer, paper, 28" × 12"	40.00	50.00
☐ **Sign,** Ivory Soap, picture of child holding soap, for a trolley car, 20" × 10"	68.00	85.00
☐ **Sign,** Kelloggs Corn Flakes, picture of infant in wicker basket, tin, rectangular	70.00	88.00
☐ **Sign,** Marvels Cigarettes, picture of two cigarette packages, tin, embossed, 3½" × 16", 1930s ...	16.00	21.00
☐ **Sign,** Narragansett Lager, red with silver and gold letters, 20" × 10"	69.00	89.00
☐ **Sign,** Old Milwaukee Beer, picture of woman in Victorian clothing, plastic, 15" x 22"	17.00	25.00
☐ **Sign,** Olympia Gold, cardboard, 12" × 10"	5.00	10.00
☐ **Sign,** Orange Crush, picture of pinup girl, cardboard, 12" × 15", 1950s	4.00	6.00
☐ **Sign,** Orange Crush, 12" × 32", 1940s	25.00	30.00
☐ **Sign,** Ritz Crackers, cardboard, rectangular	30.00	40.00
☐ **Sign,** Rochelle Lime-Dry, cardboard, embossed, 10" × 15", 1920s	2.50	3.50
☐ **Sign,** Salvation Army, red and white, porcelain, square, 16", 1940s	22.00	27.00
☐ **Sign,** Schaefer Beer, wood, barrel-shaped, 14" × 16"	24.00	30.00
☐ **Sign,** Smith Brothers Cough Drops, 5¢, for a trolley car	85.00	115.00
☐ **Sign,** Sun Maid Raisins, for a trolley car	40.00	50.00
☐ **Sign,** 2-Room Apartments, brass, 1½" × 7", c. 1940	2.00	6.00

	Price Range	
☐ **Sign,** Uneeda Biscuits, cardboard, 10″ × 13″	25.00	35.00
☐ **Sign,** Viceroy Cigarettes, tin	22.00	33.00
☐ **Sign,** Virginia Cigarettes, picture of bathing beauty, tin, 14″ × 21″, 1930s	50.00	62.00
☐ **Sign,** White Rock Mineral Water, tin, 4″ × 12″, 1910	8.00	12.00
☐ **Sign,** Whitman's Chocolate Candy, 13″ × 18″	50.00	68.00
☐ **Sign,** Wrigley's Gum, picture of Wrigley arrow boy, for a street-car, 10″ × 20″, 1920s	35.00	42.00
☐ **Sign,** Wrigley's Gum, picture of Wrigley arrow man, for a street-car, 10″ × 20″, 1920	30.00	39.00
☐ **Sign,** Woo Chong Import Co., picture of Oriental women and art objects, paper, 21″ × 31″, c. 1920	30.00	40.00
☐ **Sign,** Wonder Bread, cardboard, 6″ × 9″, 1910	8.00	12.00
☐ **Silverware,** Campbell Kid, three-piece place setting	14.00	18.00
☐ **Thermometer,** Carstairs, "Join the Carstairs Crowd," round	25.00	35.00
☐ **Thermometer,** Coca-Cola, tin, embossed, 16″, 1960s	5.00	8.00
☐ **Thermometer,** Coca-Cola, gold, bottle shape, 7″	20.00	30.00
☐ **Thermometer,** Coca-Cola, bottle shape, 27″	50.00	60.00
☐ **Thermometer,** Coca-Cola, "Things Go Better With Coke," 17½″	22.00	30.00
☐ **Thermometer,** Copenhagen Chewing Tobacco, 12″	12.00	18.00
☐ **Thermometer,** Dr. Pepper, 17″	25.00	35.00
☐ **Thermometer,** Gilbey's Gin, 9″	46.00	56.00

	Price Range	
☐ **Thermometer,** Hires Root Beer, bottle shape, 27"	45.00	55.00
☐ **Thermometer,** Morton Salt, picture of girl under umbrella, metal	6.00	8.50
☐ **Thermometer,** Old Dutch Root Beer, windmills, 26"	25.00	35.00
☐ **Thermometer,** Royal Crown Cola, 27"	24.00	30.00
☐ **Tray,** Coca-Cola, girl with menu, c. 1950	20.00	30.00
☐ **Tray,** Coca-Cola, hostess, c. 1936	50.00	70.00
☐ **Tray,** Coca-Cola, Santa Claus, c. 1973	21.00	31.00
☐ **Tray,** Coors, metal, round, 13" diameter	4.00	5.00
☐ **Tray,** Coors Beer, picture of a glass and bottle of beer	25.00	32.00

Almanacs

DESCRIPTION: Almanacs are annual publications that include astrological and meteorological data as well as general information of the year. Farmers use the information in almanacs to determine how weather and other variables may affect their crops.

VARIATIONS: A variety of almanacs have been published. Among the best known are the *Farmer's Almanac* and *Poor Richard's Almanack.*

PERIOD: Almanacs date from the 17th century.

COMMENTS: While collectors have been traditionally concerned with almanacs published before 1800, 19th-and early-20th-century almanacs are fast gaining in value for their wealth of scientific beliefs of the time, particularly those featuring colorful covers or expounding assorted patent medicine products.

ADDITIONAL TIPS: Almanacs are listed in chronological order and, where available, the name of the publisher and/or the place of origin are listed for identification purposes.

	Price Range	
☐ **The Farmer's Almanack,** Whittemore, 1714	900.00	1200.00

	Price Range	
☐ **An Almanack of the Coelestial Motions and Aspects,** Travis, 1717	300.00	375.00
☐ **The New-England Diary,** Bowen, 1724	350.00	435.00
☐ **The New-England Diary,** Bowen, 1725	330.00	390.00
☐ **The Rhode-Island Almanack,** Stafford, 1738	1100.00	1375.00
☐ **Poor Job's Almanack,** Shepherd (James Franklin), 1753	1400.00	1900.00
☐ **An Astronomical Diary; Or, An Almanack,** Ames, 1753	240.00	315.00
☐ **An Astronomical Diary,** Ames, 1764	75.00	95.00
☐ **The New-England Almanack,** West, 1775	240.00	315.00
☐ **The North-American's Almanack,** Stearns, 1775	90.00	120.00
☐ **Bickerstaff's Boston Almanack,** 1775	170.00	210.00
☐ **Bickerstaff's Boston Almanack,** 1778	150.00	180.00
☐ **American Almanack,** Russell, 1782	90.00	115.00
☐ **Webster's Connecticut Pocket Almanack,** Bickerstaff, 1787	145.00	180.00
☐ **An Astronomical Diary,** Strong, 1788	115.00	150.00
☐ **An Astronomical Diary,** Sewall, 1794	115.00	150.00
☐ **Strong's Almanack,** 1796	115.00	150.00
☐ **Farmer's Almanack,** Thomas, 1799	27.00	36.00
☐ **Greenleaf's New-York, Connecticut and New Jersey Almanack,** 1801	90.00	115.00
☐ **New England Almanack,** Daboll, 1805	35.00	47.00
☐ **New England Almanack,** Daboll, 1808	22.00	30.00

	Price Range	
☐ **Low's Almanac,** 1809	12.50	15.50
☐ **New England Almanack,** Daboll, 1810	33.00	41.00
☐ **Law's Boston,** 1812	16.00	21.00
☐ **New England Almanack,** Daboll, 1813	27.00	36.00
☐ **New England Almanack,** Daboll, 1816	28.00	35.00
☐ **Farmer's Almanack,** 1829	8.50	10.50
☐ **National Comic Almanack,** 1851	10.00	14.00
☐ **True American Almanack,** 1855	50.00	65.00
☐ **The Old Farmer's Almanack,** New Bedford, MA, 1858	20.00	25.00
☐ **The Old Farmer's Almanac,** Worcester, MA, 1872	8.00	10.00
☐ **Dr. O. Phelps Brown's Shakespearian Annual Almanac,** featuring *Taming of the Shrew,* Jersey City, NJ, 1874	10.00	12.00
☐ **The Old Farmer's Almanac,** Taunton, MA, 1878	6.00	8.00
☐ **Brandreth Annual Calendar,** New York, 1879	7.00	9.00
☐ **Rush's Almanac & Guide to Health,** New York, 1879, four-color cover	7.00	9.00
☐ **Rush's Almanac & Guide to Health,** New York, 1880, four-color cover	7.00	9.00
☐ **Home Almanac,** New York, 1881, exceptional engraved cover and inside page art	12.00	15.00
☐ **Green's Dairy Almanac,** Woodbury, NJ, 1883–1884	4.00	6.00
☐ **Morse's Indian Root Pill Almanac,** Morristown, NY, no date on cover, 1884	10.00	12.00
☐ **The New York Almanac,** New York, 1888, four-color cover	7.00	9.00

	Price Range	
☐ **Warner's Safe Cure Almanac for 1890,** St. Paul, MN, four-color cover	4.00	6.00
☐ **August Flower and German Syrup Almanac,** Woodbury, NJ, 1890, illustrated by Palmer Cox .	20.00	25.00
☐ **Ayer's American Almanac,** Lowell, MA, 1892	3.50	4.50
☐ **Capital Almanac,** 1892, exceptional four-color cover	8.00	10.00
☐ **Hostetter's Illustrated United States Almanac,** Pittsburgh, 1893	3.00	5.00
☐ **Kickapoo Indian Almanac,** New Haven, CT, 1893, exceptional four-color cover	10.00	12.00
☐ **Ayer's American Almanac,** Lowell, MA, 1894	3.00	5.00
☐ **Hostetter's Illustrated United States Almanac,** Pittsburgh, 1894	3.00	5.00
☐ **Ayer's American Almanac,** Lowell, MA, 1895	3.00	5.00
☐ **The New York Almanac,** New York, 1901, four-color cover	4.00	6.00
☐ **The Peruna Almanac for 1902,** Columbus, OH	8.00	10.00
☐ **Herrick's Almanac,** New York, 1903	3.00	5.00
☐ **Kodol Almanac,** featuring 200-year calandar (1776–1976), Chicago, 1903, four-color cover	10.00	12.00
☐ **Dr. Morse's Indiana Root Pills Almanac,** Morristown, NY, 1904, four-color cover	10.00	12.00
☐ **Bucklen's Almanac,** Chicago, 1905, four-color cover	4.00	6.00
☐ **Hostetter's Illustrated United States Almanac,** Pittsburgh, 1905	2.00	4.00

	Price Range	
☐ **Bliss Native Herb's Almanac,** Washington, DC, 1905	4.00	6.00
☐ **The Household Almanac,** Burlington, VT, 1908	2.00	4.00
☐ **Hostetter's Illustrated United States Almanac,** Pittsburgh, 1910	2.00	4.00
☐ **DeWitt's 200 Year Calendar** (1776–1976), Chicago, no date on cover, c. 1913, four-color cover .	8.00	10.00
☐ **Ayer's American Almanac,** Lowell, MA, 1916	2.00	4.00
☐ **Dr. Miles's New Weather Almanac and Handbook of Valuable Information,** Elkhart, IN, 1916	2.00	4.00
☐ **The Old Farmer's Almanac,** Dublin, NH, 1964	.50	1.00

American Indian Artifacts

TOPIC: American Indian artifacts are appreciating quickly as more and more people are attracted to these unique and historical items.

TYPES: Types of artifacts range from jewelry to woven products to weapons.

PERIOD: Though some items may be prehistoric, as a rule these collectibles will date from around 1600 to 1925. More recent artifacts are usually valued according to rarity and quality of workmanship.

ORIGIN: These artifacts may originate anywhere in the United States, but the Plains and the Southwest have provided a disproportionate number of items.

MATERIALS: The material depends on the artifact; leather, stone, wood, and ceramics are used extensively.

COMMENTS: Many collectors focus on specific tribes and items, such as Navajo rugs or Hopi Kachina dolls. Others do not limit themselves so strictly and may collect all Indian artifacts from a certain period or area.

Note: The single values shown below are the actual auction-realized prices.

	Price Range	
☐ **Acoma polychrome water jar** ...		4125.00
☐ **Alaskan Eskimo cribbage board,** walrus ivory with four wooden legs, engraved with scenes of caribou, birds and berry bushes, 19th century	200.00	400.00
☐ **Apache coil grain basket,** dark animal decoration on light ground, 9¼″ diameter, 8½″ high		200.00
☐ **Apache coil grain basket,** dark geometric and animal decoration on light ground, 8¾″ diameter, 8½″ high		200.00
☐ **Carved wood whirligig,** 19th century, depicting an Indian in a canoe, raised on a stand of later vintage, 13″ long, 24″ high	1700.00	2000.00
☐ **Cheyenne moccasins,** children's moccasins, high ankle flaps and perpendicular bands of red and blue beadwork, late 19th century	125.00	175.00
☐ **Fox hunting charm,** walrus ivory, with bushy tail outstretched, perforated underneath body, 19th century	100.00	180.00
☐ **Horn snuff box,** oval form, with applied salmon and horsehead decoration, 2″ high		60.00
☐ **Iroquois platform pipe,** clay, undecorated form with centrally placed bowl and perforation at each end, found in the area of Lake Champlain in New York, 17th century	175.00	250.00
☐ **Mono bottleneck basket**		2750.00
☐ **Panamint pictorial basket**		3025.00

Left. Mono bottleneck basket, $2750. *Right*. Panamint pictorial basket, $3025. (*Photo courtesy of Butterfield & Butterfield, San Francisco*)

	Price Range	
☐ **Kachina doll,** turn of the century, wood carved, "Salaka Mana," 14½" high		2600.00
☐ **Kachina doll,** turn of the century, wood carved, "Salaka Mana," 14" high		2400.00
☐ **Kachina doll,** Eagle Dancer, rabbit fur and eagle feather decoration with cowrie shells and turquoise, 22¾" high		200.00
☐ **Kachina doll,** Squash Dancer, leather, shell and rabbit fur decoration, 14" high		50.00
☐ **Kachina doll,** Morning Dancer, rabbit fur, leather and shell decoration, 15" high	50.00	100.00
☐ **Kachina doll,** Protection Dancer, rabbit fur, leather, shell, and yarn decoration, 15" high		50.00
☐ **Kachina doll,** "He-e-e," bearing traces of the original polychrome, 13¼" high	500.00	700.00

Price Range

☐ **Navajo blanket,** woven, black
and white crystal decorations on
red ground, 3′11″ × 6′1″ 150.00   250.00

☐ **Navajo blanket,** multicolor
wedge decoration on tan ground,
3′5″ × 5′8″ 250.00   300.00

☐ **Navajo rug,** storm pattern in red,
brown, and light brown on off-
white ground, 3′10″ × 5′4″ 300.00   400.00

☐ **Navajo rug,** double crystal pattern on red ground, the ground
scattered with various motifs, the
brown borders with spirit threads,
4′ × 6′10″ 650.00

☐ **Navajo Kachina dolls,** two,
"Spirit" and "Bee," various sizes,
each with multicolor painted dec-
oration 200.00   300.00

☐ **Tularosa bowl,** characteristic
black and white geometric design   300.00   550.00

☐ **Wayang Kulit puppet,** polychrome pierced leather, raised on
a carved wood handle, 28″ long   30.00

☐ **Wayang Kulit puppet,** polychrome pierced leather on a
carved bamboo handle, 33″ high   35.00

WORKS OF ART

☐ **Art pottery portrait vase,** by J.
B. Owens Pottery, c. 1896, "Utopian Range," the globular body
painted with the portrait of an
Indian, glazed in brown, with un-
der-the-glaze slip painting, impressed "OWENS, UTOPIAN
1025," 12″ high 650.00

☐ **Carl Kauba,** polychrome, enameled bronze, "Chief Wolf Robe,"
fully signed, 26″ high 30,000.00

Price Range

☐ **Ledger drawings,** set of 55, Southern Plains, collected in 1890 by census taker and artist Julian Scott at the Kiowa, Comanche and Wichita Agency, Oklahoma (see color section for illustration) 22,000.00

☐ **Study of an Indian,** artist: Dean Cornwell, charcoal and white chalk on paper, unframed, 20 " × 15 " 250.00   350.00

☐ **Charles Crow Chief Reevis,** artist: Warren W. Baumgartner, signed and inscribed, watercolor and pencil on heavy paper, unframed, 22 " × 19 " 500.00   700.00

☐ **Indian Scout,** artist: Carl Kauba, inscribed "C Kauba," bronze, brown patina, 18 " high 8500.00   10,000.00

☐ **Willie Jim, the Seminole,** artist: Warren W. Baumgartner, signed and inscribed, watercolor and pencil on paper, laid down on board, 29 " × 27 " 500.00   700.00

Animals

DESCRIPTION: Animal collectibles are highly popular among all types of collectors. In particular, collecting cat or elephant figurines, doorstops, bookends, plates, mugs, and many other items, as listed below, is extremely popular.

COMMENTS: All categories are listed alphabetically.

CATS

	Price Range	
☐ **Ashtray,** porcelain cat face, white with gold details, 3″ long, marked "Weltberuhmstnd Caillers shokoladen pralinen"	55.00	75.00
☐ **Book,** *The Cat Scout's Book,* Louis Wain	50.00	60.00
☐ **Bronze,** Vienna bronze miniature cat bands, 10 pieces, signed Bergman, c. 1890	750.00	850.00
☐ **Cookie jar,** "Shawnee Puss 'n' Boots," gold with decals	100.00	125.00

	Price Range	

□ **Cream pitcher,** green, with white and black cat handle, 6½″ high, marked "Germany #757/ 11″ 25.00 35.00

□ **Lamp,** KPM fairy lamp, cat-dog-owl 250.00 350.00

□ **Print,** "Queen of Persia," by Margaret Phillips, © New York Graphic Society, Fine Art Publishers, 12½″ × 17½″ 20.00 30.00

□ **Hooked rug,** depicting cat playing fiddle and dog looking on, excellent condition, 52″ × 33″, c. 1930 .... 300.00 400.00

□ **Bretby, England, pottery,** black cat with red ball of wool, glass eyes, Bretby sunburst hallmark, 10″ long, c. 1891 .... 90.00 100.00

□ **Cliftwood,** pottery, black reclining cat, 11½″ long, Cliftwood paper label 55.00 65.00

□ **Royal Worcester,** "Lily" figurine, girl in green dress, seated, holding gray kitten, 3¼″ high, artist: Ann Acheson, 1934 .... 200.00 250.00

□ **Royal Worcester,** blue Persian cat, 3½″ high, artist: James Adler, 1979 .... 55.00 75.00

DEER

□ **Cuddling deer,** pair, bronze, cast from a model by G. H. Laurent, two busts of animals, inscribed "Laurent," on beige veined marble base, in dark blackish green patina, 8″ high 400.00 600.00

□ **Three-deer figural,** gilt metal, cast from a model by A. Godard, of a stag standing guard over doe

	Price Range	

and fawn, on green and black onyx plinth, inscribed "A. GOD-ARD," 27½" long 300.00 500.00*

DOGS

☐ **Bulldog,** carved granite, by George Hilbert, French, signed "Hilbert, 1926," 15¾" high, 25" long 2000.00 3000.00

☐ **Wolfhound,** pottery, by Gold-scheider, sleek white and gray spotted animal sanding on self base, inscribed "Gemignano," and with firm's stamped mark, 12" long 300.00 500.00**

ELEPHANTS

☐ **Ashtray,** brass-backed porcelain 15.00 20.00

☐ **Flambé pottery elephants,** by Doulton, pair, sturdy animals with trunks raised, brilliant red with black detailing, marked, 4½" and 5½" high 350.00 450.00

☐ **Music box,** Dumbo, glazed ceramic 20.00 30.00

☐ **Plate,** Mother's Day plate, 1986, porcelain mother and her young elephant calf figurines 20.00 30.00

☐ **Puzzle,** unfinished hardwood 10.00 12.00

---

*Sold at auction for $330, December 1986, Christie's East, New York.
**Sold at auction for $195, June 1987, Christie's East, New York.

Price Range

GEESE

☐ **Oriental porcelain geese,** pair, turn-of-the-century, polychrome glaze decoration, 7″ high 75.00   85.00

GOATS

☐ **Goat,** bronze, cast from a model by Ary-Bitter, inscribed "Ary Bitter," with foundry mark, brown patina, on self base with wood mount, 5″ high 150.00   250.00*

LIONS

☐ **Standing lions,** pair, Staffordshire porcelain, buff-color glaze decoration with gilded highlights, 13 ½″ long 400.00   500.00
☐ **Lions,** pair, bronze figural, cast from a model by L. Riche, one of the cats reclining being groomed by a seated companion, inscribed "L. RICHE," in green patina, on self base, 23″ long 1400.00 1800.00**

RABBITS

☐ **Rabbit,** pottery, Art Deco style, white crackle glaze, from a design by C. H. Lemanceau, executed by K. G., Clement, France, 12″ long   100.00   200.00

*Sold at auction for $275, December 1986, Christie's East, New York.
**Sold at auction for $1760, December 1986, Christie's East, New York.

ROOSTERS

☐ **Roosters,** pair, Staffordshire porcelain, red and black highlights on white glazed ground, 11 3/4" high 550.00   650.00

Animated Cels

DESCRIPTION: Animated cels are sheets of celluloid with painted designs used to produce color cartoons and full-length animated features. Some films use part animation and part live actors as in Disney's *Song of the South* and the Beatles' *Yellow Submarine*. Cels that combine live actors and animation are as collectible as fully animated cels.

ORIGIN: After Walt Disney Productions' release of *Snow White* in 1937, art dealers and collectors began foreseeing a market for animated cels. The public acceptance of the fanciful characters in *Snow White* encouraged Disney to preserve the cels. During the 1930s and 1940s animated cels continued to sell well, fetching prices from $5 to $50. Today animated cels of that era sell for hundreds of dollars.

MAKER: Although the animated works of Walt Disney Productions and Fleischer Studios are highly collectible, animated cels preceding the 1920s are extremely desirable.

COMMENTS: Animated cels are produced by many notable cartoonists, including Walter Lantz, the creator of Woody Woodpecker, and Charles Jones, the originator of the Roadrunner. Disney's works are perhaps the most desirable of all since the studio often ignored production costs in order to produce detailed cels for the cartoon features.

CARE AND CONDITION: Special care should be taken with

all animated cels, especially those produced prior to 1951. Cels made before 1951 were made of cellulose nitrate, a flammable material that could be a serious fire hazard if stored incorrectly. After 1951 a less flammable celluloid was used. All cels, especially nitrate cels, should be stored individually in closed metal containers. Keep the containers in a cool, well-ventilated area. Do not wrap the cels in paper before storing.

ADDITIONAL TIPS: A glass mount is better than a cardboard mount. If one uses cardboard, it should be made of 100% rag stock. Always display any cel away from heat or humidity.

Note: Values shown below are actual auction-realized prices.

Alice in Wonderland, 1951, showing two playing cards holding red paint brushes; one holds a bucket of red paint, 7″ × 9″, $500. (*Photo courtesy of Phillips, New York*)

Ben and Me, 1953, Walt Disney Studios, 11″ × 14″, framed to 17″ × 20″, $4620. (*Photo courtesy of Phillips, New York*)

	Price Range
☐ **Alice in Wonderland,** 1951, showing two playing cards holding red paintbrushes; one holds a bucket of red paint, 7″ × 9″	500.00
☐ **Bambi,** 1942, showing Bambi and Thumper, WDP in circle appears on lower left background, 6½″ × 8½″	1500.00
☐ **Ben and Me,** 1953, Walt Disney Studios, 11″ × 14″, framed to 17″ × 20″	4620.00
☐ **Brave Little Tailor,** 1938, Mickey fighting soldiers in armor, gouache on full celluloid applied to a Courvoisier stenciled background, 8½″ × 12″	3080.00

Price Range

☐ **Chef Donald,** 1941, showing
Donald racing out of his house, 8″
× 10″ 900.00

☐ **Cinderella,** 1950, Lucifer, the
evil cat, in a crouching position,
8″ × 10″ 600.00

☐ **Daffy Duck,** Warner Brothers,
Daffy in midstride with open bill,
pen and ink, 1937, Leon Schles-
inger, 8½″ × 10½″ 225.00

☐ **Dumbo,** 1941, showing three
large pink elephants, 11″ × 14″ 350.00

☐ **Dumbo,** showing Dumbo and
Timothy, 26″ × 20″ 1150.00

☐ **Fantasia,** 1940, Nutcracker Suite,
marked "200A seq 5-5 SC20 B"
set up on obverse, 11″ × 14″,
framed to 17″ × 20″ 6500.00

Fantasia, 1940, Nutcracker Suite, marked "200A seq 5-5 SC20 B"
set-up on obverse, 11″ × 14″, framed to 17″ × 20″, $6500.
(*Photo courtesy of Phillips, New York*)

Price Range

☐ **The Honey Harvester,** 1949, partial celluloid of Donald Duck as beekeeper, applied to master background depicting an old car in a yard, 11″ × 14″ 1200.00

☐ **Jungle Book,** 1967, Bagheera the panther and Baloo the bear, 11″ × 14″, framed to 16″ × 20″ ... 4600.00

☐ **Lady and the Tramp,** 1955, 9″ × 12″, framed to 16″ × 19″ ... 1900.00

Peter Pan, 1953, Peter Pan holds Wendy in his arms, 10″ × 8″, $1700. (*Photo courtesy of Phillips, New York*)

	Price Range
☐ **Lady and the Tramp,** 1955, showing Lady, Tramp, and their two puppies, 8″ × 10″, framed to 15″ × 17″	2000.00
☐ **Mickey Mouse,** c. 1946, showing Mickey wearing red hunter's outfit, chopping wood, 9″ × 11″ ...	600.00
☐ **Peter Pan,** 1953, Peter Pan holds Wendy in his arms, 10″ × 8″ ...	1700.00
☐ **Pinocchio,** 1940, Figaro, the cat, goes fishing in the belly of the whale, 8″ × 10″	13,000.00
☐ **Sleeping Beauty,** 1959, Princess Aurora sings to "Dream Prince" owl, 10″ × 14″	1100.00
☐ **Snow White and the Seven Dwarfs,** 1937, Snow White is lifted onto the horse by Prince Charming, 7″ × 10″	650.00

Pinocchio, 1940, Figaro, the cat, goes fishing in the belly of the whale, 8″ × 10 ″, $13,000. (*Photo courtesy of Phillips, New York*)

Arcade Machines

TYPES: Trade stimulators, slot machines, mechanical amusement games.

COMMENTS: Originally, these machines were to be found in the arcades of the late nineteenth century—places like Coney Island in New York and Brighton Pier in England. But in the course of the twentieth century, these machines were transformed into gambling devices, more like the slot machines commonly found in Las Vegas and Atlantic City. Store owners would also use these machines to lure customers to their shops, offering the customer the chance to win a small prize in a test of skill or luck. Since gambling of any kind was very often illegal, manufacturers used great ingenuity to conceal the playing of the game. Thus, a slot machine might have been concealed as a gum dispenser.

	Price Range	
☐ **English coin-operated fortune-telling machine,** Ahrens, London, green and blue painted metal case with glazed front reveals a half-length gypsy woman behind curtains, raised on mask and scroll, cast legs with paw feet, 6'9" high	500.00	800.00

	Price Range	
☐ **Japanese 5-cent "Fortune The-ater,"** mechanical guitar-playing and fortune-telling tinplate mon-key automation, in a steel and chromed case, marked "Cragston, Japan," 25″ high	200.00	400.00
☐ **Jennings & Co. Standard Chief 10-cent three-reel slot ma-chine,** in original condition, 26″ high	800.00	1200.00
☐ **Midget 5-cent dice toss,** cast aluminum embossed with lady's profile, 9¼″ wide	100.00	200.00
☐ **Mills Castle 50-cent slot ma-chine,** c. 1934, in restored con-dition, 26½″ high	2000.00	3000.00
☐ **Mills Poinsettia 25-cent slot machine,** c. 1928, in restored condition, 24¼″ high	3000.00	3500.00
☐ **5-cent grip tester,** c. 1900, Pa-cific Machine Works of San Fran-cisco, cast-iron pedestal mounted with scale strength indicator, 5′4″ high	400.00	600.00
☐ **25-cent Cail-O-Scope,** c. 1900, oak with brass decoration, 6′1″ high	700.00	900.00
☐ **Penny Pack three-reel gum-vending machine,** in a domed blue and red painted cast-iron case	80.00	120.00
☐ **Penny-operated Pep Finger Striker,** cast-aluminum strength tester, 18¾″ high	100.00	200.00
☐ **Photo viewing machine,** painted oak with cast-iron owl-face han-dles, incomplete, 35¾″ high	100.00	150.00
☐ **"Uncle Sam" grip tester,** oak case with brass decoration, red, white, and blue cast-metal Uncle Sam, with personality indication dial on chest, 5′7″ high	500.00	700.00

Arms & Armor

DESCRIPTION: Some forms of protective devices have existed since earliest times. Throughout the years, however, they have varied to conform with the changing concepts of war and of the weapons employed.

COMMENTS: Collecting in this field has existed practically since time immemorial. It first began in the remote past, when victorious warriors returned from battle with arms and armor captured from the enemy. It continues today and represents one of the most exotic areas of military collecting. It possesses a fascination for nearly everyone, whether or not military-minded. Well-executed suits of armor and the weapons associated with that time are true objects of art and are highly collectible.

Note: The values shown below are the actual auction-realized prices.

	Price Range
☐ **Ax head,** late medieval, 16th or 17th century, 6½″ long	200.00
☐ **Bayonet,** continental plug, first half of the 18th century, engraved with rococo scrolls on both sides	110.00

Sporting Saxon crossbow, late 16th century, with blackened steel bow painted with the arms of the Electors of Saxony, 23 ¾" length, $17,600. (*Photo courtesy of Christie's East, New York*)

Price Range

☐ **Crossbow,** German Gothic, late 15th century, with robust composite bow covered with painted birch bark and retained by original cords, the top and bottom overlaid with panels of bone and horn, 40" long 8800.00

☐ **Saxon miner's guild ax,** dated 1679, 34" long 440.00

☐ **Rare German horseman's parade hammer,** third quarter of the 16th century, made almost entirely of steel, 24" long 3850.00

Price Range

☐ **Composite estoc,** the blade late
16th century 1980.00

☐ **Sporting Saxon crossbow,** late
16th century, with blackened steel
bow painted with the arms of the
Electors of Saxony, 23 3/4 " long .. 17,600.00

☐ **Italian gunner's stiletto,** mid-
17th century, wooden grip inlaid
with mother-of-pearl pellets,
17 1/2 " long 308.00

☐ **Long stiletto,** late 16th century,
possibly Italian, 19 3/8 " long 385.00

☐ **German left-hand dagger,** in
excavated condition, third quarter of the 16th century, 15 1/4 "
long 418.00

☐ **Bronze bollock knife,** the hilt
possibly early 16th century, with
later blade, 14 3/4 " long 275.00

☐ **Italian medieval dagger,** late
15th century, 11 " long 440.00

☐ **Hammer,** Polish horseman's war
hammer (*czakan*), early 17th cen-
tury, head 8 " long 330.00

☐ **Italian close helmet,** Savoyard
type, c. 1630, 10 1/4 " high 2640.00

☐ **Machete,** American, by Collins &
Co., stamped "Legitimus No.
376" on one side, 23 1/2 " long ... 50.00

☐ **Rapier,** ring-hilt, c. 1630–40,
possibly English, with tapering
hollow-ground blade with pro-
nounced central rib running its
entire length on both sides, blade
38 1/2 " long 605.00

☐ **North European rapier,** c.
1640, S-crowned, stamped
"Caino" on both sides, blade
45 1/4 " long 1320.00

Italian close helmet, Savoyard type, c. 1630, 10¼″ height, $2640. (*Photo courtesy of Christie's East, New York*)

Price Range

☐ **Spanish cup-hilt rapier,** third quarter of the 17th century, stamped "Shagom" within the narrow fuller on both sides, blade 47½″ long 4620.00
☐ **Italian swept-hilt rapier,** c. 1620, flattened hexagonal section stamped "Iohannis" and "Victoria" within the series of short fullers on one side at the forte, and

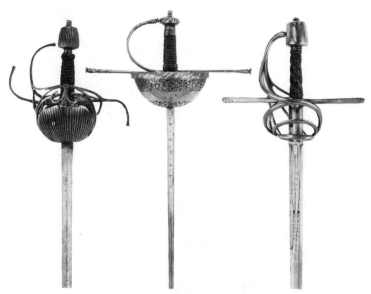

Left to right. North European rapier, c. 1640, S-crowned, stamped "Caino" on both sides, blade 45 ¼ " long, $1320. Spanish cup-hilt rapier, third quarter of the 17th century, stamped "Shagom" within the narrow fuller on both sides, blade 47 ½ " long, $4620. Italian swept-hilt rapier, c. 1620, flattened hexagonal section stamped "Iohannis" and "Victoria" within the series of short fullers on one side at the forte, and "Kirsbaum" and "Victoria Victoria" on the other, original wire-bound grip with two Turk's heads, blade 40 " long, $4400. (*Photo courtesy of Christie's East, New York*)

Price Range

"Kirsbaum" and "Victoria Victoria" on the other, original wire-bound grip with two Turk's heads, blade 40 " long 4400.00

☐ **German stone-bow,** early 17th century, with steel bow retaining its original strings and wooden spacers, the butt inlaid with engraved horn plaques, including scene of Horatius holding the

German stone-bow, early 17th century, with steel bow retaining its original strings and wooden spacers, the butt inlaid with engraved horn plaques, including scene of Horatious holding the bridge and the Roman numerals "MLIX," 27″ length, $1210. (*Photo courtesy of Christie's East, New York*)

	Price Range
bridge and the Roman numerals "MLIX," 27″ long	1210.00
☐ **Italian stone-bow,** late 16th century, with slender steel bow, lion's head carved in front of the bow, a demon mask carved at both ends of the mechanism, and the carved figure of a monster beyond, 38″ long	1430.00

Price Range

☐ **Sword,** German two-hand processional, late 16th century style,
with waved blade inscribed with
cabalistic letters on one side,
blade 55½" long 1540.00

☐ **Sword,** composite medieval,
partly early 15th century, blade
36½" long 935.00

☐ **Sword,** North European arming
sword, c. 1630, with slender tapering blade stamped with a series of letters within the narrow
fuller on both sides at the forte,
blade 34¼" long 385.00

☐ **Sword,** English officer's, c. 1780,
with short curved single-edged
blade struck with maker's mark,
"Harvey" in the body of a running wolf, blade 24½" long 220.00

☐ **Belgian curassier trooper's
helmet,** c. 1843, elaborate brass
mounts, 12½" high 990.00

☐ **French Second Empire cavalry
trooper's helmet,** c. 1860, fitted
with red ostrich plume, 12½"
high 3080.00

Art Deco

DESCRIPTION: The name *Art Deco* really came into popular usage only during the 1960s revival of interest in the interior and architectural design styles of the 1920s and 1930s. The name is derived from the title of the 1925 Parisian *Exposition des Arts Decoratifs et Modernes.* This exposition actually marked the culmination of the French Art Deco style and the emergence of the German-influenced "Modern" style, which was to become popular in America. Today both styles are generally referred to as "phases" of Art Deco.

PERIOD: Art Deco and Art Modern trace their roots to precursors in several countries, such as Italy, England, and Austria, as early as the turn of the century. However, it was the arrival of Diaghilev's *Les Ballets Russes* in Paris in 1908 and 1909 that set off the design revolution that would come to be known as Art Deco. French interior designers dominated the scene but shared the spotlight with the household production of French department stores at the 1925 Exposition. The early phases of the style were influenced by Cubist and African art, the rediscovery of Egyptian design, Orientalism, and a reaction against the lavish ornamentation of Art Nouveau. From the 1920s on, in Europe and America, the more angular Modern phase was influenced by the German

Bauhaus, modern materials, jazz and the syncopated rhythms of urban life, and the coming of age of the machine and the need to mass-produce many items. The style was the last great pervasive international style, and its influence in America was strongly felt through 1939, as evidenced by the sets, costumes, and poster designs for Hollywood films of the era and by the design of souvenirs from the New York World's Fair of 1939.

TYPES: Because the Art Deco style was so pervasive, there is hardly a design field that it did not touch, and collectors of any category of objects will find exciting examples done in the Art Deco style: furnishings, glass and pottery, graphics and posters, jewelry, sculpture, fashion and accessories, household items, from salt and pepper shakers to teapots, and more. Early French Art Deco furniture is now largely held in museums, while the "kitsch" production of later years is still amply represented in flea markets. Prices of many Art Deco objects have skyrocketed in recent years.

COMMENTS: Collectors wishing to build an Art Deco collection should familiarize themselves thoroughly with the design style, making identification simpler. Look for typical materials such as exotic woods, lacquer, chrome, mirrored glass, Bakelite plastic, and stainless steel. Watch for Art Deco design elements and motifs such as streamlining, repetitive circular or angular patterning, vivid colors, geometric designs, sleek female figures, and fast animals such as antelopes, greyhounds, and jaguars. The so-called Tropical Art Deco that flourished in Florida used a more pastel palette and often incorporated flamingos.

ADDITIONAL TIPS: Because much of the Art Deco production in this country is of relatively recent origin, be very wary of fakes and reproductions. Also, many dealers will represent lamps, radios, and other objects of the 1940s and 1950s as Art Deco because the design influence lasted beyond World War II. Art Deco of the 1920s and 1930s has become highly sought after in urban areas, and it is only in rural areas that one can still make a "find" at a flea market. Beginners may want to start with magazine covers, such as *Vogue* or *Harper's Bazaar*, because of their availability and low prices. Art Deco glass perfume bottles made in Czechoslovakia are the most accessible glass collectible. Chase chrome items such as ashtrays, candy dishes, and cocktail shakers can still be found inexpensively. Don't overlook Art Deco–styled American ceramics from Hall, Roseville, and others as a place to start. For collectors looking for a serious investment, French Art Deco furniture, posters, and dazzling Lalique glass are a few sure bets for high returns.

Note: The single values shown below are the actual auction-realized prices.

AMERICAN CERAMICS

	Price Range	
☐ **Ceramic Hall teapots,** various sizes and colors, including the "Aladdin"; "Doughnut," with a hole in the center; the "Automobile"; the "Football"; and the "Basketball"; the most popular Hall glazes are Chinese red and cobalt blue.		
☐ **Most common styles**	25.00	100.00
☐ **Aladdin**	35.00	50.00
☐ **Football style**	250.00	300.00
☐ **Trenton ceramic pottery vases,** produced in the 1930s–1940s, circular or angular stepped-back patterns and "Fiesta"-like colors in paler hues	150.00	250.00
☐ **Roseville "Mostique" style** (1915), pebble-gray background, glossy stylized flower motifs in blue, yellow, green, and brown, inside deep mossy green glaze; transitional style from Art Nouveau.		
☐ **Vase,** 8″, with no handles, streamlined conical shape with flared lip	80.00	120.00
☐ **Bowl,** 7″ diameter, 3″ high, blue, glossy vinelike line around circumference	65.00	95.00

Price Range

☐ **Roseville "Futura" style,** 1928, angular pattern with step-back motif.

☐ **Bowl,** 8″, with an oval stepped base, sharply angular sides, and a brown glaze 60.00   100.00

☐ **Jardiniere and pedestal base,** 29″ high, stacked as 2 pieces; shaded brown glaze 500.00   750.00

☐ **Roseville "Moderne" style,** 1934, spherical shapes with angular motifs and stylized handles.

☐ **Vase,** 8″, with winglike handles, white glaze with rose highlights . 80.00   120.00

☐ **Bowl,** 10″ diameter, with stylized leaf motif in low relief, turquoise glaze with gold shadings. 50.00   75.00

FASHION AND JEWELRY

☐ **Woman's black and white skirt suit** by Coco Chanel with geometric cut and broad lapels. Silk, label intact 7150.00

☐ **Trunk suitcase** by Vuitton, 24″ square × 36″ high, especially designed to hold 33 pairs of shoes; leather, with brass fittings, label intact 1250.00

☐ **Chrome cigarette case,** 4″ × 6″, with geometric pattern in a "sunray" motif; some panels varnished to brass color; felt carrying pouch 65.00   80.00

☐ **Woman's platinum ring,** with four stepped-back rows of four cut rubies and sixteen small diamonds, created around 1927, artist unknown 1000.00   2500.00

Price Range

FURNISHINGS

☐ **Bentwood bar stool,** 28″ high, designed by Josef Hoffmann, executed by J. J. Kohn in 1905. Set of six, each 2500.00

☐ **Marble-based mantel clocks with sconces,** French, 1920–1930, 12″–14″ high, with distinctive angles in design achieved through layering different colors of marble; sometimes surmounted with a reclining female figure, greyhound or other animal; statue sometimes in brass but more often in base metal; price includes pair of sconces.

☐ **Not working** 185.00   250.00
☐ **Working** 350.00   500.00
☐ **Manning-Bowman mantel clock,** 10″ high in pyramid style, with three colors of wood veneer inlaid in geometric patterns; rectangular face with stylized Roman numerals, working 150.00   250.00
☐ **Bedroom set,** 5-piece Heywood-Wakefield Deco style, with bed, bureau, vanity, and two matching chairs in a blond wood veneer, labels intact 400.00

GLASS AND POTTERY

☐ **Daum-Nancy vase,** 14″ high, 5″ diameter base, translucent white glass with lead threading and scalloped lip, signed "Daum Freres"   175.00   225.00
☐ **"Inspiration" pottery wall plaque** by Clarice Cliff, 1930s,

Price Range

13 ″ diameter, with matte glaze of greens and blues, signed 2200.00   2600.00

☐ **"Inspiration" lotus vase,** by Clarice Cliff, 12 ″ high in the "Persian" pattern, signed 7700.00   8000.00

☐ **"Age of Jazz" centerpieces,** series of four sculptural clay figures in bright colors by Clarice Cliff, 7 ″ high, depicting tuxedoed band members and elegant ballroom dancers; each 3300.00   3500.00

☐ **Table lamp,** by Rene Lalique, 22 ″, molded glass with peacocks in low relief and stained in charcoal gray, signed "R. Lalique" ...   15,000.00

☐ **Blue vase,** by Rene Lalique, 10 ″, molded glass with grasshoppers in relief; signed "R. Lalique" 3400.00

☐ **Coty perfume bottle,** c. 1915, 6 ″, clear white molded glass with black enamel panels; design attributed to Rene Lalique, good condition 250.00   400.00

☐ **"Manhattan" salad bowl,** 12 ″ diameter with small glass side handles, by Anchor-Hocking, clear glass with regular repetitive ribbing in a step-back style 35.00   50.00

☐ **Czechoslovakian perfume bottles,** various sizes and clear or translucent colors; both stoppers and bottles are cut in regular or irregular geometric faceting; marked "Czechoslovakia" on bottom; in perfect condition, depending on size, color, and detail of faceting, each 65.00   300.00

Price Range

KITSCH

☐ **Candy dish,** 6″ diameter, in chrome with black Bakelite handles, stamped Chase Chrome, glass liner, artist unknown 12.00 20.00

☐ **"Diplomat" tea service,** including tray, teapot, cream and sugar, in chrome with elongated, fluted styling and side pouring handles in ivory Bakelite, designed by Walter Van Nessen for Chase Chrome 400.00 500.00

☐ **Frankart statue,** slender female figure in cast white metal, 14″ high, painted black, holding blue glass dish; marked "Frankart, Inc. Patent Pend." 250.00 300.00

☐ **Frankart statue,** kneeling female figure in cast white metal, 12″ high, painted black, holding integrated metal dish; marked "Frankart, Inc. Patent Pend." 175.00 225.00

☐ **1933 Century of Progress bookends,** matching pair, 6″ tall, chrome greyhounds on marble base, with Century of Progress seal in metal affixed on base, excellent condition; pair 375.00 475.00

☐ **1933 Century of Progress playing cards;** two pack, depicting Art Deco rendering of Walgreen's Drug Store in monochrome green ink; one deck still in plastic wrapper with tax stamp 36.00 42.00

POSTERS AND GRAPHICS

☐ **"French Lines,"** ocean liner poster by Paul Colin, 24″ × 38″, with image of the prow of *La France* as seen through a veil-like French flag; good condition, some border repair 450.00   600.00

☐ **"L.M.S. Bestway,"** 1928 lithographic rail travel poster by A. M. Cassandre, excellent condition, mounted on linen 25,000.00

☐ **"Power, The Nerve Center of London Underground,"** 1930 lithograph by E. McKnight Kauffer, 39½″ × 25″, good to excellent condition 3000.00   5000.00

☐ **Set of three pochoir prints of women's fashions,** with hand-applied color from *Tres Parisien* magazine, 1927–1928, framed in single frame 125.00   175.00

☐ **Pochoir print of "Cinderella" gown,** by Doeuillet, rendered by Andre Marty from *Gazette du Bon Ton* magazine, 1920 .... 100.00   125.00

☐ **Magazine covers** from fashion magazines including *Vogue, Harper's Bazaar,* and others, depending on the designer featured, the illustrator, and condition: ....

☐ **Common covers** 25.00   35.00

☐ **Scarcer covers** 60.00   150.00

☐ *Wendigen Magazine,* 1922, with cover illustration by Russian graphic artist and painter El Lissitsky 2500.00   3000.00

Price Range

STATUES

☐ **Pierrot,** 12″ bronze and ivory statue by Chiparus on brown Italian marble circular base; front of clown outfit has animated bas relief of the sun, back has face in crescent moon, pointed clown cap painted silver, hands and face in ivory with meticulous detail; stepped marble base is signed 4500.00   5500.00

Reproductions and Recastings

☐ **Dancer with raised skirt,** bronze statue, 12½″ high on marble base, designed by Chiparus, cast from mold made from original statue by Sun Foundry ... 400.00   500.00

☐ **Dancer with tambourine,** 9½″ high on marble base, designed by Duchamps, cast from mold made from original statue by Sun Foundry 225.00   250.00

☐ **Modern senorita,** polychromed bronze and ivory, cast and carved from a model by P. Phillipe, the smiling figure standing in broadbrimmed hat and shawl, her left hand on her hip, her right hand holding an opened fan, inscribed "P. PHILLIPE MADE IN FRANCE," on a domed, red marble base, 18½″ high 7700.00

Modern senorita, polychromed bronze and ivory, cast and carved from a model by P. Phillipe, the smiling figure standing in broad, brimmed hat and shawl, her left hand on her hip, her right hand holding an opened fan, inscribed "P. PHILLIPE MADE IN FRANCE," on a domed, red, marble base, 18 ½" high, sold at auction for $7700. (*Photo courtesy of Christie's East, New York*)

Art Graphics

TYPES: Drawings, paintings, watercolors, sculptures, Old Masters, lithographs, etchings, serigraphs, prints.

COMMENTS: This section provides us with a small sampling of original art sold at auction during the past year.

AMERICAN—19TH AND 20TH CENTURIES

Drawings

Price Range

☐ **Ben Shahn,** *Man with a Guitar,* signed lower right, pen and ink on scored paper, 11″ × 15¾″ 1980.00

☐ **Lilly Martin Spencer,** *Isabella,* pencil on paper, 17½″ × 12½″   660.00

☐ **Mary Cassatt,** *Quietude,* drypoint, 5th State, c. 1891, 10″ × 6¾″, inscribed and signed "L.R., Ref. B.139" 6000.00

☐ **Thomas Nast,** Christmas sketch, signed, dated 1895, inscribed

Price Range

"Compliments of the Season,"
9 1/2 " × 6 1/2 " 770.00

Oil Paintings

☐ **Albert Fitch Bellows,** *Lazy Saturday Afternoon,* signed lower left, oil on canvas, 22 " × 36 " ..   4400.00

☐ **Charles Green Shaw,** abstract shapes, signed and dated 1935 on the reverse, oil on canvas, 39 1/4 " × 32 " 8800.00

☐ **Douglas Volk,** young boy sitting on a rock fishing, signed lower right, oil on canvas, 22 " × 27 "   8800.00

☐ **Frederick Arthur Bridgman,** a view of St. Servan, signed and inscribed "St. Servan, 1889," oil on canvas, 15 1/8 " × 21 1/2 " 5500.00

☐ **Frederick Judd Waugh,** East Coast, Domenica, British West Indies, signed lower right, oil on panel, 36 1/2 " × 48 1/2 " 5720.00

☐ **Jimmy Ernst,** *Floating City,* signed and dated 61, lower right, oil on masonite, 21 1/2 " × 15 " ...   2090.00

☐ **Harriet R. Lumis,** *The Winding Stream,* signed lower right, oil on canvas, 24 1/4 " × 28 1/4 " 14,300.00

☐ **Raphael Soyer,** girl in white blouse, signed lower right, dated Jan. 1948 and inscribed "Study" on the reverse, oil on canvas, 20 " × 16 " 4180.00

☐ **School of Severin Roesen,** opulent still life with grapes, watermelon, peaches, strawberries, cherries on a table, oil on canvas, 25 3/4 " × 36 " 4400.00

Price Range

☐ **Waldo Pierce,** *Paulette's Bouquet* (blackeyed susan and sumac), signed, lower right, oil on canvas, 36¼" × 29" 3740.00

Watercolors

☐ **John Henry Hill,** leaves motionless, watercolor on paper heightened with white gouache, signed, dated 1874 and inscribed "On Lake George New York," 13" × 11" 605.00

☐ **William Henry Stevenson,** composition with blue circle, signed, lower right, watercolor and black ink on paper, 23⅛" × 16¾" 880.00

☐ **William Michael Harnett,** key of color, signed and dated July 71, watercolor on paper, 8½" × 8¼" 2420.00

Sculptures

☐ **Anna Hyatt Huntington,** bronze figure of a yawning tiger, inscribed "Anna V. Hyatt," stamped GORHAM CO FOUNDERS Q402 and inscribed #98, 15½" long, including black Belgian marble base, dark reddish brown patina 2420.00

☐ **Caroline Wilson,** Mary Magdalene, white marble, inscribed on base: "Let her alone: against the day of my burying hath she kept this, John XII. Caroline Wilson, Cin. 1860." 36¼" high 6500.00

Price Range

☐ **Chaim Gross,** standing nude, wooden sculpture, inscribed "Chaim Gross," with monogram, dated 1943 on the base, 82½" high 1650.00

☐ **Richard Henry Park,** *Mignon,* 19th century, marble 12,000.00

EUROPEAN—19TH AND 20TH CENTURIES

Drawings

☐ **Camille Pissaro,** "Woman in a Cloak," crayon drawing, initialed, lower right, 14" × 9½" . 750.00

☐ **Theophile Alexandre Steinlen,** woman and child following a troll, signed lower right, charcoal on paper laid down on board, 17" × 15½" 880.00

☐ **Wilhelm Trubner,** studies of a woman painting, signed with initials and dated 74, black and red chalk on gray-green paper, 10¾" × 6⅜" 440.00

Oil Paintings

☐ **Alexandre Andre Patroff,** still life of red and white roses, signed lower left, oil on panel, 35½" × 28" 1870.00

☐ **Adolphe Weisz,** a maiden reading, signed lower left, oil on canvas, 32" × 24" 7480.00

☐ **Alfred Augustus Glendenning,** a summer afternoon, signed with

	Price Range
monogram and dated "1897," oil on canvas, 18″ × 24″	3080.00
☐ **Antonio Renya,** sailboat by the Doge's Palace, signed and inscribed "Venezia," lower left, oil on canvas, 11¾″ × 23½″	7480.00
☐ **Dutch School,** 19th century, shipping off a village, oil on cradled panel, 16½″ × 23″	3080.00
☐ **Fr. Antoine,** still life with grapes, apples, walnuts, and a green glass, signed and dated 1904, lower right, oil on panel, 14½″ × 17½″	1760.00
☐ **Henri Biva,** the Rhone Valley, signed lower left, oil on canvas, 52″ × 47″	13,200.00
☐ **Lionel Noel Royer,** *Madonna and Child,* signed lower right, oil on canvas, 42″ × 27″	6600.00
☐ **Hermann Kern,** *The Flute Player,* signed lower left, oil on panel, 27¼″ × 19″	7700.00
☐ **Segin,** *The Serenade,* signed and dated 86, lower right, oil on canvas, 17″ × 12″	16,500.00

Impressionist Paintings

☐ **Vincent Van Gogh,** *Sunflowers,* January 1889, oil on extended canvas, 39½″ × 30¼″, set a record selling price at Christie's 1987 auction (see color insert)	39,921,750.00
☐ **Vincent Van Gogh,** *Le Pont de Trinquetaille,* October 1888, oil on canvas, 28¾″ × 36¼″	20,240,000.00

Vincent Van Gogh, *Le Pont de Trinquetaille,* October 1888, oil on canvas, 28¾″ × 36¼″, $20,240,000. (*Photo courtesy of Christie's, New York*)

Price Range

Watercolors

☐ **Antoine Gaspard Truchet,** a boulevard in Paris, signed and dated "Paris 1890," watercolor, chalk and crayon on paper, 16¼″ × 27½″ 2750.00

☐ **Francis Garat,** street in Montmartre, signed lower right, watercolor and charcoal heightened with white, 7½″ × 10¼″ 1100.00

☐ **Henry Cassiers,** *The Daily Chores of a Village,* signed lower left, watercolor and gouache

Price Range

heightened with white, 15″ × 18″ 1045.00

☐ **Onorato Carlandi,** *Hanging the Wash Out to Dry,* signed and inscribed "Roma," lower right, watercolor on paper, 21½″ × 16½″ 2420.00

☐ **R. V. Meunier,** *Boar Hunt,* signed, watercolor and gouache over pencil, fan-shaped, 23″ × 10¾″ 550.00

☐ **Willem Karel Nakken,** horses in a stable, signed lower left, watercolor on paper, 15½″ × 23¼″ 1430.00

OLD MASTERS

☐ **Austrian School,** mid-18th century, portraits (two) of Joseph II of Austria and Queen Maria Teresa, oil on canvas, 32½″ × 25″ 2420.00

☐ **Flemish School,** 17th century, troopers in a landscape, oil on canvas, 27″ × 35¼″ .... 2420.00 (Auction)

☐ **German School,** 18th century, portrait of a man, half-length, in gray coat and red cloak, oil on canvas in a painted oval, 26½″ × 34″ 2420.00

☐ **Studio of John de Critz,** portrait of James I of England, oil on canvas, 80½″ × 46½″ 23,000.00

Austrian School, mid-18th century, portraits (two) of Queen Maria Teresa and Joseph II of Austria, oil on canvas, 32 ½″ × 25″, $2420. (*Photo courtesy of Christie's East, New York*)

ART NOUVEAU, ART DECO, ART MODERN

Lithographs

Price Range

☐ **Alphonse Mucha,** *Sarah Bernhardt: American Tour, 1986,* lithograph in colors with lettering, on two sheets, signed in black lower left, 75¼″ × 26″, framed 3080.00

☐ **Louis Icart** from *Dessins des Femmes,* c. 1928, of a woman playing with a puppet, approximately 17″ × 12½″, framed 715.00

Etchings

☐ **Louis Icart,** *Illusion,* c. 1940, etching and drypoint in colors, on black ground, signed lower right, with artist's blindstamp, 19″ × 9″, framed 5500.00

☐ **Louis Icart,** *Coursing II,* c. 1929, etching and drypoint in colors, pencil-signed lower right, with artist's blindstamp, 15½″ × 26″ 3300.00

☐ **Louis Icart,** *Gay Trio,* c. 1936, etching and drypoint in colors, signed lower right, with artist's blindstamp, 19½″ × 11½″, framed 1320.00

☐ **Louis Icart,** *Love's Blossom,* c. 1926, etching and drypoint in colors, pencil-signed lower right, with artist's blindstamp, 17″ × 25″, framed 1540.00

Louis Icart, *Coursing II,* c. 1929, etching and drypoint in colors, pencil-signed lower right, with artist's blindstamp, 15 ½″ × 26″, $3300. (*Photo courtesy of Christie's East, New York*)

Price Range

Oil Paintings

☐ **Alexandre Claude,** "La Valley" (1862–1927), Art Nouveau nymph, oil on canvas, signed lower left, 32″ × 25″ 495.00

Serigraphs

☐ **Erte** (Romain de Tirtoff), *Angel,* signed in pencil lower right, numbered LII/CL, published by Chalk & Vermilion, 26 ¼″ × 37 ½″, framed 1980.00

☐ **Erte** (Romain de Tirtoff), *The Arctic Sea,* 1981, embossed serigraph with foil stamping, signed in pencil lower right, inscribed "AP 36/60," 22″ × 16″, framed 2970.00

Louis Icart, *Gay Trio,* c. 1936, etching and drypoint in colors, signed lower right, with artist's blind-stamp, 19½″ × 11½″, framed, $1320. (*Photo courtesy of Christie's East, New York*)

Price Range

☐ **Erte** (Romain de Tirtoff), "Bride," from *The Twenties Remembered Suite,* 1977, serigraph in colors, signed in lower right, numbered "57 of 300," published by Circle Fine Arts, 18″ × 13½″, framed 1430.00

Grant Wood, *Approaching Storm,* lithograph, 1940, signed in pencil, from the edition of 250, image 12″ × 9″, $1900. (*Photo courtesy of Phillips, New York*)

Price Range

American Prints

☐ **Grant   Wood,** *Approaching Storm,* lithograph, 1940, signed in pencil, from the edition of 250, image 12″ × 9″ 1900.00

J. Hill (after William Guy Wall), *The Hudson River Portfolio,* fifteen (of twenty) etchings and aquatints with hand-coloring, 1821-
1825, plates 17⁷⁄₈″ × 24¼″, $65,000. (*Photo courtesy of Phillips,
New York*)

	Price Range
☐ **Grant Wood,** *Shriners' Quartet,* lithograph, 1939, signed in pencil, inscribed "To Mack & Irene Kantor in appreciation & friendship," from the edition of 250, published by Associated American Artists, image 8″ × 11¾″	1100.00
☐ **James E. Allen,** *On Top of the World,* etching, signed in pencil, plate 12¼″ × 8¾″, faint mat browning, thin line on tape on margins	1000.00
☐ **J. Hill** (after William Guy Wall), *The Hudson River Portfolio,* 15 (of 20) etchings and aquatints with	

John Taylor Arms, *Sarah Jane,* etching, 1920, signed in pencil, numbered 63/78, title by Arms, address in Arms' own hand on reverse, plate 10¼″ × 7¼″, $950. (*Photo courtesy of Phillips, New York*)

	Price Range
hand-coloring, 1821–25, plates 17⅞″ × 24¼″	65,000.00
☐ **John Taylor Arms,** *Sarah Jane,* etching, 1920, signed in pencil, numbered 63/78, title by Arms, address in Arms' own hand on reverse, plate 10¼″ × 7¼″	950.00

Wanda Gag, *Gumbo Lane,* lithograph, signed in pencil, image 10″ × 12¾″, $150. (*Photo courtesy of Phillips, New York*)

	Price Range
☐ **Roy Lichtenstein,** *Crying Girl,* 1963, signed in pencil and dated, image 17¼″ × 23″	3960.00
☐ **Stow Wengenwroth,** *Strange Visitors,* lithograph, 1944, signed in pencil, inscribed "To Lenton and Jay Roland with best wishes— Stow Wengenwroth," image 10½″ × 9½″	425.00
☐ **Wanda Gag,** *Gumbo Lane,* lithograph, signed in pencil, image 10″ × 12¾″	150.00

Modern and European Prints and Sculptures

☐ **Alberto Giacometti,** *Grand Femme Debout III,* 1960, signed

Bernard Buffet, *New York,* lithograph printed in colors, 1965, signed in pencil, annotated EA, on arches, one of the 30 artist's proofs printed before the edition of 150, 18¾" × 26⅞", $750. (*Photo courtesy of Phillips, New York*)

	Price Range
and numbered 1/6, bronze with dark brown patina, 92½" high ...	2,530,000.00
□ **Alberto Giacometti,** *Grande Femme Debout I,* 1960, signed and numbered 3/6, bronze with dark brown patina, 105⅞" high	3,080,000.00
□ **Alberto Giacometti,** *Grande Femme Debout IV,* 1960, signed and numbered 1/6, bronze with dark brown patina, 107⅞" high	3,630,000.00
□ **Bernard Buffet,** *New York,* lithograph printed in colors, 1965, signed in pencil, annotated EA, on arches, one of the 30 artist's proofs printed before the edition of 150, 18¾" × 26⅞"	750.00

Price Range

☐ **Henri Matisse,** *Nu Renverse,* etching, c. 1929, signed in pencil, numbered 16/25, image 9 3/4 " × 7 " 2600.00

☐ **Joan Miro,** *Miro,* lithograph printed in colors, signed in pencil, annotated HC, image 30 " × 22 " 900.00

☐ **Mark Chagall,** *Offering of Flowers,* lithograph printed in colors, 1964, signed in pencil, numbered 40/50, on arches, image 24 1/2 " × 18 3/4 " 3300.00

☐ **Mark Chagall,** *Les Artistes,* colored lithograph, signed lower right and numbered 11/50, 12 1/4 " × 11 " 1800.00

☐ **Mark Chagall,** *Reverie,* colored lithograph, signed lower right and annotated "epreuve d'artiste III/VII," 12 " × 16 " 1200.00

☐ **Milton Avery,** *Dawn,* woodcut printed in black and yellow, 1952, signed in pencil, from the edition of 100 published by the Collectors of Amerian Art, on japan paper, image 8 3/4 " × 7 " 900.00

☐ **Pierre Auguste Renoir,** *La Danse a la Champagne* 4950.00

☐ **Tsuguhary Foujita,** *Two Friends,* lithograph printed in colors, 1964, signed in pencil, annotated HC, image 22 " × 18 " .. 550.00

Art Nouveau

PERIOD: The period of Art Nouveau decorative and fine arts ranges from the last fifteen years or so of the nineteenth century to the second decade of the twentieth century. It came out of the Aesthetic movement in England and the belief of its founder, William Morris, that all decorative arts should be handmade. The name derives from the 1895 opening of a design shop in Paris, L'Art Nouveau.

CHARACTERISTICS: The Art Nouveau style is characterized by a return to nature in motifs executed by sensual, flowing lines with a heavy Oriental influence. Two of the most important aspects of Art Nouveau are asymmetry and femininity. There is a wide use of maidens with flowing hair, flowers, scrolls, tendrils, snakes, and anything else with sinuous curves.

BRONZES

	Price Range
☐ **Candelabra,** pair, cast from a model by Firmin Bate, inscribed "Firmin Bate," 22″ high	1320.00 (Auction)

Candelabra, pair, cast from a model by Firmin Bate, inscribed "Firmin Bate," 22″ high, sold at auction for $1320. (*Photo courtesy of Christie's East, New York*)

	Price Range
☐ **Dancer,** large patinated metal figure, by Leon Alliot, inscribed "L. Alliot," 40″ high	2090.00 (Auction)
☐ **Georgie,** bronze bust of a woman, cast from a model by Van der Straeten, of an Art Nouveau maiden in plumed hat, holding a	

Dancer, large patinated metal figure, by Leon Alliot, inscribed "L. Alliot," 40″ high, sold at auction for $2090. (*Photo courtesy of Christie's East, New York*)

Price Range

branch of cherries in her teeth, inscribed "Van der Straeten" and with foundry stamp, 20″ high ...   495.00

☐ **La Sibylle,** bronze bust, cast from a model by Emmanuel Villanis, inscribed "E. Villanis," in golden brown patina, on self pedestal base, 27½″ high ....   1980.00 (Auction)

☐ **Jeunesse: Girl with Lamb,** cast from a model by Silvestre, of a nude woman kneeling, facing a rambunctious springing lamb, inscribed "Silvestre" and "Susse Fres. Edtrs Paris," in golden

	Price Range
brown patina on self rectangular base, 32½″ long	1240.00

FURNITURE

☐ **Armchair,** carved mahogany, French, c. 1900, the heart-shaped padded back set in carved poppy frame joined by bowed armrests, to rounded seat on four legs, the front with cabriole form and carved floral crest, 40″ high 220.00

☐ **Cahier de music,** French, elm and burlwood, the rectangular burl top with tapered side supports enclosing record shelves, 41″ high, 12½″ wide, 18″ long 352.00

☐ **Cahier de music,** French, walnut, the shelved superstructure over glazed vitrine supported on leaf-carved cabriole legs with stretcher, separated with record slats, 61″ high, 21″ long, 14″ wide 605.00

☐ **Carved oak desk,** by Louis Majorelle, the three-drawer rectangular top with arched supports, on two pedestal support ends fitted with file and drawer division, having stylized brass hardware, 59″ long, 33″ diameter, 32″ high 1100.00

☐ **Carved oak chairs,** French, the tall rectangular back with openwork decoration of violent ribbon splat, on square peach upholstered seat, supporting gently tapering legs, 38″ high 950.00

☐ **Chandelier,** bronze and glass, the pillow-shaped fixture incised with

Price Range

tulips, four fully molded tulips at each corner, holding milky iridescent glass bell shades, unmarked, suspended on four chains with tulip ceiling cap, 26″ high 550.00

☐ **Dressing table,** French, mahogany, with arched rectangular mirror supported by carved leaf ends, the rectangular top with superstructure flanked by two quarter drawers over one long drawer, on four slender cabriole legs, bronze leaf handles with leaf-molded ends, 55″ high, 36″ wide, 19½″ deep 440.00

☐ **Plant stand,** mahogany, with stepped shelves above scrolled supports, 52″ high, 20½″ wide, 11½″ deep 400.00

☐ **Wall mirror,** maple and pewter, having a floral-design pewter crest and sides inset with art-glass discs, 15½″ high, 24″ wide 400.00

JEWELRY

☐ **Brooch,** probably French, c. 1900, the small openwork heart-shaped pin of boldly scrolled ribbon design bordering a cherub's head 300.00   400.00

☐ **Gold necklace,** the openwork mount with pine cone motifs set with a lozenge-shape synthetic peridot, suspended from a smaller gold and similarly set link on a fine gold, fancy link chain 400.00   500.00

☐ **Scroll pendant,** c. 1900, green, spot enameled, seed pearl set with

Price Range

baroque pearl top, and Art Nouveau gold orchid flower brooch
pendant with mauve and yellow
enamel petals, a gold curb chain
and a Victorian oval black-enamel
memorial brooch with half-pearl
and diamond flowers, locket back,
4 pieces 700.00   800.00

SCULPTURES

☐ **Bust group of a mother and
child,** French School, the child
with its arms around the mother's
neck, both in caps, 25 ³/₈ ″ high ..   700.00   1000.00
☐ **Spelter bust,** depicting a Victo-
rian maiden raised on a mottled
brown marble plinth, 11 ½ ″ high   65.00

MISCELLANEOUS DECORATIONS

☐ **Brass flower vase,** tapering cylindrical body with low-relief
sunflowers and stem handles,
signed ''B.C. Poccard,'' and dated
''Salon 1901,'' 12 ½ ″ high 350.00
☐ **Brass figural lamp,** in the form
of a female floating on a lily pad,
entitled ''La Vingbrie,'' red mar-
ble base, 24 ″ high 1100.00
☐ **Metal female figurine,** by Louis
Moreau, carrying a floral garland
and a bird, entitled ''Nymphe des
Bois,'' signed ''Louis Moreau,''
17 ½ ″ high 180.00
☐ **Pewter urn,** with baluster body,
elongated neck, stylized flowers

Price Range

in relief and branch handle, marked "AS, WMFB, I/O, 88," 14 1/2″ high 700.00

☐ **Pottery vase,** by A. Boudin, baluster form, claret to black coloration and rust and green interior, mounted in silver plate, fluid floral frame, signed, 6″ high 190.00

☐ **Silver-overlaid art glass vases,** pair, each with slightly tapered pinched sides, enameled lily reserves and floral-designed silver mounts over mottled green case glass bodies, 6″ high 700.00

Arts and Crafts

HISTORY: By the dawn of the twentieth century, a major reform movement was underway that was designed to improve the quality of American life by furnishing homes with handcrafted furniture, pottery, metalware, and other decorative arts. The Arts and Crafts movement was intended to serve dual puposes: to reform the industrialized factory system and to improve the lives of the American people.

This movement was not launched from atop empty soapboxes on busy street corners but instead came from within the workshops of designers and manufacturers such as Gustav Stickley, Elbert Hubbard, Frank Lloyd Wright, Louis Tiffany, William Fulper, Samuel Weller, William Grueby, and Robert Jarvie. They produced quality oak furniture, decorated pottery, and hand-hammered metalware in factory environments that were designed to encourage their craftsmen to take joy and pride in their work.

DESCRIPTION: The furniture from this era is almost always made of highly figured oak, often stained a dark reddish-brown. The furniture is very plain, often stark-looking, especially when compared to the elaborately carved walnut furniture of the Victorians. It is also very heavy, for the designers avoided veneers and used strong, heavy stock for their furniture. Wide slats, pegged joints, leather upholstery, and hand-hammered hardware are also characteristic of Arts and Crafts furniture from 1894 to 1923.

The pottery is often hand-painted, and the best was even hand-thrown on the potter's wheel rather than cast in a mold. The potters did a great deal of experimenting, thus we find a variety of colors and shapes; but many preferred to work with matte or dull glazes, giving their pottery a soft, satin glow.

The metalware of the period—lamp bases, candlesticks, bookends, desk sets, vases, and chandeliers—is generally copper or brass and will bear the obvious marks of the hammer rather than the smooth, glossy look of modern accessories. The hand-beaten look was highly desirable, for it implied that a person, not a machine, produced it. The hand-hammered metalware was usually treated with a mild acid to darken it, thereby simulating the aged look they sought to duplicate.

Whether it be an oak Stickley settle, a deep-green Grueby vase, or a hand-hammered Dirk Van Erp lamp, the combination of quality materials, pleasing design, and handcraftsmanship will ensure continued appreciation and lasting value for decades to come.

Note: The single values shown below are actual auction-realized prices.

	Price Range	
☐ **Oak tabouret,** by L. & J. G. Stickley, c. 1910, the octagonal top on square legs joined by a cross stretcher, white and gold decal label, Model No. 559, 20″ high, 18″ diameter	700.00	900.00
☐ **Ebonized oak "crib" settle,** by Gustav Stickley, c. 1902, original finish, red decal, Model No. 207, 39″ high, 70″ long, 33″ deep ...	10,000.00	15,000.00
☐ **Oak and leather library table,** hexagonal, by Gustav Stickley, c. 1910, branded mark, Model No. 624, 30″ high, 48″ diameter	8000.00	12,000.00

Inlaid oak chest of drawers, attributed to Stickley Brothers, c. 1910, the gallery top with pewter and ebony floral inlaid panels, with nickel-plated brass pulls, 55 ½" high, 34" wide, 22" deep, $2000–$3000. (*Photo courtesy of Phillips, New York*)

	Price Range	
☐ **Inlaid oak chest of drawers,** attributed to Stickley Brothers, c. 1910, the gallery top with pewter and ebony floral inlaid panels, nickel-plated brass pulls, 55 ½" high, 34" wide, 22" deep	2000.00	3000.00

Oak server, by Gustav Stickley, c. 1910, branded mark, Model No. 818, 38½″ high, 42″ long, 18″ deep, $1500–$2500. (*Photo courtesy of Phillips, New York*)

	Price Range	
☐ **Oak server,** by Gustav Stickley, c. 1910, branded mark, Model No. 818, 38½″ high, 42″ long, 18″ deep	1500.00	2500.00

Oak table lamp, by Gustav Stickley, c. 1909, the Japanese wicker shade above a squared standard with four corbeled supports continuing to a square base, 22″ high, stamp-marked on base "Model No. 504," $2600. (*Photo courtesy of Phillips, New York*)

Price Range

☐ **Oak table lamp,** by Gustav Stickley, c. 1909, the Japanese wicker shade above a squared standard with four corbeled supports continuing to a square base, 22″ high, stamp-marked on base "Model No. 504" 2600.00

	Price Range	
☐ **Oak and leather bench,** by Gustav Stickley, c. 1905, red decal, 32″ high, 20½″ deep, 55″ long	5000.00	7000.00
☐ **Oak round table,** by Gustav Stickley, c. 1910, branded mark, Model No. 607, 29″ high, 24″ diameter	800.00	1200.00
☐ **Oak dining table,** by Gustav Stickley, c. 1902, the circular top with two leaves, branded mark, 29″ high, 48″ diameter, leaves 12″	2500.00	3500.00
☐ **Ebonized oak single-door bookcase,** by Charles P. Limbert, c. 1910, original dark finish, branded mark, 48″ high, 32¾″ wide, 12¼″ deep	2000.00	3000.00
☐ **Oak center table,** by Charles P. Limbert, c. 1910, stamped on wood "Limbert 158 Model No. 158," 30″ high, 47½″ wide, 36″ deep		11,000.00
☐ **Oak slant-front desk,** by Lifetime Furniture Company, c. 1910, fall-front opening to reveal a fitted interior above two long drawers and an arched apron, decal stamp, 43″ high, 32″ wide, 16″ deep	700.00	900.00
☐ **Oak "Ali Baba" bench,** by Roycroft, c. 1910, carved orb mark, 19¾″ high, 42″ long, 11″ deep	1500.00	2500.00
☐ **Oak and leather armchair,** by George Washington Maher for the E. L. King house, Rockledge, in Homer, Minnesota, c. 1912, original green satin, 45¾″ high, 25¼″ wide, 22½″ deep		7500.00
☐ **Oak dining chairs,** set of seven, by the Majestic Furniture Company, c. 1910, one armchair and		

	Price Range
six side chairs, 47 ½″ high, 17 ¼″ wide, 16 ¾″ deep	6000.00
☐ **Oak tall case clock,** by George Washington Maher for the E. L. King house, Rockledge, in Homer, Minnesota, c. 1912, no clockworks, 80″ high, 31 ½″ wide, 15″ deep	27,000.00
☐ **Oak hall chair,** American, c. 1910, in the style of Rennie Macintosh, slip seat upholstered in blue velvet, 49″ high	1300.00
☐ **Oak Morris chair,** designed by David Kendall for Phoenix Furniture Co., Grand Rapids, Michigan, c. 1900, original green finish, Model No. 372, 40″ high, 31″ wide, 30 ½″ deep	4000.00
☐ **Inlaid oak china closet,** by The Shop of the Crafters, Cincinnati, c. 1906, paper label with lantern trademark on back, 63 ⅛″ high, 42″ wide, 15 ¾″ deep	17,000.00
☐ **Oak rocker,** by Charles Rohlfs, 1903, branded coping saw encircling R and carved 1903 on rear apron, 32″ high, 20″ wide, 19″ deep	8500.00

Autographs

DESCRIPTION: Original autographs of celebrities, including presidents, entertainers, writers, and artists, are fairly available and always sought after.

PERIOD: Autographs exist dating from the Middle Ages.

COMMENTS: Autographs have established cash values though they vary greatly in price because each specimen is unique. Single signatures are generally less expensive than signatures that are part of a letter. Often values depend on buyer demand.

ADDITIONAL TIPS: A holograph letter, AL, is a letter written entirely in the person's handwriting. A letter with the body written or typed by a secretary is referred to as an L. D is for a signed document, and N is for a signed note.

Listed alphabetically by celebrity name, prices are given for ALs, Ls, signed photo, manuscript page, document, and plain signatures.

Note: The value of each item shown below is the actual auction-realized price.

ARTISTS

Price Range

☐ **Dali, Salvador,** photograph, signed and inscribed, 1969, also shows Count Vassili Adlerberg, "Pour mon ami li Compte, BABA . . . Dali 1969," 8″ × 10″, small hole near upper edge 140.00

☐ **Manet, Edouard,** autograph letter, signed, in French, 1 page, 8vo, Monday, to "Mon cher Heyman," asking him for money and sayng that if any "concessions" are necessary he is prepared to make them 425.00

☐ **Matisse, Henri,** autograph letter, signed, in French, 1½ pages, 5 May 1933, to an unnamed recipient, regarding some panels he had painted 650.00

☐ **Renoir, Pierre-Auguste,** autograph letter, signed, in French, 1 page, 8vo, Cagues, Sunday morning, 5 February, to "Mon cher Berard," telling him of his visit to see Deudon, and he finishes, "If by chance you should run across young Blanche ask him about the story of Manet's painting which he sold to friends of Duret. You will be amazed!" 900.00

COMPOSERS

☐ **Liszt, Franz,** autographed letter, signed, 2 pages, 8vo, 2 July 1860, to an unknown recipient, "your excellence," giving him the address of Princess Wittgenstein in Rome and saying how her stay

Strauss, Richard, typed letter (carbon copy), signed, with autograph date and place, in German, one page, Garmisch, 5 December 1944, to "Herr Viceprasident," $800. (*Photo courtesy of Phillips, New York*)

	Price Range
there is suiting her well; some browning	450.00
☐ **Puccini, Giacomo,** autograph letter, signed, in Italian, 1 page, Torre del Lago, 25 May 1905, to Vitale, regarding "Madame Butterfly"	1100.00
☐ **Strauss, Richard,** typed letter (carbon copy), signed, with autograph date and place, in German,	

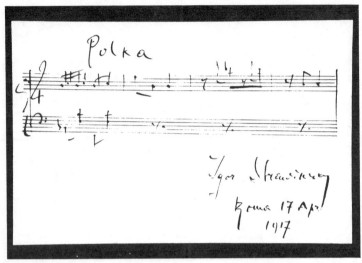

Stravinski, Igor, autograph musical quotation, signed, Rome, April 1917, four bars in treble and bass clef, entitled ''Polka,'' 4¾" × 7¼", $850. (*Photo courtesy of Phillips, New York*)

	Price Range
1 page, Garmisch, 5 December 1944, to ''Herr Viceprasident'' ...	800.00
☐ **Stravinski, Igor,** autograph musical quotation, signed, Rome, April 1917, four bars in treble and bass clef, entitled ''Polka,'' 4¾" × 7¼"	850.00
☐ **Verdi, Giuseppe,** autograph letter, signed, in Italian, 1 page, 8vo, 9 September 1879, to Signor Mola, regarding his old servant Mami	900.00
☐ **Wagner, Richard,** autograph letter, signed, in French, 1 page, to ''Cher ami,'' inviting his correspondent and wife to dinner where they will meet several friends	800.00

EXPLORERS, INVENTORS, AND SCIENTISTS

Price Range

☐ **Bell, Alexander Graham,** typed
letter, signed, 1 page, 4to, to
"Dear Master Philip," granting
him his request for an autograph;
and **Edison, Thomas A.,** autograph, in pencil on small card,
both 170.00

☐ **Curie, Marie,** autograph letter,
signed, 1 page, Faculte des Sciences de Paris, Institut de Ra-
dium, 22 May 1921, to Miss
Brooks, letter of thanks 850.00

☐ **Darwin, Charles,** autograph, cut
from a larger sheet, signed, 1
page, oblong 12mo, 24 September
1875, Down, Kent 200.00

☐ **Lindbergh, Charles,** typed letter, 1 page, small 4to, Main, Hawaii, 8 January 1970, to "Dear
Miss Cunningham," regarding the
"Whitman manuscript," and his
comments on it which he had sent
to Bill Jovanovich, a copy of
which he encloses 450.00

☐ **Livingstone, David,** autograph
letter, signed, 4 pages, 8vo, New-
stead Abbey, 28 February 1865, to
"My dear Kirk" 600.00

FAMOUS PERSONALITIES

☐ **Barnum, P. T.,** autograph senti-
ment, clipped from larger sheet,
Waldemere, 9 August 1875,
"Truly yours," tipped to larger
sheet 75.00

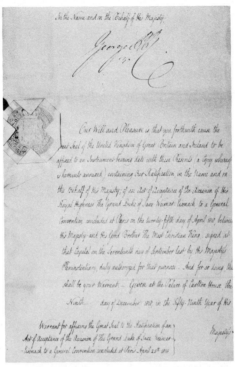

George IV, "Warrant for affixing the Great Seal to the Ratification of an Act of Acceptance of the Accession of the Swiss Confederation to a General Convention concluded at Paris April 25th 1818," document, signed "George R" at head, as Prince Regent, 23 pages, folio, Carlton House, 12 November 1818, includes a listing of the amount of reparations owed by France to the various countries involved in the years of war, totalling 12,040,000 francs, text in French and English, also signed by Viscount Sidmouth, seal on first page, slight soiling, $700. (*Photo courtesy of Phillips, New York*)

Price Range

☐ **Young, Brigham,** authograph,
on card, topped down at corner   180.00

HISTORICAL

☐ **Catherine II** (the Great), Empress of Russia, document, signed,
1 page, oblong folio, on vellum, 30

Price Range

December 1777, appointing a military position, signed by another hand, engraved decorative border, royal seal, printed 900.00

☐ **George IV,** "Warrant for affixing the Great Seal to the Ratification of an Act of Acceptance of the Accession of the Swiss Confederation to a General Convention concluded at Paris April 25th 1818," document, signed "George R" at head, as Prince Regent, 23 pages, folio, Carlton House, 12 November 1818, includes a listing of the amount of reparations owed by France to the various countries involved in the years of war, totaling 12,040,000 francs, text in French and English, also signed by Viscount Sidmouth, seal on first page, slight soiling 700.00

☐ **James I,** English king, 1603–1625, document, signed "James R" at head, 1 page, small 4vo, on vellum, Westminster, 22 December (1614), to "the keepers of Lyennalt and Chappell Lyennalt walkes," royal seal, faint browning, two small holes at joint of folds with no loss of text 1400.00

☐ **Napoleon I,** "Emperor of the French Letter," signed "Bonaparte," in French, 2 pages, 4to, Paris, 7 January 1798, to General Berthier, last seven words in Napoleon's hand, regarding an evacuation of troops "You realise of course that to have them pass by

James I, King, 1603–1625, document, signed "James R" at head, one page, small 4vo, on vellum, Westminster, 22 December (1614), to "the keepers of Lyennalt and Chappell Lyennalt walkes . . . ," royal seal, faint browning and two small holes at joint of folds with no loss of text, $1400. (*Photo courtesy of Phillips, New York*)

Price Range

the river Genes is to have them no longer." 1300.00

☐ **Nelson, Horatio,** Admiral, Viscount, document, signed "Nelson & Bronte," 1 page, folio, "Victory," 22 March 1804, enlistment paper for Michele Berlingiery of Naples 1200.00

Napoleon I, "Emperor of the French Letter," signed "Bonaparte," in French, two pages, 4to, Paris, 7 January 1798, to General Berthier, last seven words in Napoleon's hand, regarding an evacuation of troops, "You realise of course that to have them pass by the river Genes is to have them no longer . . . ," $1300. (*Photo courtesy of Phillips, New York*)

Price Range

LITERARY

☐ **Alcott, Louisa May,** autograph letter, signed, 1 page, 8vo, Boston, 9 April, to H. H. Robinson, apologizing that she has no time to write a speech for a meeting ..   190.00

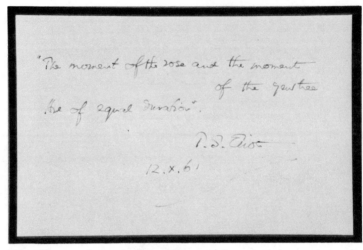

Eliot, Thomas Stearns, autograph quotation, signed, one page, oblong 8vo, dated 12 October 1961, "The moment of the rose and the moment of the yew tree are of equal duration," $700. (*Photo courtesy of Phillips, New York*)

Price Range

☐ **Eliot, Thomas Stearns,** autograph quotation, signed, 1 page, oblong 8vo, dated 12 October 1961, "The moment of the rose and the moment of the yew tree are of equal duration" 700.00

☐ **Kipling, Rudyard,** autograph letter, signed, 1 page, 8vo, Waite, VT., 6 May 1896, to an unnamed recipient regarding the setting to music of one of his songs and suggesting that the recipient contact A. P. Watt in London to check the copyright regarding public performance 250.00

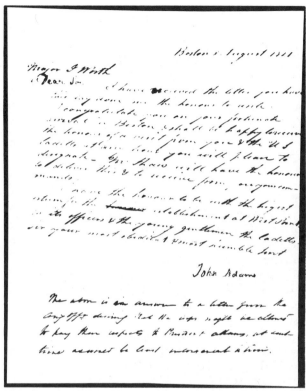

Adams, John, second president, letter, signed and with autograph salutation, 4to, Boston, 8 August 1821, to Major J. Worth, saying that he will be happy to receive him and some cadets at "any hour," $1600. (*Photo courtesy of Phillips, New York*)

Price Range

☐ **Scott, Sir Walter,** autograph letter, signed, 1 page, 4to, Edinburgh, 5 January 1821, to William S. Rose, arranging an appointment 110.00

PRESIDENTS

☐ **Adams, John,** second president, letter, signed and with autograph

Price Range

salutation, 4to, Boston, 8 August
1821, to Major J. Worth, saying
that he will be happy to receive
him and some cadets at "any
hour" 1600.00

☐ **Adams, John Quincy,** sixth
president, document, signed as
president, on vellum, 1 page, oblong 4to, 1 April 1825, on document printed during Monroe's
term of office with Monroe's
name crossed out and Adams'
substituted, granting an area of
land in Ohio to Andrew Pinneo . 150.00

☐ **Coolidge, Calvin,** 30th president, three items: typed letter,
signed, as Governor of Massachusetts, 1 page, 4to, State House,
Boston, 12 August 1920; autograph, clipped from larger sheet,
November 1919; and larger sheet
inscribed by Coolidge "Have faith
in Massachusetts" 120.00

☐ **Hoover, Herbert,** 31st president, autograph, cut from larger
sheet, 24 September 1919, "with
kind wishes of Herbert Hoover,
Stamford University, California" 180.00

☐ **Kennedy, John F.,** 35th president, photograph, signed and inscribed "Pres. Elect John F.
Kennedy," November 1965, also
signed by Edward Kennedy, ink
(red) faded, 7½" × 9½", creased 300.00

☐ **McKinley, William,** 25th president, document, signed as governor of Ohio, 1 page, folio, 28 May
1895, appointing William Bar-
nard as a notary public 130.00

Price Range

☐ **Washington, George,** first president, letter, signed as commander-in-chief of the Continental Army, 1 page, folio, Headquarters, Middlebrook, 26 February 1779, to Colonel Wigglesworth 10,000.00

Aviation Memorabilia

DESCRIPTION: Aviation memorabilia include any item dealing with airplanes. From commercial airlines to the air force, hobbyists are collecting any type of aviation memorabilia available.

TYPES: Stewardess wings, pilot goggles, pins, buttons, helmets, entire airplanes, or just parts of airplanes are all types of memorabilia collected by hobbyists.

	Price Range	
☐ **Air service insignia,** WW I, little sterling silver winged propeller, span of just over 1″, on top are crossed flags of the Army Signal Corps	15.00	25.00
☐ **Air service technical report,** Fokker D-V11, 1920, this original tech order book also contains details of the construction of the D-V11 and a test on the new Packard 1A-744 engine, many photos, 101 pp	35.00	45.00

	Price Range	

☐ **Aviators' sterling "wing" badges,** WW II and 1920s most sought after 50.00   500.00

☐ **Book,** *Meet the NP-1,* US Navy Flight School, WW II, illustrated, soft cover, issued to flight cadets, 57 photos of this rather unique and seldom seen Navy biplane ... 20.00   30.00

☐ **Book,** *Campsite and Airplane Landings Guide,* 1923, official directory of airplane landing fields, 115-page booklet, containing fold-out map, 36″ × 38″ 70.00   80.00

☐ **Charles A. Lindberg watch fob,** 1928, solid sterling silver, marked on reverse, rectangular, approx. 1½″ × 1″ 35.00   40.00

☐ **Hydraulic pressure gauge,** RCAF aircraft, WW II, from the panel of a combat aircraft, with "Lockheed Aerodraulic" pressure marked in 0–1400 lbs with green and red bands on a white 2″ face 10.00   15.00

☐ **"Lucky Lindy" Spirit of St. Louis poker chips,** 1920s; the world went crazy in 1927, and a lot of unusual memorabilia was made to honor the first solo transatlantic flight; these 1½″ poker chips were embossed with the likeness of the "Spirit of St. Louis" monoplane 5.00   7.00

☐ **Luftwaffe pilot's flying goggles,** WW II, large-lens "Lietz" type, clear glass lens of oval shape set in metal frames of the split type, rubber face cushions and green elastic strap, frame painted dark green 90.00   100.00

Price Range

☐ **Woman's Air Service Pilot's mascot pin,** "Fifinella," WW II; the lady pilots of the WASP adopted their very own female gremlin as a mascot; this "femlin" went by the name of "Fifinella" and was drawn for them by the Walt Disney Studios, designers of many of the Air Corps squadron insignia, 1½" long 40.00 45.00

☐ **Wood airplane propellers** (older and/or longer models are more expensive) 200.00 1000.00

Banks

TOPIC: Banks made saving coins more enjoyable. Besides providing a receptacle for a hoard of coins, they are interesting and amusing in themselves.

TYPES: Banks are either still or mechanical. Still banks are simply receptacles that do not move or react when a coin is deposited. Mechanical banks, however, respond to the coin (via a series of levers and springs) and put on a small show for the depositer.

PERIOD: Still banks were first made in the United States in the early 1790s; mechanical banks were introduced about seventy years later.

MATERIALS: Cast iron has been the favored material for banks.

COMMENTS: Banks make good collectibles because they are entertaining, attractive, and often ingenious.

MECHANICAL BANKS

Mechanical banks date back as early as 1793 in the United States, but full-scale production of banks with intricate, highly complex, coin-activated mechanisms actually had their inception in the 1870s, extending to the end of World

War I. Actually, mechanical banks in limited editions are still being produced. Leading makers include J. & E. Stevens, W. J. Shepard, Kyser & Rex, and J. Hall. Oddly enough, Ives produced only a few mechanicals, the "boy and bulldog" bank being an obvious exception. John Harper Ltd. was the leading toy bank maker in Great Britain. German and French toy makers stuck to tin and never entered the cast-iron mechanical bank arena. Mechanical banks are coveted by an ever-widening circle of enthusiasts, attributable to cleverness of animation as well as being almost exclusively American phenomena.

Note: Numbers in parentheses indicate reference to catalog number in *The Handbook of Old Mechanical Banks* by John D. Meyer.

	Price Range	
☐ **Acrobats,** E. L. Morris and J. & E. Stevens, 1883, 5″ high × 7¼″ long (1)	1500.00	2000.00
☐ **Always Did Spise a Mule,** J. H. Bowen, 1897, 6½″ high (4)	400.00	450.00*
☐ **Artillery** (cannon bank), C. A. Bailey, 1898 (37)	350.00	550.00
☐ **Bird on roof,** J. & E. Stevens, 1878 (16)	750.00	800.00
☐ **Blacksmith at anvil,** John Deere, 1950	50.00	75.00
☐ **Boy and bulldog,** Ives, Blakeslee & Co., patented by Enoch Morrison, 1878, 7½″ high, clockwork mechanism, one of few banks by Ives	2000.00	2500.00
☐ **Boy on trapeze,** J. Barton Smith, Philadelphia, 1880s	550.00	750.00
☐ **Boy robbing bird's nest,** Charles Bailey (Stevens), c. 1906, 8″ high	1400.00	1600.00
☐ **Boy Scout camp,** Charles Bailey, ptd., J. & E. Stevens, 1917, 4¾″		

*$1100.00 at Atlanta Museum Toy Auction, October 1986.

Price Range

height, scout raises flag when coin
drops 800.00 1000.00
- [ ] **Boy stealing watermelon** 650.00 850.00
- [ ] **Bucking goat** 300.00 400.00
- [ ] **Bull and bear,** maker unknown,
1890s 1000.00 1200.00
- [ ] **Bulldog,** E. R. Morrison, 1878,
5⅝" high 400.00 500.00
- [ ] **Bulldog** (seated), J. & E. Stevens,
1880 .... 450.00 550.00
- [ ] **Bureau,** picture pops up 3000.00 4000.00
- [ ] **Bureau,** J. Serrell, 1869 .... 1500.00 2000.00
- [ ] **Butting buffalo,** A. C. Rex, 1888 900.00 1100.00
- [ ] **Cabin,** J. & E. Stevens, 1890, 4"
long 200.00 300.00
- [ ] **Camera,** Wrightsville Hardware.
Mt. Joy, PA, c. 1890 .... 1400.00 1600.00
- [ ] **Cat and dog** (organ), Kyser &
Rex, 1882 (177) 400.00 500.00
- [ ] **Chimpanzee,** Kyser & Rex, 1880
(43) 450.00 500.00
- [ ] **Circus ticket collector,** Wm. C.
Bull, c. 1892, semimechanical 1000.00 1200.00
- [ ] **Clock,** Kingsbury, c. 1900, 7"
high 350.00 450.00
- [ ] **Clown on globe,** J. & E. Stevens,
1890, patented by Jas. Bowen,
two distinct sets of movements,
identical mechanism to "Girl
skipping rope" 1000.00 1200.00
- [ ] **Cupola,** J. & E. Stevens, 1874,
patented by D. Dieckman, New
York, cupola raises, man moves
back and forth exposing coin slot
(27) 1500.00 2000.00
- [ ] **Darktown battery,** J. H. Bowen,
J. & E. Stevens, 1888, 7¼" high,
black pitcher, catcher, batsman .. 500.00 600.00
- [ ] **Darktown battery,** J. H. Bowen,
J. & E. Stevens, 1888, 7¼" high,
white pitcher, catcher, batsman . 700.00 750.00

Price Range

☐ **Dentist,** J. & E. Stevens, black man's tooth is pulled by dentist, coin in dentist's pocket falls into gas bag receptacle, both figures lunge forward 1100.00 1300.00

☐ **Dinah,** English, John Harper Ltd., 1911, bust of black woman, cast metal 100.00 200.00

☐ **Dog Tray,** Kyser & Rex, 1880, 5″ high, weight of coin in dog's mouth tips him forward to deposit coin, crank on side (70) 300.00 400.00

☐ **Doll's head,** semimechanical, doll appears to have hatched from egg, all-white bank, bellows makes a baby sound when bank is opened 300.00 400.00

☐ **Eagle and eaglets,** J. & E. Stevens, 1883, 6″ high, 8″ length, patented by C. M. Henn (75) 300.00 500.00

☐ **Elephant three stars,** C. A. Bailey, 1880 (78) 350.00 450.00

☐ **Elephant with howdah,** C. F. Olm and J. Thalheim, 1901 (83) . 350.00 400.00

☐ **Frog on lattice,** patented by R. Frisbie, 1872 .... 200.00 300.00

☐ **Frog on rock** 150.00 250.00

☐ **Frogs,** J. & E. Stevens, 1882, patented by J. H. Bowen, 4¼″ high, 8¾″ long 500.00 600.00

☐ **Girl skipping rope,** patented by J. H. Bowen, J. & E. Stevens, 1890   2000.00 plus

☐ **Grenadier,** English, c. 1890 ...... 250.00 300.00

☐ **Guessing,** patented by E. M. McLoughlin, 1877, man sits atop round mechanism with dial (117) 2000.00 2500.00

☐ **Hall's Yankee Notion,** J. Hall, 1875 .... 1200.00 1500.00

☐ **Hindu,** Kyser & Rex, 1882, Hindu with turban, swallows coin and rolls eyes (122) 450.00 500.00

	Price Range	

- [ ] **Hoop-la,** John Harper, English, 1897, clown holds hoop and dog prepares to leap through 300.00 400.00
- [ ] **Horse race,** J. & E. Stevens, patented by John Hall, 1871, 4¾" high 1500.00 2000.00
- [ ] **Humpty-Dumpty** (clown), patented by P. Adams, Chas. Shephard, 7" high, name inspired by G. W. Fox, 19th century pantomimist, not nursery rhyme character 500.00 600.00
- [ ] **Indian shooting bear** 200.00 300.00
- [ ] **Jonah and whale,** Shepherd Hardware, 1890, patented by P. Adams; Jonah is in boat ready to be swallowed; when coin is placed on Jonah's tray, whale opens mouth to receive it, 10½" long, 4¾" high (138) 400.00 500.00
- [ ] **Jonah and whale,** Shephard, a rarer version with pedestal; Jonah emerges from whale's mouth, 3" high .... 2000.00 plus
- [ ] **Kiltie,** John Harper Ltd., English, 1931 .... 700.00 800.00
- [ ] **Leap frog** 550.00 650.00
- [ ] **Lion hunter,** C. A. Bailey, 1911 (148) 1500.00 2000.00
- [ ] **Little Jocko,** Strauss Manufacturing, New York, 1912, tin musical bank 900.00 1100.00
- [ ] **Little Joe High Hat** 100.00 200.00
- [ ] **Mammy feeding baby,** A. C. Rex, 1884 (155) 300.00 400.00
- [ ] **Mason and hod carrier,** C. G. Shephard, 1887, bricklayer with hod-carrying helper (156) 1200.00 1500.00

	Price Range	
☐ **Merry-go-round,** Kyser & Rex, 1880s, 5¾″ high, semimechanical	250.00	350.00
☐ **Milking cow,** J. & E. Stevens, 1880, cow kicks boy milker	1200.00	1400.00
☐ **Monkey and coconut,** J. & E. Stevens, 1886, Jas. Bowen patented, monkey's left hand lifts top of coconut to receive coin (163)	700.00	900.00
☐ **Mule entering barn,** J. & E. Stevens, 1880, patented by Edw. Morris, 8½″ long (169)	400.00	500.00
☐ **North Pole,** patented by Charles Bailey, J. & E. Stevens, 1910 (177)	1500.00	2000.00
☐ **Old woman who lives in shoe,** W. S. Reed, 1883		2000.00 plus
☐ **Organ bank,** Kyser & Rex, 1881, 6″ high	200.00	250.00
☐ **Owl,** turns head, J. H. Bowen, 1880, 7½″ high (182)	100.00	200.00*
☐ **Patronize the blind man,** H. H. Loetz, Chicago, 1878	1500.00	2000.00
☐ **Peg-leg beggar**	1000.00	1200.00
☐ **Professor Pug Frog's great bicycle feat,** J. & E. Stevens, 7½″ high	1450.00	1650.00
☐ **Punch and Judy,** C. G. Shephard, c. 1884, 6¾″ high (203)	500.00	600.00
☐ **Reclining Chinaman,** Jas. Bowen, 1882	1500.00	2000.00
☐ **Rooster,** Kilgore, c. 1900s, 6″ high	250.00	300.00
☐ **Shoot-the-chute,** Buster Brown and Tige, C. A. Bailey, 1906, J. & E. Stevens manufacturer (218)		2000.00 plus
☐ **Toad in den,** Jas. Fallows, 1871 (100)		2000.00 plus

*$350.00 at Atlanta Toy Museum Auction, October 1986.

	Price Range	
☐ **Trick dog,** Hubley, 1888, 9⅝″ high	150.00	200.00
☐ **Trick pony,** C. G. Shephard, 1885 (196)	350.00	450.00
☐ **World's Fair,** C. A. Bailey, 1893 (244)	400.00	600.00

STILL BANKS

Outsiders often consider the term "still" misleading, feeling that it connotes something to do with Prohibition. The term merely distinguishes banks with no mechanical motion involved when a penny is inserted. Tinplate banks predominated from the end of the Civil War to the 1890s, with Schlesingers, George Brown, William Fallows, and Adolf Bergmann as the principal makers. Mass-produced, cast-iron stills, using highly detailed molds, delighted youngsters and taught them the virtue of saving. From the late nineteenth century to the 1930s, A. C. Williams, J. & E. Stevens, Hubley, and Kenton were the leaders in their field.

Note: Figures appearing in parentheses indicate original listing numbers from the Whiting catalog.

Animal Banks

	Price Range	
☐ **Bear stealing pig,** 5½″ high, classic pose in finite detail makes this the most desirable of still banks (246)	500.00	600.00
☐ **Board of Trade,** bear and bull vie for sack of grain, 4¾″ high, black figures, silver sack, green base (264)	900.00	1100.00
☐ **Camel with pack,** 2½″ high, on all fours with pack on back (256)	300.00	400.00

	Price Range	
☐ **Cat standing,** 4½″ high, believed to be a tom, bronze finish (245)	100.00	150.00
☐ **Basset hound,** 3″ high, long-eared little fellow with oversize head, a tough bank to find (261)	450.00	550.00
☐ **Bulldog,** seated, 4⅜″ high (102), Hubley Mfgr., 1920–30 (105)	50.00	60.00
☐ **Dog with pack,** St. Bernard, 5½″ high, 8″ wide, A. C. Williams, 1905, black finish (113)	75.00	150.00
☐ **Elephant,** 4¾″ high, 7″ wide, the largest of a vast herd of elephant still banks, also probably the best detailed, gray finish (62)	100.00	150.00
☐ **Seated elephant,** 4½″ high, nice stylized features, looks like Babar (66)	75.00	150.00
☐ **Horse,** prancing, on oblong base, 7½″ high, black horse on gold platform rears on hind legs (78)	75.00	150.00
☐ **Horse with fly net,** 4″ high, gilded horse looks as if it is wearing medieval armor (80)	200.00	300.00
☐ **Decker's Iowana pig,** 2½″ high, advertising slogan (probably for hog mash) appears on both sides of gilded porker	75.00	150.00
☐ **Pig,** 1¾″ high, very uncommon miniature black piglet	250.00	350.00

Building Banks—Cast Iron

☐ **Old South Church,** famous old Boston landmark features roof with multiple slots for coins, gray with green roof, 13″ high, one of largest and rarest of building banks	400.00	500.00

Price Range

☐ **Victorian house,** George Brown design, 1870s, 6 1/4 " high, tin, ornate gingerbread with four gables and three chimneys, white with blue chimneys, red roof, gold stenciling 500.00 600.00

☐ **Woolworth Building,** 8 " high, rendering of New York City skyscraper, gold finish, also a 5 3/4 " high version 75.00 100.00

☐ **World's Fair Administration Building,** a white with gold and red trim replica of building from Columbian Exposition in 1893, Chicago, small red safe in main entrance 100.00 125.00

Baskets

TOPIC: The art of basketry is indeed a reflection of America's cultural past. Long before this nation's first colonization, the American Indian had achieved artistic excellence as a basket weaver. Indian baskets are said to be the world's finest. Each basket was woven for a specific purpose and with the utmost care. These baskets were not only used to hold food and water and for ceremonial purposes, but some were also used for cooking. The work is unique because only materials from nature—pine needles, straw, leaves, willow, porcupine quills, vines, reeds, and grass—were used. Dyes were made from bark, roots, or berries. Their distinctive designs have made them sought after by most basket enthusiasts.

TYPES: There are several types of basket construction. Wickerwork, the most common and widely used technique, is nothing more than an over-and-under pattern. Twining is similar except that two strands are twisted as they are woven over and under, producing a finer weave. Plaiting gives a checkerboard effect and can be either a tight weave or left with some open spaces. Twillwork is much the same except that a diagonal effect is achieved by changing the number of strands over which the weaver passes. Coiling is the most desirable weave for the collector. This technique has been carefully refined since its conception around 7000 B.C. Fibers are wrapped around and stitched together to form the basket's shape. Most of these pieces were used either for ceremonial purposes or for holding liquids, since the containers made in this fashion were tightly woven and leakproof.

COMMENTS: Baskets are available in a wide range of prices and types. Because of their decorative appeal they are now avidly sought by collectors. They may be collected by general category such as Indian, Appalachian, Nantucket, etc., or simply acquired in a wide variety of types and styles.

ADDITIONAL TIPS: Baskets are easy to care for, but a few basic rules must be followed.

1. Never wash an Indian basket. Dust it gently using a very soft sable artist's brush.

2. Do not subject Indian baskets to the sun as it will fade the patterns.

3. Do not wash any basket made of pine needles, straw, grass, or leaves.

4. Willow, oak, hickory, and rattan baskets may be washed in a mild solution of Murphy's Oil Soap and dried in a sunny location.

Note: The single values shown below are the actual auction-realized prices.

	Price Range
☐ **Bentwood and woven splint winnowing basket,** American, late 19th–early 20th century, 4″ diameter	165.00
☐ **Green-painted woven splint basket,** eastern Illinois, 19th century, 6″ high, 15″ long	275.00
☐ **American Indian potato-stamped woven splint basket,** early 20th century, the red and green basket stamped with geometric designs, the base inscribed "Sturtivant," 8″ high, 13″ long	137.50
☐ **Woven hickory splint basket,** American, 19th century, 7½″ high, 14″ diameter	137.50

Left to right. Woven splint basket, green-painted, eastern Illinois, 19th century, 6″ high, 15″ long, $275. American Indian potato-stamped woven splint basket, early 20th century, the red and green basket stamped with geometric designs, the base inscribed "Sturtivant," 8″ high, 13″ long, $137.50. Woven hickory splint basket, American, 19th century, 7½″ high, 14″ diameter, $137.50. (*Photo courtesy of Butterfield & Butterfield, San Francisco*)

	Price Range
☐ **Cheese curd woven splint basket,** 19th century, rounded circular basket with hexagonal woven splint design, 8½″ high, 20½″ diameter	330.00
☐ **Hupa basket,** decorated with a dark brown stepped triangle motif and band around the center, northern California, c. 1900, 13 cm diameter, 8 cm high	165.00
☐ **Monumental woven splint basket,** early 20th century, ribbed body with large bentwood loop handles, 25½″ high, 4′2″ long .	522.50
☐ **Nantucket woven splint lighthouse basket,** 19th century, cylindrical basket with rounded bottom and turned circular wood base, simple bentwood swig handles, 5¾″ high, 7½″ diameter ..	495.00

Price Range

☐ **Northwest Coast basket,** spruce root with knobbed lid, yellow and tan band of embrocaded decoration, 19th century, 17.5 cm diameter, 12 cm height 236.00

☐ **Pima basket,** oval, with stepped design woven in dark brown, late 19th century, 13 cm long, 7.5 cm wide, 4.8 cm high 178.00

☐ **Woven basket,** 19th century, fixed bentwood handle, multicolor floral painted decoration, 12″ long 68.00

☐ **Woven splint two-handled basket,** American, 19th century, 16½″ diameter, 11½″ high 192.50

Two-handled basket, woven splint, American, 19th century, 16½″ diameter, 11½″ high, $192.50. (*Photo courtesy of Butterfield & Butterfield, San Francisco*)

Left to right. Woven splint basket, American, 19th century, bentwood handle, 5″ high, 12½″ long, $55. Painted woven splint basket, American, 19th century, with large bentwood handle, the rim painted in alternating black and green panels, 7″ high, 12″ diameter, $247.50. Red-painted woven splint berry basket, 19th century, 7″ high, 10½″ diameter, $165. (*Photo courtesy of Butterfield & Butterfield, San Francisco*)

	Price Range
☐ **Woven splint basket,** American, 19th century, bentwood handle, 5″ high, 12½″ long	55.00
☐ **Painted woven splint basket,** American, 19th century, with large bentwood handle, the rim painted in alternating black and green panels, 7″ high, 12″ diameter	247.50
☐ **Red-painted woven splint berry basket,** 19th century, 7″ high, 10½″ diameter	165.00

Bells

TOPIC: Bells have been used for thousands of years to signal important events such as births, weddings, enemy attacks, and holidays.

TYPES: Bells can be divided into many categories, including closed and open mouth bells, figurine bells, jingle bells, chimes, and gongs.

PERIODS: Bells have existed for thousands of years, although they were introduced to Europe about 1500 years ago.

MATERIALS: Brass, iron, silver, gold, bronze, wood, glass, and porcelain are frequently used to make bells.

COMMENTS: Bells are very popular among collectors because of their interesting shapes and musical qualities.

Price Range

☐ **Bronze figural bell,** American, cast from a model by J. Kratina, modeled as a bare-breasted maiden in full sweeping skirt, inscribed ''J. KRATINA COPYRIGHT,'' 6″ high 200.00   300.00

	Price Range	
☐ **Dinner bell,** white brass, by Chase, c. 1930, the dome shape with green plastic finial, stamped "Chase U.S.A.," and centaur logo, 3″ high, 2″ diameter	80.00	120.00
☐ **Iron bell,** of traditional form, raised on a wooden post, 9′9″ high, with metal mount, 20″ diameter, 20″ high without the post	100.00	200.00
☐ **Smoke bell,** clear glass, good condition, 19th century	80.00	100.00
☐ **Smoke bells,** pair, milk glass, late 19th century	550.00	650.00
☐ **Strand of brass sleigh bells,** mounted on a leather strap, 18 bells total	40.00	50.00

Belt Buckles

DESCRIPTION: Belt buckles have become a very popular collectible as the interest in vintage clothing has grown. They can be found in thrift shops and secondhand clothing stores as well as in pawn shops, antique shops, and flea markets.

TYPES: Belt buckles have been made in a wide variety of styles, utilizing many different materials. As interest in vintage clothing has increased significantly, so has the collectibility of vintage belt buckles, especially the ones worked in intricate and eye-catching designs.

Note: The single values shown below are the actual auction-realized prices.

	Price Range	
☐ **Silver plate belt buckle,** Art Nouveau style, the symmetrical V-shape buckle formed by carnations and stylized intertwining foliage, 3 ½″ long, 2 ⅛″ wide, (estimated value)	100.00	200.00

	Price Range	
☐ **Silver belt buckle,** Art Nouveau style, the oval shape composed of iris blossoms, French assay marks, 2¾" long, 2½" wide (estimated value)	125.00	225.00
☐ **Silver belt buckle,** Art Nouveau style, marked "depose G.R.," 3¼" long, 2½" wide		200.00
☐ **Silver belt buckle,** Art Nouveau style, 5" long, 2½" wide		250.00
☐ **Egyptian Revival gilt metal belt buckle,** inset with five bands of rhinestones, 3¼" long, 2½" wide		160.00

Top to bottom. Egyptian Revival gilt metal belt buckle, inset with five bands of rhinestones, 3¼" long, 2½" wide, $160. Rhinestone belt buckle, Art Deco style, 4" long, 1½" wide, $70. Victorian brass-plated and enameled belt buckle, 1⅜" long, 3⅜" wide, estimated value $100–$150. (*Photo courtesy of Phillips, New York*)

Price Range

☐ **Rhinestone belt buckle,** Art
Deco style, 4″ long, 1 ½″ wide .   70.00

☐ **Victorian brass-plated and
enameled belt buckle,** 1 ⅜″
long, 3 ⅜″ wide (estimated value)   100.00   150.00

☐ **Silver plate and enamel belt
buckle,** Arts and Crafts style,
green and blue enameled dragonflies and peony blossoms, 3 ¼″
long, 2 ½″ wide 800.00

☐ **Silver belt buckle,** Art Nouveau
style, pink cabochon central
stone, 3 ½″ long, 2 ½″ wide 130.00

Left. Silver plate and enamel belt buckle, Arts and Crafts style,
green and blue enameled dragonflies and peony blossoms, 3 ¼″
long, 2 ½″ wide, $800. *Right.* Silver belt buckle, Art Nouveau style,
pink cabochon central stone, 3 ½″ long, 2 ½″ wide, $130. (*Photo
courtesy of Phillips, New York*)

Black Memorabilia

TYPES: A wide variety of items depicting blacks was produced from 1900 to 1960. Many were advertising promotions: figural Mammy kitchenware, postcards, cast-iron banks and doorstops, chalkware statues, dolls, figurines, toys, etc., all very popular.

COMMENTS: Many of these early items were extremely derogatory in nature, and it was not until the 1960s that the civil rights movement put an end to the production of racist depictions of blacks.

BANKS

	Price Range	
☐ **"A Jolly Nigger" mechanical bank,** cast iron, retaining its original polychrome painted decoration, 6½" high	400.00	500.00
☐ **"Bad Accident" mechanical bank,** cast iron, polychrome painted decoration	800.00	900.00
☐ **Darktown battery mechanical bank,** cast iron, depicting three		

Price Range

black ballplayers at play, original
polychrome painted decoration,
9³/₄ ″ long 1750.00   2000.00

DOLLS

☐ **Carved walnut and cloth black
dolls,** pair, American, c. 1920,
each with embroidered eyes,
mouth, and nose, with simple
carved, jointed arms and legs, 17 ″
high 500.00   800.00

☐ **Embroidered and stuffed cotton black doll,** American, early
20th century, simple body with
white embroidered eyebrows,
nose, and mouth, wearing a wa-
termelon print dress, 12 ½ ″ high   200.00   300.00

☐ **Folk art doll,** rare, 19th century,
depicting the figure of a standing
black man who dances when a
lever is pushed, 12 ½ ″ high 800.00

☐ **Stuffed cotton and velvet black
doll,** American, c. 1930, sawdust-
stuffed doll depicted with button
nose and embroidered eyes and
mouth, button hair, wearing a
green velvet shirt and dark blue
velvet pants with green velvet
pockets, 13 ½ ″ high 200.00   300.00

Gunthermann black tinplate musicians, c. 1880, $425. (*Photo courtesy of Phillips, New York*)

Price Range

FIGURINES

☐ **Gunthermann black tinplate musicians,** c. 1880, 8½″ × 4¼″ × 8″ 425.00

☐ **Painted dancing black man figure,** American, c. 1930, jointed standing figure dancing atop a paddle when wire support is squeezed, 16″ high 75.00 100.00

☐ **Painted dancing black man figure,** American, c. 1930, the jointed figure depicted with gray

	Price Range	

hat and pants, wearing a red jacket and black bow tie, 12½″ high 70.00   90.00

☐ **Stenciled wood dancing black man figure,** American, c. 1930, jointed, white hat, 11½″ high ...   75.00   100.00

MISCELLANEOUS

☐ **African carved-wood mask,** grotesque facial features depicting a fanged demon and set with blond braided tresses, 12″ long .   400.00   500.00

☐ **Ashanti Aquaba** (fertility doll), 11¾″ high 100.00

☐ **Bambara carved-wood mask,** traces of white painted decoration, 10½″ long 100.00   150.00

☐ **Bende carved adornments,** two, consisting of a knee mask and a cap mask, variously sized and decorated 300.00   350.00

☐ **Ebibio carved-wood mask,** white and red painted decoration and grass "beard," 19″ high without beard 500.00

☐ **Elephant mask,** Sepik River woven grass and mud, bulbous nose and big eyes, red, tan, brown, and white mud decoration, 26″ high   300.00   400.00

☐ **Fang tribal mask,** facial carving with white painted decoration and grass "beard," 15½″ high without beard 475.00

☐ **Standing "Darkie" blinking-eye clock,** cast iron, 15½″ high   3000.00   3500.00

☐ **Zulu rosewood authority stick,** with a Bambara berry bag, woven geometric rush 100.00   150.00

Books

TOPIC: Books have been extremely important in human history, for they allow people to record information and distribute it to others in unaltered form.

TYPES: American and European fiction, nonfiction, Bibles.

PERIOD: Books were first printed around 1450, although handwritten books were in existence earlier than that.

MATERIALS: Paper was used almost exclusively in producing books.

COMMENTS: Many book collectors limit themselves to one or two favorite writers or a favorite subject because the field of book collecting is vast. A collection is judged on quality rather than quantity, since the number of books that would be appropriate in a collection is so large.

CONDITION: It is important that the book be in good condition. Books with water damage, fire damage, broken bindings, or missing pages are worth significantly less than similar books in good condition.

Note: The single values of items shown are auction-realized prices.

Buck, Samuel and Nathaniel, "Panorama of London," five double-page plates forming a panorama from Westminster Bridge to the Tower, blue crushed levant morocco gilt, slightly rubbed on bottom of spine, gilt edge, binding by Riviere, oblong folio, London, 1749, $1300. (*Photo courtesy of Phillips, New York*)

Price Range

☐ **Buck, Samuel and Nathaniel,** "Panorama of London," 5 double-page plates forming a panorama from Westminster Bridge to the Tower, some slight handling marks, blue crushed levant morocco gilt, slightly rubbed on bottom of spine, gilt edge, binding by Riviere, oblong folio, London, 1749 ....   1300.00

☐ **Codex Lindisfarensis,** evangeliorum quattuor, Oltun & Lausanne 1956–60, 2 vols., original blind-stamped vellum and vellum-backed boards, printed titles on spines, limited edition, 1 of 680 copies 825.00

☐ **Collection Connaissance des Arts,** La Decoration, Paris, 1963–65, 4 vols., original buckram, upper covers with red paper labels   550.00

☐ **Dickens, Charles,** 4 vols., tooled cloth bindings, published by P. F. Collier, NY 40.00

Price Range

☐ **Dumas, Alexandre,** *The Works of Alexandre Dumas,* 9 vols., gilt tooled cloth bindings, Peter Fenelon Collier, Publisher, 1893 .... 85.00

☐ *Europe Illustrated,* 4 vols., one-third brown leather bindings, each volume set with numerous steel engravings from London Printing and Publishing Co. 200.00

☐ **Goethe, Johann Wolfgang von,** *Faust,* Berlin, Bruno Cassirer, 1927, folio, original brown morocco gilt, t.e.g., others uncut, limited edition, No. 48 of 100 copies 550.00

☐ **Goethe, Johann Wolfgang von,** *Goethes Buch Suleika von Schenkenbuch,* Frankfurt and Mainz, 1966, folio, vellum-backed orange cloth, pictorial upper cover, spine gilt-lettered, orange cloth slipcase within buckram folding case, limited edition, copy No. 1, signed by the artist and the publisher, extra set of plates signed in pencil by Max Peiffer Watenphul 495.00

☐ **Hubbard, Elbert,** *Ali Baba,* limited edition of 650, "hand illuminated" by Anna L. Paine, Ali Baba's bookplate inside back cover, signed, designed by Denslow, uncut, ooze-backed boards, slightly browning, 8vo, 1899 ..... 80.00 120.00

☐ **Hunter, Dard,** *The Book of the Roycrofters,* signed by Dard Hunter, decorative cloth-backed boards, slight staining, 4to, 1907 .... 80.00 120.00

☐ **Logan, James, and MacIan, Robert,** *The Clans of the Scottish*

Logan, James and MacIan, Robert, *The Clans of the Scottish High-lands,* two volumes, two chromolithograph titles, and 72 half-fin-ished color lithographs, London, 1845-1847, $1300. (*Photo courtesy of Phillips, New York*)

	Price Range
Highlands, 2 vols., 2 chromolith-ograph titles, and 72 half-finished color lithographs, London, 1845–47	1300.00

☐ **Moskowitz, Ira,** *Great Draw-ings of All Time,* New York 1962,

Russian Military Uniforms. Sketches of the History of His Imperial Highness Lifeguard Hussars Regiment, portfolio containing 25 chromolithographs of Russian military uniforms from the 1790s to 1860s, sheets 16¼″ × 12″, gilt initials "HK" on lower cover (possibly Grand Duke Nicolas Konstantinovich, grandson of Tsar Alexander II), c. 1879, $1200. (*Photo courtesy of Phillips, New York*)

	Price Range
4 vols., small folio, original buckram gilt, decorative slipcase	419.00
☐ **Mourlot, Fernand,** *Chagal Lithograph,* Monte Carlo, Andre Sauret, 1960, 4 vols., original buckram, slightly soiled	550.00
☐ *Russian Military Uniforms. Sketches of the History of His Imperial Highness Lifeguard Hussars Regiment,* portfolio containing 25 chromolithographs of Russian military uniforms from the 1790s to 1860s, sheets 16¼″ × 12″, some slight browning	

Price Range

around edges, gilt initials "HK"
on lower cover (possibly Grand
Duke Nicolas Konstantinovich,
grandson of Tsar Alexander II), c.
1879 ....   1200.00

☐ **Sinclair, Isabella,** *Indigenous*
Flowers of the Hawaiian Islands,
44 color plates, later cloth, slight
wear, folio, London, 1885 ....   850.00

☐ *Transactions of the Horticul-*
tural Society, 2 vols., full brown
leather bindings, containing numerous hand-colored prints, published by Wm. Savage, London,
1807 ....   140.00

BIBLES

BACKGROUND: The first Bible ever printed with movable
type was the Gutenberg Bible, printed in Latin using a German type. The Geneva Bible is the Bible of America, having
been brought here by the Puritans on the Mayflower, and it
was the first Bible to designate verses. It was the basis for
religion in early America and was used by the Continental
Congress as a guide for writing the preamble to the Constitution.

COMMENTS: The field of collecting Bibles is not widely
practiced. Number of years alone does not make a Bible a
collector's item. Also important is its size, date, language,
condition (inside and out), version, type of cover, printer,
translator, possible editor(s), faith purpose, and known pe-
culiarities (like misprints).

The supply of Bibles is down, and the values for them are
moving up, most dramatically in the last three to four years.

Price Range

☐ **Holy Bible,** Geneva, 1603–10, D
& M #210/301, small folio, 9" ×
12½" × 4", heavy leather cover
(with some repairs), New Testa-

Price Range

ment dated 1610, Robert Barker, London, "Englished by L. Tomson," translated from Greek by T. Baza, a rare Bible in quite good condition 400.00 450.00

☐ **Holy Bible,** King James Version, 1715, no printer indicated, large folio, 13 preliminary pages including "Translators to the Readers" from 1611 edition, plus a page of 8 copperplate engravings before Gen. 1:1, 6" × 4", blind-stamped design on each cover, large heavy Bible, clean and tight 250.00 350.00

☐ **Holy Bible,** OT & NT, King James Version, Robert Barker, London, 1636, black letter, Book of Common Prayer 1636 incomplete (begins with C1), old full-calf binding rebacked, D & M #502 .... 300.00 400.00

☐ **Holy Bible,** 1634, first edition, fourth printing, "The fourth distinct Folio edition of King James Version," black letter, "She" edition, 59 lines per page, rebound in reversed leather, blind-stamped, shows evidence of diamond-shaped plate once attached to front and back covers, spine contains title in gilt "Holy Bible" and "Robert Barker 1634," very tight, good display copy 2500.00 3500.00

☐ **Holy Bible,** 1617 Folio, first edition, third printing, "The third distinct folio edition, B/L, of the King James Version," first page of "Translators to the Reader" missing and page B misbound at end of immediate section, recently rebound with words "Holy Bible"

Price Range

stamped in gilt letters on front cover and spine 3500.00   4500.00

☐ **Holy Bible,** with Matthew Henry's Commentary inserted at large in distinct paragraphs, forming the most complete family Bible ever published, over 100 engravings, printed by and for J. Stratford, London, 1793, 2 vols., page edges gilt, clean copy, large folio, 11″ × 17″ × 3¾″ each vol. 350.00   450.00

☐ **Holy Bible,** Johann Gutenberg printer, Latin (Mainz, c. 1450–55), Paterson, NJ, Pageant Books, 1962, 2 vols., folio original brown morocco gilt, g.e., limited facsimile edition, No. 151 of 1000 copies, printed in color (sold at auction at Christie's East, New York) 495.00

☐ **Holy Bible,** Geneva Version, 1589, D & M #200, pp. 442–554 with portion of Matthew I missing, old calf, spine hubbed, with date at bottom, blind-stamped ... 375.00   400.00

☐ **Holy Bible,** King James Version, Rembrandt edition, Abradale Press, New York, 44 color plates and 72 drawings and etchings, 14 full-page color maps and four half-page maps in color, gilded page edges, 9″ × 11½″ × 2⅞″, gilt title, blind-stamped device on cover 140.00   180.00

☐ **Holy Bible,** King James Version, Cassell & Co. Ltd., London, c. 1875, 20 full-page Dore plates and nearly 900 wood engravings, marbled end papers with ½″ gilt stamped design inside each cover edge 125.00   150.00

Bottles

DESCRIPTION: Bottle collecting encompasses bitters, soft drinks, milk, medicine, and many more. Bottles have been free blown or machine-made, described as blob top, crown cap, or sheared lip.

TYPES: Avon, Jim Beam, porcelain, pottery, Lalique, Steuben.

AVON

DESCRIPTION: The oldest toiletry company that issues decorative bottles, Avon is the modern leader in the nonliquor bottle field.

TYPES: There are a variety of Avon bottle types, including figurals shaped as animals, people, cars, etc., cologne bottles, hand lotion bottles, among others.

PERIOD: Based on door-to-door sales, Avon began as the California Perfume Company more than 50 years ago. Since 1939 the name Avon has been used exclusively.

COMMENTS: Everything relating to Avon, including bottles, brochures, and magazine ads, is highly collectible. Older Avon memorabilia is usually of more value than recent products.

ADDITIONAL TIPS: The listings in this section are arranged by year of manufacture. The original selling price of the item is at the end of the listing in parentheses.

Gift Sets

	Price Range	
☐ **Atomizer box** (1900), three 1-oz perfumes and atomizer, clear glass, cork stopper, labels on front and neck ($1.35)	550.00	600.00

Household Specialties

☐ **Furniture polish** (1908–10), clear glass, toll neck, cork stopper, label on front, 8 oz ($.50) ...	150.00	160.00
☐ **Liquid Spots-Out** (1925–20), clear glass, flat-top cork stopper, dark blue/white label on front, 4 oz ($.37)	40.00	45.00

Perfumery and Fragrance Lines

☐ **Lavender salts** (1888), dark green glass, combination glass and rubber stopper ($.35)	250.00	275.00
☐ **Bay rum** (1898) (Bay rum was in the CPC-Avon line for more than 60 years, and Avon collectors have labeled it as a highly prized collectible), square clear glass, pointed glass stopper, label on front, 1 pint ($1.25)	225.00	250.00
☐ **Perfume** (1930), American Ideal, clear glass, pointed yellow glass stopper, 1 oz ($2.40)	100.00	110.00

Women's Fragrance Lines

Price Range

- ☐ **Bird of Paradise.**
- ☐ **Cologne fluff** (1969), 3 oz ($5) .. — 3.00
- ☐ **Emollient oils** (1969), 6 oz ($5) — 4.00
- ☐ **Cologne** (1969), 4 oz ($5) .... — 3.00
- ☐ **Half-ounce cologne** (1970) ($1.75) .... — 2.00
- ☐ **Bright Night.**
- ☐ **Toilet water** (1955), 2 oz ($2) .. — 22.00
- ☐ **Cologne** (1955), 4 oz ($2.50) .... — 22.00
- ☐ **Cologne with atomizer** (1955), 4 oz ($3.50) .... — 36.00
- ☐ **Bright Night** (1956), Magic Hours set, 2-oz toilet water and cologne stick ($3.50) .... — 50.00
- ☐ **Cologne mist** (1958), 3 oz ($2.75) .... — 24.00

"Cotillion" (1959 only), gift cologne, 4 oz, N.Y.–Pasadena label ($2.50) $75. (*Photo courtesy of Western World Publishing, CA*)

"Cotillion." Cologne (1961), 4 oz ($3), $12. Cologne (1961), 2 oz ($2), $3. Perfume oil for bath (1963), ½ oz ($4), $12. Cologne (1969), ½ oz ($1.50), $2. (*Photo courtesy of Western World Publishing, CA*)

	Price Range
☐ **Cotillion.**	
☐ **Cotillion** (1959 only), gift cologne, 4 oz, N.Y.–Pasadena label ($2.50)	75.00
☐ **Cologne** (1961), 4 oz ($3)	12.00
☐ **Cologne** (1961), 2 oz ($2)	3.00
☐ **Perfume oil for bath** (1963), ½ oz ($4)	12.00
☐ **Cologne** (1969), ½ oz ($1.50) ...	2.00

"Cotillion." Bath oil (1954), 4½ oz ($1.25), $13. Cream lotion (1954), 4½ oz ($.95), $13. Talc (1955), 3 oz ($1), $12. Body powder (1958), 3 oz ($1), $12. Talc (1956), 3 oz ($1), $14. (*Photo courtesy of Western World Publishing, CA*)

	Price Range
☐ **Cotillion.**	
☐ **Bath oil** (1954), 4½ oz ($1.25) ..	13.00
☐ **Cream lotion** (1954), 4½ oz ($.95)	13.00
☐ **Talc** (1955), 3 oz ($1)	12.00
☐ **Talc** (1956), 3 oz ($1)	14.00
☐ **Body powder** (1958), 3 oz ($1)	12.00
☐ **Cotillion.**	
☐ **Cotillion** (1948), gift perfume, 3 dr. ($3)	110.00
☐ **Cotillion** (1951), gift perfume, 3 dr. ($3.50)	110.00
☐ **Boxed**	125.00
☐ **Cologne** (1953), 4 oz ($2)	20.00
☐ **Toilet water** (1953), 2 oz ($1.50)	18.00
☐ **Cologne** (1961), 2 oz ($1.50)	23.00

Price Range

☐ **Elegante** (1956), gift perfume, ½
oz, burgundy box and ribbon
($7.50), bottle only 85.00
☐ **Boxed** 130.00
☐ **Elegante** (1957), Sparkling Bur-
gundy: beauty dust, 6 oz, cream
sachet, cologne, 4 oz, and per-
fume, 1 dr., burgundy box and
ribbon ($8.95) 120.00
☐ **Elegante** (1957), toilet water, 2
oz, burgundy box and ribbon ($2) 25.00
☐ **Boxed** 40.00
☐ **Elegante.**
☐ **Cream sachet** (1956), .66 oz
($1.50) 13.00
☐ **Perfume** (1956), 1 dram in bur-
gundy suede wrapper ($2.25) 18.00
☐ **Cologne** (1956), 4 oz, gold box,
burgundy ribbon ($2.50) 40.00
☐ **Powder sachet** (1957), .9 oz
($1.50) 19.00

JIM BEAM

DESCRIPTION: Jim Beam Bottles refer to the figural liquor
containers first issued in the 1950s by the James B. Beam
Distilling Company, Kentucky.

ORIGIN: The company was founded in 1778 by Jacob Beam.
The firm now bears the name of Jacob Beam's grandson,
Colonel James B. Beam.

TYPES: The company produces a variety of themes including Executive Series, Regal China Series, and Political Figures Series.

COMMENTS: Early Beam bottles made before the figural series are also collectible. In 1953 the company produced its
first figural decanter. When the decanters sold well, Beam
began producing decorative bottles on a larger scale.

1960

	Price Range	
☐ **Blue Cherub,** executive series ..	100.00	170.00
☐ **Kansas State,** state series	55.00	64.00
☐ **Pheasant,** trophy series	20.00	24.00
☐ **Sante Fe,** centennial series	200.00	230.00

1963

☐ **Dancing Scot Short,** glass series	80.00	110.00
☐ **Harolds Grey,** customer specialty	180.00	190.00
☐ **Harrahs Grey,** customer specialty	550.00	650.00
☐ **Harrahs Silver,** customer specialty	900.00	1000.00
☐ **Idaho,** state series	50.00	60.00
☐ **Montana,** state series	70.00	80.00
☐ **New Jersey Grey,** state series ...	60.00	70.00
☐ **West Virginia,** state series	150.00	250.00

1964

☐ **Dancing Scot Tall Couple,** glass series	300.00	350.00
☐ **First National Bank,** customer specialty	3000.00	3200.00
☐ **Harolds Club Nevada Silver,** customer specialty	180.00	190.00

1970

☐ **Agnew Elephant,** political series	1600.00	1650.00
☐ **Churchill Downs 96th,** double roses, sport series	24.00	28.00

Mississippi fire engine, 1978, $115.

	Price Range	
☐ **Harolds Club VIP,** customer specialty	60.00	65.00

1978–1981

☐ **Mississippi fire engine,** 1978 ..	115.00
☐ **Grant locomotive,** 1979	50.00
☐ **Dial telephone,** 1980	45.00
☐ **Ducks unlimited,** 1981	35.00

Price Range

MISCELLANEOUS

☐ **Continental porcelain figural perfume bottle,** depicting a seated mandarin, polychrome glazed decoration, 6¾" high ..... 120.00 (Auction)

☐ **Czechoslovakian scent bottle,** geometric form with glass decorated gilt metal mounts, 5¼" high 100.00

☐ **German pottery pilgrim bottle,** unusual, traditional form, pedestal foot, loose ring handles, lion, griffin and demon mask decoration with acanthus geometric and faces decoration in blue salt glaze, 19" high 200.00 300.00

☐ **Lalique "Bouchon Fleurs de Pommiers,"** scent bottle, clear glass bottle with satin finish, gray-stained polished relief with a pink apple blossom relief stopper, etched "R. Lalique, France," 5½" high 800.00 1200.00

☐ **Lalique "Pannier de Roses,"** scent bottle, tapered cylindrical form, stained gray with molded floral relief, etched signature 600.00 800.00

☐ **Steuben perfumer,** lobate iridescent clear body surmounted by a jade spear stopper, 4½" high .. 200.00

Boxes

DESCRIPTION: Versatile and charming, boxes not only have a variety of uses but they are also quite collectible.

MATERIALS: Boxes are made of a variety of materials including straw, wood, china, and glass.

COMMENTS: In the 18th and 19th centuries boxes were mostly for utilitarian use such as perishable food storage. Special boxes were made to hold such items as wedding dresses. Small boxes, for trinkets, matches, or cigarettes, seem to be especially intricate and collectible.

ADDITIONAL TIPS: The listings in this section are alphabetical according to type of box, followed by descriptions and date.

Note: The single values shown below are auction-realized prices.

Price Range

☐ **Butternut covered dough box,** flaring rectangular dovetailed construction with plain lid, raised on splayed legs, 31″ × 13″ × 26½″ high 90.00

☐ **Chinese leather box,** rectangular form, with overall raised animal, floral, and mythological decoration, iron swing handles, 14″ long 60.00

☐ **Decorative box,** porcelain-mounted, covered with red velvet, rectangular with canted corners, the hinged lid set with a floral, painted, porcelain plaque within a brocade frame, the body with four similar cabochon porcelain plaques, 18″ long 300.00 400.00

☐ **Decorative covered boxes,** four, the first painted with a coaching scene; the second, gilt tooled leather fitted as a jewelry box; the third, an early Continental painted wood coffer-form box decorated with figures in a landscape; the fourth, a similar example painted with chinoiserie figures, the largest 9 ½″ long 150.00 200.00

☐ **Dresser box,** oval gilt metal, lid set with a miniature painting on green guilloche enamel, 5 ½″ long 110.00

☐ **English green glass rectangular box and cover,** 19th century, cover surmounted by a gilt recumbent lion, lid and box with white and gilt painted scroll band, 2 ¼″ high, together with a modern colorless glass waisted rectangular paperweight surmounted by a frosted glass recumbent lion, 3 ¼″ high 200.00 250.00

☐ **Jewel box,** hand-hammered copper and enamel, of circular form, domed lid with crab decoration, sides with freeform multicolor enamel decoration, velvet-lined

Left. Jewel box, lady's, Chippendale mahogany, the domed, hinged lid with post and bale handle, opening to a fitted interior, the case with brass escutcheon on a molded base raised on ogee bracket, 7″ high, 9″ long, 6″ deep, $375. *Right.* Tea caddy, Empire mahogany, the hinged, rectangular lid opening to a covered compartment, on brass ball feet, 5½″ high, 4¾″ long, 4¾″ deep, $140. (*Photo courtesy of Phillips, New York*)

	Price Range
interior with liftout tray, bearing a sand dollar impress maker's mark, 5″ diameter	145.00
☐ **Jewel box,** lady's, Chippendale mahogany, domed, hinged lid with post and bale handle, fitted interior, case with brass escutcheon on a molded base raised on ogee bracket, 7″ high, 9″ long, 6″ deep	375.00
☐ **Oval covered enameled box,** with lily decoration on slate blue ground, 4½″ long	20.00
☐ **Sewing box,** black lacquered and decorated, c. 1820, rectangular hinged lid with canted corners, decorated and fitter interior, case with elaborate decoration and	

Sewing box, black lacquered and decorated, c. 1820, the rectangular, hinged lid with canted corners opening to a decorated and fitted interior, the case with elaborate decoration and central drawer opening to reveal a fitted compartment, 7″ high, 15″ long, 12″ deep, $385. (*Photo courtesy of Phillips, New York*)

	Price Range
central drawer with fitted compartment, 7″ high, 15″ long, 12″ deep	385.00
☐ **Snuff box,** 19th century, English, lacquered, rectangular form, painted decoration spelling out "I say old fellow, take a chaw!" 3½″ long	35.00
☐ **Snuff box,** 18th century, English, lacquered, circular form, lid painted with a portrait medallion of an elderly gentleman with a white beard, 4″ diameter	195.00
☐ **Tea caddy,** Chinese export, lacquered, 19th century, bombé coffer form, domed octagonal hinged lid, interior fitted with two	

Price Range

engraved pewter canisters, decorated overall with scenes of scholars in a garden, raised on four animal-paw feet, 5¾″ × 8″ 300.00   400.00

☐ **Tea caddy,** Chinese export, lacquered, rectangular-octagonal form, slightly domed hinged lid, interior fitted with two engraved pewter canisters, decorated overall with various figures in landscapes and scrolling band, raised on four animal-paw feet, 5¾″ × 8″ 300.00   400.00

☐ **Tea caddy,** Empire mahogany, hinged rectangular lid opening to a covered compartment, on brass ball feet, 5½″ high, 4¾″ long, 4¾″ deep 140.00

☐ **Writing box,** 19th century, plain rectangular form, inside of lid set with a wood engraving of a battle scene, 13¾″ long 45.00

☐ **Writing box,** walnut, rectangular box with slant lid opening to reveal assorted pigeonholes, mounted on a plateau with ink bottle holders and penholders, geometric brass mounts overall, 17″ long 40.00

Breweriana

TYPES: Breweriana, or beer-related memorabilia, includes serving trays, coasters, bottle and can openers, advertising signs, and a variety of bottle and can styles.

FLATS (12-OZ CANS)

	Price Range	
☐ **Alpine**	50.00	60.00
☐ **Bavarian,** with Penn tax stamp on top	60.00	70.00
☐ **Big State**	35.00	45.00
☐ **Bullfrog**	30.00	35.00
☐ **Old Dutch**	60.00	70.00
☐ **Penn Dutch German,** with Penn tax stamp on top	55.00	65.00

LABELS

☐ **Amberlite Temperance Beer**	10.00	20.00
☐ **Banner Milwaukee Beer**	5.00	10.00
☐ **Regal,** 11 oz	8.00	12.00

	Price Range	
☐ **Somovit**	10.00	20.00
☐ **U.S. Beer**	8.00	12.00
☐ **Lorelei,** Picnic	8.00	12.00

SIGNS

☐ **Carling's lithographed tin beer sign,** "Nine Pints of the Law," 11½″ x 21¼″	35.00	45.00
☐ **Kern's beer sign,** eglomise glass panel set in a metal frame, 19½″ in diameter	35.00	45.00
☐ **Pabst Blue Ribbon mechanical sign,** depicting a gentleman riding in an early automobile, 17″ high	80.00	120.00

TABS (12-OZ CANS)

☐ **Cloud 9**	20.00	30.00
☐ **DuBois**	30.00	40.00
☐ **Hi-En Brau**	20.00	30.00
☐ **Ski Country**	20.00	30.00
☐ **Twins Lager**	75.00	85.00

TRAYS

☐ **Ballantine Ale & Beer,** red, white on blue with yellow stars, 13″	10.00	20.00
☐ **Rheingold,** "Brewers since 1837," 13″	8.00	12.00
☐ **Pearl,** plastic, photo of waterfall, glass and can, 13″	8.00	12.00
☐ **Kruger Beer & Ale,** red, older tray with "K" emblem, 12″	20.00	30.00
☐ **Schlitz,** white with orange and brown squares around logo, 1968, 12″	6.00	10.00

British Royalty

TYPES: British Royalty commemoratives and memorabilia run the gamut of objects, from plates and porcelain to postcards and books.

COMMENTS: Americans have always been fascinated with the Royal Family of the land that colonized our continent over three centuries ago. But in recent years, particularly with the royal marriages of Prince Charles and Lady Diana, Prince Andrew and ebullient "Fergie," Americans have been thrown into a passionate affair with all things royal. What follows is a sample of the wide range of items available in this popular field of collectibles.

Price Range

☐ **Coronation of Edward VIII**, May 12, 1937, sugar bowl and creamer, sepia portrait with flags in color, no mark except "Made in England" 75.00

Price Range

☐ **Queen Elizabeth and Prince Philip**, tin tea caddy, color portraits on the large side panels, initial "E" on the other two sides, inscription on hinged lid, coronation souvenir, June 1953, 6 ¼ " high 18.00

☐ **Queen Victoria**, plate, full-color portrait, possibly made for her Diamond Jubilee 1897, decorative green and gold rim 160.00

☐ **Silver Jubilee of Queen Elizabeth II**, 1952–1977, commemorative plate, 7 ½ ", gold trim, manufactured by Crown Staffordshire, England 28.00

☐ **Silver Jubilee of Queen Elizabeth II**, 1952–1977, royal crest in full color, inscription in light blue, silver trim, manufactured by Wood & Sons, England, for the "Pride of Britain Series" 25.00

☐ **Silver Jubilee of George and Mary**, 1910–1935, mug, in color, gold trim, royal crest on reverse circled by names of certain colonies, manufactured by Longton ..   45.00

☐ **Silver Jubilee of George and Mary**, 1910–1935, mug, porcelain, 3 ½ " high, in color, silver trim, no mark 65.00

Cameras

DESCRIPTION: Camera collecting is a favorite hobby for thousands of people. Hobbyists collect not only the cameras but anything associated with photography, including film, postcards that picture cameras, ads selling cameras, and signs from photo stores.

TYPES: Box, folding, panoramic, miniature, and 35mm cameras are all favorite types to collect.

ORIGIN: Although the photographic process was invented by Louis Jacques Mande Daguerre of Paris in 1839, it wasn't until the late 1800s that photography was accessible to the masses. An American, George Eastman, was a major influence in manufacturing cameras to sell to the public.

COMMENTS: In 1888, the Eastman Company produced the first, inexpensive roll-film box camera which enabled the average individual to buy a camera and take pictures without fuss. Their motto was "You Press the Button—We Do the Rest." After the roll of film was used up, the camera and film were sent to the company, where the film was processed and the camera reloaded and returned to the owner.

Although Eastman Company was the first to market a camera for the masses, all Kodak cameras that are old are not particularly valuable because of the quantity produced.

Those to watch for are cameras cocked with a strong, all-wood cameras, and cameras of unusual shape or size.

With the adoption of the 35mm film size for still cameras, Germany and Japan produced high-quality cameras in the late 1920s and throughout the 1930s that are highly regarded by collectors. Examples are Leica, Canon, Contax, and Nikon rangefinder cameras. Current prices for those in good condition range from $500 to $3,500.

Few collectors have previously shown an interest in early movie cameras and related equipment. However, that is changing with the increase in camera collecting and the scarcity of desirable still cameras. Around the turn of the century, motion picture cameras were made by few companies. A standard-size film had not been adopted, and each company made a camera for a different-size film. Thus, for the collector, there are still a few of those early cine cameras available, either all wood or all metal. Most are hand-cranked and large and heavy. They fetch a sizable price today from knowledgeable collectors.

Stereo cameras, which take two pictures at once, are in short supply and in strong demand by collectors. Any wooden stereo camera, with or without bellows, commands a price of $400 or more in today's market.

MANUFACTURERS OF NOTE:

E & H T Anthony glass plate camera. Comes in various sizes with black or red bellows, wooden body, brass lenses; c. 1880.

Boston Camera Company box camera, c. 1890, leather-covered box with simple lens and shutter; uncommon.

Canon 35mm camera, made in Japan before WW II and during the war; compact, high quality, with leather-covered metal body.

Contax 35mm camera, similar to Canon in size and quality, c. 1932.

Daguerreotype camera, c. 1845, all wood with brass lens, the size of a shoe box or larger, often no name; priced today to $6,000.

Eastman Company cameras, c. 1888, black leather-covered wooden body smaller than shoe box, cocked by string from top; first model with rotary shutter brings $1,500, later models $300 to $400.

Ernst Leitz Company, makers of Leica cameras and numerous accessories, c. 1926 to present; early rangefinder models particularly sought, but all Leicas are collector material as well as the accessories; all are 35mm, compact, highest quality.

Folmer & Schwing Mfg. Co., 1901 to 1940, makers of Graflex cameras in a number of film sizes, famous for use of their early cameras by news photographers; large, boxy, with pop-up top and lens that runs out on track.

Nikon, Tokyo, Japan, 1948 to present; all Nikon 35mm cameras up to 1965 are considered collectible, with the early ones quite scarce; prices paid by collectors range from $200 to $2,000.

Particular movie cameras to watch for, all hand-cranked, are Akeley, Lancaster, Edison, and Tourist Multiple, as well as those unnamed.

	Price Range	
☐ **Adlake cameras**, Adams & Westlake Co., manual plate-changing box cameras for 12 plates in 3 1/4 " × 4 1/4 " and 4 " × 5 " sizes, c. 1897	45.00	65.00
☐ **Baby Hawkeye**, Blair, miniature box camera, the smallest of the Hawkeye cameras, comparable to Eastman's "Pocket Kodak" cameras, for 12 exposures 2 " × 2 1/2 " on daylight loading "Blair's Sunlight Film," c. 1897	150.00	200.00
☐ **E. Leitz, 35mm projector**, can be used horizontal or vertical, rare, c. 1930	100.00	200.00
☐ **Golden Ricoh 16**, Japan, subminiature for 25 exposures 9 × 13mm on 16mm film, f3.5/25mm synchronized shutter 50–200, c. 1955	80.00	120.00
☐ **Hansa**, 35mm cannon camera, made in Japan, forebear of Nikon camera line, c. 1944	2500.00	3500.00
☐ **Kodak**, original Kodak Brownie box camera, c. 1900	300.00	400.00

	Price Range	
☐ **Kodak 16mm movie camera**, c. 1923	200.00	250.00
☐ **Kodak 16mm tripod**, c. 1923 ..	75.00	125.00
☐ **Kodak Cine Special**, 16mm projector, a sophisticated projector of advanced design, too expensive for that period, c. 1933	250.00	350.00
☐ **Magic Lantern Light**, for projecting 3 1/4″ × 4 1/4″ glass slides provided by oil lamp, c. 1890	75.00	100.00
☐ **Minex**, Adams & Co., single lens reflex, for 3 1/4″ × 4 1/2″ exposures, similar to the Graflex, c. 1895	165.00	185.00
☐ **Pokkor lens**, 3-speed shutter, 25, 50, and 200	15.00	25.00
☐ **Premier,** pathescope 28mm projector, c. 1918	40.00	60.00
☐ **Model IIIs**, Kodak, nonfolding type, Retina Xenon f1.9 or 2.8, synchronized computer, 1959–61	60.00	100.00
☐ **Retina Reflex**, Kodak SLR, Xenon f2 or f2.8/50mm, synchronized computer, c. 1958–59	50.00	80.00
☐ **Ricoh 35**, Leica-style 35mm, f3.5, 2.8, or f2 lens, c. 1955	15.00	25.00
☐ **Ricohflex**, Japan, 6 × 6 cm TLR, Ricoh Anastigmat f3.5, c. 1953 ..	15.00	25.00
☐ **Samoca Super**, Japan, 35mm camera for 36 exposures, 24 × 36mm on standard cartridges, Ezumar f3.5/50mm, shutter 10–200, CRF, built-in selenium meter, c. 1956	25.00	35.00
☐ **Scat**, Italy, subminiature for 8 × 11mm exposures on 5mm film in Minox cassettes, f3.5 lens, revolving shutter, leather-covered metal body, uncommon, c. 1950	125.00	175.00

	Price Range	
☐ **Signet 80,** Kodak, interchangeable f2.8/50mm Ektanar in bayonet mount, Synchro 250 shutter, CRF, BIM, originally $130.00, 1958–62	50.00	80.00
☐ **Stereo Hawkeye**, Blair, Stereo Weno, leather-covered wood bodied stereo rollfilm camera for 3 1/2″ × 3 1/2″ exposure, maroon bellows, simple B & W stereo shutter in brass housing	225.00	275.00

Carousel Animals

DESCRIPTION: Carousel animals are hand-carved and sculptured creations—true examples of a lost art.

PERIOD: Although the concept of the carousel has been recorded since early Byzantine times, the name has been traced to twelfth-century Arabian games of horsemanship (which Italian and Spanish cusaders called *carousellos* or "little wars"). Crudely carved carousels, fashioned by wheelwrights, blacksmiths, and carpenters in their spare time, were introduced to America early in the nineteenth century. In 1867 German cabinetmaker Gustav Dentzel formed the first successful American carousel company in Philadelphia.

COMMENTS: In contrast to European figures, the more imaginatively posed and ornately decorated American carousel animals can be identified by their elaborately carved right side, which is the side facing the viewer. This distinguishing feature is due to the clockwise movement of most European machines and counterclockwise rotation of American carousels. The most intricate carvings and elaborate trappings were concentrated on the outside-row animals, and competition among American carvers produced an array of exciting horses and whimsical menagerie animals.

Dentzel goat, outside row, c. 1895, stripped to traces of old paint, $11,000. (*Photo courtesy of Phillips, New York*)

Note: Single values shown below are the actual auction-realized prices.

	Price Range
☐ **Dentzel goat**, outside row, stripped to traces of old paint, c. 1895	11,000.00
☐ **Dentzel zebra**, outside row, rare, exceptional carving with fine restoration, c. 1895	23,000.00

Dentzel zebra, outside row, rare, c. 1895, exceptional carving with fine restoration, $23,000. (*Photo courtesy of Phillips, New York*)

Price Range

☐ **English carved- and painted-wood carousel horse**, the outside-row horse with elaborately carved acanthus leaves, finished in orange and black show paint with stars and a purple carved saddle, 74″ long, c. 1880 .... 3300.00

☐ **English carved- and painted-wood carousel horse**, middle-row horse with carved snake and dove motifs and a large tassle at the front of the mane, reins inscribed "Trevor," finished in

Price Range

green, yellow, blue, red, and silver show paint, 68″ long, c. 1880 .... 3850.00

☐ **English savage running cockerel**, large, 64″ long, 45″ high, c. 1900 .... 4250.00

☐ **English savage cockerel**, small, 34″ long, 33″ high, c. 1912 ...... 2400.00

☐ **French carved-wood fairground bear**, with glass eyes and carved to simulate bear fur, carved saddle and bow tie, stripped and finished, 34″ long, c. 1875 .... 1430.00

☐ **French carved-wood fairground donkey,** with central brass handle, stripped and finished, 32″ long, c. 1875 .... 1320.00

☐ **French carved-wood fairground rabbit**, with glass eyes and a bow tie around his neck, 38″ long, c. 1885 .... 2310.00

☐ **German leaping tiger**, most likely Hubner, painted as a cheetah, 58″ long, 26″ high, c. 1900 4750.00

☐ **Herschell-Spillman ostrich**, from park carousel, feather details, simple trappings, 42″ long, 65″ high, c. 1914 .... 4250.00

☐ **Heyn elephant**, large, exciting elephant with upholstered railed seat as howdah, fancy draped skirt and rosette trim, wonderful large clown is perched on elephant's head, c. 1911 .... 13,000.00

Looff armored jumper, outside row, rare, c. 1910, $15,000. (*Photo courtesy of Phillips, New York*)

	Price Range
☐ **Looff armored jumper**, outside row, rare, c. 1910	15,000.00
☐ **Looff greyhound**, outside row, old paint, rare, c. 1895, sold at record-setting price (see color section)	59,400.00
☐ **Looff prancing goat**, outside row, nice old paint, c. 1895	9000.00

Looff stander, 60″ height, 66″ length, $18,700. (*Photo courtesy of Phillips, New York*)

	Price Range
☐ **Looff stander,** 60″ high, 66″ long	18,700.00
☐ **Looff stander**, large horse, outside row, 66″ long, 58″ high	18,700.00
☐ **Looff jumping camel**, outside row, c. 1910	12,000.00

Looff jumping camel, outside row, c. 1910, $12,000. (*Photo courtesy of Phillips, New York*)

	Price Range
☐ **Muller-Dentzel tiger**, original trappings removed, nice body paint, c. 1895	12,000.00
☐ **P. T. C. deer**, outside row, elegant standing pose, fine fur detail, c. 1905	15,000.00

P.T.C. stander, outside row, c. 1915, fine restoration, $15,000.
(*Photo courtesy of Phillips, New York*)

	Price Range
☐ **P.T.C. stander,** outside row, fine restoration, c. 1915	15,000.00
☐ **Spooner centaur,** English, small, 44″ long, 30″ high, c. 1900	4800.00

Cars (Classic)

COMMENTS: The cars included here are defined as *classic* cars by the Classic Car Club of America, Chicago. These automobiles are not necessarily old but rank as classics because of workmanship, reputation, scarcity, and/or uniqueness of design. The Classic Car Club of America sets the beginning of the "classic" era at 1925 and the end of 1948. Though some of the more popular lines from later periods are not yet considered classics, particular models may soon fit the rigorous standards of this organization.

Note: Because of limitations of space, we are including only four models from each maker. Prices reflect the range from fair to excellent condition. Further information may be found in *The Official Price Guide to Collector Cars*.

	Price Range	
A.C. (Great Britain)		
☐ 1927, 2-passenger	2800.	9100.
☐ 1936, sport roadster	10,000.	35,000.
☐ 1938, cabriolet	6700.	23,000.
☐ 1947, sedan	5000.	21,000.
Adler (Germany)		
☐ 1925, 6/25, touring sport	5700.	25,000.
☐ 1930, sport roadster	11,000.	37,500.

	Price Range	
☐ 1936, sport touring	9000.	36,000.
☐ 1937, roadster	8500.	50,000.
Alfa-Romeo (Italy)		
☐ 1926, GS 1750, sport	4600.	27,500.
☐ 1933, 8C 2300	6700.	25,000.
☐ 1939, GP 2500, 12 cyl. roadster .	12,700.	75,000.
☐ 1947, 6C-2500, sport convertible	5500.	27,500.
Alvis (Great Britain)		
☐ 1925, 12/50, touring	11,000.	50,000.
☐ 1929, Silver Eagle, sedan	10,000.	27,500.
☐ 1933, Firefly, sport roadster	15,000.	62,000.
☐ 1946, TA-14, saloon sedan	4000.	18,000.
Amilcar (France)		
☐ 1925, CGS, touring	7500.	37,500.
☐ 1930, C8, touring	10,000.	50,000.
☐ 1936, Pegase, drop-head coupe ..	4500.	18,000.
☐ 1939, Compound, sedan	4000.	12,500.
Armstrong-Siddeley (Great Britain)		
☐ 1930, 12, coupe	3,000.	10,000.
☐ 1935, 30, Sedanca de Ville	3500.	15,000.
☐ 1939, limousine	3700.	19,000.
☐ 1952, Hurricane, drop-head		
coupe	3500.	9000.
Aston-Martin (Great Britain)		
☐ 1931, Le Mans, touring	5600.	35,000.
☐ 1934, Mark II	22,000.	88,000.
☐ 1937, touring	7500.	36,500.
☐ 1939, sport roadster	8200.	30,000.
Auburn (United States)		
☐ 1925, 6–66, roadster	12,500.	43,000.
☐ 1928, 8–88, roadster	17,500.	53,000.
☐ 1930, 125, cabriolet	18,500.	62,500.
☐ 1936, 852, phaeton	25,000.	87,500.
Austro-Daimler (Austria; the firm closed in 1936)		
☐ 1910, 22/80, touring	5700.	22,500.
☐ 1914, ADV, town	5700.	22,500.
☐ 1932, ADR-8, drop-head coupe ..	12,500.	48,000.
Bentley (Great Britain)		
☐ 1931, Speed 6, cabriolet	15,000.	78,000.
☐ 1935, Speed 6, cabriolet	13,000.	50,000.

Price Range

☐ 1938, Continental, drop-head
   coupe .... 9000.   50,000.
☐ 1940, MK-V, convertible .... 10,000.   40,000.
Benz (Germany; merged with
Mercedes in 1926)
☐ 1914, racer .... 45,000.   82,000.
Blackhawk (United States; the firm
closed in 1903)
☐ 1902, phaeton .... 5000.   18,000.
Brewster (United States; taken over
by Ford in 1934 and closed in 1936)
☐ 1917, roadster .... 11,000.   37,000.
☐ 1934, town car .... 11,000.   32,000.
☐ 1934, limousine .... 12,000.   50,000.
Bugatti (Italy)
☐ 1927, Type 35-C, convertible ..... 35,000.   130,000.
☐ 1930, Type 50, sport saloon ...... 26,000.   210,000.
☐ 1936, Type 57-C, sport .... 26,000.   135,000.
☐ 1940, Type 57-C, grand sport .... 25,000.   140,000.
Cadillac (United States)
☐ 1931, 370, V-12 7-passenger ...... 14,000.   50,000.
☐ 1932, 452, 16-cyl. convertible
   coupe .... 26,000.   180,000.
☐ 1936, 80, 12-cyl. limousine .... 10,000.   50,000.
☐ 1937, 90, 7-passenger cabriolet .. 37,000.   125,000.
Chrysler (United States)
☐ 1929, Imperial 80, sport roadster 23,000.   70,000.
☐ 1931, Imperial CG, limousine .... 50,000.   175,000.
☐ 1932, Imperial CL, phaeton .... 42,000.   180,000.
☐ 1941, Newport, dual-cowl phaeton 61,000.   262,000.
Cord (United States)
☐ 1929, L-29, sports roadster .... 47,000.   225,000.
☐ 1931, L-29, Sedanca de Ville ...... 28,000.   130,000.
☐ 1936, 810, phaeton .... 26,000.   112,000.
☐ 1937, 812, convertible coupe ..... 28,000.   235,000.
Cunningham (United States)
☐ 1925, V6, touring .... 8,200.   37,500.
☐ 1927, V7, touring .... 15,000.   70,000.
☐ 1929, V9, Roadster .... 14,000.   61,000.
☐ 1935, Town .... 8200.   32,000.

	Price Range	
Dagmar (United States)		
☐ 1923, 6T, touring	5600.	23,000.
☐ 1924, 6–70, touring	5600.	23,000.
☐ 1925, 25–70, sedan	4000.	18,000.
☐ 1926, 70, 7-passenger sedan	5500.	22,000.
Daimler (Great Britain)		
☐ 1927, Double Six, touring	11,500.	53,000.
☐ 1933, 15, touring	6700.	48,500.
☐ 1936, limousine	3500.	14,500.
☐ 1949, limousine	4600.	17,500.
Darracq/Talbot (France)		
☐ 1920, 12/16, racing	6000.	23,000.
☐ 1928, 12/32, sedan	1500.	7500.
☐ 1938, Grand Prix racing	5200.	26,000.
☐ 1949, sport sedan	3800.	15,000.
Delage (France)		
☐ 1925, 12-cyl. racing	15,000.	75,000.
☐ 1926, DI touring	8000.	32,000.
☐ 1933, D6–11 drop-head coupe ...	5000.	18,000.
☐ 1934, D8–15 roadster	11,500.	83,000.
Delahaye (France)		
☐ 1935, Superlux, roadster	9000.	31,000.
☐ 1936, Dragonfly, convertible	41,000.	280,000.
☐ 1937, Des Alpes, convertible coupe	17,000.	70,000.
☐ 1938, Type 145, roadster	40,000.	275,000.
Delaunay-Belleville (France)		
☐ 1904, roadster	4000.	16,000.
☐ 1909, 10 CV, touring	4000.	16,500.
☐ 1924, drop-head coupe	4200.	17,000.
☐ 1928, Greyhound, sedan	3000.	12,000.
Doble (United States)		
☐ 1923, D, steam roadster	22,000.	100,000.
☐ 1924, E, steam touring	17,500.	81,000.
☐ 1925, E, steam roadster	20,000.	100,000.
☐ 1931, Deluxe, 2-cyl. steam	37,500.	125,000.
Dorris (United States)		
☐ 1921, Pasadena, phaeton	5000.	32,000.
☐ 1923, 6–80 sedan	4000.	15,000.
☐ 1923, 6–80, sport	4200.	23,000.
☐ 1925, Custom, touring	4000.	17,500.

Price Range

Duesenberg (United States)
- [ ] 1926, A, phaeton .... 25,000.   190,000.
- [ ] 1927, X 7 Ps limousine .... 21,000.   92,000.
- [ ] 1928, Murphy-J convertible
  roadster .... 90,000.   400,000.
- [ ] 1929, Derham J phaeton .... 120,000.   420,000.

Du Pont (United States)
- [ ] 1923, touring .... 6200.   38,000.
- [ ] 1925, D, touring .... 6800.   42,000.
- [ ] 1928, G, Speedster .... 12,000.   93,000.
- [ ] 1931, H, touring .... 7000.   44,000.

Excelsior (Brazil)
- [ ] 1907, Adex, 6-cyl. sport .... 1600.   11,000.
- [ ] 1914, 14/20, coupe .... 1200.   6000.
- [ ] 1921, touring .... 1500.   11,000.
- [ ] 1922, Albert I, sport touring ...... 2500.   12,000.

Farman (France)
- [ ] 1902, 12 CV, racing .... 4500.   19,000.
- [ ] 1925, A 6 B, touring .... 6000.   21,000.
- [ ] 1925, coupe .... 6000.   21,000.
- [ ] 1930, NF 2, Sedanca de Ville ..... 8100.   32,000.

Fiat (Italy)
- [ ] 1915, Tipo 5, racing .... 31,000.   125,000.
- [ ] 1921, 12-cyl. Coupe de Ville ...... 4000.   28,000.
- [ ] 1927, Tipo 520, racing .... 32,000.   125,000.
- [ ] 1929, Tipo 528, Sport .... 2000.   10,000.

Franklin (United States)
- [ ] 1925, II, roadster .... 4000.   32,000.
- [ ] 1926, II B, Speedster .... 6000.   51,000.
- [ ] 1930, 14, Pursuit phaeton .... 12,500.   80,000.
- [ ] 1933, Airman, sedan .... 5000.   31,000.

Frazer Nash (Great Britain)
- [ ] 1932, roadster .... 6200.   30,000.
- [ ] 1935, Type 319, sport .... 5000.   21,000.
- [ ] 1948, High Speed, racing .... 6400.   41,000.
- [ ] 1953, coupe .... 2100.   10,000.

Graham-Paige (United States)
- [ ] 1929, 621, touring .... 7500.   34,000.
- [ ] 1930, 837, phaeton .... 5000.   36,000.
- [ ] 1932, 57 Blue Streak, cabriolet .. 4000.   23,000.
- [ ] 1941, Hollywood convertible ..... 5000.   32,000.

	Price Range	
Hispano-Suiza (Spain)		
☐ 1930, H6, phaeton	22,500.	175,000.
☐ 1930, touring	15,000.	92,000.
☐ 1937, Tipo 49, sedan	12,500.	41,000.
☐ 1938, Tipo 64, touring	27,500.	150,000.
Horch (Germany)		
☐ 1930, 450, touring	12,500.	60,000.
☐ 1932, 12-cyl. cabriolet	21,500.	110,000.
☐ 1937, 12-cyl. cabriolet	15,000.	105,000.
☐ 1939, 12-cyl. sport cabriolet	13,000.	87,000.
Hotchkiss (France)		
☐ 1907, 15.3-litre, racing	6000.	33,000.
☐ 1931, AM 80, touring	2000.	17,000.
☐ 1934, 15 CV, sport	2200.	16,500.
☐ 1939, limousine	2100.	16,000.
Hudson (United States)		
☐ 1916, Super Six, touring	6000.	25,000.
☐ 1919, Super Six, touring	6100.	23,000.
☐ 1927, Standard Six, phaeton	5000.	22,500.
☐ 1929, Greater Hudson, roadster .	11,000.	57,000.
Humber (Great Britain)		
☐ 1927, 14/40, racing	2200.	11,000.
☐ 1930, Pullman, coupe	1000.	6500.
☐ 1937, Twelve, drop-head coupe .	4000.	16,000.
☐ 1939, Super Snipe, sedan	2200.	11,000.
Invicta (Great Britain)		
☐ 1925, touring	4200.	17,500.
☐ 1928, drop-head coupe	3200.	13,500.
☐ 1930, phaeton	4600.	22,500.
☐ 1933, 12/90, sedan	4200.	18,500.
Isotta Fraschini (Italy)		
☐ 1922, Tipo 8, sport touring	20,000.	90,000.
☐ 1926, 8 A, cabriolet	35,000.	175,000.
☐ 1929, Special, convertible coupe	44,000.	250,000.
☐ 1930, 8 A, phaeton	44,000.	250,000.
Italia (Italy)		
☐ 1906, Targa Florio, touring	4000.	20,000.
☐ 1909, 35, limousine	4000.	17,500.
☐ 1922, 51-F, racing	3200.	13,000.
☐ 1929, 61, roadster	3400.	14,000.

Price Range

S.S. Jaguar (Great Britain)
- ☐ 1934, SS-1, roadster .... 6400. 39,000.
- ☐ 1935, SS-100, roadster .... 9000. 60,000.
- ☐ 1938, SS-100, supercharged
  roadster .... 17,500. 83,000.
- ☐ 1939, SS-100, drop-head coupe .. 11,500. 60,000.

Jensen (Great Britain)
- ☐ 1936, sport touring .... 6000. 22,000.
- ☐ 1938, DC, phaeton .... 4800. 21,500.
- ☐ 1938, 4-dr, sedan .... 1800. 11,000.
- ☐ 1950, Interceptor, cabriolet .... 1500. 10,000.

Jordan (United States)
- ☐ 1920, Playboy, roadster .... 7000. 38,000.
- ☐ 1925, L, touring .... 5,600. 30,000.
- ☐ 1929, Playboy, roadster .... 8200. 36,000.
- ☐ 1930, Series T, speedster .... 6000. 35,000.

Kissel (United States)
- ☐ 1920, Gold Bug, runabout .... 22,500. 50,000.
- ☐ 1923, 45, Boattail speedster .... 11,000. 36,000.
- ☐ 1929, White Eagle 6, speedster .. 12,000. 48,000.
- ☐ 1929, 8-cyl. coupe .... 3200. 14,000.

Lagonda (Great Britain)
- ☐ 1930, Boattail speedster .... 6700. 50,000.
- ☐ 1934, Selector-Special, sport
  touring .... 8000. 36,000.
- ☐ 1937, 12-cyl. convertible sedan .. 10,700. 70,000.
- ☐ 1939, 12-cyl. convertible Victoria 11,000. 72,000.

Lanchester (Great Britain)
- ☐ 1921, Twenty-one, sport .... 6000. 32,500.
- ☐ 1923, Landaulet .... 5200. 31,500.
- ☐ 1932, roadster .... 5300. 22,500.
- ☐ 1938, Roadrider de Luxe, drop-
  head coupe .... 3500. 14,500.

Lancia (Italy)
- ☐ 1920, DiKappa, touring .... 9500. 46,500.
- ☐ 1920, Torino, roadster .... 7500. 35,000.
- ☐ 1923, Lambda, Torpedo .... 3800. 15,000.
- ☐ 1940, Ardea, convertible coupe .. 3800. 17,500.

LaSalle (United States)
- ☐ 1927, 303, dual-cowl phaeton .... 26,000. 93,000.
- ☐ 1928, 328, dual-cowl phaeton .... 25,000. 100,000.

	Price Range	
☐ 1930, 340, touring	14,000.	65,000.
☐ 1932, 345B, cabriolet	14,000.	59,000.

Lincoln (United States)

☐ 1932, dual-cowl phaeton	21,500.	115,000.
☐ 1933, convertible Victoria	21,500.	115,000.
☐ 1936, LeBaron, convertible	16,000.	93,000.
☐ 1937, K, phaeton	22,000.	77,000.

Lincoln-Continental (United States)

☐ 1940, coupe	6300.	40,000.
☐ 1941, 12-cyl. convertible	6100.	40,000.
☐ 1946, convertible cabriolet	6300.	32,000.
☐ 1948, convertible	8500.	38,000.

Marmom

☐ 1927, 4-passenger, roadster	8750.	35,000.
☐ 1930, Roosevelt, sedan	7500.	32,500.
☐ 1932, 16, convertible sedan	125,000.	72,500.
☐ 1933, 5-passenger, convertible	7500.	40,000.

McFarlan

☐ 1910, 5-passenger, touring	3750.	27,500.
☐ 1915, 7-passenger, touring	5000.	36,250.
☐ 1920, Knickerbocker, cabriolet	11,250.	56,250.
☐ 1923, SV, touring	10,000.	40,000.

Mercedes Benz

☐ 1926, K, touring	16,250.	97,500.
☐ 1933, 170, roadster	10,625.	32,500.
☐ 1936, 500K, sport convertible	62,500.	48,750.
☐ 1948, 190, sedan	3,250.	12,125.

Mercer

☐ 1910, 35-R, roadster	12,500.	110,000.
☐ 1925, L-Head, touring	7500.	37,500.
☐ 1931, 140-hp., touring	7500.	33,750.

MG

☐ 1929, Midget, cabriolet	2250.	8125.
☐ 1934, LeMans, roadster	2875.	19,375.
☐ 1936, PB, touring	2250.	22,500.
☐ 1939, WA, convertible, coupe	2125.	20,940.

Nash

☐ 1925, 161, phaeton	2875.	20,940.
☐ 1950, 470, sedan	2375.	11,560.
☐ 1939, Ambassador, convertible	4375.	20,000.
☐ 1947, Super, coupe	1125.	7440.

Price Range

Packard
- [ ] 1926, 243, touring .... 10,625.   48,750.
- [ ] 1934, 1100, sedan .... 7375.   18,750.
- [ ] 1940, Darrin, Victoria
      convertible............................. 13,750.   87,500.
- [ ] 1946, 2016, coupe .... 6000.   17,500.

Peugeot
- [ ] 1930, Type 201, touring .... 2250.   9000.
- [ ] 1935, Type 601, coupe .... 815.   3125.
- [ ] 1939, Darl mat, coupe .... 875.   3500.
- [ ] 1947, Type 203, sedan .... 690.   2750.

Pierce-Arrow
- [ ] 1928, 80, cabriolet .... 5750.   25,000.
- [ ] 1932, 53, rumble seat coupe ...... 9000.   48,750.
- [ ] 1934, 1240 A, sedan .... 7625.   47,500.
- [ ] 1938, 1802, formal sedan .... 11,500.   55,000.

Railton
- [ ] 1933, sport .... 3250.   11,875.
- [ ] 1934, sedan .... 2750.   10,310.
- [ ] 1935, sedan .... 2875.   10,625.
- [ ] 1939, sedan convertible .... 6250.   32,500.

Renault
- [ ] 1930, Reinasetta, sport .... 6250.   37,500.
- [ ] 1936, sport .... 815.   5625.
- [ ] 1940, sport sedan .... 875.   6250.
- [ ] 1946, sedan .... 815.   5625.

Reo
- [ ] 1927, Flying Cloud, coupe .... 2500.   13,625.
- [ ] 1930, 6–25, roadster .... 4375.   30,000.
- [ ] 1931, 6–6–25, sport coupe .... 2500.   14,000.
- [ ] 1933, Royale 8, cabriolet .... 7500.   35,000.

Revere
- [ ] 1917, Speedster .... 18,750.   37,500.
- [ ] 1920, C, roadster .... 5625.   22,500.

Riley
- [ ] 1930, Fourteen, touring .... 1375.   10,625.
- [ ] 1934, convertible .... 2500.   13,125.
- [ ] 1938, sport .... 2500.   12,500.
- [ ] 1946, sedan .... 940.   6250.

Roamer
- [ ] 1916, touring .... 6250.   28,750.

	Price Range	
☐ 1919, sport	17,500.	43,750.
☐ 1923, Model 75-E, touring	6250.	27,500.
☐ 1925, Model 8–88, sedan	5000.	18,750.
Rohr		
☐ 1928, Type R, sedan	11,250.	37,500.
☐ 1930, Type RA, sedan	11,250.	37,500.
☐ 1935, Type F, sedan	11,250.	37,500.
Rolls-Royce		
☐ 1935, de, coupe	13,750.	60,000.
☐ 1940, Wraith, convertible sedan .	21,250.	86,250.
☐ 1946, Silver Wraith, brougham sedan	13,250.	57,500.
☐ 1947, Silver Wraith, sedan	10,500.	45,000.
Ruxton		
☐ 1929, front-wheel drive, roadster	11,250.	90,000.
☐ 1930, sedan	7500.	43,750.
☐ 1930, roadster	11,250.	90,000.
☐ 1931, town car	15,000.	81,250.
Straker-Squire		
☐ 1919, 20/25, touring	3875.	17,500.
☐ 1921, 24/90, sport	3750.	15,625.
☐ 1924, 24/90, touring	4375.	18,750.
☐ 1926, coupe	2750.	12,500.
Studebaker		
☐ 1931, Dictator, roadster	5500.	37,500.
☐ 1933, Commander, Victoria	3250.	17,500.
☐ 1940, President, sedan	2500.	11,250.
☐ 1948, Commander, convertible coupe	3000.	20,000.
Stutz		
☐ 1927, rumble seat coupe	7500.	35,000.
☐ 1929, dual-cowl phaeton	36,250.	130,000.
☐ 1930, Boattail speedster	23,750.	102,500.
☐ 1933, DV-32, club sedan	15,000.	51,250.
Sunbeam		
☐ 1924, Sprint	7500.	40,000.
☐ 1933, Speed Model, sport	2315.	9375.
☐ 1934, Dawn, sedan	1875.	6000.
☐ 1938, sedan	940.	4815.
Talbot		
☐ 1929, 14/45, sedan	2500.	15000.

	Price Range	
☐ 1930, 75, touring	4375.	22500.
☐ 1931, sedan	2250.	8750.
☐ 1935, 110, sport	5625.	20,000.
Tatra		
☐ 1926, Type 30, touring	1125.	3440.
☐ 1930, Type 49, Tri-car	690.	4000.
☐ 1934, Type 77, sport	940.	5000.
☐ 1939, Type 97, sedan	500.	4700.
Triumph		
☐ 1900, Stanhope	3750.	17,500.
☐ 1906, tonneau	2750.	16,875.
☐ 1909, touring	3125.	17,190.
Vauxhall		
☐ 1930, Cadet, sedan saloon	3500.	11,250.
☐ 1935, Big Six, Landaulet	3625.	11,250.
☐ 1940, Ten, coupe	1125.	4250.
☐ 1948, Velox, sedan	1500.	9000.
Voisin		
☐ 1927, sedan	1875.	8500.
☐ 1931, coupe	2815.	11,250.
☐ 1934, Chamant, sedan	3750.	15,000.
☐ 1938, coupe	5415.	18,750.
Wills Sainte Claire		
☐ 1922, roadster	7500.	36,250.
☐ 1923, brougham	3625.	13,750.
☐ 1925, sport roadster	8750.	42,500.
☐ 1926, roadster	7500.	40,000.

Cartoon Art (Original)

DESCRIPTION: Original cartoon art is original art as created by the artist for comic strips, printed illustrations, and the like, as opposed to prints, newspaper pages, etc. We are dealing primarily here with comic strips and cartoons that were distributed by syndicates to daily and Sunday newspapers. There is a collector's market in the original drawings for such material. Modern collectors regard Richard Outcault's "Yellow Kid" as the first major, modern comic strip character, according to *Comics Buyer's Guide*, Iola, Wisconsin. The strip first appeared in the *New York Journal* on October 18, 1896, and gave its name to "yellow journalism."

COMMENTS: Many collectors frame and hang fine specimens of work in this field.

Note: The single values shown below are the actual auction-realized prices.

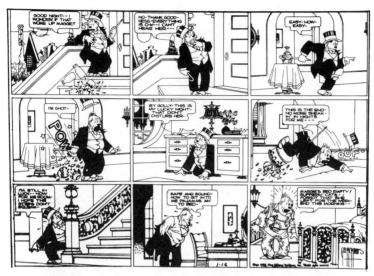

"Bringing Up Father," George McManus, Sunday page, January 16, 1938, with signature, $425. (*Photo courtesy of Phillips, New York*)

	Price Range
☐ **"B. C.,"** Johnny Hart, Sunday page, February 17, 1982, signed, 11″ × 16″	275.00
☐ **"B. C.,"** Johnny Hart, Sunday page, July 26, 1981, signed "All Good Wishes From Johnny Hart," 11½″ × 16″	200.00
☐ **"Beetle Bailey,"** Mort Walker, Sunday page, August 25, 1982, with signature, featuring Sarge, Beetle, and the Lieutenant, 10″ × 15″	150.00
☐ **"Bringing Up Father,"** George McManus, Sunday page, January 16, 1938, with signature	425.00
☐ **"For Better or for Worse,"** Lynn Johnston, Sunday page, August 24, 1986, with signature, 9″ × 13″	175.00

"Little Nemo in Slumberland," Winsor McCay, full Sunday page, c. 1900, some hand-coloring, with signature, framed to 30″ × 24″, $2400. (*Photo courtesy of Phillips, New York*)

	Price Range
☐ **"Hagar the Horrible,"** Dick Browne, Sunday page, September 12, 1982, with signature, features Hagar and Helga, 10″ × 15″	180.00
☐ **"Little Nemo in Slumberland,"** Winsor McCay, full Sunday page, c. 1900, some hand coloring, with signature, framed to 30″ × 24″ ..	2400.00
☐ **"Mutt and Jeff,"** Bud Fisher, daily strip, June 7, 1923, 8½″ × 29″ ..	110.00

"Prince Valiant," Hal Foster, full Sunday page, June 10, 1962, with signature, 33 ½ ″ × 22 ½ ″, $1300. (*Photo courtesy of Phillips, New York*)

	Price Range	
☐ **"Peanuts,"** Carl Schultz, daily strip, January 23, 1986, with signature, 5 ″ × 21 ″ (estimated value)	500.00	600.00
☐ **"Polly and Her Pals,"** Cliff Sterrett, full Sunday page, October 12, 1958, with signature, 17 ½ ″ × 24 ¼ ″		300.00
☐ **"Prince Valiant,"** Hal Foster, full Sunday page, June 10, 1962, with signature, 33 ½ ″ × 22 ½ ″ .		1300.00

"Tarzan," Hal Foster, Sunday page, December 13, 1936, with signature, No. 301, titled "Flint's Surprise," Tarzan with the Golden Lion battle sequence, 26″ × 20″, $1900. (*Photo courtesy of Phillips, New York*)

	Price Range
☐ **"Ripleys Believe It Or Not,"** King Features Syndicate, daily panel, September 23, 1963, 12″ × 15″	110.00
☐ **"Tarzan,"** Hal Foster, Sunday page, December 13, 1936, with signature, No. 301, titled "Flint's Surprise," Tarzan with the Golden Lion battle sequence, 26″ × 20″	1900.00
☐ **"The Little King,"** Otto Soglow, Sunday page with signature, October 24, 1960, 13″ × 19″	200.00

Cash Registers

HISTORY: The cash register was introduced in 1884 by James Ritty. Its primary purpose was to deter salesclerks from stealing money. One of Ritty's customers bought controlling interest in Ritty's business and eventually started the National Cash Register Company, which has become the best-known maker of cash registers. Other manufacturers include St. Louis, Ideal, and Michigan.

DESCRIPTION: Prior to World War I, cash registers were ornately made and decorated. Popular materials used were oak, brass, and bronze. Registers made before 1916 are the most sought after because of their decoration. Age, rarity, beauty, and size of the machine are the top factors when buying a cash register.

Note: The single values shown below are the actual auction-realized prices.

	Price Range	
☐ **National cash register**, brass, No. 1346371, with an art glass nameplate, on a polished mahogany base, 30½″ wide	800.00	1200.00

Price Range

☐ **National cash register**, nickel steel, two-drawer, large, No. 110377, 30½" wide 500.00   800.00

☐ **National cash register**, Model No. 313, with "Amount Purchased" sign, 21" high 750.00

☐ **National cash register**, nickel-plated brass, Model No. 313, 9¾" × 16" × 17" 525.00

☐ **National cash register**, nickel-plated brass, Model No. 410, side-mounted crank arm, 18¼" × 15" × 19" 325.00

Left. Steel Barber Shop register, #2196348, 9¾" wide, estimated value $200–$300. *Right*. Michigan cast brass Barber's Shop register, #571, 9¼" wide, sold for $192.50. (*Photo courtesy of Butterfield & Butterfield, San Francisco*)

	Price Range	
☐ **Steel barber shop register**, No. 2196348, 9¾″ wide (estimated value)	200.00	300.00
☐ **Michigan cast-brass barber shop register**, No. 571, 9¼″ wide (sale price)		192.50
☐ **"World" nickled-iron sale record register**, in scroll cast case, 18¼″ wide		605.00

"World" nickeled iron sale record register, in scroll cast case, 18¼″ wide, $605. (*Photo courtesy of Butterfield & Butterfield, San Francisco*)

Circus
Memorabilia

DESCRIPTION: All circus-related items are considered collectible, including posters, photographs, ticket stubs, and programs, as well as large items such as cages and tents.

ORIGIN: The first American circus opened in 1793 in Philadelphia. About thirty years later, tents and big tops were introduced. In 1919 the top two competing circuses, Barnum and Bailey and Ringling Brothers, combined their shows.

Note: The single values shown below are the actual auction-realized prices.

	Price Range	
☐ **Circus scene diorama**, Continental, mounted in glass vitrine, two-ring circus with German flat-painted lead figures engaged in varied activities, the rectangular vitrine decorated on the exterior with bosses and swags, 14″ high	300.00	400.00

Schoenhut Humpty Dumpty Circus, in original pictorial box, 21 pieces, $1870. (*Photo courtesy of Christie's East, New York*)

	Price Range
☐ **Mammoth Circus,** Britains, display set No. 1539, with ringmaster, lion tamer, man on stilts, boxing clowns and kangaroo, elephants, tigers, prancing horses, equestrienne, tub, ring, and other figures, in original box	1300.00
☐ **Posters,** two: Cole Bros. Circus lithograph in colors, 17¼″ × 26″, framed; and Hagenbeck—Wallace Circus, lithograph in colors, 50″ × 25½″, framed	176.00
☐ **Schoenhut Humpty Dumpty Circus,** in original pictorial box, 21 pieces	1870.00
☐ **Schoenhut Humpty Dumpty Circus,** Delvan set, comprising ringmaster, four clowns, elephant, horse, donkey, three chairs, five ladders, pedestals, barrels, balls, barbells, dividers and tent, in original box with literature, 1950s	625.00

Price Range

CLOWN TOYS

☐ **Balancing clown**, German, 1910, hand-painted tin, cloth-dressed clown on wood platform with balancing bar 600.00 650.00

☐ **Balancing toy clown**, German, 1915, hand-painted composition wood, iron-weighted balancing bar, 11″ high 550.00 650.00

☐ **Carnival strong man**, German, 1920s, clown hits gong on strength machine with large hammer, 4½″ long 100.00 150.00

☐ **Cirko clown cyclist**, maker unknown, 1924, lithographed circus figure appears on large wheel of high-wheeler, clown wears high peaked cap, 8½″ high 250.00 300.00

☐ **Clown and Black on see-saw**, Watrous Mfg. Co., 1905, tin and cast-iron bell pull toy, 5¾″ long 300.00 500.00

☐ **Clown and goat**, German, 1920s, lithographed tin mechanical with cloth clown outfit, clown has whip, goat butts cart from behind 200.00 250.00

☐ **Clown and poodle**, gong bell, 1903, clown swings dog who rings bell attached to muzzle, 8¼″ long, cast-metal, painted ... 350.00 450.00

☐ **Clown balancing bears**, German, 1900s, painted and stenciled tin, 11½″ high, clown is on back, resting on platform with feet in air balancing a spinning ball with bar, at each end of bar is a bear suspended in a swing, small bells at each end of bar ring as toy is activated 1400.00 1600.00

Price Range

☐ **Clown barrel walker**, Chein, 1940s, lithographed tin mechanical, 7¾" high (variation of Chein's Popeye and Barnacle Bill toys) 150.00   200.00

☐ **Clown bell toy**, gong bell, 1910, clown rides in cart pulled by pig   350.00   450.00

Civil War Memorabilia

DESCRIPTION: The Civil War produced some of the most collectible antiques in today's marketplace. Items are available all over the world. Collecting Civil War memorabilia can be a most gratifying hobby for the collector as he or she delves into the history of each item and discovers the principles on which this country has grown.

COMMENTS: The most sought-after collectible in this category is that of firearms. This period marked a technological transition from a single-shot gun to one that would shoot several times, including the first machine gun. Other collectible areas include uniforms, buttons, belt buckles, canteens, knapsacks, insignias, and personal effects, such as diaries, letters, and photographs.

ADDITIONAL TIPS: Auctions are a great place to pick up such items as well as dealer shops. Prices are as varied as the items, so even the novice can afford to begin this type of collection.

	Price Range	
☐ **Book**, *History of the 6th N.H. Regiment*, 1897, 630 pp.	50.00	60.00
☐ **Book**, *The Soldier in Our Civil War*, 2 vols, each 400 + pp., with illustrated picture history, published 1885 by Stanley Bradley; covers show wear, insides are very good	80.00	100.00
☐ **Carte de visite**, signed, Capt. J. W. Kimball, killed in action June 22, 1864	30.00	40.00
☐ **Diary**, James McBride, 88 pp., small 8vo, May 18, 1863, to July 1, 1864; text mainly in pencil, though with a few pages in ink, some pages faded, a few leaves loose, red/brown stain in upper corner on most pages, cloth, worn	400.00	600.00
☐ **Diary**, James Wren, Major, 48th Regiment of Pennsylvania Volunteers, Infantry; seven manuscript diaries covering Wren's military service from April 17, 1871, to May 25, 1863, and his honorable discharge; text in pancil and ink, some pencil faded, four diaries cloth-bound and three leather, some wear, one cover detached .	1500.00	2500.00
☐ **Engravings, steel, 1865:**		
☐ **Lincoln, U. S. Grant**	20.00	25.00
☐ ***Monitor*** and ***Merrimack*** battle	20.00	25.00
☐ **General Burnside at Newbern**	20.00	25.00
☐ **Death of General Lyon**	20.00	25.00
☐ **Greatcoat**, worn primarily by cavalary soldiers in the Union Army	400.00	500.00
☐ **Jacket**, Union naval jacket, rank of commodore	600.00	650.00
☐ **Letter**, George B. McClellan, signed, 1 ¾ pp., 4to, Washington,		

	Price Range	
August 10, 1861, to President Lincoln, apologizing for the remarks made in a letter, two days earlier, to Lieutenant-General Scott	200.00	300.00
☐ **Map**, the southern and western states, hand-colored, dated 1855	12.00	15.00
☐ **Print**, "The Battle of Manassas"	600.00	700.00
☐ **Print**, engraved Abraham Lincoln print by J. C. Buttre, late 1865 ...	550.00	750.00
☐ **Reunion medal**, Massachusetts Gettysburg, 1913, suspended medal with Lincoln bust	25.00	30.00
☐ **Stamped envelope**, with Jefferson Davis stamp, CS #11, postmarked Macon, 1874	30.00	40.00
☐ **Tintype**, unidentified soldier, mounted as carte de visite	20.00	25.00
☐ **Tintype**, Confederate General Beauregard	55.00	75.00

Clocks

TOPIC: Clocks, of course, are devices that measure time in hours, minutes, and sometimes seconds. Usually they have circular faces with Arabic or Roman numerals. Two or three hands on the face are standard.

TYPES: There are numerous types of clocks, including alarm clocks, atmospheric clocks, dresser clocks, gingerbread clocks, tall case (grandfather) clocks, mantel clocks, regulator clocks, travel clocks, and wall clocks.

PERIOD: Most collectors focus on eighteenth- and nineteenth-century clocks. Domestic clocks originated around the 1500s.

ORIGIN: Clocks developed in Europe.

MATERIALS: Clock cases may be of wood, glass, plastic, metal, or porcelain. The works are metal.

MAKERS: Seth Thomas is one of the most famous clockmakers from New England. Well-known clock companies include Ansonia, W. L. Gilbert, E. Ingraham, Jerome, New Haven, and Waterbury.

COMMENTS: Clocks cover a great range of sizes, varieties, and designs. The collector can focus on a specific type of clock, such as a wall clock, and further specialize in banjo-style specimens.

Austrian ebonized and giltwood shelf clock, 19th century, 22″ high, $922. (*Photo courtesy of Christie's East, New York*)

Note: The single values shown below are the actual auction-realized prices.

	Price Range
☐ **Austrian ebonized and giltwood shelf clock**, 19th century, 22″ high	922.00
☐ **Brass mantel clock**, beveled-glass panels, mercury pendulum, 9″ high	160.00
☐ **Ceramic figural clock**, Art Nouveau style, by Goldcheider, titled "The Sinner," the domed face set	

Price Range

in the molded form of a woman, inset with mother-of-pearl and opals, 35″ high, bears plaque "Exhibited at the World's Fair 1937" .   2000.00

☐ **Continental skeleton clock**, 19th century, scrolling brass front and back plates with scalloped dial, 14″ high 400.00

☐ **Empire architectural onyx mantel clock**, repousse gilt metal dial with Father Time decoration, 16¾″ long, 13¼″ high 100.00

Federal cherrywood tall case clock, early 19th century, 90″ high, $750. (*Photo courtesy of Phillips, New York*)

Price Range

☐ **French onyx and gilt metal desk clock**, of acroterium form, 7 ½ " high 90.00

☐ **Desk clock**, highly unusual, Roman numeral dial, bearing two patent dates, for August 1855 and July 1856, covered in a blown-glass dome, 6¾" high 225.00

☐ **Federal cherrywood tall case clock**, early 19th century, 90" high 750.00

☐ **French Empire-style mantel clock**, gilt bronze dial on blue glass melon-form body, 15 ½" high 225.00

☐ **German tall case clock**, turn of the century, Elite time-and-strike movement with second hand and phases of the moon dial, 26" × 14 ½" × 90" 700.00

☐ **Herschede tall case clock,** broken-arch pediment with urn finials over a nickel-plated dial with phases of the moon and second hand, 26 ½" × 16" × 100" 1650.00

☐ **Louis XV–style gilt bronze mantel clock**, second half of 19th century, the white enameled dial inscribed "E. Funnello a Paris," the backplate stamped "H.P. & Co. Paris," 21¾" high .   1210.00

Louis XV-style gilt bronze mantel clock, second half of the 19th century, the white enameled dial inscribed "E. Funnello a Paris," the back plate stamped "H.P. & Co. Paris," 21¾" high, $1210. (*Photo courtesy of Butterfield & Butterfield, San Francisco*)

Clothing

TYPES: Vintage clothing, especially items from the Victorian era, are most sought after, as well as clothes from the 1920s–1940s. What makes vintage clothes so interesting is the elaborate workmanship and detail, combined with the use of finest fabrics and materials.

Note: The single values shown below are the actual auction-realized prices.

	Price Range
☐ **Battenberg lace coat,** with buttoned-back lapels and flared skirt, c. 1910	440.00
☐ **Calico day dress**, red floral print on cream, with bateau neckline and long fitted sleeves, c. 1840; together with an 1870s calico wrapper trimmed with red piping	110.00
☐ **Cocktail dress**, black silk crepe, the ruched sheath-style dress with wide band shoulder straps, late 1950s	66.00

Price Range

☐ **Evening coat**, sapphire-blue velvet, the deep cape collar and full sleeves with corded detailing, late 1910s 132.00

☐ **Evening coat**, gold lamé and black velvet, the fabric woven in an Art Deco pattern of linear and elliptical forms and lined with deep red velvet, late 1920s 660.00

☐ **Fortuny brown velvet robe**, gilt-printed, with foliate borders and medallions, knee length with pale gold charmeuse lining, label 3850.00

☐ **Fortuny amethyst silk Delphos**, with short laced sleeves, trimmed with black and white opaque glass beads 1650.00

☐ **Fortuny black velvet coat**, gilt-printed in a bold, scrolling, foliate pattern, knee length with dolman sleeves, pale green rolled edging and cream charmeuse lining, label 4620.00

☐ **Fortuny kimono-style robe**, black velvet, gilt-printed, with medieval-style borders and roundels, lined with pale peach silk, label 2860.00

☐ **Fortuny medieval-style gown**, black velvet, gilt-printed, with interlacing Islamic-style designs, long tapering sleeves and pleated silk insets at the sides, label 5280.00

☐ **Fortuny robe**, shaded red velvet, reverse-printed in gilt to create a Renaissance-style "artichoke" pattern, floor-length robe with slit sleeves cut to drape below, lining of gold silk faille, label 4400.00

☐ **Fortuny tea gown**, cream silk gauze printed in a gilt, floral pattern, with puffed, elbow-length

Left to right. "Fortuny" brown velvet robe, gilt-printed with filiate borders and medallions, knee-length with pale gold, charmeuse lining, with label, $3850. "Fortuny" amethyst, silk delphos, with short, laced sleeves, trimmed with black and white opaque glass beads, $1650. "Fortuny" black velvet coat, gilt-printed in a bold, scrolling, foliate pattern, knee-length with dolman sleeves, pale green rolled edging and cream charmeuse lining, with label, $4620. (*Photo courtesy of Christie's East, New York*)

	Price Range
sleeves and pleated side panels trimmed with striped glass beads, lined with cream silk de chine ...	3300.00

☐ **Fortuny black velvet coat**, gilt-printed in an all-over foliate pattern, knee length, dolman sleeves,

Left to right. "Fortuny" robe of shaded red velvet, reverse-printed in gilt to create a Renaissance-style "artichoke" pattern, the floor-length robe with slit sleeves cut to drape below, the lining of gold silk faille, with label, $4400. "Fortuny" tea gown, of cream silk gauze printed in a gilt, floral pattern, with puffed, elbow-length sleeves and pleated side panels trimmed with striped glass beads, the gown lined with cream silk de chine, $3300. "Fortuny" black velvet coat, gilt-printed in an all-over foliate pattern, the knee-length coat with dolman sleeves, green velvet rolled edging and deep rose charmeuse lining, with label, $4180. (*Photo courtesy of Christie's East, New York*)

	Price Range
green velvet rolled edging and deep rose charmeuse lining, label	4180.00

☐ **Irish lace dress**, two-piece, with embroidered net sleeves caught

	Price Range
and draped at the elbow, label: Fox, c. 1900	242.00
☐ **Irish lace dress,** skirt and bodice inset with bands of foliate-embroidered net, label: Fox, c. 1905	550.00
☐ **Irish lace dress**, ivory gauze over satin with deep lace hem and bodice, label: Denova, Paris, c. 1908	660.00
☐ **"Monkey" fur jacket**, with long sleeves and round collarless neck, c. 1940	275.00
☐ **Opera coat**, black velvet, embroidered with silver beads and sequins in a peacock feather design, label: Yvonne May, Paris, c. 1920	660.00
☐ **Paisley shawl**, square, pieced, and worked in red, pale green, blue, black, and magenta wools ..	440.00

Coca-Cola

DESCRIPTION: Coca-Cola collectibles are any items made by or for the largest soft drink company in the world, the Coca-Cola Company. Although this company produces several types of cola, its most popular soft drink is Coke.

ORIGIN: First produced in 1886, Coca-Cola was first sold in Atlanta, Georgia, only in glasses at the soda fountain. The beverage was not bottled until 1894 in Vicksburg, Missouri, by Joseph Biedenharm. Coca-Cola was created by John Pemberton, an Atlanta pharmacist. The familar Coca-Cola logo was created by Pemberton's bookkeeper, Frank Robinson.

COMMENTS: Although the company produced thousands of different items promoting its soft drinks, because of the large number of Coca-Cola collectors, many items are valued higher than similar objects for other soft drink companies' advertising memorabilia.

	Price Range	
☐ **Ashtray**, aluminum, c. 1955	4.00	6.00
☐ **Ashtray and match holder**, c. 1940	200.00	250.00
☐ **Ashtray**, metal, c. 1963	5.00	6.00
☐ **Ashtray**, Mexican, painted aluminum, c. 1970	3.00	5.00

	Price Range	
☐ **Ashtray**. picture of Atlanta plant, c. 1958	18.00	25.00
☐ **Ashtray,** set of card suites, c. 1950s, red glass	75.00	125.00
☐ **Bank**, Coca-Cola, plastic, c. 1950s	8.00	12.00
☐ **Bank**, pop bottle machine, c. 1950s	35.00	40.00
☐ **Bingo game**, plastic, c. 1950s ...	35.00	45.00
☐ **Blackboard**, menu, c. 1939	50.00	60.00
☐ **Blotter**, "Delicious and Refreshing," c. 1904	75.00	100.00
☐ **Blotter**, "Duster Girl" in auto, c. 1910	175.00	300.00
☐ **Blotter**, "Icy Style COLD Refreshment," c. 1939	7.00	10.00
☐ **Blotter**, "Restores Energy and Strengthens Nerves," c. 1906	75.00	125.00
☐ **Blotter**, sprite with bottle-top hat, c. 1953	2.00	3.00
☐ **Blotter**, sprite with bottle-top hat, dated, 1951	2.00	3.00
☐ **Book cover**, c. 1939	6.00	8.00
☐ **Book cover**, c. 1951	6.00	8.00
☐ **Bookmark**, Hilda Clark, c. 1903	175.00	250.00
☐ **Bookmark**, Lillian Russel, Nordica, c. 1904	175.00	225.00
☐ **Bookmark**, owl on perch, celluloid, c. 1906	250.00	350.00
☐ **Bookmark**, Valentine, celluloid, c. 1899	250.00	350.00
☐ **Bookmark**, Victorian lady, 1905	300.00	350.00
☐ **Bottle**, "Best by a Dam Site," c. 1936	35.00	45.00
☐ **Bottle**, display, 20″ high, green, c. 1923	125.00	175.00
☐ **Bottle carrier,** six-bottle type, paper, c. 1933	35.00	45.00
☐ **Calendars**, 1950s	20.00	30.00
☐ **Calendars**, 1960s	10.00	20.00
☐ **Can**, large diamond, c. 1960s	15.00	30.00
☐ **Can**, checkerboard, c. 1963	5.00	15.00

	Price Range	
☐ **Cardboard cutout,** with Eddie Fisher, 1953–57	30.00	40.00
☐ **Cigarette lighter**, Coke can, c. 1950	8.00	10.00
☐ **Cigarette lighter**, music box, plays "Dixie"	35.00	45.00
☐ **Cigarette lighter**, musical, c. 1960	35.00	45.00
☐ **Clock**, brass, mantel type, c. 1954	300.00	400.00
☐ **Clock**, dome style, c. 1930s	600.00	700.00
☐ **Clock**, leather, boudoir, c. 1910	350.00	425.00
☐ **Clock**, reissue of Betty, c. 1974 .	20.00	35.00
☐ **Clock**, small, boudoir style, c. 1915	300.00	400.00
☐ **Clock**, spring-operated, wall style, brass pendulum	650.00	750.00
☐ **Clock**, walnut, wall model, battery-operated, c. 1970s	100.00	125.00
☐ **Cooler**, c. 1930	250.00	300.00
☐ **Cuff links**, bottle cap, c. 1954 ...	6.00	10.00
☐ **Door pull**, bottle shape, aluminum	75.00	85.00
☐ **Glass**, 5¢ with arrow, c. 1913 ...	300.00	375.00
☐ **Glass**, flare-type, c. 1900	200.00	250.00
☐ **Glass**, flared lip, c. 1923	50.00	60.00
☐ **Glass,** fountain-type with syrup line, c. 1900	180.00	225.00
☐ **Glass**, fountain-type, no syrup line, acid-etched, 1930s	15.00	20.00
☐ **Glass**, pewter, c. 1930	150.00	200.00
☐ **Ice pick and opener,** c. 1940 ..	8.00	12.00
☐ **Key chain**, car key style, c. 1950	20.00	30.00
☐ **Key chain**, 50th anniversary celebration, c. 1936	12.00	18.00
☐ **Menu board**, tin, c. 1940	40.00	60.00
☐ **Milk glass**, light shade, c. 1920 .	1000.00	1200.00
☐ **Mirror**, pocket-size, "Bathing Beauty," rare, c. 1922	450.00	500.00
☐ **Mirror**, pocket-size, "Coca-Cola Girl," c. 1909	200.00	225.00

	Price Range	
☐ **Mirror**, pocket-size, "Coca-Cola Girl," c. 1911	150.00	175.00
☐ **Notebook**, brown leather, embossed, c. 1903	100.00	150.00
☐ **Note pad**, celluloid-covered, c. 1915	200.00	250.00
☐ **Opener**, bone-handle knife, c. 1908	75.00	100.00
☐ **Opener**, Nashville anniversary, c. 1952	35.00	45.00
☐ **Opener**, skate key style, c. 1920	40.00	50.00
☐ **Opener**, "Starr X," c. 1925	5.00	10.00
☐ **Pocket secretary**, leather-bound, c. 1920	30.00	40.00
☐ **Postcard**, "All Over the World," c. 1913	10.00	15.00
☐ **Postcard**, "Duster Girl" driving car, c. 1910	300.00	350.00
☐ **Postcard**, girl with picture hat, "Hamilton King," c. 1910	300.00	350.00
☐ **Poster**, "Bathing Beauty," c. 1920s	300.00	400.00
☐ **Poster**, "Betty," c. 1914, 30″ × 38″	500.00	600.00
☐ **Poster**, "Early Display with Young Lovers," c. 1891	400.00	500.00
☐ **Record**, 45-rpm, from Eddie Fisher's Coketime show, 1953–57	5.00	10.00
☐ **Tray**, "Johnny Weismuller and Maureen O'Sullivan," c. 1934	200.00	250.00
☐ **Tray**, oval, "Juanita," c. 1905 ...	800.00	1000.00
☐ **Tray**, "Topless," c. 1908	1000.00	1500.00
☐ **Tray**, "Two Girls at Car," c. 1942	50.00	60.00
☐ **Tray**, "Vienna Art Nude," Western Coca-Cola, c. 1905	80.00	100.00
☐ **Tray**, "Western Bottling Co." (seven different), c. 1905	400.00	450.00
☐ **Wallet**, Coke bottle emblem, c. 1920s (1915 bottle)	20.00	25.00
☐ **Wallet**, Coca-Cola script, c. 1922	35.00	45.00

Coins

DESCRIPTION: Coins are metallic objects, usually circular, designed as a medium of exchange. The earlier series of U.S. coins comprised base metal for the lowest denominations, silver for the medium to high denominations, and gold for very high denominations, up to $50. Today almost all U.S. coins relegated for commercial circulation, regardless of denomination, are made out of base metal; neither silver nor gold is used. For present-day U.S. coins of 10¢ and higher denominations, a nickel exterior coating is bonded to a copper interior. Periodically, a gold and silver commemorative series of coins is issued, usually containing 90% silver or gold. The front of a coin, which on U.S. issues carries a portrait, is called the obverse. The back is the reverse.

MATERIALS: When precious metal was used in U.S. coins, it was usually a .900 grade. That is, silver coins were 90% silver, 10% copper; gold coins were 90% gold, 10% copper. The very earliest U.S. coins did not precisely conform to these standards, but all later ones did. Thus, the term *coin silver* means .900 silver.

PERIOD: U.S. coins were first struck in 1793, though earlier coins issued by the colonial governments had preceded them. They have been struck continually since then, though with various changes in denominations and, of course, in

233

designs. The United States has had coins with face values of 2¢, 3¢, 20¢, $3, and other odd amounts.

MARKS: While there are numerous types of marks that could potentially be found on coins (double strikes, small letters, etc.), the most frequent are the Mint marks, which are placed intentionally. These are small letters indicating the mint of origination, S for San Francisco, D for Denver, O for New Orleans, CC for Carson City, and just recently a new Mint mark for West Point. Traditionally, the Mint did not place any mark on its Philadelphia coins, but this practice has been changed in recent years.

ADDITIONAL TIPS: Do not attempt to clean or polish coins; the surfaces are much more delicate than you may imagine and can be easily injured. Though coin collecting is a hobby and pastime, coin buying is more akin to a science. Coin fakes are very numerous, often of high quality and undetectable except by a trained expert. It is therefore important to buy, as much as possible, from the recognized coin dealers rather than from flea markets or other questionable sources.

GRADING CONDITIONS: The grading standard recognizes in the uncirculated category 11 intermediate grades of Mint State 60 to Mint State 70: In the circulated scale, About Circulated (AU-50), Extremely Fine (EF-45 and EF-40), Very Fine (VF-30 and VF-20), Fine (F-12), Very Good (VG-8), Good (G-4), and About Good (AG-3). Coins that are damaged are worth less than those without defects. Flawless uncirculated bring an additional premium in price. Slightly worn coins ("sliders") that have been cleaned or conditioned ("whizzed") to simulate uncirculated luster are worth less than uncirculated pieces. For those readers who desire more detailed description of all coin grades, I recommend the publication, *Official ANA Grading Standard for United States Coins* by the American Numismatic Association.

VALUATIONS: Coin valuations listed are averaged from data supplied from several coin publications. The coin market is so active in some categories that values can easily change in a short period of time. Therefore, prices are shown only as a guide and are not intended to serve as a price list for those from dealers' stocks.

ORGANIZATIONS: It is highly recommended that the collector or investor join a local coin club, for these organizations provide an educational forum covering all aspects of numismatics. The major numismatic organization is called the American Numismatic Association (ANA). This association is an educational, nonprofit entity whose principal objectives are to advance the knowledge of numismatics and to bring about better cooperation and closer relations between numismatists. It offers a certification and grading service. In addition, it publishes an excellent monthly periodical called *The Numismatist* and also offers to its membership a numismatic library of over 22,000 books, periodicals, and catalogs. The ANA address is American Numismatic Association, P.O. Box 2366, Colorado Springs, CO 80901. Their membership fee is $20.

PUBLICATIONS: The following numismatic publications are obtainable by subscription. Complimentary copies may be obtained by writing to the individual publishers.

Coin World, P.O. Box 150, Sydney, OH 45367 (weekly).
Numismatic News, Iola, WI 54990 (weekly).
The Coin Dealer Newsletter, Dept CDN, P.O. Box 1099, Torrance, CA 90510 (monthly).
Rare Coin Market Digest, P.O. Box 8094, Newport Beach, CA 92658–8094 (monthly).

LINCOLN CENTS

	G-4	VG-8	F-12	VF-20	EF-40	MS-60	MS-65
☐ 1909-SVDB* ..	220.	235.	265.	285.	300.	430.	1000.
☐ 1909-S ..	31.00	35.00	40.00	52.50	82.50	135.	320.
☐ 1910	.16	.21	.35	.75	1.50	21.00	85.
☐ 1910-S ..	5.50	6.00	7.50	9.25	16.75	73.50	325.
☐ 1911-D .	3.00	3.25	5.40	9.50	25.00	105.	400.
☐ 1911-S ..	8.25	9.00	11.15	15.15	27.50	110.	545.
☐ 1912-D .	3.25	3.90	5.50	10.50	30.00	95.00	400.
☐ 1912-S ..	8.50	9.00	11.00	14.75	26.50	100.	545.
☐ 1913-D .	1.40	1.80	2.35	6.00	16.00	67.50	375.
☐ 1913-S ..	5.50	6.00	7.25	11.00	21.00	85.00	715.
☐ 1914	.30	.40	1.25	2.60	5.75	45.00	225.
☐ 1914-D*	48.00	52.50	80.00	125.	360.	765.	1850.
☐ 1914-S ..	7.50	9.00	11.00	15.00	28.00	150.	1200.

	G-4	VG-8	F-12	VF-20	EF-40	MS-60	MS-65
☐ 1915	.85	1.00	2.65	6.00	25.50	95.00	300.
☐ 1915-D .	.55	.70	1.50	2.65	7.50	34.00	375.
☐ 1915-S ..	6.00	7.00	8.00	9.85	24.00	85.00	715.
☐ 1916-D .	.25	.35	.60	1.25	5.15	41.50	295.
☐ 1916-S ..	.65	.80	1.10	2.00	6.00	49.00	400.
☐ 1917	.15	.20	.30	.70	1.50	9.50	90.00
☐ 1917-D .	.20	.30	.60	1.70	4.40	41.50	285.
☐ 1917-S ..	.21	.32	.62	1.55	4.25	49.00	385.
☐ 1918	.15	.20	.30	.70	1.50	9.50	90.00
☐ 1918-D .	.21	.32	.62	1.70	4.40	41.50	275.
☐ 1918-S ..	.25	.35	.55	1.55	4.20	49.00	375.
☐ 1919-D .	.20	.33	.55	1.30	3.15	37.50	170.
☐ 1919-S ..	.19	.25	.40	1.00	2.40	27.50	245.
☐ 1920-D .	.20	.27	.50	1.25	3.50	42.50	205.
☐ 1920-S ..	.20	.25	.50	1.15	3.00	46.50	375.
☐ 1921	.17	.21	.40	1.05	3.15	32.50	195.
☐ 1921-S ..	.60	.80	1.10	2.70	10.75	95.00	1050.
☐ 1922							
P1.*	125.	165.	210.	365.	650.	2300.	8300.
☐ 1922-D .	3.00	3.75	5.75	9.00	17.50	60.00	365.
☐ 1923-S ..	1.15	1.40	2.25	3.50	14.00	160.	1050.
☐ 1924	.12	.16	.25	.75	2.40	18.00	130.
☐ 1924-D .	8.25	9.15	10.50	16.00	38.00	200.	890.
☐ 1924-S ..	.60	.75	1.15	1.90	6.50	90.00	830.
☐ 1925	.12	.16	.20	.60	1.80	7.00	77.50
☐ 1925-D .	.20	.35	.65	1.05	3.75	42.00	390.
☐ 1925-S ..	.16	.25	.45	.80	2.75	52.50	575.
☐ 1926-D .	.20	.30	.60	1.05	3.35	40.00	375.
☐ 1926-S ..	1.85	2.25	3.25	4.00	9.50	82.50	650.
☐ 1927-D .	.20	.30	.50	.75	2.35	23.00	325.
☐ 1927-S ..	.40	.60	.90	1.90	5.00	50.00	575.
☐ 1928	.11	.16	.22	.55	1.65	5.50	73.50
☐ 1928-D .	.20	.30	.50	.75	2.25	18.50	255.
☐ 1928-S ..	.25	.35	.60	1.20	3.25	40.00	415.
☐ 1929	.11	.16	.25	.40	.90	4.25	36.50
☐ 1929-D .	.20	.30	.40	.60	1.55	12.75	135.
☐ 1929-S ..	.15	.20	.30	.55	1.10	6.75	81.00
☐ 1930	.10	.15	.20	.55	1.00	3.60	25.00
☐ 1930-D .	.13	.20	.40	.60	1.60	9.25	80.00
☐ 1930-S ..	.17	.25	.35	.60	1.10	5.00	55.00

	G-4	VG-8	F-12	VF-20	EF-40	MS-60	MS-65
☐ 1931	.45	.60	.75	.90	1.90	14.00	77.50
☐ 1931-D .	1.75	2.00	2.50	3.25	6.25	39.00	185.
☐ 1931-S ..	27.50	30.00	31.50	35.00	37.50	59.00	125.
☐ 1932	1.10	1.25	1.50	2.05	2.65	15.00	58.00
☐ 1932-D .	.70	.80	.90	1.25	1.65	12.75	60.00
☐ 1933	.75	.90	1.10	1.45	2.00	13.60	72.50
☐ 1933-D .	1.50	1.65	2.00	2.50	3.15	17.75	68.00

	F-12	VF-20	EF-40	MS-60	MS-65
☐ 1934	.18	.25	.55	2.50	12.50
☐ 1934-D	.25	.55	.90	19.00	67.50
☐ 1935	.12	.18	.45	1.25	6.40
☐ 1935-D	.18	.30	.60	2.75	12.75
☐ 1935-S	.18	.30	.70	6.50	68.00
☐ 1936	.12	.18	.35	.95	5.30
☐ 1936-D	.18	.25	.40	1.80	7.75
☐ 1936-S	.18	.30	.55	1.85	8.25
☐ 1937	.12	.18	.35	.85	5.50
☐ 1937-D	.18	.30	.40	1.55	6.40
☐ 1937-S	.18	.30	.40	1.40	8.65
☐ 1938	.12	.18	.35	1.15	6.00
☐ 1938-D	.25	.30	.50	1.80	7.60
☐ 1938-S	.40	.45	.70	2.05	9.50
☐ 1939	.12	.18	.35	.65	3.65
☐ 1939-D	.40	.45	.70	2.25	10.75
☐ 1939-S	.20	.30	.45	1.30	8.15
☐ 1940	.07	.12	.19	.50	3.45
☐ 1940-D	.12	.18	.25	.75	4.55
☐ 1940-S	.12	.18	.25	1.00	5.75
☐ 1941	.07	.12	.19	.60	3.50
☐ 1941-D	.07	.12	.30	1.75	7.25
☐ 1941-S	.12	.18	.30	2.25	8.50
☐ 1942	.07	.12	.19	.45	2.90
☐ 1942-D	.07	.12	.19	.50	3.50
☐ 1942-S	.12	.18	.45	3.00	18.75
☐ 1943	.18	.20	.35	.55	2.50
☐ 1943-D	.20	.25	.40	1.00	4.00
☐ 1943-S	.20	.25	.40	1.80	7.00
☐ 1944	.07	.12	.19	.30	1.30
☐ 1944-D	.07	.12	.19	.35	1.50
☐ 1944-S	.07	.12	.19	.35	1.45

	F-12	VF-20	EF-40	MS-60	MS-65
☐ 1945	.07	.12	.19	.35	1.20
☐ 1945-D	.07	.12	.19	.35	1.40
☐ 1945-S...................	.07	.12	.19	.40	1.45
☐ 1946	.07	.12	.19	.25	1.20
☐ 1946-D	.07	.12	.19	.28	1.25
☐ 1946-S..................	.07	.12	.19	.35	1.35
☐ 1947	.07	.12	.19	.40	1.45
☐ 1947-D	.07	.12	.19	.35	1.30
☐ 1947-S..................	.12	.18	.25	.38	1.65
☐ 1948	.07	.12	.19	.35	1.45
☐ 1948-D	.07	.12	.19	.45	1.60
☐ 1948-S..................	.12	.18	.25	.60	1.80
☐ 1949	.07	.12	.19	.65	2.05
☐ 1949-D	.07	.12	.19	.60	2.00
☐ 1949-S..................	.12	.18	.25	.90	3.75

	VF-20	EF-40	MS-60	MS-65	Proof-65
☐ 1950	.12	.19	.45	1.40	40.00
☐ 1950-D	.07	.13	.25	1.25	—
☐ 1950-S...............	.12	.25	.50	1.40	—
☐ 1951	.12	.30	.50	1.45	26.00
☐ 1951-D	.07	.13	.25	1.10	—
☐ 1951-S...............	.18	.25	.65	2.55	—
☐ 1952	.12	.19	.45	1.30	20.00
☐ 1952-D	.06	.13	.33	1.15	—
☐ 1952-S...............	.12	.19	.50	1.90	—
☐ 1953	.07	.13	.20	1.05	11.25
☐ 1953-D	.06	.13	.32	1.15	—
☐ 1953-S...............	.12	.19	.33	1.25	—
☐ 1954	.18	.28	.40	1.40	7.00
☐ 1954-D	.06	.13	.20	1.00	—
☐ 1954-S...............	.07	.13	.23	1.10	—
☐ 1955	.06	.13	.20	.95	5.75
☐ 1955 Dbl. Die	305.	350.	645.	2650.	—
☐ 1955-D	.06	.13	.20	.90	—
☐ 1955-S...............	.15	.20	.36	1.15	—
☐ 1960 SD	.75	1.00	1.75	4.50	11.50
☐ 1960-D SD.........	.04	.06	.15	.85	—
☐ 1972 Dbl. Die	105.	115.	165.	265.	—

	Proof-65
☐ 1975-S	4.25
☐ 1976-S	2.00
☐ 1977-S	2.50
☐ 1978-S	2.55
☐ 1979-S Var.1	1.90
☐ 1980-S	1.25
☐ 1981-S Var. 1	1.25
☐ 1982-S	2.50
☐ 1983-S	8.50
☐ 1984-S	7.00
☐ 1985-S	6.75

BUFFALO NICKELS

VARIETY 1

	VG-8	F-12	VF-20	EF-40	AU-50	MS-60	MS-65
☐ 1913							
Var. 1...	3.15	3.50	6.00	10.25	17.00	31.50	525.
☐ 1913-D							
Var. 1...	6.25	8.25	10.75	19.25	36.50	67.50	750.
☐ 1913-S							
Var. 1...	10.50	14.50	22.50	35.50	50.00	95.00	850.

VARIETY 2

	VG-8	F-12	VF-20	EF-40	AU-50	MS-60	MS-65
☐ 1913							
Var. 2...	3.25	4.00	6.00	9.50	20.00	33.50	675.
☐ 1913-D							
Var. 2...	37.50	42.50	56.00	69.00	105.	190.	1800.
☐ 1913-S							
Var. 2...	76.50	97.50	125.	170.	235.	450.	2450.
☐ 1914	4.25	5.25	7.25	12.50	27.50	110.	675.
☐ 1914-D.	28.50	37.50	55.00	88.50	125.	285.	1500.
☐ 1914-S..	5.40	8.50	15.00	31.00	45.00	92.50	1555.
☐ 1915	3.25	3.90	5.40	10.00	23.50	47.50	735.
☐ 1915-D.	7.00	15.75	30.50	45.00	62.50	135.	1550.
☐ 1915-S..	12.25	21.00	56.00	90.00	140.	245.	1825.
☐ 1916							
All							
Vars.	.95	1.50	2.35	4.65	14.50	37.50	675.
☐ 1916-D.	5.50	8.75	19.50	41.00	65.00	140.	1250.
☐ 1916-S..	3.50	6.00	16.25	37.00	62.50	120.	1350.

	VG-8	F-12	VF-20	EF-40	AU-50	MS-60	MS-65
☐ 1917	1.00	1.55	3.00	8.00	23.00	40.00	725.
☐ 1917-D.	5.65	11.00	36.50	70.00	120.	215.	2050.
☐ 1917-S..	5.35	11.25	34.00	57.50	210.	225.	2300.
☐ 1918	1.10	2.00	5.00	15.00	34.00	65.00	900.
☐ 1918/ 17-D	450.	675.	1000.	2350.	4000.	7500.	26500.
☐ 1918-D.	5.50	11.75	50.00	77.00	265.	270.	2550.
☐ 1918-S..	4.50	10.50	34.00	70.00	125.	230.	2300.
☐ 1919	.75	1.25	2.25	6.50	18.00	35.00	735.
☐ 1919-D.	6.00	13.75	57.50	90.00	315.	330.	2350.
☐ 1919-S..	3.50	7.75	39.00	67.50	275.	270.	3450.
☐ 1920	.75	1.20	2.25	7.00	20.00	38.00	725.
☐ 1920-D.	4.00	9.25	47.50	80.00	285.	290.	3250.
☐ 1920-S..	2.85	5.75	25.00	67.50	280.	190.	4000.
☐ 1921	1.00	2.00	5.75	17.50	37.00	75.00	775.
☐ 1921-S..	15.00	34.00	135.	290.	440.	675.	3350.
☐ 1923	.60	1.00	1.90	6.10	16.50	35.00	800.
☐ 1923-S..	2.00	4.35	22.50	44.00	72.50	140.	3850.
☐ 1924	.65	1.05	2.50	8.50	25.00	49.50	755.
☐ 1924-D.	3.00	6.00	39.00	66.00	150.	195.	1900.
☐ 1924-S..	6.25	13.50	140.	325.	465.	850.	2850.
☐ 1925	.65	1.05	2.50	6.25	18.00	36.00	700.
☐ 1925-D.	5.25	10.00	45.00	72.50	155.	265.	2000.
☐ 1925-S..	2.75	5.50	20.00	43.50	77.50	190.	3100.
☐ 1926	.45	.85	1.60	4.50	15.00	30.00	675.
☐ 1926-D.	3.35	8.00	45.00	75.00	97.50	140.	2350.
☐ 1926-S..	6.75	11.50	57.50	215.	400.	625.	3900.
☐ 1927	.45	.85	1.40	4.35	14.25	32.00	700.
☐ 1927-D.	1.35	2.65	10.50	35.00	55.00	87.50	1350.
☐ 1927-S..	1.00	1.75	12.00	45.00	62.50	145.	1550.
☐ 1928	.45	.85	1.65	4.50	15.00	31.50	665.
☐ 1928-D.	1.05	1.75	5.85	13.50	26.50	46.00	900.
☐ 1928-S..	.65	1.25	2.75	11.50	27.50	60.00	1050.
☐ 1929	.45	.85	1.25	3.00	12.00	28.50	535.
☐ 1929-D.	1.05	1.45	3.75	11.00	25.00	47.00	1075.
☐ 1929-S..	.45	.90	1.40	7.75	17.00	36.00	950.
☐ 1930	.45	.85	1.10	3.50	12.50	27.50	350.
☐ 1930-S..	.65	1.15	1.55	6.25	22.50	43.50	675.
☐ 1931-S..	3.15	3.50	4.90	9.50	24.00	49.50	590.
☐ 1934	.40	.50	1.00	3.75	10.25	26.00	330.

	VG-8	F-12	VF-20	EF-40	AU-50	MS-60	MS-65
☐ 1934-D.	.45	.90	2.65	7.75	18.00	46.00	450.
☐ 1935	.35	.50	.85	1.75	7.00	17.50	220.
☐ 1935-D.	.60	1.00	2.30	6.50	18.50	44.50	650.
☐ 1935-S..	.40	.65	1.30	3.25	11.00	25.00	290.
☐ 1936	.35	.50	.90	1.50	6.50	14.25	175.
☐ 1936-D.	.45	.60	1.15	2.50	8.75	17.25	200.
☐ 1936-S..	.40	.55	1.15	2.00	9.75	19.00	250.
☐ 1937	.35	.50	.90	1.50	5.50	12.75	135.
☐ 1937-D.	.45	.60	1.15	2.10	7.50	16.00	165.
☐ 1937-D 3 Legs ..	90.00	105.	145.	190.	290.	475.	5050.
☐ 1937-S..	.55	.65	1.20	2.20	7.75	16.10	180.
☐ 1938-D.	.50	.60	1.00	2.00	6.50	13.25	125.
☐ 1938-D/S	4.25	4.90	6.75	9.25	15.50	24.75	140.

MERCURY DIMES

	VG-8	F-12	VF-20	EF-40	AU-50	MS-60	MS-65
☐ 1916	2.15	3.85	5.85	8.00	14.75	23.50	135.
☐ 1916-D.	375.	725.	950.	1200.	1775.	2250.	2850.
☐ 1916-S..	2.65	4.75	7.50	13.75	20.50	35.00	165.
☐ 1917	1.45	2.15	4.50	6.00	11.75	18.25	125.
☐ 1917-D.	2.75	6.00	12.50	30.00	55.00	87.50	525.
☐ 1917-S..	1.65	2.85	4.90	7.65	18.00	5.00	190.
☐ 1918	1.45	3.20	8.00	19.50	33.50	52.50	175.
☐ 1918-D.	1.65	3.15	7.50	18.00	35.00	60.00	535.
☐ 1918-S..	1.45	2.75	5.25	10.50	22.50	39.50	390.
☐ 1919	1.30	2.50	4.50	6.00	13.25	24.50	220.
☐ 1919-D.	2.25	4.85	12.00	27.00	60.00	120.	625.
☐ 1919-S..	1.70	3.70	10.15	23.50	60.00	135.	535.
☐ 1920	1.20	2.00	4.00	5.75	12.00	18.00	150.
☐ 1920-D.	1.75	3.05	5.50	12.00	28.00	60.00	525.
☐ 1920-S..	1.75	2.90	5.25	10.75	22.50	57.50	435.
☐ 1921	27.00	56.00	110.	310.	550.	685.	1325.
☐ 1921-D.	36.00	79.00	165.	340.	565.	675.	1350.
☐ 1923	1.25	2.00	3.35	5.00	9.50	17.00	160.
☐ 1923-S..	1.65	3.15	6.25	16.50	36.00	67.50	530.
☐ 1924	1.30	2.00	4.00	6.75	16.75	37.50	265.
☐ 1924-D.	1.50	3.05	7.25	15.00	36.00	80.00	345.

	VG-8	F-12	VF-20	EF-40	AU-50	MS-60	MS-65
☐ 1924-S..	1.50	2.75	5.75	13.00	33.50	77.50	575.
☐ 1925	1.20	1.90	3.50	5.90	14.25	32.50	225.
☐ 1925-D.	3.50	7.00	19.00	55.00	120.	215.	585.
☐ 1925-S..	1.70	2.75	6.00	14.75	42.00	96.50	490.
☐ 1926	1.20	1.70	3.50	4.65	8.50	15.75	140.
☐ 1926-D.	1.55	3.10	5.25	11.00	25.50	57.50	400.
☐ 1926-S..	8.00	12.50	26.00	66.00	180.	400.	1350.
☐ 1927	1.20	1.70	3.50	4.50	8.50	15.75	150.
☐ 1927-D.	2.35	3.85	9.50	28.00	68.50	150.	490.
☐ 1927-S..	1.50	2.35	4.50	10.00	28.50	67.50	575.
☐ 1928	1.20	1.70	3.50	4.50	8.50	16.25	150.
☐ 1928-D.	2.35	5.25	12.00	27.50	57.50	115.	360.
☐ 1928-S..	1.45	2.25	4.00	8.50	22.50	45.00	350.
☐ 1929	1.15	1.70	3.00	3.75	7.00	12.25	67.50
☐ 1929-D.	2.00	3.40	5.65	7.85	16.75	35.00	130.
☐ 1929-S..	1.25	1.75	3.50	4.60	11.75	36.50	145.
☐ 1930	1.30	1.85	3.35	4.50	10.75	18.00	97.50
☐ 1930-S..	2.60	3.75	5.00	10.00	33.50	60.00	260.
☐ 1931	1.45	2.50	4.00	7.75	16.00	29.50	120.
☐ 1931-D.	7.00	8.85	14.25	25.50	48.50	82.50	225.
☐ 1931-S..	3.00	3.90	5.00	10.00	29.00	60.00	240.
☐ 1934	.70	.90	1.25	2.25	6.25	15.00	62.00
☐ 1934-D.	1.45	1.85	3.00	5.00	16.00	28.00	90.00
☐ 1935	.70	.90	1.25	2.00	4.25	12.50	57.50
☐ 1935-D.	1.20	1.45	2.75	7.00	17.00	37.50	130.
☐ 1935-S..	1.20	1.45	1.75	3.25	6.50	20.50	75.00
☐ 1936	.70	.90	1.25	1.85	2.50	9.85	47.50
☐ 1936-D.	1.20	1.45	1.70	4.00	13.50	25.00	85.00
☐ 1936-S..	1.20	1.45	1.70	2.75	7.40	16.00	60.00
☐ 1937	.70	.90	1.25	1.85	2.80	10.10	42.50
☐ 1937-D.	1.20	1.45	1.70	2.60	6.50	21.00	85.00
☐ 1937-S..	1.20	1.45	1.70	2.60	6.25	15.50	55.00
☐ 1938	.70	.90	1.25	1.85	3.75	12.00	47.50
☐ 1938-D.	1.45	1.75	2.00	3.25	9.50	18.50	82.50
☐ 1938-S..	1.20	1.45	1.70	3.20	6.75	12.50	56.50
☐ 1939	.70	.90	1.25	1.85	2.90	10.00	40.00
☐ 1939-D.	1.20	1.45	1.55	1.90	4.00	10.20	45.00
☐ 1939-S..	1.45	1.85	2.10	2.65	6.50	15.50	64.00
☐ 1940	.70	.90	1.25	1.50	2.25	7.00	37.50
☐ 1940-D.	.70	.90	1.25	1.65	4.20	11.50	45.00

	VG-8	F-12	VF-20	EF-40	AU-50	MS-60	MS-65
☐ 1940-S..	.70	.90	1.25	1.50	2.75	7.10	38.50
☐ 1941	.70	.90	1.25	1.50	2.05	6.25	35.00
☐ 1941-D.	.70	.90	1.25	1.65	2.75	10.50	45.00
☐ 1941-S..	.70	.90	1.25	1.65	2.80	8.50	40.00
☐ 1942/1 .	180.	190.	210.	245.	375.	875.	2050.
☐ 1942/ 1-D	190.	205.	225.	280.	390.	950.	2400.
☐ 1942	.70	.90	1.25	1.40	2.00	7.00	34.50
☐ 1942-D.	.70	.90	1.25	1.50	2.45	10.00	42.50
☐ 1942-S..	.70	.90	1.25	1.50	4.10	13.50	50.00
☐ 1943	.70	.90	1.25	1.40	2.00	6.50	34.50
☐ 1943-D.	.70	.90	1.25	1.50	2.25	9.50	39.00
☐ 1943-S..	.70	.90	1.25	1.50	2.75	10.50	40.00
☐ 1944	.70	.90	1.25	1.40	2.00	6.50	34.50
☐ 1944-D.	.70	.90	1.25	1.50	2.25	8.75	37.50
☐ 1944-S..	.70	.90	1.25	1.50	2.25	8.50	37.50
☐ 1945	.70	.90	1.25	1.40	2.00	6.75	35.00
☐ 1945-D.	.70	.90	1.25	1.50	2.25	10.50	38.00
☐ 1945-S..	.70	.90	1.25	1.50	2.50	10.75	38.50

STANDING LIBERTY QUARTERS

	G-4	F-12	VF-20	EF-40	AU-50	MS-60	MS-65
☐ 1916 Var. 1...	1025.	1275.	1400.	1800.	2300.	3050.	4750.
☐ 1917 Var. 1...	9.50	12.25	27.50	55.00	95.00	165.	1250.
☐ 1917-D Var. 1...	14.75	22.50	48.50	85.00	110.	175.	1265.
☐ 1917-S Var. 1...	13.50	19.75	45.00	75.00	115.	175.	1275.
☐ 1917 Var. 2...	12.50	17.50	21.50	35.00	60.00	110.	1225.
☐ 1917-D Var. 2...	17.75	42.50	55.00	85.00	110.	160.	1335.
☐ 1917-S Var. 2...	17.50	27.75	47.50	67.50	95.00	140.	1335.
☐ 1918	14.25	20.00	28.50	43.00	75.00	135.	1310.
☐ 1918-D .	20.00	35.00	52.50	77.50	115.	200.	1375.

	G-4	F-12	VF-20	EF-40	AU-50	MS-60	MS-65
☐ 1918-S..	13.00	20.75	25.00	41.00	75.00	135.	1300.
☐ 1918/ 7-S	950.	1550.	2050.	2800.	4950.	7350.	23000.
☐ 1919	23.00	41.50	47.50	59.00	80.00	145.	1275.
☐ 1919-D .	42.00	95.00	125.	205.	265.	515.	1900.
☐ 1919-S..	41.00	79.50	105.	175.	235.	415.	1725.
☐ 1920	13.00	18.75	22.00	33.00	59.00	115.	1225.
☐ 1920-D .	21.50	48.50	70.00	92.50	145.	200.	1375.
☐ 1920-S..	15.00	22.50	29.00	44.00	72.50	135.	1300.
☐ 1921	50.00	110.	140.	205.	300.	400.	1425.
☐ 1923	13.25	20.00	22.75	36.50	59.00	120.	1250.
☐ 1923-S..	85.00	155.	215.	335.	425.	525.	1400.
☐ 1924	13.15	20.00	22.75	36.00	59.00	120.	1250.
☐ 1924-D .	21.50	45.00	60.00	85.00	100.	135.	1265.
☐ 1924-S..	14.25	22.50	26.00	40.00	70.00	140.	1325.
☐ 1925	2.50	5.25	13.10	25.00	50.00	105.	1215.
☐ 1926	2.50	5.25	13.00	25.00	50.00	105.	1230.
☐ 1926-D .	5.00	12.00	20.00	42.50	75.00	110.	1240.
☐ 1926-S..	4.00	11.50	19.50	49.50	85.00	175.	1650.
☐ 1927	2.50	5.25	13.00	24.75	55.00	110.	1215.
☐ 1927-D .	6.50	12.75	25.00	52.50	82.50	140.	1265.
☐ 1927-S..	6.25	40.00	115.	425.	725.	1250.	3000.
☐ 1928	2.75	5.25	13.00	24.75	52.00	105.	1240.
☐ 1928-D .	4.25	11.00	16.00	35.00	62.00	125.	1275.
☐ 1928-S..	2.60	5.75	13.25	29.00	60.00	115.	1235.
☐ 1929	2.50	5.25	13.00	24.75	55.00	95.00	1200.
☐ 1929-D .	4.50	11.00	16.00	29.00	60.00	115.	1230.
☐ 1929-S..	2.50	5.25	13.00	25.50	55.00	110.	1215.
☐ 1930	2.50	5.25	13.00	25.00	55.00	110.	1200.
☐ 1930-S..	2.50	5.25	13.00	25.25	55.00	105.	1210.

MORGAN DOLLARS

	F-12	VF-20	EF-40	AU-50	MS-60	MS-63	MS-65
☐ 1878 8TF.....	15.00	17.50	20.75	29.75	63.50	145.	2200.
☐ 1878 7TF.....	14.50	16.50	18.00	22.00	56.50	97.50	1625.

	F-12	VF-20	EF-40	AU-50	MS-60	MS-63	MS-65
☐ 1878							
7/8F	16.50	19.00	24.75	38.25	67.50	155.	2650.
☐ 1878-							
CC	23.75	30.75	36.25	50.00	140.	210.	1450.
☐ 1878-S	13.75	15.50	18.00	22.50	56.50	135.	1100.
☐ 1879	12.00	13.75	16.60	21.50	45.00	90.00	1500.
☐ 1879-							
CC	38.50	72.50	200.	425.	1375.	2200.	8500.
☐ 1879-O	12.00	13.75	18.75	23.50	50.00	185.	2550.
☐ 1879-S	13.75	15.50	17.25	22.00	57.50	120.	675.
☐ 1880	12.00	13.75	16.00	20.75	45.00	92.50	1150.
☐ 1880-							
CC	36.50	52.50	78.50	115.	215.	330.	1200.
☐ 1880-O	12.00	13.75	19.00	25.00	60.00	190.	3450.
☐ 1880-S	13.75	15.00	17.25	21.75	57.50	110.	475.
☐ 1881	12.00	14.00	15.75	21.25	45.00	92.50	1150.
☐ 1881-							
CC	60.00	75.00	87.50	125.	250.	425.	1200.
☐ 1881-O	11.90	13.75	17.00	19.00	40.00	90.00	1600.
☐ 1881-S	13.50	15.25	17.75	21.50	56.50	110.	675.
☐ 1882	11.90	13.75	17.25	21.25	44.00	92.50	900.
☐ 1882-							
CC	27.00	35.00	47.50	65.00	135.	225.	975.
☐ 1882-O	11.90	13.75	16.35	19.50	40.00	92.50	1250.
☐ 1882-S	15.75	17.00	19.75	24.75	60.00	125.	490.
☐ 1883	12.00	14.00	16.75	20.75	41.50	93.00	800.
☐ 1883-							
CC	24.75	35.00	47.50	65.00	120.	220.	925.
☐ 1883-O	12.00	14.00	16.40	19.00	33.50	80.00	725.
☐ 1883-S	15.75	17.50	22.50	105.	400.	865.	5300.
☐ 1884	12.00	14.50	16.75	22.00	42.50	120.	950.
☐ 1884-							
CC	35.50	46.50	57.50	70.00	120.	220.	925.
☐ 1884-O	12.00	13.50	17.00	19.50	28.00	75.00	650.
☐ 1884-S	15.85	18.50	29.50	180.	1550.	3450.	34000.
☐ 1885	12.00	13.50	17.00	19.50	28.00	75.00	675.
☐ 1885-							
CC	155.	165.	175.	190.	265.	360.	1750.
☐ 1885-O	12.00	13.50	17.00	19.25	28.00	75.00	625.
☐ 1885-S	15.25	17.00	20.00	44.25	125.	245.	1800.
☐ 1886	12.00	13.50	17.00	19.50	28.00	77.50	590.

	F-12	*VF-20*	*EF-40*	*AU-50*	*MS-60*	*MS-63*	*MS-65*
☐ 1886-O	12.00	15.25	19.50	46.25	325.	710.	5150.
☐ 1886-S.	16.75	19.75	25.75	37.25	175.	300.	2100.
☐ 1887....	12.00	13.50	16.75	19.00	28.00	75.00	585.
☐ 1887-O	12.00	13.50	18.00	22.75	52.00	110.	1750.
☐ 1887-S.	14.25	16.00	19.25	24.75	87.50	245.	2000.
☐ 1888....	12.00	13.50	16.35	19.00	28.00	85.00	750.
☐ 1888-O	13.75	15.25	17.50	20.75	27.50	87.50	975.
☐ 1888-S.	17.75	20.75	26.00	39.75	185.	325.	2350.
☐ 1889....	12.00	13.40	16.50	18.50	29.00	87.50	1150.
☐ 1889-CC	160.	250.	575.	2050.	5350.	8100.	26000.
☐ 1889-O	12.00	15.00	17.00	22.50	80.00	245.	3500.
☐ 1889-S.	18.50	23.50	27.75	38.75	150.	280.	1950.
☐ 1890....	12.00	14.50	17.50	20.25	29.00	100.	1350.
☐ 1890-CC	23.00	35.00	49.00	75.00	225.	375.	2050.
☐ 1890-O	12.00	15.25	17.25	22.50	57.50	115.	1750.
☐ 1890-S.	13.75	16.00	18.00	27.50	75.00	150.	1150.
☐ 1891....	12.25	15.25	18.00	33.25	71.00	160.	2500.
☐ 1891-CC	23.50	35.00	49.00	73.50	215.	365.	1850.
☐ 1891-O	12.00	15.00	17.75	27.00	71.00	200.	4400.
☐ 1891-S.	14.25	16.00	18.00	23.50	75.00	150.	1075.
☐ 1892....	14.50	16.50	20.00	40.00	140.	350.	2500.
☐ 1892-CC	28.00	48.00	77.50	175.	370.	550.	2400.
☐ 1892-O	13.25	16.25	20.00	41.75	130.	400.	3950.
☐ 1892-S.	16.10	40.00	130.	700.	4250.	7600.	30000.
☐ 1893....	36.00	42.50	75.00	155.	305.	615.	2750.
☐ 1893-CC	49.00	120.	275.	410.	750.	1750.	9300.
☐ 1893-O	37.50	67.50	155.	300.	985.	2150.	22000.
☐ 1893-S.	825.	1300.	2850.	8150.	17000.	27500.	75000.
☐ 1894....	215.	240.	325.	500.	850.	1500.	10250.
☐ 1894-O	14.25	17.50	24.75	67.50	400.	1100.	15500.
☐ 1894-S.	16.75	35.00	70.00	145.	310.	665.	3250.
☐ 1895 ...	Very Rare—Proof 67						30500.
☐ 1895-O	40.00	75.00	155.	325.	1950.	5300.	39500.

	F-12	VF-20	EF-40	AU-50	MS-60	MS-63	MS-65
☐ 1895-S.	70.00	130.	290.	450.	755.	1450.	9250.
☐ 1896....	12.00	14.50	17.00	19.00	29.00	82.50	800.
☐ 1896-O	12.50	15.75	19.50	75.00	700.	1475.	30500.
☐ 1896-S.	13.75	35.00	95.00	215.	535.	900.	6250.
☐ 1897....	12.00	14.50	17.00	19.50	29.00	87.50	875.
☐ 1897-O	12.50	15.25	19.00	40.75	515.	925.	9500.
☐ 1897-S.	14.25	16.25	17.50	23.50	77.50	200.	1125.
☐ 1898....	12.00	14.50	17.00	19.50	29.00	85.00	825.
☐ 1898-O	14.00	16.50	18.00	23.50	29.50	85.00	690.
☐ 1898-S.	14.25	16.75	21.50	41.75	175.	335.	2350.
☐ 1899....	24.25	32.00	46.00	62.50	95.00	200.	1600.
☐ 1899-O	14.25	16.25	17.00	22.00	29.00	88.50	700.
☐ 1899-S.	14.50	17.50	21.25	52.50	150.	325.	2200.
☐ 1900....	13.25	15.00	17.00	19.50	28.50	75.00	950.
☐ 1900-O	14.25	16.25	18.00	22.00	31.50	84.00	710.
☐ 1900-S.	14.25	16.75	19.50	39.75	130.	300.	1750.
☐ 1901....	21.50	29.75	40.00	155.	950.	2450.	35500.
☐ 1901-O	15.50	18.00	20.00	24.50	29.00	90.00	1100.
☐ 1901-S.	15.00	19.00	28.50	62.50	265.	625.	3750.
☐ 1902....	12.25	14.50	16.50	25.00	56.50	130.	1700.
☐ 1902-O	14.25	16.25	17.00	22.50	29.00	89.50	825.
☐ 1902-S.	23.00	37.00	65.00	125.	215.	400.	2350.
☐ 1903....	12.25	14.50	17.00	24.25	52.50	130.	925.
☐ 1903-O	150.	160.	175.	190.	235.	325.	1350.
☐ 1903-S.	15.50	41.50	150.	580.	1650.	3150.	8000.
☐ 1904....	12.25	15.75	17.50	30.25	87.50	280.	2150.
☐ 1904-O	14.25	16.50	17.50	23.50	30.50	72.00	635.
☐ 1904-S.	21.25	40.00	100.	390.	850.	2050.	5300.
☐ 1921....	10.60	12.00	12.50	14.50	27.00	55.00	600.
☐ 192-D..	10.75	12.35	12.75	15.50	42.00	90.00	1300.
☐ 1921-S.	10.75	12.35	12.75	15.50	32.50	100.	2050.

U.S. GOLD DOLLARS

	F-12	VF-20	EF-40	MS-60	MS-65
☐ 1849 Op. WR L					
Type I......................	175.	195.	245.	920.	8750.
☐ 1849 Cl. WR............	175.	195.	245.	895.	8450.

	F-12	VF-20	EF-40	MS-60	MS-65
☐ 1849-C Cl. WR	300.	435.	905.	4250.	—
☐ 1849-D	275.	435.	855.	3250.	10500.
☐ 1849-O	190.	225.	390.	1925.	8200.
☐ 1850	180.	200.	245.	840.	8050.
☐ 1850-C	385.	665.	1250.	4850.	—
☐ 1850-D	355.	600.	1100.	4450.	—
☐ 1850-O	275.	475.	725.	1925.	10850.
☐ 1851	175.	190.	240.	820.	7850.
☐ 1851-C	275.	325.	550.	1675.	11050.
☐ 1851-D	290.	410.	905.	3050.	11250.
☐ 1851-O	230.	235.	295.	975.	8050.
☐ 1852	175.	190.	240.	820.	7850.
☐ 1852-C	280.	400.	810.	1875.	12000.
☐ 1852-D	350.	675.	1150.	4450.	—
☐ 1852-O	190.	235.	295.	1100.	10500.
☐ 1853	175.	200.	245.	820.	7850.
☐ 1853-C	265.	400.	1000.	4500.	—
☐ 1853-D	350.	750.	1650.	4850.	17500.
☐ 1853-O	190.	225.	305.	840.	8050.
☐ 1854	175.	190.	240.	820.	7950.
☐ 1854-D	585.	925.	2250.	8150.	—
☐ 1854-S	315.	425.	700.	5050.	27750.
☐ 1854 Type II	225.	305.	540.	6000.	28500.
☐ 1855	225.	305.	540.	6000.	—
☐ 1855-C	900.	1500.	2650.	7500.	—
☐ 1855-D	1950.	3000.	6750.	—	—
☐ 1855-O	515.	735.	975.	6750.	—
☐ 1856-S	540.	760.	1075.	6100.	—
☐ 1856 Up 5 Type III	180.	205.	280.	805.	6650.
☐ 1856 Sl. 5	170.	190.	250.	760.	6250.
☐ 1856-D	2900.	4800.	7850.	—	—
☐ 1857	170.	190.	240.	755.	6800.
☐ 1857-C	300.	600.	1100.	4750.	—
☐ 1857-D	315.	675.	1275.	6100.	—
☐ 1857-S	350.	575.	1000.	—	—
☐ 1858	170.	190.	250.	755.	6250.
☐ 1858-D	385.	650.	1450.	6100.	—
☐ 1858-S	360.	500.	775.	—	—
☐ 1859	180.	205.	285.	815.	6150.

	F-12	VF-20	EF-40	MS-60	MS-65
☐ 1859-C	325.	450.	1000.	4000.	9150.
☐ 1859-D	475.	825.	1625.	5250.	—
☐ 1859-S	375.	455.	640.	—	—
☐ 1860	195.	220.	260.	765.	6350.
☐ 1860-D	2375.	3700.	5450.	20000.	—
☐ 1860-S	315.	380.	655.	1275.	7100.
☐ 1861	170.	190.	240.	770.	6300.
☐ 1861-D	4750.	7100.	9650.	26500.	67500.
☐ 1862	170.	190.	240.	770.	6500.
☐ 1863	355.	490.	740.	1875.	7100.
☐ 1864	330.	455.	605.	930.	6350.
☐ 1865	330.	455.	615.	1150.	6900.
☐ 1866	330.	455.	615.	1100.	6750.
☐ 1867	340.	505.	665.	1150.	6300.
☐ 1868	295.	335.	455.	975.	6350.
☐ 1869	345.	405.	665.	1125.	6750.
☐ 1870	295.	305.	420.	1025.	6300.
☐ 1870-S	—	555.	715.	1775.	7050.
☐ 1871	295.	305.	420.	895.	6600.
☐ 1872	305.	325.	445.	930.	7100.
☐ 1873 Cl. 3	—	340.	640.	2750.	—
☐ 1873 Op. 3	170.	190.	240.	725.	6150.
☐ 1874	170.	190.	240.	725.	6150.
☐ 1875	2075.	2350.	3250.	8200.	20500.
☐ 1876	235.	270.	305.	1150.	7050.
☐ 1877	205.	245.	280.	930.	7050.
☐ 1878	235.	260.	290.	1000.	7100.
☐ 1879	205.	245.	280.	805.	6600.
☐ 1880	185.	215.	260.	775.	6150.
☐ 1881	185.	215.	260.	775.	6150.
☐ 1882	195.	220.	260.	785.	6350.
☐ 1883	185.	215.	260.	775.	6150.
☐ 1884	185.	215.	260.	775.	6150.
☐ 1885	185.	215.	260.	775.	6150.
☐ 1886	185.	215.	260.	775.	6150.
☐ 1887	185.	215.	260.	775.	6150.
☐ 1888	185.	215.	260.	775.	6150.
☐ 1889	185.	215.	260.	775.	6150.

QUARTER EAGLE, $2.50 GOLD, INDIAN HEAD TYPE

	F-12	VF-20	EF-40	AU-50	MS-60	MS-65
☐ 1908	175.	190.	205.	235.	400.	5440.
☐ 1909	175.	190.	205.	235.	400.	5500.
☐ 1910	175.	190.	205.	235.	415.	5800.
☐ 1911	175.	190.	205.	235.	400.	5650.
☐ 1911-D	540.	675.	1000.	1450.	2850.	8500.
☐ 1912	175.	190.	205.	235.	400.	5900.
☐ 1913	175.	190.	205.	235.	400.	5650.
☐ 1914	180.	195.	215.	255.	450.	6000.
☐ 1914-D	175.	190.	215.	265.	390.	6000.
☐ 1915	175.	190.	205.	235.	370.	5500.
☐ 1925-D	175.	190.	205.	235.	370.	5700.
☐ 1926	175.	190.	205.	235.	370.	5470.
☐ 1927	175.	190.	205.	235.	370.	5450.
☐ 1928	175.	190.	205.	235.	370.	5450.
☐ 1929	175.	190.	205.	235.	370.	5460.

$3.00 GOLD

	F-12	VF-20	EF-40	MS-60	MS-65
☐ 1854	460.	555.	855.	2750.	16350.
☐ 1854-D	5500.	8250.	17000.	4250.	—
☐ 1854-O	475.	555.	975.	3250.	17450.
☐ 1855	460.	540.	850.	42500.	—
☐ 1855-S	580.	750.	1350.	—	—
☐ 1856	460.	540.	950.	5000.	17150.
☐ 1856-S	485.	680.	1100.	5150.	—
☐ 1857	460.	545.	950.	4950.	16400.
☐ 1857-S	655.	825.	1550.	—	—
☐ 1858	850.	1025.	1700.	5400.	—
☐ 1859	460.	545.	900.	4800.	16000.
☐ 1860	460.	560.	975.	4850.	16350.
☐ 1860-S	655.	705.	1300.	—	—
☐ 1861	555.	665.	1050.	5100.	17000.
☐ 1862	555.	665.	1150.	5200.	17000.
☐ 1863	570.	680.	1050.	5200.	16350.

	F-12	VF-20	EF-40	MS-60	MS-65
☐ 1864	580.	690.	1100.	5300.	16800.
☐ 1865	780.	975.	1500.	6350.	23500.
☐ 1866	705.	715.	1150.	5250.	17750.
☐ 1867	680.	690.	1075.	5250.	17500.
☐ 1868	630.	685.	1025.	5150.	17750.
☐ 1869	655.	725.	1075.	5350.	17750.
☐ 1870	655.	715.	1075.	5250.	17750.
☐ 1870-S Only One Known EF-40 $687,500.					
☐ 1871	695.	715.	1150.	5150.	17750.
☐ 1872	685.	690.	1050.	5100.	17750.

HALF EAGLES, $5.00 GOLD, INDIAN HEAD TYPE

	F-12	VF-20	EF-40	AU-50	MS-60	MS-65
☐ 1908	235.	255.	270.	295.	980.	8300.
☐ 1908-D	235.	255.	270.	305.	985.	8650.
☐ 1908-S	280.	325.	425.	625.	2500.	9250.
☐ 1909	235.	255.	270.	295.	955.	8550.
☐ 1909-D	235.	255.	270.	295.	940.	8400.
☐ 1909-O	345.	415.	865.	1650.	6000.	50000.
☐ 1909-S	275.	315.	385.	700.	1700.	13000.
☐ 1910	235.	255.	270.	295.	955.	8750.
☐ 1910-D	250.	270.	290.	460.	1025.	8850.
☐ 1910-S	265.	305.	355.	650.	2100.	14000.
☐ 1911	235.	255.	270.	295.	940.	8450.
☐ 1911-D	305.	380.	440.	925.	4100.	—
☐ 1911-S	245.	280.	305.	390.	1100.	9100.
☐ 1912	235.	255.	270.	295.	940.	8450.
☐ 1912-S	270.	310.	365.	775.	1900.	13000.
☐ 1913	235.	255.	270.	295.	940.	8450.
☐ 1913-S	295.	325.	395.	850.	2800.	—
☐ 1914	240.	260.	275.	325.	970.	8450.
☐ 1914-D	240.	260.	280.	340.	950.	8550.
☐ 1914-S	250.	265.	305.	460.	1100.	—
☐ 1915	240.	260.	275.	315.	940.	8450.
☐ 1915-S	265.	300.	350.	800.	2600.	—
☐ 1916-S	245.	260.	295.	475.	1100.	9100.
☐ 1929	—	—	3550.	4500.	6750.	17500.

EAGLES, $10 GOLD, INDIAN HEAD TYPE

	F-12	VF-20	EF-40	AU-50	MS-60	MS-65
☐ 1907 Wire Rim, Periods	—	—	—	—	10500.	24000.
☐ 1907 Rolled Rim, Periods AU-50 ..			32000.			
☐ 1907 No Prds...........	470.	555.	555.	605.	1050.	8450.
☐ 1908 N.M...	480.	560.	630.	755.	1300.	8250.
☐ 1908-D N.M.	480.	560.	610.	695.	1200.	7850.
☐ 1908 Motto	480.	530.	535.	560.	1010.	8800.
☐ 1908-D	505.	580.	630.	705.	1150.	10500.
☐ 1908-S	485.	600.	675.	790.	3250.	10500.
☐ 1909..........	470.	555.	555.	620.	1050.	7700.
☐ 1909-D	480.	560.	590.	635.	1060.	8000.
☐ 1909-S	480.	555.	585.	660.	1500.	8100.
☐ 1910..........	480.	530.	535.	550.	1000.	7750.
☐ 1910-D	480.	530.	535.	550.	1000.	7700.
☐ 1910-S	480.	540.	540.	595.	1325.	8000.
☐ 1911..........	455.	490.	505.	545.	1000.	7000.
☐ 1911-D	580.	690.	875.	1400.	5500.	25000.
☐ 1911-S	470.	530.	560.	690.	2250.	8900.
☐ 1912..........	470.	515.	530.	550.	1000.	7100.
☐ 1912-S	485.	555.	570.	660.	1950.	8150.
☐ 1913..........	455.	490.	505.	545.	1000.	7750.
☐ 1913-S	505.	610.	700.	1050.	6750.	42000.
☐ 1914..........	465.	515.	525.	545.	1010.	7800.
☐ 1914-D	455.	490.	505.	545.	1025.	7950.
☐ 1914-S	480.	530.	535.	620.	1750.	8100.
☐ 1915..........	470.	515.	525.	545.	1040.	7900.
☐ 1915-S	485.	540.	570.	715.	2400.	19500.
☐ 1916-S	455.	490.	505.	620.	1250.	8600.
☐ 1920-S	—	—	7500.	10000.	16000.	5500.
☐ 1926..........	445.	485.	505.	530.	975.	7350.
☐ 1930-S	—	—	—	—	12000.	25500.
☐ 1932..........	445.	485.	505.	530.	975.	7500.
☐ 1933..........	—	—	—	—	55000.	140000.

DOUBLE EAGLES, $20 GOLD, ST. GAUDENS TYPE

	VF-20	*EF-40*	*AU-50*	*MS-60*	*MS-63*	*MS-65*
☐ 1907 Ex. High Relief Proofs Only, Proof 65: $265,000.						
☐ 1907 H.R.-R.N. Wire Ed.	2700.	4050.	5500.	8650.	14000.	25500.
☐ 1907 H.R.-R.N. Flat Ed.	2750.	4300.	5650.	8750.	14250.	26000.
☐ 1907	530.	550.	575.	620.	1275.	3800.
☐ 1908	530.	550.	575.	620.	1200.	3525.
☐ 1908-D	555.	575.	610.	660.	1350.	4050.
☐ 1908 Motto	540.	565.	600.	700.	1300.	4900.
☐ 1908-D Motto	555.	580.	605.	700.	1450.	4400.
☐ 1908-S Motto	715.	850.	1150.	3500.	5250.	15750.
☐ 1909/8	530.	550.	650.	1050.	2200.	5100.
☐ 1909	555.	585.	715.	850.	1600.	4500.
☐ 1909-D	615.	685.	950.	2700.	5750.	28500.
☐ 1909-S	530.	550.	590.	645.	1325.	4050.
☐ 1910	530.	550.	590.	645.	1350.	4025.
☐ 1910-D	530.	550.	590.	645.	1325.	4050.
☐ 1910-S	530.	550.	590.	645.	1375.	4100.
☐ 1911	530.	555.	605.	670.	1500.	4250.
☐ 1911-D	530.	550.	590.	645.	1225.	3800.
☐ 1911-S	530.	555.	605.	660.	1385.	4150.
☐ 1912	530.	555.	605.	685.	1575.	4350.
☐ 1913	530.	555.	605.	680.	1600.	4350.
☐ 1913-D	530.	550.	580.	645.	1350.	4150.
☐ 1913-S	550.	590.	695.	1150.	2100.	4750.
☐ 1914	540.	565.	605.	685.	1500.	4350.
☐ 1914-D	530.	555.	605.	660.	1350.	3950.
☐ 1914-S	530.	550.	590.	635.	1300.	3850.
☐ 1915	540.	565.	590.	660.	1600.	4300.
☐ 1915-S	530.	555.	605.	650.	1300.	3800.
☐ 1916-S	530.	550.	590.	645.	1375.	3950.
☐ 1920	530.	555.	605.	635.	1350.	4200.
☐ 1920-S	—	7000.	8750.	13250.	21000.	—
☐ 1921	—	8750.	11000.	18750.	29500.	—
☐ 1922	530.	550.	590.	615.	1225.	4000.

	VF-20	EF-40	AU-50	MS-60	MS-63	MS-65
☐ 1922-S........	570.	650.	780.	1250.	2600.	4550.
☐ 1923	530.	550.	575.	610.	1275.	4100.
☐ 1923-D.......	530.	550.	575.	635.	1375.	3850.
☐ 1924	530.	550.	575.	610.	1200.	3575.
☐ 1924-D.......	—	950.	1250.	1950.	2900.	7750.
☐ 1924-S........	—	—	1150.	1900.	2950.	8800.
☐ 1925	530.	550.	575.	610.	1225.	3600.
☐ 1925-D.......	—	—	1300.	2100.	3250.	8250.
☐ 1925-S........	—	800.	1200.	2200.	3100.	—
☐ 1926	530.	550.	575.	630.	1250.	3750.
☐ 1926-D.......	—	—	1250.	2200.	3350.	—
☐ 1926-S........	—	—	1050.	1700.	2300.	5900.
☐ 1927	530.	550.	575.	610.	1200.	3550.
☐ 1927-D—Extremely Rare, MS-65: $290,000.						
☐ 1927-S........	—	—	3250.	7600.	13500.	24500.
☐ 1928	530.	550.	575.	610.	1200.	3550.
☐ 1929	—	—	—	7400.	11000.	—
☐ 1930-S........	—	—	—	17500.	—	—
☐ 1931	—	—	—	14500.	23500.	—
☐ 1931-D.......	—	—	—	16500.	24000.	—
☐ 1932	—	—	—	17000.	26500.	38000.
☐ 1933 NOT LEGAL TO OWN.						

COMMEMORATIVE SILVER DOLLARS, HALVES, QUARTERS

	AU-50	MS-60	MS-63	MS-65
☐ 1892 Columbian...............	18.50	67.50	120.	945.
☐ 1893 Columbian...............	16.50	66.50	115.	935.
☐ 1893 Isabella 25¢	280.	550.	1000.	5000.
☐ 1900 Lafayette $1.............	350.	1000.	2250.	10300.
☐ 1915 Pan-Pacific...............	270.	550.	975.	5250.
☐ 1918 Illinois	67.50	120.	245.	1350.
☐ 1920 Maine......................	80.00	145.	250.	1700.
☐ 1920 Pilgrim....................	36.50	60.00	120.	875.
☐ 1921 Pilgrim	95.00	170.	265.	1550.
☐ 1921 Alabama 2 × 2	185.	350.	700.	4000.
☐ 1921 Alabama Plain	87.50	240.	525.	3800.
☐ 1921 Missouri Plain	260.	490.	950.	4500.

	AU-50	MS-60	MS-63	MS-65
☐ 1921 Missouri 2 × 4..........	365.	525.	1000.	4650.
☐ 1922 Grant	52.50	120.	235.	1550.
☐ 1922 Grant Star...............	375.	750.	1750.	7000.
☐ 1923 Monroe	28.50	65.00	135.	1700.
☐ 1924 Huguenot	65.00	115.	235.	1350.
☐ 1925 Lexington...............	35.00	50.00	100.	1300.
☐ 1925 Stone Mtn...............	22.50	42.00	105.	600.
☐ 1925 California	80.00	155.	290.	1450.
☐ 1925 Vancouver..............	285.	400.	550.	2050.
☐ 1926 Sesqui	27.50	46.00	105.	3300.
☐ 1926 Oregon...................	85.00	120.	165.	850.
☐ 1926-S Oregon	87.50	125.	170.	840.
☐ 1928 Oregon...................	175.	275.	365.	1100.
☐ 1933-D Oregon	210.	305.	400.	1350.
☐ 1934-D Oregon	115.	230.	345.	1900.
☐ 1936 Oregon...................	92.50	165.	280.	1100.
☐ 1936-S Oregon	165.	250.	355.	1450.
☐ 1937-D Oregon	90.00	145.	235.	800.
☐ 1938 Oregon Set PDS	—	600.	750.	2750.
☐ 1939 Oregon Set PDS	—	1200.	1500.	4400.
☐ 1927 Vermont.................	175.	240.	400.	1800.
☐ 1928 Hawaiian	750.	950.	1800.	6000.
☐ 1934 Boone	95.00	120.	170.	775.
☐ 1934 Boone Set Sm. 4.......	—	950.	1300.	3800.
☐ 1935 Boone Set PDS........	—	325.	525.	2200.
☐ 1936 Boone Set PDS........	—	325.	515.	2150.
☐ 1937 Boone Set PDS........	—	600.	950.	1850.
☐ 1938 Boone Set PDS........	—	1200.	1400.	2000.
☐ 1934 Maryland.................	125.	140.	285.	1250.
☐ 1934 Texas	110.	145.	240.	500.
☐ 1935 Texas Set PDS..........	—	400.	685.	1550.
☐ 1936 Texas Set PDS..........	—	425.	700.	1500.
☐ 1937 Texas Set PDS..........	—	440.	750.	1500.
☐ 1938 Texas Set PDS..........	—	725.	1025.	1700.
☐ 1935 Ark. Set PDS............	—	280.	375.	3900.
☐ 1936 Ark. Set PDS............	—	280.	375.	3900.
☐ 1936 Ark. Single...............	72.50	82.50	130.	1150.
☐ 1937 Ark. Set PDS............	—	290.	425.	3500.
☐ 1938 Ark. Set PDS............	—	485.	700.	5050.
☐ 1939 Ark. Set PDS............	—	900.	1250.	7050.

	AU-50	MS-60	MS-63	MS-65
☐ 1935 Conn......................	185.	240.	400.	1500.
☐ 1935 Hudson	385.	500.	825.	3800.
☐ 1935-S San Diego	70.00	110.	185.	625.
☐ 1936-D San Diego	77.50	125.	210.	750.
☐ 1935 Spanish Trail...........	615.	725.	950.	2300.
☐ 1936 Albany	235.	260.	390.	1100.
☐ 1936 Bridgeport..............	130.	165.	250.	1300.
☐ 1936 Cincinnati Set	—	825.	1200.	7250.
☐ 1936 Cincinnati Single......	240.	280.	410.	2350.
☐ 1936 Cleveland	77.50	115.	160.	1050.
☐ 1936 Columbia Set PDS	—	975.	1150.	2100.
☐ 1936 Columbia Singles......	215.	275.	325.	975.
☐ 1936 Delaware.................	190.	250.	385.	1750.
☐ 1936 Elgin, Ill.	180.	235.	375.	1350.
☐ 1936 Gettysburg...............	190.	240.	350.	1250.
☐ 1936 Long Island.............	64.50	90.00	150.	1075.
☐ 1936 Lynchburg	175.	210.	290.	1700.
☐ 1936 Norfolk	315.	375.	450.	1150.
☐ 1936 Rhode Is. Sing.........	85.00	125.	175.	1150.
☐ 1936 Rhode Is. Set	—	350.	550.	3600.
☐ 1936 Robinson.................	92.50	120.	165.	1025.
☐ 1936 San Francisco Bay Bridge	77.50	120.	175.	1300.
☐ 1936 Wisconsin................	180.	235.	335.	1150.
☐ 1936 York County	175.	235.	315.	1000.
☐ 1937 Antietam	265.	375.	500.	1350.
☐ 1937 Roanoke..................	160.	210.	305.	1125.
☐ 1938 New Rochelle	335.	425.	525.	1300.
☐ 1946 Iowa	77.50	85.00	150.	600.
☐ 1946 B.T. Wash. (3)	—	35.00	47.50	375.
☐ 1946 B.T. Wash. (1)	10.75	12.00	16.75	110.
☐ 1947 B.T. Wash. (3)	—	55.00	72.50	490.
☐ 1948 B.T. Wash. (3)	—	125.	160.	765.
☐ 1949 B.T. Wash. (3)	—	175.	245.	1200.
☐ 1950 B.T. Wash. (3)	—	150.	190.	950.
☐ 1951 B.T. Wash. (3)	—	92.50	135.	700.
☐ 1951 Wash.-Car (3)..........	—	87.50	130.	700.
☐ 1951 Wash.-Car (1)..........	11.00	13.00	17.75	110.
☐ 1952 Wash.-Car (3)..........	—	115.	175.	800.
☐ 1953 Wash.-Car (3)..........	—	145.	200.	850.

COMMEMORATIVE GOLD COINS

	AU-50	MS-60	MS-63	MS-65
☐ 1903 La.Pur Jeff.$1	390.	650.	1100.	3750.
☐ 1903 La.Pur Mckin.$1	375.	625.	1075.	3800.
☐ 1904 Lew. & Clark $1	525.	1100.	2100.	7300.
☐ 1905 Lew. & Clark $1	550.	1125.	2150.	7360.
☐ 1915-S Pan-Pac $1	360.	675.	1075.	4100.
☐ 1915-S Pan-Pac $2.50	825.	1700.	2850.	7100.
☐ 1915-S Pan-Pac $50 Rnd ...	21000.	29000.	36500.	49500.
☐ 1915-S Pan-Pac $50 Oct....	16750.	23000.	30000.	49500.
☐ 1916 McKin. $1	345.	730.	1000.	4950.
☐ 1917 McKin. $1	360.	750.	1175.	4950.
☐ 1922 Grant Star $1	625.	1125.	2050.	4950.
☐ 1922 Grant Plain $1	565.	1075.	1850.	4950.
☐ 1926 Sesqui $2.50	310.	575.	925.	4900.

Comic Books

TOPIC: Comic books are collections of sequential cartoons that tell a story. Each illustrated frame moves the story line along. In recent years the comic book has become a recognized art form in the world of pop culture.

TYPES: Comic books are categorized by publisher, examples being D-C National Periodical, Fawcett, and Marvel. The comic books included in this section are first editions only.

PERIOD: Most comic books covered were published from 1940 to the early 1970s, now considered a prime collectible period.

COMMENTS: Comic books make wonderful collectibles. The comic book is fun reading material and often has true artistic merit. In many cases it is regarded as a historical document as well. Condition is all-important in the matter of pricing comics, as the reader will note from the wide price range cited in the following list. Grading runs from "Poor" (i.e., damaged, weathered, soiled, torn) to "Pristine Mint" (i.e., absolutely perfect in every way). The most worthless comic, however, is the coverless comic. It takes such ingenuity as a color Xerox to make the item worth anything in the market.

Note: Prices listed indicate the range of specific comics from good to mint condition.

Price Range

☐ **Action Comics,** June 1938. Featuring the first appearance of Superman 4000.00 25,000.00

☐ **Archie Comics,** No. 1, scarce, with the first appearance of Jughead and Veronica (prices vary widely on this book) 225.00 1775.00

☐ **Batman,** National Periodical Publishing/Detective Comics/DC Comics, origin of the Batman retold by Bob Kane; Detective No. 33 originally published this story (prices vary widely on this book) 950.00 7600.00

☐ **Captain America,** March 1941, origin and first appearance, Captain America and Bucky by S&K, Red Skull appearance (prices vary widely on this book) 815.00 5700.00

☐ **Captain Marvel,** 1941, no number; Captain Marvel and Sivana by Jack Kirby; cover was printed on unstable paper stock and is rarely found in fine or mint condition .. 800.00 5700.00

☐ **Detective Comics,** No. 1, March 1937, Slam Bradley and Spy by Siegel and Shuster, Speed Saunders by Guardineer, Flat Foot Flannigan by Gustavson, Cosmo the Phantom of Disguise, Buck Marshall, Bruce Nelson begins (no known copy to exist beyond very fine condition) 1300.00 7500.00

☐ **Detective Comics,** No. 27, first appearance of the Batman and Commissioner Gordon by Bob Kane (no copy known to exist beyond very fine to near mint condition; prices vary widely on this book) 2800.00 17,500.00

Price Range

☐ **Dick Tracy**, May 1937, David McKay Publications, Feature Books, no number, 100 pp., appeared before Large Feature Comics, very rare, with only three copies known to exist 400.00   2800.00

☐ **Flash Comics**, January 1940, with "No. 1" on inside, origin and first appearance of Captain Thunder; eight copies of *Flash* exist (all available copies of *Flash* sold in 1986 for between $4000 and $10,000 each) 4000.00 10,000.00

☐ **Flash Comics**, National Periodical Publications, The Flash by Harry Lambert 550.00   3850.00

☐ **Star Trek**, No. 1, 1967, published by Gold Key, based on television series of same name 5.75   40.00

☐ **Superman**, No. 1, the first four action stories reprinted, origin of Superman by Siegel and Shuster . 2900.00 18,000.00

☐ **Walt Disney's Comics and Stories**, first edition contains a reprint by Al Taliaferro, and Gottfredson's Mickey Mouse begins 300.00   2900.00

Credit Cards

DESCRIPTION: A credit card establishes the privilege of the person to whom it is issued to charge bills.

VARIATIONS: Credit cards fall into one of three categories: paper, laminated paper, and plastic.

PERIOD: Paper credit cards were first issued in the early 1900s. They were easily damaged, so in the 1940s some companies began laminating them with clear plastic. The plastic cards we know today replaced the laminated cards in the late 1950s.

COMMENTS: Collectors generally specialize in one of the following areas: airlines, gasoline, department stores, banks, or travel and entertainment cards.

ADDITIONAL TIPS: Paper and laminated paper credit cards are rare. Plastic credit cards before 1970 are scarce.

PERIODICALS OF INTEREST: *Credit Card Collector,* 150 Hohldale, Houston, TX 77022.

	Price Range	
☐ **American Express**, 1958, paper	125.00	150.00
☐ **American Express Violet Card**, 1967, centurion on upper left	20.00	25.00

Gulf Travel Card. (*Photo courtesy of Greg Tunks*)

	Price Range	
☐ **American Oil Company**, 1969, red, white, and blue map of the United States	7.00	9.00
☐ **Bank Americard**, with magnetic stripe	5.00	7.00
☐ **Carte Blanche**, 1974, blue on whie, gold border	6.00	8.00
☐ **Diners Club**, 1966, colored blocks	10.00	12.00
☐ **Eastern Wings**, 1979, couple at seaside	2.00	3.00
☐ **Enco Happy Motoring!**, 1971, bar code	8.00	10.00
☐ **Frederick's of Hollywood**, Fabulous Filmland Fashions, pink on white	6.00	8.00
☐ **Gulf, Land, Sea, or Air**, bar code	8.00	10.00
☐ **Husky**, 1978, husky dog on white background	4.00	5.00
☐ **MasterCard**, pre-hologram	2.00	4.00
☐ **Master Charge**, with magnetic stripe	4.00	6.00

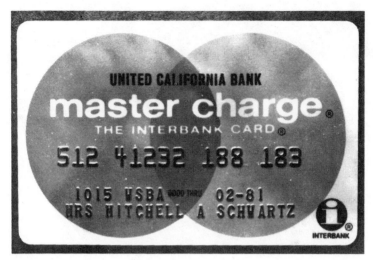

Master Charge became MasterCard, $4–$6.

	Price Range	
☐ **Montgomery Ward**, National Chargall, data punch card	10.00	12.00
☐ **Sinclair Credit Card**, drawing of gas station	10.00	12.00
☐ **Standard Oil Company Courtesy Card**, 1937, paper	20.00	25.00
☐ **Sunoco**, 1971, drawing of custom blended pump	4.00	6.00
☐ **Texaco**, 1960, red, white, and green stripes	6.00	8.00
☐ **The Texas Company** (Texaco), 1936, paper	20.00	25.00
☐ **Tide Water Associated Oil Co.**, 1949, laminated paper, flying red A	15.00	20.00
☐ **TWA Getaway Card**, 1974, swimsuited couple	6.00	8.00
☐ **Visa**, pre-hologram	2.00	4.00
☐ **Western Union**, 1934, paper, authorizes acceptance of collect messages	10.00	12.00

Dairy Collectibles

DESCRIPTION: All items pertaining to the American dairy industry.

TYPES: Dairy collectibles include articles used on dairy farms such as pails, milking devices, and churns; containers to transport and retail milk and other dairy products; and advertising items, brochures, and signs generated by the dairy industry.

PERIOD: Though dairy farming in America dates to the early colonial era, collectibles available on the market date from the 1700s. Most of them are of the period from about 1850 to the early 1900s. This era ushered in large-scale factory production of such items as milk cans and store bottles.

COMMENTS: This is another of various fields of collecting in which charm and historical appeal take precedence over immaculate condition.

BOTTLES

Price Range

☐ **Round embossed pint**, Rosedale Dairy Co. Inc., 1680 Park Ave, NY City, store bottle 9.00

Price Range

☐ **Round embossed pint**, Maine Dairy Inc., Milk, Portland, on banner Maine seal 8.00

☐ **Round embossed pint**, Ball Mountain Milk, Springfield, Mass, on reverse "S.C.Co." 9.00

☐ **Round embossed pint**, Mountain View Farm, R.J. Breisch, Catawissa, PA, complete tin on top . 30.00

☐ **Round pyro pint**, Larose Bros., Lowell, Mass, "Pasteurized for Safety Larose Bros., Health in every bottle," boy and girl with bottle of milk, orange and black . 12.00

☐ **Round pyro pint**, "Enjoy Miss Georgia Dairy Products, Georgia Milk Producers Confederation Inc. Atlanta, Ga.," red girl in old-fashioned dress and hat holding bottle 15.00

☐ **Round pyro quart**, Village Dairy Sutherland, Nebraska, "Drink milk for health," man dressed in armor with shield and spear, green 22.00

☐ **Square pyro quart**, plain green glass bottom, Sealed LC One Quart Liquid, 644–1 registered 25.00

☐ **Square pyro quart**, H. E. Johnson, Rutland, Vt., Tel. 3–9544, "Nature's Best Food," half circle with baby arms reaching up, amber with white pyro 12.00

☐ **Square pyro ½ pint**, short, Hope Dairy Farms, Madison, N.J., "Build 'Em Healthy with Lots of Milk" bucking horse and rider, orange with orange dots around shoulders 7.00

☐ **Square pyro ½ pint**, tall, Indian Hill Farm Dairy, Greenville, Me.,

Price Range

Tel. 76–2, Indian chief in head-
dress, two sides orange 7.00

BOXES

☐ **Porch box**, property of H. P.
Hood & Sons, Inc., holds 6 round
qts, metal embossed, 10 3/4 " high   18.00
☐ **Porch box**, Elmhurst Dairy,
metal, red on front, 6 qts, 10 1/2 "
high 16.00

CREAMERS

☐ **Brandt's Dairy**, Great Bend, Pa.,
2 sides red 20.00
☐ **Dairylea**, two sides red, 1/2 oz ..   12.00
☐ **Ewald Brothers**, Golden Guern-
sey, with trademark, 1/2 oz, red ..   15.00
☐ **Helfand Dairy Products**, two
sides green, 1/2 oz 17.00
☐ **Raritan Valley Farms**, Somer-
ville, N.J., Dairy Products, 3/4 oz,
orange 18.00

DAIRY GO-WITHS

☐ **Bank**, chalkwear baby in diaper
hugging giant bottle of milk, hole
for money in bottle, printed
"Peek-A-Boo Here's Health for
you Save to buy milk Natures Perfect food" (was given to new ba-
bies from their dairy) 15.00
☐ **Chocolate mold**, metal, em-
bossed "Loft Milk Chocolate
Cream," 3 " × 3 ", some rust 10.00

Price Range

☐ **Churn**, National Ideal Chick Fount Toledo, Ohio, embossed on bottom glass, has Greek key pattern around shoulders and around bottom, all metal, 2-blade beater, wooden handle on crank 45.00

☐ **Cylinder churn**, new style white cedar, No. 1, made in USA, 3 gallons, all stamped in black on front of wooden churn, complete 90.00

☐ **Fan**, cardboard, "Compliments of E. A. Strout Co., World's Largest Farm Dealers, N.Y., Philadelphia, Boston, Syracuse, N.Y., Scottsville, Va., Kents Hill, Me.," front depicts cow and two milkmaids in long dresses and bonnets sitting on a fence, one standing with milk pail, reverse shows banker giving money to farmer in exchange for a deed and horse-drawn buggy with realtor showing farm to buyer, dated 1908 in pencil 15.00

☐ **Hawley dash churn**, 1 gallon, 3-part dasher 55.00

☐ **Hood Farm puzzle box**, "C. I. Hood Co., Lowell, Mass, Copyright 1905," box of six puzzles ..   55.00

☐ **Matchbook**, empty, "Cleaner Milk Faster Milking with The Surge Milker Surge Dairy Farm Equipment" advertising inside and out 2.00

☐ **Metal tray**, "Otto's Suburban Dairy Milk That Best Food" in center of tray and in small letters at bottom "Kemper-Thomas Co. Cincinnati, Ohio," cream color with black letters and border, 10 1/4 " × 13 " 30.00

Price Range

☐ **Testrite floating dairy thermometer**, easy-reading scale guaranteed accurate, 9″ long, in original box 8.00

SIGNS

☐ **"Better than the Best,"** Vermont Dairy, V. D's Ice Cream Mfg. at Old Orchard Beach, Maine, yellow and black, 4″ × 28″ 65.00

☐ **Frojoy Ice Cream "Youth Units,"** metal with wood frame, 36″ × 36″, in upper left a man carrying ice cream on a plate, red, yellow, and black 60.00

☐ **Metal sign**, "Wiseman Farms Ice cream" embossed across a large ice cream cone, "The Old Fashioned Kind" embossed under cone, navy blue with white, yellow, and red, 28″ × 20″ 70.00

Decoys

TOPIC: A decoy is a representation of some animal used to lure others of that species within shooting range.

TYPES: Decoys most often represent waterfowl, but frog, fish, owl, and crow decoys are not uncommon. Decoys can be solid, hollow, or slat-bodied. They can be either of the floating variety or the "stick-up" variety, which is driven into the ground.

PERIOD: Decoys produced after the mid-19th century are most popular among collectors.

ORIGIN: American Indians have made and used decoys since 1000 A.D.

MAKERS: Famous decoy carvers include Ira Hudson, Charles Wheeler, Albert Laing, and Mark Whipple.

MATERIALS: Decoys are usually carved out of wood, although metal and other materials are found.

COMMENTS: Enthusiasts usually collect decoys by carver, species, or flyway (the path of migration). Decoys made for actual use are more favored by collectors than those intended only for show.

TIPS: The condition of the paint on a decoy is a good indicator of age. Many cracked layers of paint mean that the

269

decoy is probably old. Original paint is favored by collectors.

	Price Range	
☐ **American scoter**, rare, by "Gus" Wilson (So. Portland, ME), with swivel head, fluted tail, and raised wings, one of only two known, near mint condition, three tight checks in one side	2500.00	3000.00
☐ **Black duck**, sleeping, exceedingly rare, by Charles Perdew (Henry, IL), c. 1910, Edna's finest paint, early three-piece body style, $\frac{1}{2}'' \times 3''$ slice missing from the center body section on one side	7500.00	8800.00
☐ **Bluewing teal pair**, Mason's, premier grade, drake has minor wear, small, old, in-use repair to a slice and a crack in the top of the bill, head has been reset with three tiny nails, hen has been lightly dusted by shot, otherwise mint	3000.00	3600.00
☐ **Bluebill**, extremely rare and important, by Nathan Cobb, Jr., c. 1890, hollow, with inlet head, original paint with moderate wear	15,000.00	18,000.00
☐ **Brant**, swimming, in the style of Nathan Cobb, made by Frank Finney (Virginia Beach, VA), hollow with glass eyes, several coats of paint with minor wear on the top coat	400.00	425.00
☐ **Canada goose**, Mason's, rare early style, exceptional feathering on back, excellent dry original paint with minor crazing and wear	1400.00	1700.00
☐ **Curlew**, well sculptured, from the eastern shore of Virginia, near		

	Price Range	

mint original paint with good patina, bill missing 200.00   250.00

☐ **Goldeneye**, pair, by "Gus" Wilson (So. Portland, ME), both have inlet heads and raised carved primaries, the white on both decoys has old in-use repaint with good patina, both have minor age splits 4500.00   5500.00

☐ **Golden plover**, oversize, by A. E. Crowell (E. Harwich, MA), c. 1890, with finely carved primary feathers and glass eyes, near mint condition with fantastic patina ... 30,000.00 40,000.00

☐ **Green-winged teal**, drake, Mason's, excellent original paint, very rare 1500.00   1800.00

☐ **Eider**, drake, extremely early turtleback, by Thomas Alexander (Harpswell, ME), large serif initials "T.A." carved in underside and date "1846," one-piece construction with detailed bill carving, excellent old paint which has mellowed to a fine patina 3500.00   4400.00

☐ **Mallard**, drake, by Bert Graves (Peoria, IL), near mint original paint, structurally excellent 1000.00   1650.00

☐ **Merganser**, drake, by Charles Perdew (Henry, IL), Edna's paint, raised primaries, excellent original paint with minor crazing on a small area of the neck and bill, bill has been cracked and reglued, most of plaster foot is missing, feather missing from the crest 800.00   1400.00

☐ **Owl**, extremely rare, great horned, from Windham, ME, carved crossed primaries and fluted tail carving, highly detailed carving with feathering on horns, slightly open beak, wonderful

	Price Range	

muted paint with feathering on breast, wooden painted perch with copper sleeve for attaching to pole, near mint original paint — 4500.00 — 6500.00

☐ **Pintail**, drake (early), by Robert Elliston (Bureau, IL), c. 1890, "A.A.A." is painted on underside — 250.00 — 350.00

☐ **Redhead drake**, Mason's, premier grade, good original paint with minor wear, very slightly dusted by shot .... — 500.00 — 700.00

☐ **Snipe**, from Wachadreque, VA, c. 1890, branded "P" on bottom, original paint with slight wear, lightly hit by shot .... — 250.00 — 300.00

☐ **Squaw**, pair, very rare, old, by "Gus" Wilson (So. Portland, ME), both have swivel heads, carved eyes, and raised wings, hen has fluted tail, the drake has a small crack in the tail, otherwise both in mint condition with good patina .... — 7500.00 — 9000.00

☐ **Western grebe**, preening, by Harold Haertel (Dundee, IL), "Western Grebe by Harold Haertel 1974" is written on the bottom, highly detailed precise wing tip carving and fine feather painting, mint condition .... — 1000.00 — 1600.00

☐ **Widgeon**, drake exceptionally early, found in southern New Jersey, finely blended paint with intricate feather painting on back, tack eyes, near mint original paint with several rubs and string marks — 1500.00 — 1800.00

☐ **Willet**, extremely rare, oversize, by A. E. Crowell (E. Harwich, MA), c. 1890, with finely carved primary feathers and glass eyes, 11½" long, near mint condition — 15,000.00 — 20,000.00

Price Range

☐ **Yellowlegs**, rare, by Chief Chaffey, raised primaries and split tail, original paint with very slight wear, old coat of varnish, small rough area on tip of tail 200.00   250.00

Disneyana

BACKGROUND: The debut of a little pie-eyed rodent named Mickey Mouse on November 18, 1928, the eve of the Great Depression, took place in "Steamboat Willie," the first sound animated cartoon, at New York's Colony Theater. The legacy of Mickey, his pals Minnie, Donald, Goofy, Dumbo, Bambi, Snow White and the Seven Dwarfs, and all of the beloved cartoon characters are not only enshrined in films, videos, comic strips, books, and world-famous tourist attractions but in the countless products created in their image for well over fifty years by over four hundred licensees in the United States, Canada, Great Britain, Japan, Germany, and Taiwan. Walter Ewing Disney's cartoon characters have inspired more toys, in numerous variations, than all other cartoonists combined. Many collectors stick strictly to the vast field of Disneyana.

CLARA CLUCK

This operatic hen was introduced in the Disney short, "The Orphan's Benefit," in 1934.

	Price Range	
☐ **Clara Cluck pull toy,** Fisher Price, 1934, litho and wood platform toy, 8″ long	75.00	125.00

DONALD DUCK

Donald, who in recent years may well have overshadowed his sidekick, Mickey, made his first appearance in a cameo role in "The Wise Little Hen" in 1934. He was his usual obstreperous self in Mickey's first color cartoon, "The Band Concert," 1935. His first starring role did not come until 1937 in "Donald's Ostrich."

	Price Range	
☐ **Donald Duck and Pluto rail car,** Lionel, 1936, 10″ long, Pluto is in doghouse while Donald stands in rear, composition and metal	750.00	850.00
☐ **Donald Duck and Pluto roadster,** Sun Rubber, 1930s, 7″ long	35.00	50.00
☐ **Donald Duck car,** Paperino Politoys, Italy, 1960s, litho tin, Donald drives with nephews in rumble seat	50.00	75.00
☐ **Donald Duck drummer,** Line Mar, 1950s, litho tin windup, 6″ high	75.00	100.00
☐ **Donald Duck fireman on ladder,** Line Mar, 1950s	125.00	150.00
☐ **Donald Duck in open roadster,** Sun Rubber, 1933–34, hard rubber, painted push toy, 6½″ long	25.00	35.00

ELMER ELEPHANT

Price Range

☐ **Elmer Elephant pull toy,** Fisher Price, 1936, litho and wood, 7 ½" long 35.00   50.00

FERDINAND THE BULL

Disney adapted the book *The Story of Ferdinand,* by Munro Leaf and Robert Lawson, to a special short feature film in 1938.

Price Range

☐ **Ferdinand,** composition-jointed figure, Ideal, 1938, 9" long 50.00   75.00
☐ **Ferdinand the Bull,** Marx, 1938, litho tin windup (tail spins), 7 ½" long 100.00   150.00

GOOFY

☐ **Goofy Gardiner,** Line Mar, 1940s (see also Donald Duck Duet, with Goofy playing bass fiddle) 25.00   35.00
☐ **Goofy Walker,** Line Mar, 1940s, 7" high, tin litho windup 25.00   35.00

LUDWIG VON DRAKE

☐ **Ludwig Von Drake,** Line Mar, 1950s, litho tin windup, 6" high   75.00   100.00

Price Range

MICKEY AND MINNIE MOUSE

☐ **Climbing Mickey,** Dolly Toy Co., Dayton, Ohio, early 1930s, copyrighted by Walt Disney Enterprises, 9″ high, die-cut pasteboard 150.00   200.00

☐ **Dancing Mickey and Minnie,** Japan, 1930s, celluloid windup, 3½″ high, variations include Minnie and Elmer the Elephant, Donald and Elmer dancers 250.00   300.00

☐ **Fun-E-Flex Mickey and Minnie on dogsled,** pulled by Pluto, George Borgfeldt, 10¾″ long, wood and composition 250.00   300.00

☐ **Fun-E-Flex Minnie and Mickey,** 1931, distributed by George Borgfeldt, wood-jointed bodies with composition heads, 7″ high, figures produced separately for Minnie, Mickey and Pluto (ears were leatherette or felt), each 100.00   125.00

☐ **Mickey and Donald acrobats,** Line Mar, 1950s, litho tin, steel with celluloid figures, 17″ high (also Minnie and Mickey acrobats versions) 300.00   350.00

☐ **Mickey and Minnie standing figures,** Japan, 1930s, celluloid, heads attached by elastic, nonanimated, each 200.00   250.00

☐ **Mickey and Pluto in three-wheel cart,** Japan, litho tin and celluloid, 4½″ long 150.00   200.00

☐ **Mickey in bathing suit,** Japan, 1930s, celluloid, 5½″ high 200.00   300.00

☐ **Mickey in life preserver,** Japan, 1930s, hard rubber, 4½″ high (serves as both toy and baby rattle) 300.00   350.00

	Price Range	
☐ **Mickey in roadster pull toy,** licensed by Walt Disney, Japan, 1934, 12″ long, roadster is tinted celluloid, Mickey figure is string-jointed wooden beads	500.00	600.00
☐ **Mickey jack-in-the-box,** Japan, 1930s, celluloid Mickey figure, box is paper-covered wood, 6″ high	350.00	400.00

THREE LITTLE PIGS

Another Grimm's fairy tale–based film, "The Three Little Pigs," came to the screen in 1933, the most famous of all of Disney's Silly Symphonies.

	Price Range	
☐ **Big Bad Wolf walker,** Line Mar, late 1940s, 6″ high, litho tin windup	50.00	75.00
☐ **Drummer Pig, Fiddler Pig, and Fifer Pig,** Schuco, mid-1930s, felt on tin windups, 6″ high	350.00	400.00
☐ **Fiddler Pig walker,** Line Mar, late 1940s, 6″ high, litho tin windup	50.00	75.00
☐ **Three Little Pigs acrobats,** Line Mar, 1950s, celluloid and metal (variation of Mickey and Donald acrobat toys)	150.00	200.00

Dollhouses

PERIOD: Dollhouses have been manufactured by toy companies since the Industrial Revolution. The most elaborate American dollhouses date from the Victorian period, which is considered to be the golden age of toys.

COMMENTS: Many of the loveliest examples are handmade. Traditionally, fathers and grandfathers have made dollhouses for their little girls, often a miniature version of their actual house.

ADDITIONAL TIPS: Because of the tremendous popularity of all types of miniature collectibles, the demand for vintage dollhouses is at its greatest peak ever.

Note: The values shown below are the actual auction-realized prices.

	Price Range
☐ **Bliss-type,** small, two-story, "brick" with blue pitched roof and covered porch, open at rear to reveal two rooms, 12½″ × 11″ × 6″	462.00
☐ **Bliss-type,** small, two-story neo-Gothic "brick" with covered porch, balcony, and angel-head	

Price Range

decoration in the eaves, the facade opening to reveal two papered rooms, 14″ × 9″ × 6″, c. 1890 ....   990.00

☐ **Bliss-type,** small, German, with papered "brick" facade and blue pitched roof with gable, the hinged facade opening onto two rooms, 11″ × 6″ × 5″, c. 1900   330.00

☐ **Cottage,** German, 1920s, painted yellow with steep red roof, trellised porch and green stenciled shutters, lower facade opening to reveal two rooms, one furnished with painted, blue metal bedroom suite, the dormer window opens onto a large attic, 15″ × 16″ × 11″ 308.00

☐ **Fretwork,** two-story, yellow with blue roof and green fenced porch, 15″ × 13″ × 10″, c. 1900 ....   275.00

☐ **Bliss-type,** German, two-story, with papered "brick" exterior, five curtained windows, painted green pitched roof with dormer, roofed porch and metal railings, facade opening to reveal two rooms, 1890–1900, 18″ × 12″ × 8″ 660.00

☐ **Lancaster County farmhouse,** large, two-story, painted red brick exterior with hand-split shingled roof, green shutters, dormer, covered porches on three sides, and small separate outhouse, rear and side doors opening to reveal upper and lower floors, 34″ × 38″ × 23″, c. 1890 ....   8250.00

☐ **"Mystery" house,** four rooms, gray exterior with mahogany-stained paneled door and pairs of

Left to right. Bliss-type, small, two-story, "brick" with blue pitched roof and covered porch, open at rear to reveal two rooms, 12 ½ " × 11 " × 6 ", $462. Bliss-type, small, two-story, neo-Gothic "brick" with covered porch, balcony, and angel-head decoration in the eaves, the facade opening to reveal two papered rooms, 14 " × 9 " × 6 ", c. 1890, $990. Bliss-type, small, German, with papered "brick" facade and blue pitched roof with gable, the hinged facade opening onto two rooms, 11 " × 6 " × 5 ", c. 1900, $330. (*Photo courtesy of Christie's East, New York*)

Left to right. Cottage, German, 1920s, painted yellow with steep red roof, trellised porch and green stencilled shutters, lower facade opening to reveal two rooms, one furnished with painted, blue metal bedroom suite, the dormer window opens onto a large attic, 15 " × 16 " × 11 ", $308. Fretwork, two-story, yellow with blue roof and green fenced porch, 15 " × 13 " × 10 ", c. 1900, $275. Bliss-type, German, two-story, with papered "brick" exterior, five curtained windows, painted, green pitched roof with dormer, roofed porch and metal railings, facade opening to reveal two rooms, 1890–1900, 18 " × 12 " × 8 ", $660. (*Photo courtesy of Christie's East, New York*)

"Mystery" house, four-room, the gray exterior with Mahagony-stained paneled door and pairs of windows on front and sides with scroll-cut lintels, the "slate" roof with glittered double cornice and brick chimney, the exterior trimmed with chamfered black strips, the facade opening cabinet-style to reveal two upper and two lower papered rooms with pale blue connecting doors, each room with parquetry floors stained tan, forest green and red, three rooms with original gilt and white glass chandeliers, $15,400. (*Photo courtesy of Christie's East, New York*)

Price Range

windows on front and sides with scroll-cut lintels, "slate" roof with glittered double cornice and brick chimney, exterior trimmed

Price Range

with chamfered black strips, facade opening cabinet-style to reveal two upper and two lower
papered rooms with pale blue
connecting paneled doors, each
room with parquetry floors
stained tan, forest green, and red,
three rooms with original gilt and
white glass chandeliers 15,400.00

☐ **"Mystery" house,** six rooms,
blue-green exterior with two mahagony-stained paneled doors and
pairs of windows on front and
sides with scroll-cut lintels, slate
roof with two hinged dormers for
access to attic, brick chimney and
tricolored glittered cornice, exterior trimmed with chamfered
black strips, three hinged doors in
the facade opening onto three upper and three lower repapered
rooms with blue-green paneled
connecting doors, each room with
parquetry floors stained light
brown, dark brown, and black ...   13,200.00

☐ **New Jersey farmhouse,** two-
story, blue clapboard exterior
with double-hung pedimented
windows, large front porch with
turned columns and railings and
gray shingled roof with bracketed
cornices, the rear open for access
to six furnished rooms with connecting interior doors, furnishings include Schoenhut painted
bedroom suite, a pair of Marklin
painted metal beds and a five-
piece upholstered Duncan Phyfe–
style parlor suite 6050.00

☐ **Pennsylvania house,** large, 19th
century, two-story with white

Price Range

clapboard exterior, two-story front bay and covered porch with swing, each side opening to reveal four rooms (eight total), stairway on the right, fully furnished with period and later pieces, including Tiny Toy, Schoenhut, and Columbia, 41″ × 36″ × 38″ 7480.00

☐ **Victorian model,** with yellow clapboard exterior, covered porch extending along length and width of house and around octagonal bay, gray, shingled roof with widow's walk and weathervane, the rear of the house open for access to upper and lower floors, 17″ × 16″ × 14″, c. 1900 .... 1320.00

☐ **Victorian doll's mansion,** two-story, cream-painted facade with two large six-windowed bays flanking the pedimented front door and French-doored balcony, each bay surmounted by a belvedere with two chimneys and widow's walk, the facade opening to reveal four rooms with fireplaces, hallways, and staircase, probably German in origin, 33″ × 33″ × 19″, c. 1890 .... 1760.00

FURNISHINGS

☐ **Biedermier dining room,** comprising marble-topped sideboard, Gothic-style china cabinet, hall tree, mirrored armoire, five upholstered Gothic-style side chairs, all 19th century Waltershausen, brass chandelier with glass globes,

Victorian model, with yellow clapboard exterior, covered porch extending along length and width of house and around octagonal bay, the gray, shingled roof with window's walk and weathervane, the rear of the house open for access to upper and lower floors, 17″ × 16″ × 14″, c. 1900, $1320. (*Photo courtesy of Christie's East, New York*)

	Price Range
marble-top dining table, grandfather's clock watch holder, mirrored curio stand, and various glass and porcelain ornaments, all contained in a painted wood bookcase with glass door, 15″ × 24″ × 17″	3520.00
☐ **Biedermier bedroom suite,** comprising mirrored dressing table, bed, armoire, night table, table, and three side chairs	495.00

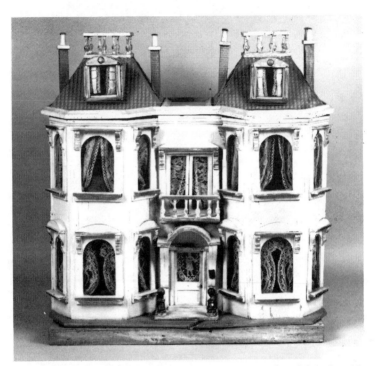

Victorian doll's mansion, the two-story, cream-painted facade with two, large, six-windowed bays flanking the pedimented front door and French-doored balcony, each bay surmounted by a belvedere with two chimneys and widow's walk, the facade opening to reveal four rooms with fireplaces, hallways and staircase, the house probably German in origin, 33″ × 33″ × 19″, c. 1890, $1760. (*Photo courtesy of Christie's East, New York*)

Price Range

☐ **Parlor furnishings,** gilt metal, comprising mirrored fireplace, what-not shelf, three faux-bamboo chairs, writing table with three picture frames, a table lamp with white glass globe, mantel clock with cherub top, a glass-globed chandelier, three porcelain vases and a radiator 2530.00

Parlor furnishings, gilt metal, comprising mirrored fireplace, what-not shelf, three faux-bamboo chairs, writing table and three picture frames, a table lamp with white glass globe, mantel clock with cherub top, a glass-globed chandelier, three porcelain vases and a radiator, $2530. (*Photo courtesy of Christie's East, New York*)

Dolls

ORIGIN: We know that doll-like creations date back to ancient times, but it is not easy to determine what was considered a plaything in those early days. Small painted statuettes made of baked clay, representing different activities, have been found in the graves of noble Egyptians. It is not very likely that they were designed as children's toys. Crudely carved wooden dolls have been recorded dating from the Roman time of the Caesars, which takes doll-making back about 1,900 years.

COMMENTS: Dolls have been called the most emotion-inducing collectibles, and their appeal is such that they rank within the top four forms of collectibles in popularity.

Note: The single values shown are the actual auction-realized prices.

	Price Range
☐ **Bru bisque-headed bebe,** large, with closed mouth, blue paperweight eyes, pierced ears, auburn-hair wig and jointed body (unstrung), incised "Bru Jne 14," (minor body damages), 30″ high	8800.00

Bru bisque-headed bebe, large, with closed mouth, blue paper-weight eyes, pierced ears, auburn hair wig and jointed body (un-strung), incised "Bru Jne 14," 30″ height, $8800. (*Photo courtesy of Christie's East, New York*)

Price Range

☐ **Bru child doll,** cup and saucer bisque shoulder plate head on a kid gusseted body with perfect bisque hands and well-defined kid feet and toes, original human-hair wig, 29″ high 14,300.00

☐ **Eden bisque-headed bebe,** large, with blue paperweight eyes, pierced ears, brown-hair wig, and jointed body, incised "Eden Bebe Paris 14," 29″ high 2420.00

☐ **Jimeau bisque-headed bebe,** large, with pierced ears, brown paperweight eyes, replaced blond-hair wig, and jointed body,

Left to right. Eden bisque-headed bebe, large, with blue paper-weight eyes, pierced ears, brown hair wig and jointed body, incised "Eden Bebe Paris 14," 29" height, $2420. Jimeau bisque-headed bebe, large, with pierced ears, brown paperweight eyes, replaced blond hair wig and jointed body, incised "1907 16," (hands repainted), 32" height, $2420. F. G. bisque-headed bride doll, large, with closed mouth, pierced ears, blue paperweight eyes, blonde mohair wig, swivel neck, bisque shoulder plate and straight-limbed kid body, incised "11, F. G." on shoulder, 28" height, $2860. Steiner bisque-headed lady waltzing doll, with swivel neck, bisque shoulder plate, pale blue paperweight eyes, pierced ears, blond mohair wig, composition arms and wheeled carton base housing the mechanism, wearing original ivory satin dress trimmed with lace, doll turns in circles and lifts arm when key is wound (partially operative), 15" height, $2200. (*Photo courtesy of Christie's East, New York*)

	Price Range
incised "1907 16" (hands re-painted), 32" high	2420.00

☐ **F. G. bisque-headed bride doll,** large, with closed mouth, pierced ears, blue paperweight eyes, blonde mohair wig, swivel neck, bisque shoulder plate, and

Price Range

straight-limbed kid body, incised
"11, F. G." on shoulder, 28″ high   2860.00

☐ **Steiner bisque-headed lady waltzing doll,** with swivel neck, bisque shoulder plate, pale blue paperweight eyes, pierced ears, blonde mohair wig, composition arms, and wheeled carton base housing the mechanism, wearing original ivory satin dress trimmed with lace, doll turns in circles and lifts arm when key is wound (partially operative), 15″ high 2200.00

☐ **German closed-mouth, turned shoulder-headed doll,** large, with solid-dome head, blue paperweight eyes, blonde mohair wig, and kid body with bisque arms, incised "639," 26″ high ...   715.00

☐ **Jimeau bisque-headed bebe,** with pierced ears, blue paperweight sleeping eyes, replaced brown-hair wig, and jointed body (repainted, shows wear), redressed in deep plum velvet, stamped "Tete Jumeau 12," 27″ high 2089.00

☐ **Simon & Halbig closed-mouth, bisque-headed doll,** with swivel neck and bisque shoulder plate, pierced ears, blue paperweight eyes, blonde-hair wig, and jointed pink kid body with bisque forearms, incised "949" (minor eye scratches), 18″ high 880.00

☐ **German closed-mouth, bisque shoulder-headed doll,** large, with blue paperweight eyes, auburn-hair wig and kid body with bisque forearms, incised "698," 28″ high 880.00

Left to right. German closed-mouth, turned shoulder-headed doll, large, with solid dome head, blue paperweight eyes, blond mohair wig and kid body with bisque arms, incised "639," 26″ height, $715. Jimeau bisque-headed bebe, with pierced ears, blue paperweight sleeping eyes, replaced brown hair wig and jointed body (repainted, shows wear), redressed in deep plum velvet, stamped "Tete Jumeau 12," 27″ height, $2089. Simon & Halbig closed-mouth, bisque-headed doll, with swivel neck and bisque shoulder plate, pierced ears, blue paperweight eyes, blond hair wig and jointed pink kid body with bisque forearms, incised "949," (minor eye scratches), 18″ height, $880. German closed-mouth, bisque shoulder-headed doll, large, with blue paperweight eyes, auburn hair wig and kid body with bisque forearms, incised "698," 28″ height, $880. (*Photo courtesy of Christie's East, New York*)

	Price Range
☐ **Steiner bisque-headed bebe,** small, with closed mouth, pierced ears, blue paperweight eyes, and five-piece composition body, wearing a gray velvet dress trimmed with rose and matching hat, incised "A3," 11″ high	1100.00

☐ **Heubach Koppelsdorf bisque-headed "Stuart Baby,"** rare version with separately molded cap, closed mouth, blue sleep eyes, and bent-limb body, re-dressed in pink silk trimmed with lace, incised with the sunburst "79 75" (finger chipped), 12″ high 3080.00

☐ **Rohmer bisque-headed lady doll,** with swivel neck, bisque shoulder-plate, closed mouth, fixed blue eyes, curly blonde mohair wig, and jointed kid body with wood upper arms and tinted china forearms, redressed in black silk and lace over period undergarments and ivory leather shoes, stamped "Mme. Rohmer, Paris" in blue on chest, 18″ high 2860.00

☐ **Bisque-headed closed-mouth doll,** large, with blue paperweight eyes, replaced brown hair wig, and jointed body (repainted), wearing a cream silk dress trimmed with lace and ribbons, white fur cape, muff, and silk bonnet, incised "a8," probably Kestner for the French market, 30″ high 1890.00

☐ **Heuback Koppelsdorf black bisque-headed character doll,** with brown sleep eyes, brass hoop earrings, pierced nostrils, and five-piece straight-legged body, redressed as a harem boy, incised "399," 10″ high 308.00

☐ **"Uncle Sam" doll,** 20th century, dressed in a blue felt hat and coat and red and white nylon pants, 16½″ high 180.00

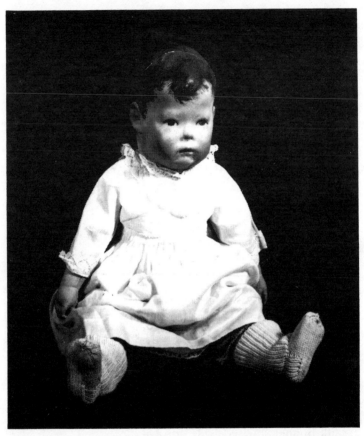

Kathe Kruse boy doll, Model #1, with painted brown eyes and brown hair, wearing a white cotton smock, stamped on feet "Germany" and "Kathe Kruse H 344," 17″ high, $850. (*Photo courtesy of Phillips, New York*)

Price Range

☐ **Kathe Kruse boy doll,** Model No.1, with painted brown eyes and brown hair, wearing a white cotton smock, stamped on feet "Germany" and "Kathe Kruse H 344," 17″ high 850.00

Left to right. French market S & H bisque-headed doll, with closed mouth, large blue paperweight eyes, pierced ears, blond hair wig and jointed body with fixed wrists, wearing a whitework dress, 27″ high, incised "749 DEP 12," $2420. Large Handwerck bisque-headed doll, with pierced ears, blue sleep eyes, blond hair wig and jointed body, wearing a white lawn dress, 31″ high, incised "Simon & Halbig," $605. Large B. F. bisque-headed bebe, with closed mouth, pierced ears, blue paperweight eyes, brown hair wig and jointed body, 27″ high, wearing a white cotton dress, incised "B12F," head probably by Jumeau, $2090. Schmidt bisque-headed bebe, with closed mouth, blue paperweight eyes, pierced ears, brown hair wig and jointed body with fixed wrists, wearing a later blue lace dress, 23″ high, incised with the shield mark on head and body, $6600. (*Photo courtesy of Christie's East, New York*)

Price Range

☐ **French Market S & H bisque-headed doll,** with closed mouth, large blue paperweight eyes, pierced ears, blonde-hair wig, and jointed body with fixed wrists,

Price Range

wearing a whitework dress, incised "749 DEP 12," 27″ high ..   2420.00

☐ **Large Handwerck bisque-headed doll,** with pierced ears, blue sleep eyes, blonde-hair wig, and jointed body, wearing a white lawn dress, incised "Simon & Halbig," 31″ high 605.00

☐ **Large B.F. bisque-headed bebe,** with closed mouth, pierced ears, blue paperweight eyes, brown-hair wig, and jointed body, wearing a white cotton dress, incised "B12F," head probably by Jumeau, 27″ high 2090.00

☐ **Schmidt bisque-headed bebe,** with closed mouth, blue paperweight eyes, pierced ears, brown-hair wig, and jointed body with fixed wrists, wearing a later blue lace dress, incised with the shield mark on head and body, 23″ high   6600.00

☐ **Kestner closed-mouth, bisque-headed doll,** with fixed brown eyes, blonde mohair wig, and jointed body with fixed wrists, wearing a later pink wool jumper, incised "13," 19″ high 1430.00

☐ **Rabery & Delphieu bisque-headed bebe,** with closed mouth, pierced ears, brown paperweight eyes, brown-hair wig, and jointed body with fixed wrists, wearing an embroidered pink dress, incised "R2D," 22″ high 2145.00

☐ **German closed-mouth, bisque, turned shoulder-headed doll,** with fixed blue eyes, blonde mohair wig, and kid body with bisque forearms, wearing a period white lawn dress, 21″ high 352.00

Left to right. Kestner closed-mouth, bisque-headed doll, with fixed brown eyes, blond mohair wig and jointed body with fixed wrists, wearing a later pink wool jumper, 19″ high, incised "13," $1430. Rabery & Delphieu bisque-headed bebe, with closed mouth, pierced ears, brown paperweight eyes, brown hair wig and jointed body with fixed wrists, wearing an embroidered pink dress, 22″ high, incised "R2D," $2145. German closed-mouth, bisque, turned shoulder-headed doll, with fixed blue eyes, blond mohair wig and kid body with bisque forearms, wearing a period white lawn dress, 21″ high, $352. German closed-mouth, bisque, shoulder-headed boy doll, with fixed brown eyes, blond hair wig and kid body with bisque hands, wearing a black velvet suit and lace-trimmed shirt, 18″ high, estimated value $500–$700.

Price Range

☐ **German closed-mouth, bisque, shoulder-headed boy doll,** with fixed brown eyes, blonde-hair wig, and kid body with bisque hands, wearing a black velvet suit and lace-trimmed shirt, 18″ high (estimated value) 500.00 700.00

Eyeglasses

TOPIC: Eyeglasses are devices that enhance eyesight. They consist of one or two glass or plastic lenses and a frame to help the user keep the lenses in front of his eyes.

TYPES: Common types of eyeglasses that collectors are interested in include the quizzing glass, scissors-glasses, temple spectacles, and the lorgnette. The quizzing glass was an early version of the monocle. Scissor-glasses consisted of two eyepieces connected by a hinged handle that was held under the nose. Temple spectacles employ two bars that press against the temples; these are modern eyeglasses. The lorgnette is a pair of eyepieces with a handle on one side.

PERIOD: Although eyeglasses have been available since the 1200s, they did not come into general use until the 1780s.

COMMENTS: Wild styles of eyeglasses from the 1960s are currently in demand among collectors. Prices for these and other types of eyeglasses are still reasonable.

ADDITIONAL TIPS: Old eyeglasses can be found through Lions and Rotary clubs, which collect eyeglasses for the needy. Optometrists' offices are another good source for collectible specimens.

Price Range

☐ **Coin silver,** octagonal lenses, long temporal pieces ending in loops, marked "COIN," in velvet-lined cigar-shaped case 62.00

☐ **Coin silver,** octagonal lenses, with turnpin-type temporal pieces ending in loops, marked "McAllister" 275.00

☐ **Coin silver,** oval lenses, wide, extendable temporal pieces ending in loops, marked "20" 65.00

☐ **Coin silver,** oval lenses, long temporal pieces ending in damaged loops, marked "HARWOOD BROTHERS" 18.00

☐ **Gold-plated,** scissorlike, folding out, oval lenses, decorated short handle with circular loop, catch on handle 65.00

☐ **Green,** oval lenses, turnpin-style temporal pieces with circular loop attachment and small oval loops at ends, in felt-lined tin case 85.00

☐ **Lorgnette,** short decorated handle, oval lenses with spring action, marked "CROWN GOLD PLATED" 45.00

☐ **Lorgnette,** oval lenses with central spring and releasing knob on decorated handle, marked "CROWN SILVER" 45.00

☐ **Lorgnette,** silver frame, folding out, oval lenses, cloth on handle 48.00

☐ **Pince-nez,** patented 1892, in decorated brass case with velvet lining 20.00

☐ **Pince-nez,** oval lenses, movable, padded nasal pieces, short handle 6.00

☐ **Pince-nez,** green oval lenses, padded nasal pieces, short handle 6.00

Price Range

☐ **Pince-nez,** large oval lenses, folding, short decorated handle marked "sterling" 30.00

☐ **Pince-nez,** oval lenses, folding, hard rubber frame, c. 1880, marked "38" 20.00

☐ **Protective,** in original oval tin case 10.00

☐ **Quadrangular lenses,** coin-silver frame with narrow extendable temporal pieces ending in loops, marked "24," in felt-lined tin case, marked "F. Parker, 1868" 60.00

☐ **Quadrangular lenses,** brass frame with narrow extendable temporal pieces ending in loops . 46.00

☐ **Turnpin,** steel frame with wide temporal pieces and large oval loops, lenses missing, in original steel case, 18th century 140.00

☐ **Wire frame,** oval lenses, long temporal pieces ending in loops, in cigar-shaped, leather-covered case 20.00

Firearms

TYPES: Flintlock, breech-loader, revolver.

COMMENTS: Guns have been both weapons of war and a means of survival as well as a source of sport over the centuries. They disrupted the balance of power in Europe by rendering vulnerable the once-invincible knight on horseback. Enthusiasts tend to gravitate between antique and modern weapons. In antique firearms, particular attention is paid to the maker, then to the ornament and detail. Modern firearm collectors concentrate on the type of gun. The following is primarily a list of antique firearms.

Note: Values shown are the actual auction-realized prices.

Price Range

☐ **German 8mm C.F. single-shot, falling-block target rifle,** Schuetzen type, by Ad. Frohn, Suhl, No. 2269, late 19th century, breech-block stamped "Syst Aydt D.R. Patent 793," 31¾″ long 660.00

☐ **Small-bore custom bench-rest single-shot target rifle,** built on a Stevens rolling-block action, by

302

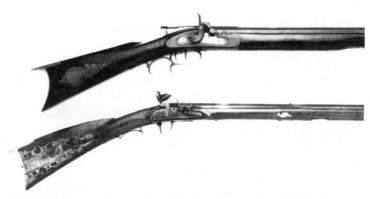

Top. Percussion Kentucky rifle, by George Fay, Blair County, Pennsylvania, mid-19th century, 42 ¼ ″ barrel, $4950. *Bottom.* Flintlock Kentucky rifle, reconverted from percussion, early 19th century, lock signed Josh Golcher, 42 ″ barrel, $550. (*Photo courtesy of Christie's East, New York*)

	Price Range
A. W. Peterson, Denver, Colorado, No. 12903, 30 ¼ ″ barrel ...	4400.00
☐ **Percussion Kentucky rifle,** by George Fay, Blair County, Pennsylvania, mid-19th century, 42 ¼ ″ barrel	4950.00
☐ **Flintlock Kentucky rifle,** reconverted from percussion, early 19th century, lock signed Josh Golcher, 42 ″ barrel	550.00
☐ **Rare Pauly patent breechloading D.B. sporting gun,** signed "Invention Pauly, No. 219," c. 1820, 27 ″ barrel	308.00
☐ **Pauly patent breech-loading D.B. sporting gun,** signed "Inv. on. Pauly a Paris," early 19th century, 30 ″ barrel	462.00

Top. French flintlock carbine, rare, reconverted from percussion, by Valentin Delacroix, Paris, c. 1724, 29 ½ " length, $49,500. *Bottom*. Bohemian D.B. flintlock rifled carbine, unsigned, Taus, mid-18th century, double lock inscribed "In Taus," 33 ½ " length, $2420. (*Photo courtesy of Christie's East, New York*)

	Price Range
☐ **French flintlock carbine,** rare, reconverted from percussion, by Valentin Delacroix, Paris, c. 1724, 29 ½ " long	49,500.00
☐ **Bohemian D.B. flintlock rifled carbine,** unsigned, Taus, mid-18th century, double lock inscribed "In Taus," 33 ½ " long ...	2420.00
☐ **Fine cased German pair of .32 R.F. hammer-rifled target pistols,** by J. P. Sauer & Sohn, Berlin, 16 ¾ "	1085.00
☐ **Cased English .450 C.F. Tranter patent six-shot double-action revolver,** No. 50071, c. 1865, barrel inscribed "Examined, by Wm Moore & Grey, 43 Old Bond Street, London," 10 ¼ "	1210.00
☐ **Cased 11mm Galand patent self-extracting six-shot double-action revolver,** No. 2479, 10 "	4400.00

Cased English .450 C.F. Tranter patent six-shot double-action revolver, No. 50071, c. 1865, barrel inscribed "Examined, by Wm Moore & Grey, 43 Old Bond Street, London," 10¼", $1210. (*Photo courtesy of Christie's East, New York*)

Price Range

☐ **Belgian 6.35mm Le Novo five-shot pocket revolver,** No. 1913, with 1¼" sighted take-down barrel inscribed "P. Huet Lille," 3¾" 275.00

☐ **.32 calibre Moore's patent front-loading six-shot teat-fire revolver,** No. 7092, c. 1865, 7" 462.00

☐ **.31 calibre Sharps patent breech-loading single-shot disk priming pistol,** 1st Model, No. 300, c. 1855, the frame stamped "Sharps Patent Arms Mfed. Fairmont Phila PA.," 9¼" 1760.00

☐ **French 7mm pinfire combined six-shot "Apache" revolver, knife, and knuckleduster,** by L. Dolne Inv. ur, No. 4775, late 19th century, 4¼" long (folded) 2640.00

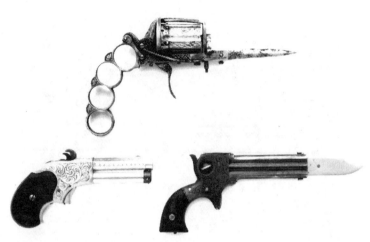

Top. French 7mm pinfire combined six-shot "Apache" revolver, knife and knuckleduster, by L. Dolne Inv. ur, No. 4775, late 19th century, 4 ¼ " long (folded), $2640. *Bottom left*. .32 R.F. Remington-Rider magazine pistol, with engraved barrel stamped "Remington & Sons Ilion NY" and "Riders Pat Aug 15th 1871," 5 ¾ ", $770. *Bottom right*. .22 R.F. Marston patent three-barrel derringer pistol, with retractable knife blade, No. 75, c. 1858, 6 ", $638. (*Photo courtesy of Christie's East, New York*)

	Price Range
☐ **.32 R.F. Remington-Rider magazine pistol,** with engraved barrel stamped "Remington & Sons Ilion NY" and "Riders Pat Aug 15th 1871," 5 ¾ "	770.00
☐ **.22 R.F. Marston patent three-barrel derringer pistol,** with retractable knife blade, No. 75, c. 1858, 6 "	638.00
☐ **.22 R.F. Reid patent knuckleduster revolver,** No. 9841, c. 1883, with engraved silver-plated brass frame stamped "My Friend. Patd. Dec. 2. 1865," 4 ¼ "	550.00
☐ **Chicago Fire Arms Co. revolving seven-shot palm pistol,**	

Top. .22 R.F. Reid patent knuckleduster revolver, No. 9841, c. 1883, with engraved silver-plated brass frame stamped "My Friend. Patd. Dec. 2. 1865," 4 ¼″, $550. *Bottom left*. Chicago Fire Arms Co. revolving seven-shot palm pistol, "The Protector," No. 1380, c. 1894, 5 ¼″, $44,000. *Bottom right*. Chicago Fire Arms Co. revolving seven-shot palm pistol, fitted with Norris double-ring finger guard, No. 2618, c. 1896, stamped "Mfd. by John T. Norris" on one side, and "Springfield, Ohio," on the other, 5 ⁵/₁₆″, $4180. *(Photo courtesy of Christie's East, New York)*

	Price Range
"The Protector," No.1380, c. 1894, 5 ¼″	44,000.00
☐ **Chicago Fire Arms Co. revolving seven-shot palm pistol,** fitted with Norris double-ring finger guard, No. 2618, c. 1896, stamped "Mfd. by John T. Norris" on one side, and "Springfield, Ohio," on the other, 5 ⁵/₁₆″	4180.00
☐ **French Jarre patent breech-loading six-shot pistol,** unsigned, No. 370, 9 ¾″	660.00

Price Range

☐ **French Jarre patent six-barrel breech-loading "Harmonica" pistol,** No. 103, 5½″ 2750.00

☐ **Genhard patent ten-shot turret target pistol,** No. 1011, c. 1853–60, 15¾″ 6820.00

☐ **French 7mm pinfire twenty-shot double-action revolver,** with over-and-under barrels, by E. Lefaucheus, Bte. Paris, No. 1251, c. 1880, 10¼″ 4950.00

☐ **Mexican 9mm pinfire Lefaucheaus-type eighteen-shot double-action revolver,** with over-and-under barrels, unsigned, late 19th century, stamped "Mexico" on the inner face, 11¼″ 1320.00

☐ **Cased French six-shot percussion double-action revolver,** rare, by L. Perrin, Inveur. Bte. a Paris, c. 1840–45, the case's interior lid signed "L. Perrin Bte, Rue Laffitte 51, a Paris," in gilt letters, 11⅞″ 6600.00

☐ **Irish flintlock four-shot "Ducksfoot" tap-action volley pistol,** rare, by McDermot, Dublin, c. 1815, barrel maker's mark "R & W," with spurious London proof marks beneath, 9¼″ 2200.00

Irish flintlock four-shot "Ducksfoot" tap-action volley pistol, rare, by McDermot, Dublin, c. 1815, barrel maker's mark "R & W," with spurious London proof marks beneath, 9 1/4", $2200. (*Photo courtesy of Christie's East, New York*)

Fishing Tackle

DESCRIPTION: Rods, reels, and lures comprise the majority of collectible fishing tackle. The manufacture of fishing tackle did not begin in the United States until around 1810. Prior to that time, all fishing supplies were imported from Europe.

MAKERS: Reels made by J. F. and B. F. Meeks, B. Milan, and Talbot are favored, as are rods made by Hiram Leonard. Some popular companies making lures were Heddon, Shakespeare, Pflueger, Winchester, South Bend, and Jameson, and there are thousands of smaller manufacturers. Ice-spearing decoys (fish decoys), a folk art collectible, have become increasingly desirable among tackle enthusiasts.

COMMENTS: "Silver" used as description of tackle material refers to German silver (alloy), not pure or solid silver.

	Price Range	
☐ **Artificial lure,** Arbogast "tinliz"	10.00	18.00
☐ **Casting rod,** Heddon, split bamboo, 6', c. 1920	80.00	100.00
☐ **Casting rod,** split bamboo, straight handle, 5', c. 1800	45.00	55.00
☐ **Casting rod,** Tonkin, cane, 5½', c. 1900	25.00	45.00

Price Range

☐ **Casting rod,** Union Hardware, 5', c. 1920 .... 15.00 25.00

☐ **Casting rod,** Winchester, split bamboo, c. 1925 .... 20.00 30.00

☐ **Creel fishing basket,** splint weave, pine lid, c. 1900 .... 45.00 75.00

☐ **Creel fishing basket,** splint weave, pine lid, centered hole, c. 1900 .... 45.00 75.00

☐ **Creel fishing basket,** wicker with leather straps, c. 1880 .... 85.00 110.00

☐ **Fishhooks,** set of 50, c. 1910 ... 10.00 15.00

☐ **Flies,** English, set of 12, c. 1880 420.00 440.00

☐ **Fly box,** metal, round, c. 1910 .. 25.00 35.00

☐ **Fly box,** wooden, 6" × 10", c. 1900 .... 55.00 65.00

☐ **Fly rod,** Heddon, split bamboo, 9½', c. 1922 .... 65.00 75.00

☐ **Fly rod,** H. L. Leonard, 8½', c. 1890 .... 165.00 185.00

☐ **Fly rod,** H. L. Leonard, 7', c. 1885 .... 320.00 340.00

☐ **Lure,** Heddon, wooden plug, Dowagiac Minnow 25.00 50.00

☐ **Lure,** Heddon, wooden plug, Heddon's Minnow, #100 series .. 25.00 50.00

☐ **Lure,** Heddon, wooden plug, Meadow Mouse, #4000 series 8.00 10.00

☐ **Lure,** Shakespeare, wooden plug, Darting Shrimp, #135 series 25.00 50.00

☐ **Reel,** Billinghurst, fly, nickel-plated, c. 1869 .... 190.00 250.00

☐ **Reel,** Coxe, casting, aluminum, c. 1940 .... 120.00 140.00

☐ **Reel,** English fly, c. 1850 .... 520.00 620.00

☐ **Reel,** Heddon, casting, c. 1925 .. 55.0 85.00

☐ **Reel,** Hendryx, fly, brass, c. 1890 25.00 35.00

☐ **Reel,** Leonard, fly, bronze, silver trim, c. 1878 .... 470.00 570.00

☐ **Reel,** Leonard, fly, c. 1925 .... 270.00 300.00

	Price Range	
☐ **Reel,** Meek, casting, brass, c. 1855	300.00	500.00
☐ **Reel,** Meek, casting c. 1930	145.00	185.00
☐ **Reel,** Meisselbach, casting, c. 1920	55.00	75.00
☐ **Reel,** Meisselbach, fly, nickel-plated, c. 1895	50.00	70.00
☐ **Reel,** Meisselbach, trolling, wood, c. 1910	25.00	35.00
☐ **Reel,** Milam, casting, brass, c. 1865	250.00	350.00
☐ **Reel,** Milam, casting, c. 1898	170.00	230.00
☐ **Reel,** Mills, fly, nickel, c. 1895	120.00	170.00
☐ **Reel,** Orvis, fly, nickel-plated, c. 1874	120.00	170.00
☐ **Reel,** Orvis, fly, c. 1874	620.00	720.00
☐ **Reel,** Pennell, casting, nickel-plated, c. 1920	40.00	60.00
☐ **Reel,** Pfleuger, casting, brass, c. 1910	25.00	35.00
☐ **Reel,** Pfleuger, casting, c. 1925	60.00	110.00
☐ **Reel,** Pfleuger, fly, rubber, c. 1905	120.00	170.00
☐ **Reel,** Pfleuger, trolling, brass, c. 1915	30.00	40.00
☐ **Reel,** Pfleuger, trolling, c. 1890	40.00	60.00
☐ **Reel,** Sage, fly, c. 1848	350.00	600.00
☐ **Reel,** Shakespeare, casting, plastic, c. 1940	50.00	70.00
☐ **Reel,** Shakespeare, casting, level wind, c. 1922	40.00	60.00
☐ **Reel,** Shakespeare, universal, take-down, c. 1922	12.00	15.00
☐ **Reel,** Shipley, casting, brass, c. 1885	190.00	270.00
☐ **Reel,** Snyder, casting brass, c. 1820	520.00	670.00
☐ **Reel,** South Bend, fly, aluminum, c. 1940	45.00	65.00
☐ **Reel,** Talbot, casting, c. 1920	95.00	145.00

Price Range

☐ **Reel,** Union Hardware, fly, nickel-plated, c.1920	8.00	10.00
☐ **Reel,** Vom Hofe, fly, nickel, small, c. 1890	145.00	195.00
☐ **Reel,** Vom Hofe, trolling, rubber, c. 1918	170.00	240.00
☐ **Reel,** Yawman and Erbe, fly, aluminum, c. 1889	120.00	170.00
☐ **Reel,** Zwarg, trolling, rubber, c. 1950	195.00	275.00
☐ **Rod case,** wood, brass trim, 5′, c. 1880	100.00	120.00
☐ **Spearing decoy,** maker unknown, Michigan, Wisconsin, and Minnesota	25.00	75.00
☐ **Spearing decoy,** Ocsar Pererson, Michigan	200.00	500.00
☐ **Steel casting rod,** Wards, telescopic, 9″, c. 1922	35.00	45.00
☐ **Steel casting rod,** Wards, with case, agate guides, 5½′, c. 1922	35.00	45.00
☐ **Tackle box,** wooden and brass trim, 14″, c. 1910	55.00	65.00
☐ **Tackle box,** metal and brass trim, 16″, c. 1925	55.00	65.00
☐ **Wrought iron fish spear**	15.00	25.00

Flasks

DESCRIPTION: Flasks are containers with a broad body and narrow neck, often fitted with a closure. Usually they were used to hold alcoholic beverages.

TYPES: There were many variations of flask bottles produced, including figural and portrait flasks.

PERIOD: Usually collectors search for flasks from the early 1800s through the early 1900s. Before 1810 few glass containers were manufactured.

COMMENTS: Flasks with portraits of presidents or other politicians are highly sought after by collectors.

Note: The values shown are the actual auction-realized prices.

	Price Range
☐ **Bennington pottery book flask,** mottled green and brown flint glaze, 6″ high, spine marked "Bennington Battle"	450.00
☐ **Bennington brownware book flask,** mottled brown glaze, 5¾″ high, spine marked "Departed Spirits"	450.00

Left to right. German circular powder-flask, early 17th century, the body inlaid with horn pellets, central plug of turned bone, brass top with nozzle and spring-lever cover, $250. Italian powder flask, entirely of steel, early 17th century, 7½″ height, $275. German circular powder flask, late 16th or early 17th century, body with a central horn-lined hole and profusely inlaid in black, white, and green-stained horn with designs of circular medallions framed by overlapping concentric circles of brass wire, the cap cast with initials "GR" within a wreath, retaining its original woven suspension cord with two silk tassels, 4¾″ height, $935. (*Photo courtesy of Christie's East, New York*)

	Price Range
☐ **English silver overlay glass flask,** slender cylindrical body of clear glass with decorative floral overlay, separable sterling jigger that fits the base snugly, 6¼″ long, together with a silver-mounted crystal decanter, retailed by Saks with key for unlocking the stopper, in leather case	165.00
☐ **German circular powder flask,** early 17th century, body inlaid with horn pellets, central plug of turned bone, brass top with nozzle and spring-lever cover	250.00

Price Range

☐ **Italian powder flask,** entirely of steel, early 17th century, 7½″ height 275.00

☐ **German circular powder flask,** late 16th or early 17th century, central horn-lined hole and profusely inlaid in black, white, and green-stained horn with designs of circular medallions framed by overlapping concentric circles of brass wire, cap cast with initials "GR" within a wreath, retaining its original woven suspension cord with two silk tassels, 4¾″ high 935.00

☐ **German powder flask,** late 16th or early 17th century, flattened cowhorn body of curved triangular form with later brass mounts, engraved on the outer face with a circular cartouche containing a demifigure in pseudo-Classical armor, flanked by designs of flowers, 12″ 275.00

☐ **German circular powder flask,** early 18th century, turned wooden body inlaid with engraved horn and bone hounds, foxes and hares in patterns of running foliage and ball-flowers, 6¼″ height 440.00

☐ **German staghorn powder flask,** late 16th or early 17th century, forked body of natural horn, the outer face carved with the figures of King David and Bathsheba, 6½″ high 440.00

☐ **German staghorn powder flask,** late 16th or early 17th century, forked body, the inner face engraved with foliage, the outer

face finely engraved with the allegory of ill fortune, involving a
winged female figure raising her
skirts to a harpie, a crayfish at her
feet, and the inscription "Inforv-
nium Das Vnglvck," 9 ½ ″ high ..   825.00

Folk Art

DESCRIPTION: Originally the term used to describe painting and sculpture done by untrained artists; today the term is given to all handcrafted items.

TYPES: Various types of folk art sculpture include dolls, toys, animals, jewelry, and bottlecap sculpture. Four types of folk art painting include paintings done by stencil, called theorems; drawings that display unique penmanship skills, called calligraphic; frakturs, which were ornately designed certificates of birth, baptism, or marriage; and mourning pictures, to commemorate the death of a loved one.

PERIOD: Folk art has no specific period; it is still made today.

ORIGIN: The original popularity of folk art dates to the 1920s and the first folk art exhibits at the Whitney Studio Club (later the Whitney Museum of American Art) and the Museum of Modern Art.

COMMENTS: Until the 1920s the value of folk art was largely ignored because its distortion of size and scale was not considered artistic. Today such Americana collectibles are much sought after. Reasonably priced pieces can be found, especially those from the 19th and 20th centuries.

Price Range

☐ **Banjo,** snakeskin head, three-string, 31″ 60.00 80.00

☐ **Barber's pole,** with hitching post 150.00 170.00

☐ **Bird,** cloth, Victorian 40.00 75.00

☐ **Bird in hoop,** green and yellow painted wood parrot perched in a wrought-iron hoop; 19th century, 14″ 675.00 725.00

☐ **Blanket chest,** Chippendale, front is painted with a compote filled with red and yellow flowers and bordered with yellow floral vines on a painted red and black background, signed Miss H. Taylor in pencil inside lid, 19th century, 8″ × 19″ × 7¼″ 1000.00 1500.00

☐ **Boat,** model, wood, c. 1900 ...... 40.00 70.00

☐ **Bootjack,** wooden, unpainted ... 10.00 20.00

☐ **Bottlecap sculpture,** snake 160.00 190.00

☐ **Bottlecap sculpture,** carved heads of a man and woman, c. 1930 .... 80.00 115.00

☐ **Box,** hinged lid has three overlapping hearts carved, edge is painted black, green sponge decoration on bottom, 14″ × 9″ × 5″ 75.00 95.00

☐ **Bride's box,** painted bentwood, late 18th century, 6½″ × 18¼″ 395.00 495.00

☐ **Butcher's shop sign,** carved pig painted pink-orange, inscribed MEAT in black letters, wrought-iron tail, iron suspension rings, c. 1930, 12″ × 26″ 1400.00 1500.00

☐ **Candle box,** pine planked construction, painted red, 14″ 300.00 350.00

☐ **Carving,** bird, wood, painted, 6″ 40.00 60.00

☐ **Cigar store Indian,** Princess, c. 1880, 61″ 4500.00 5500.00

	Price Range	
☐ **Coffeepot,** Toleware, decorated with painted red flowers on green stems with yellow leaves, dark brown background, convex hinged lid, conical shape, 19th century, 8¼″	900.00	950.00
☐ **Cow,** felt, painted face, 9″	30.00	40.00
☐ **Cradle,** doll, pine, original paint, 18th century	225.00	275.00
☐ **Crock,** marked White's-Utica 3, decorated with a dark blue flower, stem and leaves, open top	160.00	180.00
☐ **Decoy,** swan, original paint, hollow construction, cedar	950.00	1075.00
☐ **Decoy,** wooden bluebill, glass eyes, weighted bottom, some bullet marks	35.00	55.00
☐ **Decoy,** wooden bluebill, painted eyes, original paint	45.00	55.00
☐ **Decoy,** wooden, Canadian goose in gray, white, black, and brown, 27″	40.00	50.00
☐ **Dentzel carousel cat,** with fish in mouth	3400.00	3600.00
☐ **Doll,** dancer, jointed wood, hand operated, 14½″, 19th century	200.00	240.00
☐ **Doll,** reversible face, dress and color, 14″	275.00	320.00
☐ **Face mask,** carved, man's face	125.00	145.00
☐ **Figure,** Black preacher, carved and painted wood, initials DC carved on chest, 10″	3000.00	3120.00
☐ **Figure,** cast-iron form of a woman holding two trays in her hands, painted polychrome, 12⅝″ × 11″	1000.00	1100.00
☐ **Flute,** pine, 15″	60.00	80.00
☐ **Footstool,** wooden, pumpkin top with two ends, black and red underneath, 12″ × 8″ × 7″	55.00	75.00

Price Range

☐ **Footstool,** wooden with turned legs, square nailed construction, 10″ × 9″ × 6″ 40.00   50.00

☐ **Fraktur,** part printed, part hand-colored, Victorian frame 50.00   70.00

☐ **Game,** checkered game board, splined, signed, 19″ × 29″ 80.00   115.00

☐ **Game,** ring toss, 5 rings, c. 1900   50.00   80.00

☐ **Game,** skittles, ornate steeple in center, 19th century 200.00   250.00

☐ **Gatepost finial,** carved Statue of Liberty finial made of pine, wrought-iron crown spokes, traces of black and yellow poly-chrome, c. 1900, 19¾″ 2500.00   3500.00

☐ **Hooked rugs,** picture of dog in the middle encircled by dark blue with purple border, set of two, c. 1910, 45″ × 26″ 300.00   400.00

☐ **Hooked rug,** two black and two white horses on vertical striped background, 49″ × 26″ 150.00   250.00

☐ **Indian beaded box/purse,** cat design on one side, 1908 on opposite side 55.00   75.00

☐ **Miniature,** bookcase on chest, accessories, 11¾″ × 9½″ 160.00   200.00

☐ **Miniature,** furniture, set of 3 chairs, painted 60.00   80.00

☐ **Miniature,** windmill, wood, tin blades, 21″ 75.00   100.00

☐ **Mourning picture,** embroidery on silk, 16″ × 20″ 330.00   365.00

☐ **Oil on board,** little girl in hooded cape, 7″ × 9″, c. 1820 .... 125.00   175.00

☐ **Oil on board,** rat terrier with rat, 19th century 275.00   325.00

☐ **Oil on canvas,** apples and book, 8″ × 10″ 390.00   425.00

☐ **Oil on canvas,** boy, girl, lamb, mid-19th century 130.00   170.00

	Price Range	
☐ **Oil on canvas,** fruit and bird, unframed, 24″ × 18″, c. 1835	550.00	650.00
☐ **Oil on canvas,** Irish setter, 16″ × 19″, framed	325.00	380.00
☐ **Picture,** cut paper, white cut into a design against a red background, c. 1850	425.00	500.00
☐ **Portraits,** man and woman (pair), unsigned, 19th century	350.00	400.00
☐ **Portrait,** miniature, on ivory, bust of man in coat, gold frame with leaves and flowers, 19th century	1900.00	2400.00
☐ **Portraits,** pair, signed, G. H. Blackburn, 30″ × 28″ framed, c. 1886	325.00	375.00
☐ **Rag doll,** Amish, embroidered face	90.00	100.00
☐ **Rag doll,** Amish, faceless, Amish outfit	65.00	75.00
☐ **Rag doll,** handmade of floss eyes, nose, mouth, and hair, blue and white dress, 11″	20.00	50.00
☐ **Rag doll,** made from a printed pattern, c. 1930s	40.00	50.00
☐ **Rocking horse,** wooden shoofly, with seat between sides of horse	100.00	200.00
☐ **Sewing stand,** to hang on wall, set of 3 spool holders on top shelf, hand-carved diamond design around top border, carved heart and three initials on second shelf, natural pine darkened with time	55.00	75.00
☐ **Shelves,** two shelves, stripped down with blue, red, and gray showing, checkerboard showing on the back, 10″ × 14″ × 4″ ..	45.00	55.00
☐ **Spreaders,** wooden, original mustard-colored paint, set of two, 29″	20.00	30.00

Price Range

☐ **Storks,** carved and painted, c. 1910, 20″ pair 380.00 420.00

☐ **Toy,** baby rattle, hand-carved, 9″ 80.00 115.00

☐ **Toy,** climbing clown, flat, made of cardboard in red and blue polka dots 10.00 25.00

☐ **Toy,** "Froggie" of the Andy Devine Show, green, red, white, and black rubber, 5″ 10.00 20.00

☐ **Toy,** monkey on pole, hand-carved 70.00 100.00

☐ **Toy,** pecking chicken, hand-carved 60.00 85.00

☐ **Toy,** rocking horse, handmade .. 60.00 85.00

☐ **Toy,** sheep on wheels, hand-carved 130.00 170.00

☐ **Toy,** train, hand-carved, painted, 23″, 19th century 110.00 135.00

☐ **Whirligig,** Black man made of wood wearing a yellow hat and jacket, red pants, and black boots, paddle baffles on the arms, round base, Maine, early 20th century .. 3900.00 4400.00

☐ **Whirligig,** cast-iron, painted, man turning grindstone 475.00 545.00

☐ **Whirligig,** wooden duck, glass eyes, mounted on a wood fence post 60.00 75.00

☐ **Whirligig,** wooden Indian, carved and painted, 11½″ 1700.00 1800.00

Furniture

COMMENTS: Interest in antique and collectible furniture is growing, according to auction houses and dealers around the country. Record prices were realized for American Federal and Victorian period pieces this year. European furniture is also very strong. Experts feel that the current design trends featuring "country" and Victorian styles have had a major impact on this upward movement in the popularity of antique furniture.

Note: The values shown are the actual auction-realized prices.

	Price Range
☐ **Aesthetic Movement walnut desk,** by Kimbel and Cabus, with scrolled strap work, 65 ½″ high, 38″ wide, 20 ½″ deep	3100.00
☐ **Aesthetic Movement fireplace surround,** carved and inlaid with walnut, by Herter Brothers, c. 1880, stamped "Herter Bros," 74″ wide, 15 ½″ deep	17,600.00
☐ **Anglo-Indian rosewood sofa,** c. 1840, carved cane backrest	

Aesthetic Movement walnut desk, by Kimbel and Cabus, with scrolled strap work, 65 ½″ high, 38″ wide, 20 ½″ deep, $3100. (*Photo courtesy of Phillips, New York*)

	Price Range
continuing to scrolled arms above a cane seat on shaped French feet, 83 ½″ long	1500.00
☐ **Art Deco desk and chair,** double pedestal, by Rene Prou, c. 1933, with four drawers in each undulating pedestal, the swivel chair en suite, 86 ½″ wide, 39 ¼″ deep, 29″ high	2200.00

Art Moderne bar cabinet, marquetry-inlaid walnut, by Andrew Szoeke, 41″ high, 68″ long, 19″ wide, $2200. (*Photo courtesy of Christie's East, New York*)

	Price Range
☐ **Art Deco sideboard,** marble top, Maccassar ebony, bombé, attributed to Dominique, shaped black marble top over arched four-door cabinet with elm interior, 43″ high, 84″ long, 24″ wide	1870.00
☐ **Art Moderne bar cabinet,** marquetry-inlaid walnut, by Andrew Szoeke, 41″ high, 68″ long, 19″ wide	2200.00
☐ **Arts and Crafts oak armchair,** possibly by Cincinnati Shop O'The Crafters	600.00
☐ **Bentwood music stand,** by Thonat, shaped folio rack above a plywood undertier etched with a lyre	1200.00
☐ **Bentwood coatrack,** by Thonet, 78″ high	600.00

Arts and Crafts oak armchair, possibly by Cincinnati Shop O'The Crafters, $600. (*Photo courtesy of Phillips, New York*)

Price Range

☐ **Chippendale-style mahogany dining chairs,** set of ten, comprising two arms and eight sides, shaped crest over pierced splat with leather-upholstered slip seat, on cabriole legs ending in claw-and-ball feet .... 4600.00 •

Chippendale mahogany and giltwood wall mirror, 18th century, the carved and scrolled gilt pediment centering a spread-wing phoenix above a carved and gilt mahogany frame, 23″ high, $6500. (*Photo courtesy of Phillips, New York*)

Price Range

☐ **Chippendale mahogany and giltwood wall mirror,** 18th century, the carved and scrolled gilt pediment centering a spread-wing phoenix above a carved and gilt mahogany frame, 23″ high .. 6500.00

☐ **Chippendale reverse serpentine mahogany chest of drawers,** Massachusetts, c. 1780, the molded serpentine top above the case with four graduated drawers, molded base ending in claw-and-ball feet, 35″ high, 45½″ long, 24″ deep 6600.00

Chippendale reverse serpentine mahogany chest of drawers, Massachusetts, c. 1780, the molded serpentine top above the case with four graduated drawers, molded base ending in claw-and-ball feet, 35″ high, 45½″ long, 24″ deep, $6600. (*Photo courtesy of Phillips, New York*)

	Price Range	
☐ **Continental painted blanket chest,** dated 1790, hinged lid opening to a fitted interior, two floral-decorated front panels, molded base, 20″ high, 47″ long, 24″ deep	1000.00	1500.00
☐ **Federal mahogany fine sofa,** made in New England, c. 1805 ..		46,000.00

Continental painted blanket chest, dated 1790, the hinged lid opening to a fitted interior, the case with two floral, decorated front panels, on molded base, 20″ high, 47″ long, 24″ deep, $1000–$1500. (*Photo courtesy of Phillips, New York*)

Federal mahogany fine sofa, made in New England, c. 1805, $46,000 (estimate was $6000–$9000). (*Photo courtesy of Phillips, New York*)

Federal inlaid mahogany console table, Massachusetts, c. 1810, 35″ high, 24″ long, 16½″ deep, $18,700 (estimate was $800–$1200). (*Photo courtesy of Phillips, New York*)

	Price Range
☐ **Federal inlaid mahogany console table,** Massachusetts, c. 1810, 35″ high, 24″ long, 16½″ deep	18,700.00
☐ **Louis XVI semanier,** petite, ormolu-mounted tulipwood and kingwood, late 18th century, 45″ high, 19½″ wide, 12″ deep	2640.00

Modern Gothic oak dresser, attributed to Kimbel and Cabus, mirror enclosed in a carved and incised frame, 92″ high, 50″ wide, 23″ deep, $1500. (*Photo courtesy of Phillips, New York*)

Price Range

☐ **Modern Gothic oak dresser,** attributed to Kimbel and Cabus, mirror enclosed in a carved and incised frame, 92″ high, 50″ wide, 23″ deep 1500.00

Neo-classic Continental side table, walnut, late 18th century, probably German, 28½" high, 33" wide, 16½" deep, $1760. (*Photo
courtesy of Christie's East, New York*)

	Price Range
☐ **Neo-classic Continental side table,** walnut, late 18th century, probably German, 28½" high, 33" wide, 16½" deep	1760.00

Renaissance, Italian, buffet, walnut, 16th century, 49″ high, 76″ wide, 25½″ deep, $2640. (*Photo courtesy of Christie's East, New York*)

	Price Range
☐ **Italian Renaissance buffet,** walnut, 16th century, 49″ high, 76″ wide, 25½″ deep	2640.00
☐ **Renaissance Revival rosewood parlor suite,** attributed to Jeliff, comprising a sofa, a gentleman's armchair and three side chairs, fully carved Minerva-head arms	2400.00
☐ **Rococo, Continental, center table,** green-painted and parcelgilt, 18th century, 30″ high, 31″ wide, 20½″ deep	2420.00

Rococo, German, oak armoire, mid-18th century, 105 ¼ " high, 56 ½ " wide, 15 " deep, $8800. (*Photo courtesy of Christie's East, New York*)

	Price Range
☐ **Rococo, Continental, open armchairs,** pair, mid-18th century	7700.00
☐ **Rococo, German, oak armoire,** mid-18th century, 105 ¼ " high, 56 ½ " wide, 15 " deep	8800.00

Rococo, German, library cabinets, pair, giltwood-mounted, mid-18th century, 93″ high, 58″ wide, 22″ deep, $16,500. (*Photo courtesy of Christie's East, New York*)

Price Range

☐ **Rococo, Italian, open arm-chairs,** pair, walnut, mid-18th century, upholstered in yellow and white cotton damask 4400.00

Victorian overstuffed sofas, pair, c. 1880, upholstered and tufted in a rust brocade with a tasseled trim, 4″ long, $1100. (*Photo courtesy of Phillips, New York*)

	Price Range
☐ **Rococo, German, library cabinets,** pair, giltwood-mounted, mid-18th century, 93″ high, 58″ wide, 22″ deep	16,500.00
☐ **Victorian overstuffed sofas,** pair, c. 1880, upholstered and tufted in a rust brocade with a tasseled trim, 4″ long	1100.00

20th century "Skyscraper" bookcase, Paul T. Frankl, painted black with silver edging, 83″ high, 79″ total width, $18,700. (*Photo courtesy of Phillips, New York*)

Price Range

☐ **20th-century "Skyscraper" bookcase,** Paul T. Frankl, painted black with silver edging, 83″ high, 79″ total width 18,700.00

Glassware

COMMENTS: Collecting glassware is one of the most enjoyable hobbies because the properties of the glass itself contribute so much to the pleasure in collecting. There is something so aesthetically pleasing in seeing light pass through colored glass or reflect off the countless facets of cut lead crystal. Glass is so pristine and pure in its look, feel, and sound. Glassware is also so abundant that nearly everyone collects glass whether or not they consider themselves to be collectors. Regardless of economic level, there has always been glassware that was affordable to all and that has now probably become highly collectible.

TYPES: American, Carnival, cut, Daum Nancy, Depression, Emile Galle, European, Lalique, Steuben, Tiffany, Thomas Webb.

Note: Values shown are the actual auction-realized prices.

AMERICAN GLASS

Price Range

☐ **Bud vase,** royal Flemish enameled glass, by Mt. Washington,

Price Range

footed diamond body with shaped cylindrical neck, in mottled yellow glass, the foot in blue enamel, the midsection with gilt honeycomb pattern, the neck with Persian-inspired ogee design in orange, blue, and pink enamels with gilt detailing, marked "1193/1, B347," 10¼" high 418.00

☐ **Plates,** set of ten, Chintz glass, by Nash, with blue and green internal decoration fanning from the center, inscribed "403" and "Nash," 8⅝" diameter 605.00

☐ **Vase,** two-handled Sicilian lava vase, by Mt. Washington, black with irregularly shaped inclusions of bright-colored glass, unmarked, 9" high 4620.00

CARNIVAL GLASS

DESCRIPTION: In 1905, Taffeta, or Carnival glass as it has come to be known, was born out of the turn-of-the-century craze for iridescent art glass. Using mass production and new chemical techniques, Carnival glass was widely produced toward the end of the Art Nouveau period. Tastes changed, however, ushering in the streamlined Art Deco period. Even though it continued to be produced until 1930, by 1925 Carnival glass was on the way out. With a dwindling market, this glass was sold by the trainload to fairs and carnivals to be given away as prizes. Hence, it has come to be called Carnival glass.

ADDITIONAL TIPS: Intense collector interest has already driven the prices of Carnival glass into the astronomical range. An amethyst Carnival farmyard plate sold for $8,000 just this year. The tables have really been turned in this field over the years as this originally cheap imitation of art glass now far exceeds in value the high-quality glass it sought to imitate. Long regarded with disdain by serious dealers,

Vase, two-handled Sicilian lava vase, by Mt. Washington, black with irregularly shaped inclusions of bright-colored glass, unmarked, 9″ high, $4620. (*Photo courtesy of Christie's East, New York*)

collectors, and auction houses, Carnival glass is now turning up on the more prestigious auction blocks in the country. Carnival glass auctions demonstrated one thing clearly: Carnival glass continues to command higher and higher prices with no ceiling in sight. Examples of auction results are: rare, one-of-a-kind Acorn Burrs aqua-opalescent punch bowl, base, and five cups, $12,500; purple Christmas compote, $1550; large green Hobstar and Feather rosebowl, $1150; amethyst Inverted Thistle pitcher, $2100; teal blue Grape and Cable plate, $1150; and amethyst Farmyard bowl, $1400.

	Price Range
☐ **Acorn Burrs,** punch cups, two, each	35.00
☐ **Apple Tree,** tumbler	45.00
☐ **Bushel Baskets**	
☐ purple	70.00

	Price Range
☐ blue	75.00
☐ marigold	60.00
☐ white, 8-sided	140.00
☐ **Daisy and Plume,** footed candy dish, Raspberry interior pattern	125.00
☐ **Fenton,** 5-piece berry set, deep marigold	175.00
☐ **Fernery,** footed	40.00
☐ **French Knots,** hattie	45.00
☐ **Golden Wedding,** pint whiskey bottle	35.00
☐ **Grape and Cable,** master ice cream bowl, white	245.00
☐ **Grape and Cable,** footed bowl, ice blue, 8 1/2″ diameter	395.00
☐ **Millersburg Trout and Fly,** ice cream bowl, radium finish, rare	595.00
☐ **Northwood Grape and Cable,** punch set	
☐ purple	375.00
☐ marigold	400.00
☐ **Orange Tree,** breakfast set	135.00
☐ **Orange Tree,** bowl, 8 1/2″ diameter	115.00
☐ **Peach,** covered butter dish, frosty color	295.00
☐ **Persian Garden,** 5-piece ice cream set, white, very rare	795.00
☐ **Singing Bird,** individual berry bowls, each	35.00
☐ **Stork and Rushes,** punch cup	20.00
☐ **Wishbone,** footed bowl	65.00
☐ **Wreath Cherry,** tumbler	45.00
☐ **Wreath of Roses,** 8-piece punch set, purple	375.00

CUT GLASS

DESCRIPTION: Cut glass features deep prismatic cutting in elaborate, often geometrical designs. The edges are very sharp, thus allowing light to be refracted easily. Its high lead content makes it heavier than most blown glass. It also has a distinct bell tone when struck.

ORIGIN: It developed during the 16th century in Bohemia and was very popular until the invention of molded pressed glass in America about 1825, which was an inexpensive imitation of cut glass. It enjoyed a revival during the Brilliant period of cut glass in America, which dated from 1876 to 1916.

PROCESS: The making of cut glass was a time-consuming process requiring the patience and talent of master craftsmen. The glass was handblown of the finest 35 to 45% lead crystal and poured into molds to produce the shaped piece, called a blank. These blanks were anywhere from $1/4''$ to $1/2''$ thick in order to achieve the deep cutting that distinguished this glass from later periods. The resulting finished product was therefore exceedingly heavy.

The cutting and polishing was accomplished in four steps. The first step involved making the desired pattern on the blank with crayons or paint. Next the deepest cuts were made by rough cutting. This was accomplished by pressing the blank on an abrasive cutting wheel of metal or stone that was lubricated by a small stream of water and sand. In the third step the rough cuts were smoothed with a finer stone wheel and water only. Finally, polishing or "coloring" was done on a wooden wheel with putty powder or pumice in order to produce the gleaming brilliant finish.

	Price Range	
☐ **Center bowl,** crystal, circular flaring form, scroll and foliate cut decoration, $11\,3/4''$ diameter	100.00	150.00
☐ **Fruit bowl,** circular form with scalloped rim, traditional cut decoration, $8''$ diameter	80.00	120.00
☐ **Liquor set,** comprising a stoppered $9''$ decanter and four cordials, fan, notch, and floral cut decoration overall	100.00	150.00
☐ **Liquor decanter,** Canadian, inverted pear form with faceted lid and wooden spigot, $29\,1/2''$ high .		50.00

	Price Range
☐ **Stoppered decanter,** spherical form, stick neck, cranberry cut through to clear, depicting cherry blossoms, 13″ high	75.00
☐ **Tray,** circular form, fan and diamond cut decoration, 2″ diameter	140.00
☐ **Vase,** Hawkes crystal, flaring cylindrical form on square pedestal base with floral and foliate cut decoration, 10¼″ high	95.00

DAUM NANCY

☐ **Vase,** art glass, egg form, mottled black and green ground with gold expanded foil decoration, signed Daum Nancy with the Cross of Lorraine and bearing a paper label numbered 33770, 27″ high	1000.00	1200.00

DEPRESSION GLASS

DESCRIPTION: Colored glassware was machine-made during the Depression years of the late 1920s and early 1930s. The glass was available in ten-cent stores, given away at filling stations, and theaters, and used for promotional purposes. There are approximately 150,000 collectors, and the popularity is steadily increasing each year. There are over eighty Depression Glass clubs that sponsor shows, with attendance in the thousands.

COMMENTS: Of the approximately 100 different patterns and colors produced, rose pink remains the favorite color. Luncheon sets of 16 pieces sold new for as low as $1.29. Today a dinner service, depending on the scarcity of the pattern, may cost from $100 to $1000.

	Price Range
☐ **American Sweetheart,** pink	
☐ cup	8.50
☐ sugar bowl	6.50
☐ creamer	7.00
☐ **Blue Bubble,** plate, 9⅜″ diameter	3.50
☐ **Concave,** tumbler	17.00
☐ **Crystal Harp**	
☐ cup	4.00
☐ plate	3.00
☐ **Doric,** tall candy dish, green	20.00
☐ **Floragold,** pitcher	15.00
☐ **Florentine**	
☐ pitcher, 7½″ high	120.00
☐ salt and pepper	35.00
☐ covered butter dish	110.00
☐ custard cup	35.00
☐ **Georgian,** butter dish, green	55.00
☐ **Iris Crystal**	
☐ cup	7.50
☐ plate, 5½″ diameter	6.00
☐ plate, 9″ diameter	8.50
☐ **Laurel Ivory,** candlesticks, pair	15.00
☐ **Manhattan,** wine glasses, set of 12	288.00
☐ **Pink Holiday,** 52-oz pitcher	20.00
☐ **Pink Holiday,** plate, 9″ diameter	8.50
☐ **Rock Crystal,** compote, 7″ diameter	25.00
☐ **Sierra Pink,** creamer	5.00

EMILE GALLE

☐ **Vase,** amber and cherry sprig triple overlay, mold-blown glass, translucent amber ground with burgundy leaves and red cherries, burgundy rim and foot, signed

Price Range

with the cameo signature, 11 3/8″ high 6000.00

☐ **Vase,** two-color, cameo, burnt umber cut to clear, signed, 9 1/2″ high 1300.00

☐ **Vase,** art glass, amber, ribbed form with flaring neck, enameling over gold leaf, signed Emile Galle, also bearing a floral signature and various annotations, 8 1/2″ diameter, 8 1/4″ high 1500.00   2000.00

EUROPEAN GLASS

☐ **Bohemian decanter and two glasses,** amethyst, gilt and colorless cut glass, decanter 11 1/2″ high 275.00

☐ **Venetian glass decanters,** pair, silver-mounted, silver collars marked, 9 1/2″ high 495.00

☐ **Jar,** Verrerie de Sevres, c. 1900, floral cameo cut glass surmounted by bronze mounts and raised on silver-plated mounts, signed "VS" with sailing ship, 6″ high 130.00

LALIQUE GLASS

☐ **Chrysis,** opalescent glass car mascot, etched "R.LALIQUE/ FRANCE" with wooden mount, 4 3/4″ high, ...   12,100.00

☐ **Bacchantes,** gray stained opalescent glass vase, etched "R.LALIQUE FRANCE," 9 3/8″ high 15,400.00

☐ **Sirenes,** opalescent glass brule parfum, molded "R. LALIQUE," 6 5/8″ high 1100.00

Bohemian decanter and two glasses, amethyst, gilt and colorless cut glass, the decanter 11 ½ " high, $275. (*Photo courtesy of Christie's East, New York*)

	Price Range
☐ **Formose,** brown patinated glass vase, bulbous, molded with Japanese goldfish, inscribed "R. Lalique, France," 7 " high	440.00
☐ **Meplat Sirenes,** frosted glass cologne bottle, large, inscribed "R. Lalique, France," stopper frozen, 14 ¼ " high	2420.00
☐ **Oran,** wrought-iron mounted opalescent glass vase, by Paul Kiss and R. Lalique, vase inscribed "R. LALIQUE FRANCE," base marked "PAUL KISS PARIS," together 16 " high	6380.00
☐ **Vase,** turquoise glass	3850.00

Vase, turquoise glass, $3850. (*Photo courtesy of Butterfield & Butterfield, San Francisco*)

Price Range

STEUBEN GLASS

☐ **Candlesticks,** pair, blue Aurene glass, inscribed "Aurene 2933," 10¼" high 880.00

☐ **Vase,** gold Aurene glass, inscribed "Steuben Aurene 6627," 6¼" high 660.00

☐ **Vase,** blue Aurene floriform, inscribed "Aurene 312," 12" high 935.00

Left to right. Candlesticks, pair, blue Aurene glass, inscribed "Aurene 2933," 10¼" high, $880. Vase, gold Aurene glass, inscribed "Steuben Aurene 6627," 6¼" high, $660. Vase, blue Aurene floriform, inscribed "Aurene 312," 12" high, $935. Vase, blue Aurene floriform, inscribed "Steuben Aurene 312," 8¼" high, $825. (*Photo courtesy of Christie's East, New York*)

	Price Range
☐ **Vase,** blue Aurene floriform, inscribed "Steuben Aurene 312," 8¼" high	825.00
☐ **Caviar bowl and liner,** blue Aurene glass, conical bowl with inverted rim, round liner on three conical feet, inscribed "Aurene 3078," 6" high, 10" diameter	880.00

Left to right. Cluthra urn, pink mottled glass with twin opal handles, unsigned, 10¼″ high, $1650. Cluthra rose jar, in mottled blue glass, stamped "Steuben," 9″ high, $770. Cintra two-handled bowl, orange bowl trimmed in blue, clear handles holding blue twist rings on blue, knopped circular foot, model 2942, unsigned, 9″ high, $2860. (*Photo courtesy of Christie's East, New York*)

	Price Range
☐ **Cluthra urn,** pink mottled glass with twin opal handles, unsigned, 10¼″ high	1650.00
☐ **Cluthra rose jar,** mottled blue glass, stamped "Steuben," 9″ high	770.00
☐ **Cintra two-handled bowl,** orange bowl trimmed in blue, clear handles holding blue twist rings on blue knopped circular foot, Model 2942, unsigned, 9″ high ..	2860.00
☐ **Footed bowl,** gold Aurene glass, circular pedestal foot supporting deep bowl, inscribed "Aurene 2899," 11½″ diameter	286.00

☐ **Loving cup,** intaglio-carved crystal, two-handled, c. 1940, Strawberry Mansion pattern, square faceted base supporting flared cup with decoration of eagle above medallion encircled by floral wreaths, drapery swag border, inscribed "Steuben," 13″ high 2200.00

☐ **Pedestal candy dish,** gold Aurene glass, circular foot supporting bulbous stem and low bowl, inscribed "Aurene 2642," with remnants of paper label, 8″ high 462.00

☐ **Vase,** blue Aurene floriform, circular foot, supporting tapered vase with ruffled rim, inscribed "Aurene 312," 12″ high 935.00

☐ **Verre de soie glass bowl,** wide circular bowl with ruffled rim, green twined border, unsigned, 15 3/4″ diameter 198.00

TIFFANY STUDIOS

☐ **Compote,** gold Favrille glass, flared rim, short stem, and circular foot, inscribed "L.C. Tiffany-Favrille," 3 3/8″ high 264.00

☐ **Vase,** iridescent Rosaline glass, with silver resist, signed L.C. Tiffany, 3 3/4″ diameter 800.00

☐ **Vase,** gold Favrille glass, ovoid body with vertical ridges, bulbous neck and scalloped rim in gold iridescence, inscribed "L.C. Tiffany Favrille 1100-91581," 4 5/8″ high 385.00

Vase, large, applied gold Favrille glass, inscribed "L.C. Tiffany Favrille 8157C" and with firm's paper label, 18½" high, $3190. (*Photo courtesy of Christie's East, New York*)

Price Range

☐ **Vase,** large, applied gold Favrille glass, inscribed "L.C. Tiffany Favrille 8157C" and with firm's paper label, 18½" high 3190.00

Left to right. Vase, decorated green Favrille glass, decorated with silvery trailing lily pads and stems, inscribed "L.C. Tiffany-Favrille 670H," 6″ high, $1320. Vase, green Favrille glass, decorative pulled design in iridescent gold at the shoulder, with paper label, 4½″ high, $935. Loving Cup, three-handled, in gold iridescence decorated with green trailing vines at the rim and large, green ivy leaves in between the handles, inscribed "L.C. Tiffany-Favrille 9657C," 5¼″ high, $1210. (*Photo courtesy of Christie's East, New York*)

	Price Range
□ **Vase,** decorated green Favrille glass, decorated with silvery trailing lily pads and stems, inscribed "L.C. Tiffany-Favrille 670H," 6″ high	1320.00
□ **Vase,** green Favrille glass, decorative pulled design in iridescent gold at the shoulder, with paper label, 4½″ high	935.00
□ **Loving cup,** three-handled, in gold iridescence decorated with green trailing vines at the rim and large green ivy leaves in between the handles, inscribed "L.C. Tiffany-Favrille 9657C," 5¼″ high	1210.00
□ **Wine glasses,** set of six, gold iridescent, signed L.C. Tiffany Favrille, No. 208, 3¾″ high	625.00

Price Range

THOMAS WEBB

☐ **Cameo glass tray,** yellow, signed "THOMAS WEBB & SONS CAMEO," 14″ long 1320.00

☐ **Cameo glass vase,** cherry red overlaid in white, with firm's mark, 8¼″ high 1760.00

Cameo glass vase, in cherry red overlaid in white, with firm's mark, 8¼″ high, $1760. (*Photo courtesy of Christie's East, New York*)

Holiday Memorabilia

DESCRIPTION: The category of holiday memorabilia encompasses all holidays and all manner of decorations and ephemera.

BACKGROUND: Among the most popular forms of holiday memorabilia are Christmas items, Halloween costumes, Thanksgiving postcards from the turn of the century, and Fourth of July banners, badges, and trappings.

Note: The single values shown below are the actual auction-realized prices.

CHRISTMAS

	Price Range	
☐ **Kugel ball,** hand-blown, blue, with original brass cap, 6″ diameter	60.00	80.00
☐ **Kugel ball,** hand-blown, lime		

	Price Range	
green, with original brass cap, 6″ diameter	60.00	80.00
☐ **Kugel ornament,** hand-blown, in the form of a bunch of grapes in cobalt blue with original brass cap, 4″ long		180.00
☐ **Clip-on popcorn head ornament,** rare, with painted features		300.00
☐ **"Clown in a Barrel,"** unusual, the blue barrel banded with gold paint, trimmed with tinsel rope, a two-faced sad/happy clown fitting in the top of the barrel, 3½″ high		225.00
☐ **Clip-on Indian head,** glass		190.00
☐ **Cotton Santa Claus,** with molded clay face and painted features, 4″ high		170.00
☐ **Chenille Santa bell,** decorated with molded Santa face and glass silver beads	60.00	80.00
☐ **Santa holding a Christmas tree,** together with a Mrs. Santa Claus ornament	70.00	90.00
☐ **"Santa in Shoe,"** net candy container, Japan, c. 1930, 3″ high ...		20.00

CRECHE FIGURES, 19TH-CENTURY NEAPOLITAN

DESCRIPTION: The figures have hand-painted molded composition hands, legs, and heads with glass eyes and bodies of straw-filled fabric, clad in handmade costumes.

☐ **Three peasants,** dressed in costumes of silk, velvet, suede, wool, and cotton, appointed with a basket of berries, bagpipes, and a hat, 18½″, 12½″, and 18″ high		850.00

Three peasants, dressed in costumes of silk, velvet, suede, wool, and cotton, appointed with a basket of berries, bagpipes, and a hat, 18½″, 12½″, 18″ high, $850. (*Photo courtesy of Phillips, New York*)

	Price Range
☐ **Three peasants,** dressed in Continental costumes of silk, velvet, and cotton with gold thread trim, 17″, 17″, and 12″ high	750.00
☐ **Three blackamore attendants,** figures dressed in colorful costumes of court, made of silk, decorated with ribbons, 17″ high ...	800.00
☐ **Two angels,** in flight, dressed in blue and gold silk gowns with "gold" decoration, and painted paper wings, 15″ and 16″ high .	950.00
☐ **Angels,** pair, in flight, dressed in "jeweled" silk robes with stiff velveteen "feathered" wings, 18½″ and 15″ high	550.00
☐ **Two Chinese guardsmen,** dressed in festive silk costumes in	

Two angels, in flight, dressed in blue and gold silk gowns with "gold" decoration, and painted paper wings, 15″ and 16″ high. $950. (*Photo courtesy of Phillips, New York*)

	Price Range
tones of purple, green, blue, red, and gold, wearing hats and long braids, 18″ high	225.00
☐ **Figural group,** the Holy Family—Mary, Joseph, and Baby Jesus—dressed in costumes of silk and cotton decorated with gold thread, leather sandals, and gilt metal halos, the child reclining in a basket, 14″ and 18½″ high, 4½″ long	2100.00
☐ **Two peasants,** a man and a woman dressed in Continental costumes of silk, velvet, and cotton, the woman carrying a basket of fruit, 17½″ and 16½″ high ..	500.00
☐ **Manger animals,** of carved and painted wood, comprising a mule, three ewes, one reclining, and a ram, together with a rolled mat-	

Two Chinese guardsmen, dressed in festive silk costumes in tones of purple, green, blue, red, and gold, wearing hats and long braids, 18″ high, $225. (*Photo courtesy of Phillips, New York*)

	Price Range
tress and a milk churn, 10″, 6½″, 7″, 5″, and 4½″ high	275.00

EASTER

☐ **Bunny Express,** Marx 1936, Easter Rabbit Express, scale-model train toy, large tin rabbit with glass eyes, engine pulls two hopper cars, originally sold at Easter filled with jelly beans, 18″ long — 600.00 700.00

Figural group, comprising: The Holy Family, Mary, Joseph, and Baby Jesus dressed in costumes of silk and cotton, decorated with gold thread, with leather sandals and gilt metal halos, the child reclining in a basket, 14″ and 18½″ high, 4½″ long. $2100. Two peasants, a man and a woman, dressed in Continental costumes of silk, velvet, and cotton, the woman carrying a basket of fruit, 17½″ and 16½″ high, $500. Manger animals, of carved and painted wood, comprising a mule, three ewes, one reclining, and a ram, together with a rolled mattress and a milk churn, 10″, 6½″, 7″, 5″, and 4½″ high, $275. (*Photo courtesy of Phillips, New York*)

	Price Range	
☐ **Peter Rabbit Chickmobile,** Lionel 1935, yellow hand car, steel, tin and composition, rabbit is on one end and Easter basket on other, 9½″ long	800.00	900.00
☐ **Rabbit bowling game,** German, 1870s, papier-mâché with glass eyes, also believed to be a pull toy, 24″ long	1000.00	1200.00

HALLOWEEN

☐ **Pumpkin-head walker,** German, 1910, composition, cloth clockwork, 7″ high	600.00	650.00

Price Range

☐ **Spook bank,** maker unknown, contemporary, cast aluminum, pumpkin-headed figure with black cat, 6″ high 50.00   75.00
☐ **Witch riding goose,** Strauss, 1920s, lithograph tin wind-up 100.00   125.00

VALENTINES

☐ **Dobbs,** lacy folder, 5″ × 7″, c. 1840s 15.00   25.00
☐ **Dobbs,** fancy lace, 7″ × 9″, c. 1840s 25.00   45.00
☐ **Mansell,** gilded lace folder, 4″ × 6″, c. 1865 ....   10.00   20.00
☐ **Mansell,** lacy with handwritten verse, 1845, hand-applied floral wreath on front, 8″ × 10″ 75.00   100.00
☐ **Postcard,** novelty kaleidoscope   10.00   20.00
☐ **Whitney,** Art Nouveau, 3-layer, lacy, 7″ × 10″ 8.00   15.00

Inkwells and Inkstands

TOPIC: Inkwells have been in use since people first began to write. The inkwell itself is the container for holding ink, and an inkstand is composed of two or more wells on a stand. One well, as part of a decorative piece, can be either an inkwell or an inkstand. Inkwell collections often include related accessories, including blotters, seals, letter openers, sponge dishes, and other items used by a writer. Inkwells and inkstands, as well as their accessories, are often very elaborate and very beautiful.

PERIOD: Most of the collectible inkwells and inkstands date from the 1800s and early 1900s, although there are pieces that date from earlier periods. Different eras produced very distinctive pieces; there are many different periods of inkwell styles within the two centuries of their prominence. And as inkwells have been in use for over 4,500 years, it is always possible to come across some very old inkwells.

ORIGIN: Inkwells have been in use since people began to write, more than 4,500 years ago. The "modern" period is usually dated from the late 1700s.

MATERIAL: Most of the actual inkwells are made of glass or porcelain. Inkstands and inkwells are most commonly made of glass or porcelain, but other popular materials include brass, silver, bronze, pewter, wood, stone, seashells, ceramics, and just about anything else that can be imagined.

TREND: Today one sees many desk sets in catalogs and sales rooms. These are of various materials, porcelain, brass, or ceramics. Most of the sets include blotters, stamp box, letter holder, pen tray, letter opener, picture frame, everything except an inkwell. Another accessory observed frequently is the letter opener, usually brass or sterling with an ornate handle of cut glass, an animal head, or monogrammed initials.

	Price Range
☐ **Art Nouveau pewter figural inkstand,** on a stylized floral base, marked "WMF," 7 3/4 " high	170.00
☐ **Art Nouveau figural metal inkstand,** white metal rococo-style stand with two greyhounds in relief, 14 " long, 8 1/2 " high	450.00
☐ **Bronze inkwell and pen tray,** Austrian, rectangular with circular inkwell at one end, at the other end two vultures on rocky promontory, inscribed "HK" and "LW," 16 1/2 " long	275.00
☐ **Glass,** "octagonal teakettle," clear, mouth-ground base, 3 3/8 " high, 2 5/8 " diameter	50.00
☐ **Glass,** "Benjamin Franklin head fountain inkwell," clear, ground mouth-smooth base, 2 3/4 " high, 4 1/2 " long, metal cap missing	90.00
☐ **Glass,** rare freeblown funnel-type inkwell on pedestal base, deep golden amber, tool mouth-scarred base, 2 7/8 " high, 2 1/4 " diameter .	225.00
☐ **Glass,** unique six-ringed inkwell with two quill holes, olive amber, tool mouth-scarred base, 1 3/4 " high, 2 1/4 " diameter	675.00

Price Range

☐ **Glass,** "Smith's Perpetual Calendar," ink bottle, aqua, tool mouth-smooth base, 3 1/4″ high, 2 1/4″ diameter, small base flake and light 150.00

☐ **Glass,** rare "cabin" ink bottle, clear, ground mouth-smooth base, 3 1/8″ high, 2 1/2″ long 50.00

☐ **Glass and metal,** fountain inkwell, clear with black-painted cast-iron and gold decoration, tooled mouth-smooth base, 3 1/2″ high, 5 3/8″ long 30.00

Insulators

DESCRIPTION: Insulators are the nonconducting glass figures used to attach electrical wires to poles.

ORIGIN: The first insulator was invented in 1844 for a telegraph line.

COMMENTS: Insulators became collectible after World War II. Old electrical lines with insulators were taken down during the early postwar stages of urban development.

Color, age, and design determine value. Threadless insulators are older, more rare, and usually more valuable than threaded ones.

Clear glass is most common. Colors, including green, milk white, amber, amethyst, and cobalt blue, are more valuable.

ADDITIONAL TIPS: The listings are alphabetical according to manufacturer. Other information including color and size is also included.

	Price Range	
☐ **Amber ponies**	16.00	20.00
☐ **Armstrong,** 51-C1A, red amber .	10.00	20.00
☐ **California,** CD 260, purple Roman helmet, very low pin hole shows lots of glass in dome, slight scuffing around lower portion of		

	Price Range	
outer skirt, minute stress crack from right ear to upper wire ridge	180.00	220.00
☐ **Canadian Pacific RY Co.,** CD 143, royal purple	15.00	25.00
☐ **Canadian pony,** CD 102, small drips and number	20.00	30.00
☐ **Clear mouse**	20.00	30.00
☐ **Colorado Springs,** 1971, 2nd National, black glass	120.00	130.00
☐ **Columbia,** no inner skirt, aqua, very rare	120.00	130.00
☐ **Columbia,** No. 2, cobalt	20.00	30.00
☐ **Eared Jumbo,** CD 269, deep aqua	240.00	260.00
☐ **EC & M Co.,** San Francisco, CD 123, dark blue aqua	45.00	55.00
☐ **Floy,** aqua, open rim bubble	90.00	100.00
☐ **H. G. Co./Petticoat,** tall narrow skirt variety, dark purple, $3/4''$ × $1/2''$ shallow flake on front outer skirt, rest of insulator is mint and very clean glass	90.00	100.00
☐ **Hemingray,** No. "0" Provo, super-rare especially when mint	240.00	260.00
☐ **Hemingray E-3,** made in USA, aqua	80.00	100.00
☐ **Hemingray High Voltage,** No. 3, triple petticoat, inner skirt chips, aqua	90.00	110.00
☐ **Hutchinson,** 1973, 4th National, dark carnival	50.00	60.00
☐ **Jumbo,** Oakman on rim, aqua ...	120.00	130.00
☐ **Kansas City,** 1972, 3rd National, cobalt	50.00	60.00
☐ **Knowles,** $5 1/2''$, aqua, very rare	240.00	260.00
☐ **Oakman,** light aqua, eared version	150.00	170.00
☐ **Porcelain,** No. 5, brown	90.00	110.00
☐ **Prism,** attractive lime green color	70.00	80.00
☐ **Pyrex 401,** light carnival	30.00	40.00
☐ **San Diego,** 1975, 6th National, red	70.00	80.00

Ivory

COMMENTS: Depending on where a piece was produced, the ivory used in it would come from either Africa or India. Popular for the way in which it colors with age and the ease with which it can be carved, ivory has, since the late nineteenth century, become a precious commodity, due primarily to the popularity of the piano. Over 12 million pianos were built and sold in the United States by the first decade of the twentieth century, each piano requiring over a pound and a half of ivory for the keyboard. The subsequent depletion of the elephant herds in both India and Africa and the ensuing wildlife and environment concerns have led to severe restrictions in the use of ivory in our own day.

	Price Range	
☐ **African carved elephant tusk horn,** the wide end with alligator skin binding, high-relief geometric carved decoration, 27″ long .	800.00	1000.00
☐ **Asian carved ivory figure of a standing elephant,** raised on an elaborate rectangular carved ivory plinth, on a conforming carved teakwood stand, 15″ long, 20″ high	700.00	900.00

Price Range

☐ **Buccellati ivory, carved emerald, gold, and ruby plaque,** oval, depicting the Holy Family trilogy and attendant angels, surrounded by carved emerald bits and interspersed with small round-cut rubies, set under glass in a carved yellow gold frame, the ivory inscribed on the verso "Inciso nella bottega di M. Buccellati," 5 1/2" high 500.00   800.00

☐ **Carved ivory tusk,** depicting Kipling's allegory, "How the Elephant Got Its Trunk," 27 1/4" long   100.00   150.00

☐ **Carved ivory netsuke,** depicting a peasant with an umbrella ...   25.00   35.00

☐ **European carved ivory,** depicting a small standing boy, raised on a circular turned plinth, 3 1/2" high 200.00   300.00

☐ **Japanese carved ivory netsuke,** depicting a turtle crawling on a human skull, 1 1/2" high 65.00   85.00

☐ **Japanese carved ivory netsuke,** depicting a dog with a stinging bee, 1 1/2" high 75.00   100.00

☐ **Japanese carved ivory snuff bottle,** in the form of a swimming fish, 3" high 65.00   85.00

☐ **Oriental carved ivory koro,** undercut architectural and landscape finial, 16 1/4" high 400.00   500.00

☐ **Oriental carved ivory koro,** massive, raised on an octagonal ivory pedestal, 49" high 500.00   700.00

☐ **Oriental carved ivory plateau,** depicting a pagoda with pendant bells, 8" high 40.00   60.00

☐ **Oriental carved ivory snuff bottle,** in the figure of a doctor's lady, raised on a native wood stand, 3" long 40.00   60.00

Jewelry

PERIOD: Some of the major style periods for jewelry include 18th-century Georgian, 19th-century Victorian, Art Nouveau, and Art Deco.

COMMENTS: Usually the value of a piece of jewelry depends on the quality of material used. Designer status also accounts for some high prices. To judge material quality, the collector should use a loupe, an eyepiece magnifier. A 10-power loupe is recommended. A touchstone should be used to assess gold content in jewelry.

Note: The single values shown below are the actual auction-realized prices.

Price Range

☐ **Art Nouveau insect brooch,** rare, c. 1905, of fine quality, the outspread wings decorated with pale green plique-a-jour enamel and mounted with clusters of small sapphires and diamonds, the flexible body set with rubies and rose-cut diamonds, the forelegs clasp a brilliant-cut diamond, and

Price Range

twin pendant pearls suspend from chain connections, signed "MAS-RIERA H." 10,000.00

☐ **Bracelet,** sapphire and diamond, c. 1950, composed of 13 graduating, jointed, clustered set with cabochon sapphires bordered by drop marquise and brilliant-cut diamonds, platinum mount, total estimated weight of sapphires approximately 50 carats, diamonds 24 carats 20,000.00

☐ **Brooch,** lady's, 14k yellow, white gold, and diamond, containing 139 round-cut diamonds, weighing approximately 8.3 carats total, double-leaf form 4000.00

☐ **Brooch,** lady's, 14k white gold, diamond, ruby, emerald and pearl, of arched form, containing 103 single-cut diamonds weighing approximately 3.0 carats total, 7 foliate-cut rubies weighing approximately 3.5 carats total, 8 foliate-cut emeralds weighing approximately 4.8 carats total, and 23 2mm pearls 3800.00

☐ **Dinner ring,** lady's, platinum and diamond, containing 3 emerald-cut diamonds weighing approximately 2.4 carats total 2500.00

☐ **Engagement ring,** lady's, platinum and diamond, containing 1 emerald-cut diamond weighing approximately 3.2 carats and 20 single-cut diamonds weighing approximately .10 carats total 11,500.00

☐ **Necklace,** South Sea cultured pearls, composed of a single row of 37 pearls graduated from 14.3 mm to 11.1 mm, approximately,

Fancy cut diamond necklace, c. 1912, $18,700. (*Photo courtesy of Phillips, New York*)

Price Range

secured by an oval openwork 18k yellow gold clasp with five bands of diamonds 35,000.00

☐ **Necklace,** fancy-cut diamond, of flexible design, the front mounted with a square step-cut diamond bordered by baguettes and flanked by lines of three marquise diamond clusters, between two lines of graduating baguettes, the front tapering with fancy-cut diamonds to a single line of small brilliants in leaf settings, probably French, c. 1912 .... 18,700.00

☐ **Pin,** lady's, 18k yellow and white gold enamel, diamond and ruby sea horse, containing 22 round-cut diamonds weighing approximately 1.4 carats total and 2 small round-cut rubies 1250.00

☐ **Ring,** lady's, platinum, diamond and ruby, containing 7 emerald-cut rubies weighing approximately 3.5 carats total, 25 emerald-cut rubies weighing approximately 1.04 carats total and 28 round-cut diamonds weighing approximately .84 carats total 1500.00

☐ **Ring,** lady's, 14k white gold, emerald, and diamond, containing 1

Price Range

emerald-cut emerald weighing approximately 9.05 carats, 2 half-round-cut diamonds weighing approximately 1.30 carats total, and 2 tapered baguette diamonds weighing approximately .50 carats total 5000.00

☐ **Ring,** lady's, 14k white gold, platinum, diamond, and pink sapphire, containing 1 oval-cut pink sapphire weighing approximately 55 carats and 26 round-cut diamonds weighing approximately 2.6 carats total; provenance, ex-collection of Helena Rubenstein . 24,000.00

☐ **Stickpin,** 14k white gold, diamond, and red jade, containing one carved red jade hoi toi and approximately 77 old mine-cut diamonds 1200.00

☐ **Stickpin,** 14k white gold, diamond and green jade, containing one carved green jade hoi toi and approximately 77 old mine-cut diamonds 1000.00

Kitchenware

TYPES: Kitchen collectibles cover a wide variety of items, including utensils, boxes, molds, tools, wares, as well as advertising items and cookbooks.

	Price Range
☐ **Butter mold,** 19th century, sheaf of wheat pattern, bearing a patent date from April 17, 1866, 5″ diameter	70.00
☐ **Butter print,** cast iron, sunburst pattern with wooden handle	35.00
☐ **Cake mold,** cast iron, two-piece chicken	125.00
☐ **Cake mold,** cast iron, two-piece small lamb	94.00
☐ **Cake mold,** cast iron, the 866 Griswold lamb, two-piece	52.00
☐ **Cake mold,** cast iron, two-piece Griswold Santa Claus, embossed "Hello Kiddies!!"	215.00
☐ **Cake mold,** cast iron, two-piece Griswold rabbit	135.00
☐ **Cake mold,** cast iron, fluted tube pan	32.00

Cake mold, cast iron, two-piece chicken, $125. (*Photo courtesy of Marilyn Kelley*)

Coffee grinder, American, inlaid burl walnut, late 19th century, 10½″ high, 7⅛″ wide, $605. (*Photo courtesy of Butterfield & Butterfield, San Francisco*)

	Price Range
☐ **Cookie press,** cast iron, black boy on pot pattern	45.00
☐ **Cookie press,** cast iron, lyre pattern	48.00
☐ **Candy mold,** cast iron, pony, makes two pieces	38.00
☐ **Candy mold,** Kriss Kringle, cast iron, makes four pieces	54.00
☐ **Candy mold,** cast iron, egg-shaped, 8-oz chocolate mold	40.00
☐ **Coffee grinder,** American, inlaid burl walnut, late 19th century, 10½″ high, 7⅛″ wide	605.00
☐ **Coffeepot,** American, punch-work-decorated tin, inscribed "made in 1848," brass finial, 10⅝″ high	1100.00

Coffeepot, American, punchwork-decorated tin, inscribed "made in 1848," brass finial,10⅝″ high, $1100. (*Photo courtesy of Butterfield & Butterfield, San Francisco*)

Left. Tea caddie, pear shaped, $1210. *Right*. Tea caddie, pear shaped, $1100. (*Photo courtesy of Butterfield & Butterfield, San Francisco*)

	Price Range
☐ **Corn stick pan,** cast iron, double, makes 14, marked "Wagner Ware, Krusty Korn Kobs"	65.00
☐ **Hudson apple parer and wall-mounted coffee mill,** 19th century, patented	100.00
☐ **Tea caddie,** pear-shaped	1210.00
☐ **Tea caddie,** pear-shaped	1100.00
☐ **Muffin pan,** cast iron, 18 sections, cannonball shaped cups	50.00
☐ **Muffin pan,** cast iron, 7-section doughnut ring	65.00
☐ **Muffin pan,** cast iron, 13 sections, hexagon-shape cups, marked "W.C. Davis & Co. Cin'ti"	50.00
☐ **Muffin pan,** cast iron, 3-cup with small skillet handle	45.00
☐ **Muffin pan,** cast iron, 9 sections, heart-shaped cups	70.00

VAN GOGH, VINCENT: *SUNFLOWERS* (JAN. 1889), OIL ON EXTENDED
CANVAS, 39½″ x 30¼″.

Sold at Christie's, London, on March 30, 1987 for $39,921,750 to a
Japanese insurance company, *Sunflowers* set a trend in the '87 auction year
that culminated in the Sotheby's, New York, sale of the same artist's *Irises* for
$53.9 million. In all, three of Van Gogh's works in 1987 brought in a hefty
$112 million at the auction block. Of the three, this was perhaps the most
surprising, as the estimated value of the work prior to sale had been placed
at *only* $15 million. *(Photo courtesy of Christie's, New York)*

When the Norweb Coin Collection went up for auction in October, 1987—in the first of three sessions—12 records were broken for Colonial and United States coins, according to *Coin World* magazine. The single, largest sale was that of *a)* an 1829 Capped Head half eagle gold coin, which brought in $320,000. Other items that brought record or near-record prices included: *b)* 1694 Carolina Elephant token ($32,000), *c)* 1864-S Coronet half eagle ($100,000), and *d)* 1652 Willow Tree shilling ($48,000). *(Photos courtesy of Auctions by Bowers and Merena Galleries, Inc.)*

There are only six like this in the world. This 56-year-old automobile has had only two owners—the Bugatti family (who occasionally used the car to go shopping) and Briggs Cunningham. The last Bugatti Royale, chassis #41.150, went for a reported $8 million in a private sale at the end of 1986. The auction including this one, chassis #41.141, occurred on November 19, 1987 at the Albert Hall in London. Christie's estimated the value at $8 to $10 million. The actual price paid by a London vintage car dealer was $9 million. *(Photo courtesy of Christie's, New York)*

Ten-year-old Ruthy Rogers was living in Marblehead, Massachusetts in 1788 when she embroidered this fine sampler. Exceptional because of its size—only 9½″ x 10½″—and compactness of design—it is considered a masterpiece, an example of American needlework at its best. Its estimated value had been placed at $20,000-$30,000, but it set a new record when it finally sold for $198,000 on June 6, 1987. *(Photo courtesy of Robert W. Skinner, Inc.)*

Among the few Titanic relics on the open market—the controversial Franco-American salvage expedition will not offer any of the materials recovered for sale—are postcards and other items that had been mailed from the ship during its ill-starred maiden voyage. In a London auction in April, 1987 (the 75th anniversary of the disaster), a card featuring the Titanic and her sister ship, the Olympic, that had been mailed from on board by a 7-year-old girl, sold for $4,000 (pictured is a reproduction of that card).

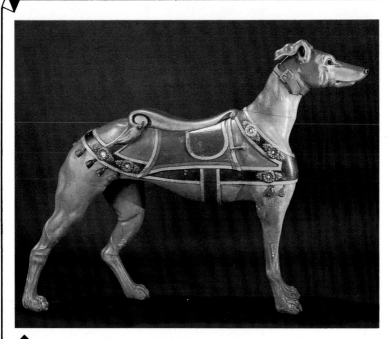

Carousel horses may be sedentary animals, but in the auction houses, the gavel seems to have become a checkered flag, with Loofs, Dares, Dentzels, and Bayols racing to achieve prices unimaginable a few years ago. Pictured is a Charles Loof carousel greyhound that sold at Phillips for $59,400—roughly 150% of the estimate. *(Photo courtesy of Phillips of New York)*

In a year that saw the sale of the collection of the Duchess of Windsor's jewelry by Sotheby's, Geneva—by all accounts an extraordinary social, as well as auction, event—this little red diamond quietly set an extraordinary standard of its own at Christie's. Only 0.95 carats in size, this little drop of purplish-red, estimated at $100,000-$150,000, actually sold for $880,000, setting a world record per carat of $926,000. *(Photo courtesy of Christie's, New York)*

GUTENBERG BIBLE, BIBLIA LATINA (MAINZ: JOHANN GUTENBERG AND JOHANN FUST, 1455), VOL. I (*GENESIS* TO *PSALMS*).

There are bestsellers and then there are *bestsellers.* Another shocker on the auction block this year came in the first session of the Christie's sale of rare books from the Estelle Doheny Collection. *The Gutenberg Bible* is celebrated as the first work published in the western world with movable type, with 47 copies of the book—some printed on vellum, the rest on paper—surviving. Estimated at $1.5 to $2 million, this volume actually brought $5.39 million on October 22, 1987. *(Photo courtesy of Christie's, New York)*

In December, 1986, military figures from the Boer War were still marching into history. This time, the soldiers, horses, and supply wagons were made of lead, and the battlefield was Phillips of New York, where the ten soldiers, the two wagons-and-four (complete with driver and rider), and the leader on horseback commandeered $12,100—a world record for a lead soldier set. This extremely rare item was manufactured by Britains. *(Photo courtesy of Phillips of New York)*

▼

This copper locomotive once rested atop the Providence and Worcester Railway depot. Estimated at $60,000-$80,000, this tender weathervane broke through to a new record high of $203,000 at Skinner on March 21, 1987. *(Photo courtesy of Robert W. Skinner, Inc.)*

▼

This rare Shaker dining table was made in Canterbury, New Hampshire during the first half of the 19th century at a Shaker house on Coles Island, Gloucester, Massachusetts. The clean line is typical of the style with which Americans of the 20th century have become so enamored. This example of "the gift to be simple" set a record for Shaker artifacts when it sold at Skinner for $96,000. *(Photo courtesy of Robert W. Skinner, Inc.)*

Frank Lloyd Wright's architecture was not merely designs for buildings, but designs for *living.* He generally designed the decorations and the furnishings as well. The dining table and eight spindle chairs from the George Barton House in Buffalo, New York went for an extraordinary $594,000 in June, 1987. *(Photo courtesy of Christie's, New York)*

The celebration of the bicentennial of the Constitution was not missed in the auction world. Two items associated with Thomas Jefferson were particularly noteworthy. A bottle of 1784 Chateau d'Yquem, bottled for the American statesman, sold in London for $56,390, while Jean Antoine Houdon's painted plaster bust of the third American president sold in New York for $2,860,000—a record for an 18th-century sculpture. *(Photo courtesy of Christie's, New York)*

Edward Steichen did several nude figure studies in Paris at the turn of the century. There are only two known copies of "La Cigale"—one, printed in 1907, is in the Metropolitan Museum of Art in New York. The other, printed in 1908, was sold for $82,500 on October 29, 1987, setting a world record for a single-image photo. Sotheby's sold the multiple image "The Seven Words," featuring the photographer F. Holland Day as Christ on the Cross, for $93,500. *(Photo courtesy of Christie's, New York)*

	Price Range
☐ **Kettle,** cast iron, American, New England, 18th century, 9½" high	440.00
☐ **Springerle mold,** cast iron, 2 designs, flower patterns	55.00
☐ **Springerle mold,** cast iron, 6 designs, various patterns	85.00
☐ **Springerle mold,** 12 designs, various patterns	85.00
☐ **Waffle iron,** with stand, five-heart design with German recipe embossed on top	65.00

Waffle iron, with stand, five-heart design with German recipe embossed on top, $65. (*Photo courtesy of Marilyn Kelley*)

Knives

HISTORY: Knives are man's oldest tools, first as stone implements, then as one of the first things fashioned from metals. Their utilitarian value has always made them a desired object, functioning as both tool and weapon.

Most knives were made in towns that offered the necessary natural resources for manufacturing cutlery: running water to run the grinding wheels, stone deposits nearby suitable for making grinding wheels, coal deposits for the tempering fires, and usually some sort of steel manufacturing. Each country seemed to have one town that fit the bill. Here's a brief list of cutlery towns and their respective countries: Solingen, Germany; Thiers, France; Maniago, Italy; Seki City, Japan; Sheffield, England.

For America the first knives were usually made in England. Prior to the Civil War a cutlery industry emerged, sparked for the most part by John Russell. Soon the mountain men heading into the Rockies were carrying John Russell knives right alongside their English-made I. Wilson scalpers. Nearly all of the early factories in America were established by Sheffield expatriates pursuing their craft in the small towns of the Connecticut Valley.

As the industrial revolution began, knife manufacturing rolled right along with it. One group of ex-Sheffielders left the Connecticut Valley in favor of the Hudson River Valley and there formed the New York Knife Company, which, along with the Cattaraugus Cutlery Corp., would dominate American cutlery until the beginning of the twentieth century.

During the first twenty years of this century, the United States imposed heavy tariffs on importers, forcing them to search out their own manufacturing facilities, among them Aldoph Kastor, who formed Camillus Cutlery Company; Milard F. Robeson, who started his company in Rochester, New York; and Schatt & Morgan, who started in Gowanda, New York. Boker, Germany, opened its own American plant. Also seeing opportunity at the time were the Case Brothers, who started W. R. Case & Sons Cutlery Company.

ORGANIZED KNIFE COLLECTING: Today there are nearly one hundred regional clubs, two national organizations, four major publications, and shows in most major cities.

CATTARAUGUS CUTLERY COMPANY

	Price Range
☐ **Mother-of-pearl handle,** 32173, 3⅞″, fine stock pattern, large clip, sheepfoot and spey blades, brass lined, nickel silver bolster, crocus finish	165.00
☐ **Stag handle,** 2269, 4″, large spear point and long pen blades, brass lined, nickel silver bolsters, glaze finish, shielded	120.00

HUBBARD, SPENCER AND BARTLET, CHICAGO

☐ **Black bone handle,** 1H, 3⅜″, one blade, iron lined	120.00
☐ **Black bone handle,** 2H, 3⅜″, two blades, iron lined	120.00
☐ **Cocoa handle,** 144, 5¾″, one blade, iron lined	150.00
☐ **Cocoa handle,** 125, 5⅜″, one blade, iron lined	150.00

	Price Range	

☐ **Stag handle,** 146, 5 3/8 ″, one blade, iron lined 150.00

☐ **Stag handle,** 51086D, 3 1/8 ″, two blades, polished, brass lined, nickel silver cap, bolster, and shield 65.00

KA-BAR CUTLERY COMPANY, INC.

☐ **Imitation pearl handle,** P269 J, stamped UNION CUT CO. 80.00

☐ **Genuine stag handle,** 2269 J, stamped UNION CUT CO. 140.00

☐ **Bone stag handle,** 6269 J, stamped UNION CUT CO. 120.00

☐ **Genuine stag handle,** 2269 J, stamped KA-BAR 110.00

PARKER KNIVES

☐ **Brass handle,** Art Nouveau, 3″   4.00   8.00

☐ **Genuine stag handle,** The Trapper, discontinued, 2,400 released, 4 1/2 ″ 20.00   40.00

☐ **Mother-of-pearl handle,** Bearclaw, 2 ″ 10.00   20.00

☐ **Pickbone handle,** knife-ax combo, 600 released, 10 1/2 ″ 40.00   80.00

☐ **Smoothbone handle,** Apache Teardrop, discontinued, 12,000 released, 3 7/8 ″ 10.00   20.00

☐ **Continental multi-blade clasp knife,** probably late 19th century, outer surface decorated with a design in gold and silver, 6 ″ long 242.00

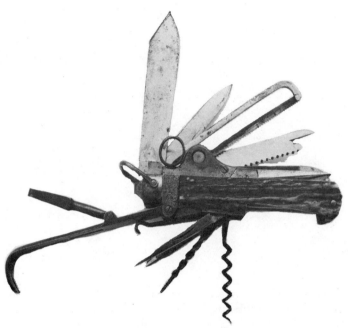

Continental multi-blade clasp knife, probably late 19th century, outer surface decorated with a design in gold and silver, 6″ long, sold at auction for $242. (*Photo courtesy of Christie's East, New York*)

Labels

TYPES: There is a wide variety of collectible labels, including cigar box labels, pictorial cigar bands, fruit crate labels, firecracker labels, cigarette cards, and can labels, to name a few.

COMMENTS: Attractive design and pleasing coloring has made labels very popular in the field of collectibles. Pre-1910 labels are much sought after, especially citrus labels from California and Florida, as well as related ephemera—books and promotional items, advertising cards, and postcards.

CIGAR BOX LABELS

TYPES: Inner lid label, usually 6″ × 9″, is the large label on the inside top of the box. This was used to grab the customer's eye and make the big retail sale.

Top sheet, usually 6″ × 9″, is a paper or piece of felt placed unattached on top of the cigars and almost always discarded when the box was opened. The theme was the same as the inner lid label with less detail.

Top wrap, having the image of wood grain, was glued to the top of the cigar box.

Out label is any label placed on the outside of the box. The most prevalent type is $4\,1/2''\times4\,1/2''$, affixed on the side of the box; it seals the lid.

Inner Lid Labels

	Price Range
☐ **Arizona**	24.00
☐ **General Hale**	12.75
☐ **Sir Loraine**	9.00
☐ **Tom Mix**	22.00
☐ **Dime Bank**	3.75
☐ **Turnover Club**	30.00
☐ **King of Cuba**	35.00
☐ **Captain Corker**	19.50
☐ **Huguenot**	12.00
☐ **Susquehanna**	9.50
☐ **Cigarros Primeros**	7.00
☐ **Bulldog**	4.50
☐ **Valencia**	4.50
☐ **Uncle Sam**	27.00
☐ **Camel**	9.00
☐ **The Radio Queen**	35.00
☐ **Alexander the Great**	14.00
☐ **Mephisto**	4.50

Outer Side Labels

☐ **Tom Mix**	12.00
☐ **National League**	7.00
☐ **American League**	7.00
☐ **Flor de Astro**	12.75
☐ **After Dinner**	12.00
☐ **Inventor**	12.50
☐ **Jim**	9.00
☐ **Stradella**	8.00
☐ **Turnover Club**	12.00
☐ **Honest Labor**	38.00
☐ **Uncle Sam**	12.00
☐ **Lord Badge**	8.00

Valencia, $4.50. (*Photo courtesy of Cerebro Lithographs*)

Uncle Sam, $27. (*Photo courtesy of Cerebro Lithographs*)

Camel, $9. (*Photo courtesy of Cerebro Lithographs*)

The Radio Queen, $35. (*Photo courtesy of Cerebro Lithographs*)

Alexander the Great, $14. (*Photo courtesy of Cerebro Lithographs*)

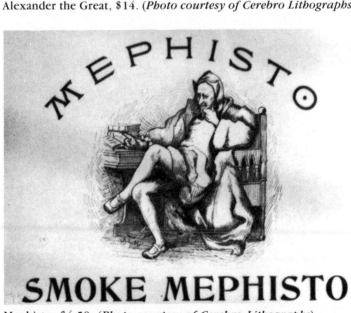

Mephisto, $4.50. (*Photo courtesy of Cerebro Lithographs*)

	Price Range
☐ **White Thief**	12.00
☐ **Gisela**	14.00
☐ **Nabobs**	18.00
☐ **Greenbacks**	24.00
☐ **Leo Grande**	4.00
☐ **Fidelio**	10.00
☐ **Cupido**	6.00

FRUIT LABELS

☐ **Washington Brand Apples** 8.00

Washington Brand Apples, $8. (*Photo courtesy of Cerebro Lithographs*)

Lucky Trail Brand Apples, 1915, $12.50. (*Photo courtesy of Cerebro Lithographs*)

	Price Range
☐ **Lucky Trail Brand Apples,** 1915	12.50
☐ **Yakima Chief Brand Apples,** 1930	8.00
☐ **Montecito Valley Brand, 1920**	24.00
☐ **Uncle Sam Brand Apples, 1920**	6.00
☐ **Appleton Brand Apples, 1915** .	6.00

Yakima Chief Brand Apples, 1930, $8. (*Photo courtesy of Cerebro Lithographs*)

Price Range

VEGETABLE LABELS

☐ **Pride of the River Green Asparagus,** 1930 .... 6.50
☐ **Champ Louisiana Brand Yams** 3.75
☐ **Bare Foot Boy Brand** 1.00
☐ **Anne Arundel Pride** 6.00

Montecito Valley Brand, 1920, $24. (*Photo courtesy of Cerebro Lithographs*)

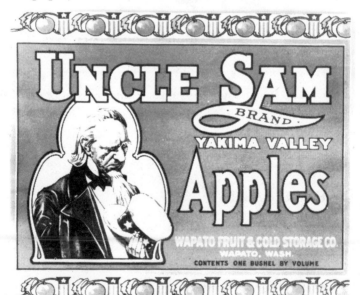

Uncle Sam Brand Apples, 1920, $6. (*Photo courtesy of Cerebro Lithographs*)

Appleton Brand Apples, 1915, $6. (*Photo courtesy of Cerebro Lithographs*)

Lamps and Lighting Fixtures

TYPES: There are many different types of lighting fixtures, from grease-burning to kerosene to electric. Styles of lamps and other fixtures may be named for the designer who innovated them or a distinctive feature of the lamp itself. For instance, the "Emeralite" light is a green-glass-shaded office lamp.

PERIOD: Lamps and lighting fixtures have been popular since the early 1700s. Collectors focus on the periods that saw significant developments in the field, such as the Art Nouveau period.

ORIGIN: Clay oil lamps have existed for at least two thousand years.

MAKERS: The most prominent makers of lamps and lighting fixtures are Tiffany, Quezal, Handel, and Pairpoint. These companies produced some of the finest and most artistic lamps in existence.

COMMENTS: Although few individuals collect lamps and lighting fixtures as a hobby, these items are eagerly sought as accent pieces. Many lamps, especially the most expensive ones, are works of art as much as functional pieces.

Ball lamp, Tiffany, Favrille glass and bronze, 1902–1911, $35,750. (*Photo courtesy of Butterfield & Butterfield, San Francisco*)

Note: The single values shown are the actual auction-realized prices.

	Price Range
☐ **Ball lamp,** Tiffany, Favrille glass and bronze, 1902–1911	35,750.00
☐ **Boudoir lamp,** by Pairpoint, shade in pink and yellow roses, paper label, base stamped "PAIRPOINT B3079," with firm's mark, 10½" high	1320.00
☐ **Brass kerosene lamp,** Classical style, by Cornelius and Co., Philadelphia, 1845, brass tag, 26" high, 13" diameter	400.00

Brass kerosene lamp, classical, by Cornelius and Co., Philadelphia, 1845, brass tag, 26″ high, 13″ diameter, $400. (*Photo courtesy of Phillips, New York*)

Price Range

☐ **Bronze lamps,** pair, possibly by Edgar Brandt, each in the form of a serpent, extended in a menacing pose supporting a trumpet-form mottled salmon and pink glass shade, probably Daum Nancy, 22″ high 3300.00

☐ **Chandelier,** turtleback tile and bronze, by Tiffany Studios, the circular shade set with seven gold turtleback tiles on a four-branch

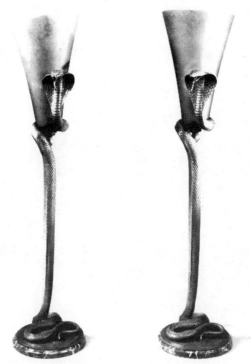

Bronze lamps, pair, possibly by Edgar Brandt, each in the form of a serpent, extended in a menacing pose supporting a trumpet-form mottled salmon and pink glass shade, probably Daum Nancy, 22″ high, $3300. (*Photo courtesy of Phillips, New York*)

	Price Range
bronze mount, unmarked, 7 3/4″ diameter shade	2090.00

☐ **Chandelier,** Favrille glass and turtleback tile, by Tiffany Studios, domed shade with central circular turtleback jewel and rows of gold geometric glass ascending to

Counterbalance table lamp, by Tiffany Studios, Favrille glass and silvered bronze, the circular shade with green and silvery blue damascene decoration, unsigned, 7″ diameter; in a silvered bronze adjustable counterbalance base, impressed "Tiffany Studios #415," 17″ high, $3080. (*Photo courtesy of Christie's East, New York*)

	Price Range
upper band of 18 square turtleback tiles, 14¾″ diameter	7150.00
☐ **Counterbalance table lamp,** by Tiffany Studios, Favrille glass and silvered bronze, circular shade with green and silvery blue damascene decoration, unsigned, 7″ diameter; in a silvered bronze adjustable counterbalance base, impressed "Tiffany Studios #415," 17″ high	3080.00

Dick Van Erp hammered copper and mica lamp, $11,000. (*Photo courtesy of Butterfield & Butterfield, San Francisco*)

Price Range

☐ **Dick Van Erp hammered copper and mica lamp** 11,000.00

☐ **Figural candelabra,** pair, Louis XVI–style gilt-bronze, patinated, 19th century, each formed as a strident nude nacchic female figure holding aloft in one hand a vining branch issuing four candle arms centering another; in the other hand, each holds a gilt chalice raised on a gilt bronze-

mounted rouge marble square
base, 28″ high 1200.00   1800.00

□ **"Hurricane" lamps,** pair, marble and ormolu, with bell-shaped glass shades on a floral socket and a green veined-marble base, 19″ high 1700.00

□ **Lantern,** by Tiffany Studios, Favrille glass and bronze, an iridescent green feather pull bell shade trimmed in blue/gold on golden ivory ground, inscribed "L.C.T.," 5¼″ high, the bronze mount 12″ high 1760.00

□ **Lily lamp,** Favrille glass and gilt-bronze, 12-light, by Tiffany Studios, gold-patinated lily pad standard supporting 12 curved stems, holding pendant, gold Favrille lily shades, inscribed "L.C.T.," 21½″ high 17,600.00

□ **"Pansy" leaded-glass shade,** by Tiffany Studios, green mottled-glass ground with wide border of light and dark flowerheads against green and blue leaves and stems, impressed "TIFFANY STUDIOS," 16″ diameter, 22″ high, ...   12,100.00

□ **"Peony" leaded-glass lamp shade,** by Tiffany Studios, dome with green ground and mottled pink and white flowerheads, border and some ground in yellow with fractured glass pieces, impressed "Tiffany Studios," 22″ diameter, on a later American green patinated metal floor base fitted for 6 lights, in classical style, 65″ high 40,700.00

□ **Table lamp,** gilt bronze, American, neoclassical style, 26″ high   3080.00

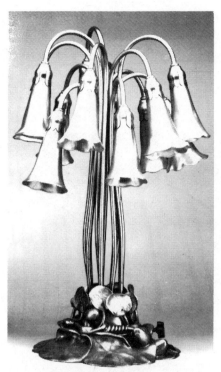

Lily lamp, Favrille glass and gilt-bronze, twelve-light, by Tiffany Studios, the gold-patinated lily pad standard supporting twelve curved stems, holding pendant, gold Favrille lily shades, inscribed "L.C.T.," 21½" high, $17,600. (*Photo courtesy of Christie's East, New York*)

	Price Range
☐ **Table lamps,** pair, Empire style, bronze, each with a classical maiden playing two horns supported by her outstretched arms, standing on a triangular base, 30" high	1100.00
☐ **Table lamp,** Chinese porcelain and French bronze, 18th century, 13" high	425.00
☐ **Wall light,** Louis XV–style gilt-bronze and cut glass,	

"Pansy" leaded glass shade, by Tiffany Studios, the green, mottled glass ground with wide border of light and dark flowerheads against green and blue leaves and stems, impressed "TIFFANY STUDIOS," 16″ diameter, 22″ high, $12,100. (*Photo courtesy of Christie's East, New York*)

	Price Range	
7-branch, late 19th century, ribbon-mounted flaming urn backplate issuing two tiers of the cornucopia-form candle arms, each with fluted urn-form nozzles and circular platform drip pans hung with drops and suspending beaded chains with amethyst glass drops, 27″ high	300.00	500.00

"Peony" leaded glass lamp shade, by Tiffany Studios, the dome with green ground and mottled pink and white flower-heads, the border and some ground in yellow with fractured glass pieces, impressed "Tiffany Studios," 22″ diameter, on a later American green-patinated metal floor base fitted for six lights, in classical style, 65″ high, $40,700. (*Photo courtesy of Christie's East, New York*)

Price Range

☐ **Wall lights,** pair, giltwood, mirrored and cut glass, 2-branch, possibly Swedish, 19th century, each with pierced rectangular backplate surmounted by a ribbon and pendant husks, intersected by a circular mirrored plate, issuing from the sides two scrolled candle arms joined by beaded chains, the drip pans hung with prism drops, 36″ high 600.00   900.00

Limited Editions

DESCRIPTION: Collector plates and figurines have a painting or design, usually by a well-known studio or artist. There are two types of limited editions: either the number produced or the number of production days it was limited to.

TYPES: Dorothy Doughty birds, Hummels, limited-edition plates, Royal Doulton figurines.

DOROTHY DOUGHTY BIRDS

Note: The following listings are prices realized from a Christie's East auction in New York in 1987.

Price Range

☐ **Bob White quail,** pair, the male bird standing on a naturalistic base, the female standing with two chicks at her breast, both figures glazed, *Colinus virginianus,* 1940, edition 22, 6¼″ high 4000.00
☐ **Cactus wrens and prickly pear,** pair, male with mottled shades of brown-and-white speckled plumage and pale orange breast,

Bob White quail, pair, the male bird standing on a naturalistic base, the female standing with two chicks at her breast, both figures glazed, *Colinus virginianus,* 1940, edition 22, 6¼″ high, $4000. (*Photo courtesy of Christie's East, New York*)

Cactus wrens and prickly pear, pair, the male with mottled shades of brown and white speckled plumage and pale orange breast, perched with uplifted tail on a cactus plant of thick and thorny violet and green leaves with brilliant yellow blossoms and buds, a desert snake concealed below; the mate on a similar perch, *Heleodytis brunei-capillus covesi,* 1959, edition 500, 10¾″ height (2), $650. (*Photo courtesy of Christie's East, New York*)

Price Range

perched with uplifted tail on a cactus plant of thick and thorny violet and green leaves with brilliant yellow blossoms and buds, a desert snake concealed below; the mate on a similar perch, *Heleodytis brunei-capillus covesi,* 1959, edition 500, 10¾" high (2) 650.00

☐ **Chicadees and larch,** pair, male with pale greenish-rose breast, a blue-gray head, and matching extended wings and tail feathers, clutching a branch with cones and needles supported by a tall trunk; female with similar plumage clinging to similar branch from below, *Parus atricapillus,* 1938, edition 325, 9¾" high (2) 1200.00

☐ **Hooded warblers and Cherokee rose,** pair, male with greenish-yellow back tipped in black, yellow breast, tail feathers shaded at the sides with white, perched alertly on a thorny green branch above a beautiful white rose with a bud below; female of similar plumage, perched similarly, *Wilsonia citrina,* 1961, edition 500, 12" high (2) 1200.00

☐ **Indigo buntings and blackberry,** pair, blue male perched in a flowering, fruited branch; orange female with wings and tail extended on a similar perch, *Passerina cyanea,* 1941, edition 500, 9¼" high 1700.00

☐ **Oven birds with crested iris and lady's slipper,** pair, green male with brown markings on wings and tail feathers, orange-brown crest, and cream breast

Hooded warblers and Cherokee rose, pair, the male with greenish-yellow back tipped in black, yellow breast, tail feathers shaded at the sides with white, perched alertly on a thorny green branch above a beautiful white rose with a bud below; the female of similar plumage, perched similarly, *Wilsonia citrina,* 1961, edition 500, 12″ height (2), $1200. (*Photo courtesy of Christie's East, New York*)

Price Range

with black speckles, open beak, perched on a small branch over a path of blue dwarf irises; mate of similar coloring, standing on fallen oak leaves, beside two lady's slipper orchids, *Seirus aurocapillus,* 1957, edition 500, 10¾″ high (2) 1900.00

☐ **Vireos and swamp azalea,** pair, male bird with yellow, light green, lavender, and brown plu-

Indigo buntings and blackberry, pair, the blue male perched in a flowering, fruited branch; the orange female with wings and tail extended on a similar perch, *Passerina cyanea,* 1941, edition 500, 9 1/4 " height, $1700. (*Photo courtesy of Christie's East, New York*)

Price Range

mage, lavender crest, singing from his perch among branches of blooming pink and white azaleas; female of similar coloring poised amid beautiful blossoms, *Vireo olivaceus,* 1952, edition 500, 8 1/4 " high (2) 1100.00

GOEBEL HUMMEL FIGURINES

☐ **Adventure Bound,** No. 347, 8 " long, bearing the Goebel V mark   475.00

Price Range

☐ **Ring around the Rosie,** No. 348, 7″ high, bearing the firm's stylized bee mark 750.00

☐ **Appletree Girl,** No. 141 3/0, full bee mark, 4¼″ high 70.00

☐ **Umbrella Boy,** No. 152 A II, full bee mark, 7¾″ high 350.00

☐ **Umbrella Girl,** No. 152 B II, full bee mark, 7½″ high 450.00

☐ **Be Patient,** No. 197 2/0, major differences between this figure and later editions can be seen, full bee mark, 4⅜″ high 95.00

☐ **We Congratulate,** No. 220 2/0, varying from later version, bearing the firm's bee mark, 4″ high 150.00

☐ **Sister,** No. 98, full bee mark, 5¾″ high 65.00

☐ **Schoolboy,** No. 82/0, full bee mark, 5¾″ high 80.00

PLATES

☐ **Bareuther,** 1985, 15th issue in the Thanksgiving series, under-glazed in cobalt blue 43.00

☐ **Edwin M. Knowles,** 1986, Edna Hibel, "Emily and Jennifer," 8½″, the third in Mother's Day plate series 29.50

☐ **Lynell Studios,** 1981 Ronald Reagan–George Bush Inaugural collectors plate, single issue, 10¼″ diameter, 17,500 issued ... 45.00

☐ **Rockwell Society,** 1982, Norman Rockwell's Mother's Day plate, "The Cooking Lesson" 25.00   30.00

☐ **Royal Copenhagen,** 1983, "Mother Cat and Kitten," bas-relief porcelain, 6″ diameter 29.50

	Price Range	
☐ **Wedgwood,** 1983, third in the series "My Memories," "Our Garden" by Mary Vickers, earthenware, 8″ diameter	27.00	35.00

ROYAL DOULTON FIGURINES

Note: the following listings are prices realized at a Frank H. Boos Gallery auction in 1987 in Michigan.

☐ **Marie,** HN1370, 4¾″ high	30.00
☐ **The Little Bridesmaid,** HN1433, 5¼″ high	70.00
☐ **Sweet Anne,** HN1496, 7″ high .	90.00
☐ **Biddy,** HN1513, 5½″ high	80.00
☐ **Janet,** HN1537, 6¼″ high	85.00
☐ **Ruby,** HN1724, 5¼″ high	135.00
☐ **Day Dreams,** HN1731, 5¾″ high	70.00
☐ **Top o'the Hill,** HN1834, 7″ high	55.00
☐ **Spring Morning,** HN1922, 7½″ high	60.00
☐ **Marguerite,** HN1928, 8″ high ..	130.00
☐ **Autumn Breezes,** HN1934, 7½″ high	50.00
☐ **Sweeting,** HN1935, 6″ high	60.00
☐ **Lady Charmian,** HN1948, 8″ high	115.00
☐ **Lavinia,** HN1955, 5″ high	35.00
☐ **Genevieve,** HN1962, 7″ high ...	115.00
☐ **Her Ladyship,** HN1977, 7¼″ high	145.00
☐ **The Ermine Coat,** HN1981, 6¾″ high	80.00
☐ **Rosebud,** HN1983, 7½″ high ...	100.00
☐ **Blithe Morning,** HN2021, 7¼″ high	130.00
☐ **Judith,** HN2089, 7″ high	150.00
☐ **Uriah Heep,** HN2101, 7½″ high	150.00
☐ **Abdullah,** HN2104, 6¾″ high ..	275.00

	Price Range
☐ **The Skater,** HN2117, 7 ¼ ″ high	140.00
☐ **Good King Wenceslas,** HN2118, 8 ½ ″ high	200.00
☐ **The Tailor,** HN2174, 5 ″ high ...	350.00

Magazines

DESCRIPTION: Magazines are periodicals usually containing articles and illustrations.

TYPES: There are many types of magazines including nature, sports, home, garden, and news.

COMMENTS: Hobbyists enjoy magazine collecting because periodicals capture a part of history. Magazines detail world events that make interesting reading decades later.

ADDITIONAL TIPS: Many hobbyists collect the issues of only one magazine such as *Life*, *National Geographic*, or *Playboy*. Others collect magazines topically, buying periodicals with photographs and articles about their favorite Hollywood stars, presidents, or sport heroes. Another way to collect magazines is by subject.

	Price Range	
☐ *The American*, January 1952 ...	5.00	7.00
☐ *The Brown Book of Boston*, July 1903	9.00	11.00
☐ *The Farmer's Wife*, June 1930	2.00	4.00

The American, January, 1952, $5–$7.

	Price Range	
☐ *The Flapper*, May 1923	25.00	30.00
☐ *Harper's New Monthly Magazine*, August 1897	8.00	10.00
☐ *Hollywood*, February 1943	13.00	15.00
☐ *Human Life*, January 1908	17.00	19.00

The Flapper, May, 1923, $25-$30.

	Price Range	
☐ ***The Illustrated Blue Book***, November 1928	30.00	35.00
☐ ***The Ladies' Home Journal***, June 1903	17.00	19.00
☐ ***Liberty***, July 1943	5.00	7.00
☐ ***Life***, May 1939	14.00	16.00

The Illustrated Blue Book, November, 1928, $30–$35.

	Price Range	
☐ *Life*, October 1941	18.00	20.00
☐ *Life*, April 1945	17.00	19.00
☐ *Life*, November 1945	14.00	16.00
☐ *Life*, November 1963	18.00	20.00
☐ *Look*, September 1940	18.00	22.00
☐ *Look*, December 1954	9.00	11.00
☐ *Peter Max Magazine*, Vol. 1, No. 1, 1969	40.00	45.00
☐ *Popular Science*, May 1930	16.00	18.00

Liberty, July, 1943, $5–7.

	Price Range	
☐ *The Saturday Evening Post*, October 1946	22.00	24.00
☐ *The Saturday Review of Literature*, August 1944	14.00	16.00
☐ *Science Fiction Plus*, December 1953	23.00	25.00
☐ *Silver Screen*, May 1942	13.00	15.00
☐ *Stage*, October 1937	20.00	25.00
☐ *Sunset*, October 1905	15.00	17.00
☐ *Theatre Magazine*, September 1925	30.00	35.00

Life, October, 1941, $18–$20.

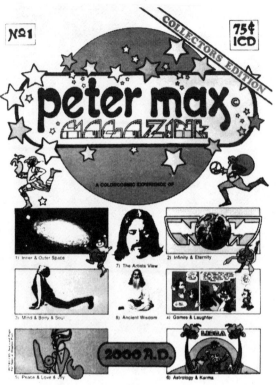

Peter Max magazine, No. 1, Vol. 1, 1969, $40–
$45.

Marbles

DESCRIPTION: Marbles are constructed of many materials but generally are categorized as either handmade or machine-made. Handmade marbles were made up to World War I; machine-made, from that time to the present.

TYPES COVERED: Handmade, machine-made, contemporary handmade.

HANDMADE MARBLES

	Mint	Near Mint	Good	Collectible
Agate, natural				
☐ To 7⁄8″	10.00	7.00	5.00	3.00
☐ 1″ to 1½″	30.00	15.00	10.00	5.00
☐ 1⅝″ to 1⅞″	65.00	45.00	25.00	10.00
☐ 2″ and over	150.00	125.00		
Agate, dyed				
☐ To 7⁄8″	30.00	20.00	10.00	5.00
☐ 1″ to 1½″	80.00	60.00	30.00	10.00

	Mint	Near Mint	Good	Collectible
Banded Lutz swirls				
☐ To 7/8″	40.00	25.00	15.00	10.00
☐ 1″ to 1½″	150.00	75.00	50.00	30.00
☐ 15/8″ to 17/8″	300.00	175.00	50.00	30.00
Banded swirls				
☐ To 7/8″	10.00	7.00	5.00	2.00
☐ 1″ to 1½″	50.00	35.00	20.00	10.00
Carpet bowl				
☐ 2″ and over	60.00	40.00	20.00	10.00
☐ Black on white, diameter 3¼″	55.00	35.00	15.00	8.00
End of Day Lutz				
☐ To 7/8″	60.00	40.00	25.00	10.00
☐ 1″ to 1½″	225.00	175.00	125.00	40.00
End of Day				
☐ To 7/8″	15.00	12.00	8.00	5.00
☐ 1″ to 1½″	75.00	45.00	25.00	15.00
☐ 15/8″ to 17/8″	150.00	100.00	50.00	25.00
☐ 2″ and over	225.00	150.00	75.00	35.00
End of Day with mica				
☐ To 7/8″	25.00	15.00	10.00	8.00
☐ 1″ to 1½″	100.00	65.00	40.00	20.00
☐ 15/8″ to 17/8″	250.00	200.00	100.00	50.00
Latticino swirls				
☐ To 7/8″	8.00	6.00	3.00	1.00
☐ 1″ to 1½″	40.00	20.00	12.00	8.00
☐ 15/8″ to 17/8″	85.00	40.00	20.00	12.00
☐ 2″ and over	150.00	65.00	35.00	20.00
Lobed swirls				
☐ To 7/8″	20.00	15.00	10.00	5.00
☐ 1″ to 1½″	75.00	40.00	20.00	12.00
☐ 15/8″ to 17/8″	150.00	100.00	50.00	25.00
☐ 2″ and over	225.00	150.00	75.00	35.00

	Mint	Near Mint	Good	Collectible
Open-core swirls				
☐ To 7/8″	8.00	6.00	3.00	1.00
☐ 1″ to 1½″	40.00	20.00	12.00	8.00
☐ 15/8″ to 17/8″	85.00	40.00	20.00	12.00
☐ 2″ and over	150.00	65.00	35.00	20.00
Pottery, glazed, blue and brown Benningtons				
☐ To 7/8″	.30	.25	.05	.05
☐ 1″ to 1½″	10.00	5.00	2.00	1.00
Pottery, glazed, mottled, or fancy				
☐ To 7/8″	1.00	.50	.25	.10
☐ 1″ to 1½″	10.00	5.00	2.00	1.00
Ribbon swirls				
☐ To 7/8″	15.00	12.00	8.00	5.00
☐ 1″ to 1½″	75.00	45.00	25.00	15.00
☐ 15/8″ to 17/8″	150.00	100.00	50.00	25.00
☐ 2″ and over	225.00	150.00	75.00	35.00
Solid-core swirls				
☐ To 7/8″	12.00	10.00	8.00	3.00
☐ 1″ to 1½″	75.00	40.00	20.00	12.00
☐ 15/8″ to 17/8″	125.00	85.00	40.00	20.00
☐ 2″ and over	200.00	125.00	65.00	30.00

Contemporary Glass Marbles

	Mint Price Range	
Brian Lonsway		
☐ To 7/8″	7.00	10.00
☐ 1″ to 1½″	12.00	15.00
☐ 15/8″ to 17/8″	20.00	25.00
☐ 2″ and over	30.00	50.00
Jim Cooprider		
☐ To 7/8″	7.00	10.00
☐ 1″ to 1½″	12.00	15.00

	Mint Price Range	
☐ 1⅝″ to 1⅞″	20.00	25.00
☐ 2″ and over	30.00	50.00

Jody Fine

☐ To ⅞″	7.00	10.00
☐ 1″ to 1½″	12.00	15.00
☐ 1⅝″ to 1⅞″	20.00	25.00
☐ 2″ and over	30.00	50.00

Steve Maslach

☐ To ⅞″	7.00	10.00
☐ 1″ to 1½″	12.00	15.00
☐ 1⅝″ to 1⅞″	20.00	25.00
☐ 2″ and over	30.00	50.00

Sulfides

Sulfides are clear-core marbles with figural subjects in the center. Rare or unique subjects such as the salamander, for example, are worth 50 percent more than the more common animal figures such as dogs, cats, birds, etc. Inanimate objects such as numbers or toys, are worth two to three times the value of animal figures. Any of the sulfides that have colored glass or colored figures could more than double the value of the normal marble.

	Mint	Near Mint	Good	Collectible
☐ 1″ to 1½″	60.00	50.00	40.00	15.00
☐ 1⅝″ to 1⅞″	80.00	65.00	50.00	20.00
☐ 2″ and over	110.00	90.00	60.00	30.00

MACHINE-MADE GLASS MARBLES

	Mint	Near Mint	Good	Collectible

Akro agate, Master Glass (aggies, slags, mibs, etc.)

	Mint	Near Mint	Good	Collectible
☐ To 7/8″	.30	.20	.10	.05
☐ 1″ to 1 1/2″	5.00	3.00	2.00	.50

Marble King, C. E. Bogard (mibs, aggies, cat's-eyes, etc.)

☐ To 7/8″	.02	.02	.01	n/a
☐ 1″ to 1 1/2″	.25	.10	.05	n/a

Peltier Glass, Ravenswood (mibs, aggies, etc.)

☐ Comics	40.00	25.00	15.00	5.00
☐ To 7/8″	.02	.02	.01	n/a
☐ 1″ to 1 1/2″	.25	.10	.05	n/a

Champion agate, Gladding Vitro Agate
(mibs, aggies, etc.)

☐ To 7/8″	.02	.02	.01	n/a
☐ 1″ to 1 1/2″	.25	.10	.05	n/a

Mechanical
Music Machines

JUKEBOXES

DESCRIPTION: A coin-operated phonograph that automatically plays records is a jukebox.

PERIOD: The most collectible jukeboxes were manufactured from 1938 to 1948.

MAKER: The most popular machines were manufactured by Wurlitzer. They were prized for their imaginative cabinetry and see-through mechanisms. Favored models are the 850, 950, and 1015.

Price Range

☐ **Rock-Ola jukebox,** c. 1939, series D type, serial #64374a with 20 multiselector programs, in a wood and veined, orange plastic case, 4′9¾″ high 500.00   700.00

☐ **Wurlitzer Model 1100,** c. 1948, with a glazed front revealing 24 selections with 45-rpm records

flanked by columns of rotating lights, veneered wood case (restored), 57″ high	4000.00	5000.00
☐ **Wurlitzer Model 1015,** c. 1946, with bubble tubes framing a glazed front revealing 24 selections, a veneered wood case (restored), 60″ high	10,000.00	11,000.00

MUSIC BOXES

DESCRIPTION: This section deals with cylinder music boxes. The cylinder has an arrangement of tiny metal pins that pluck the teeth of a tuned metal comb as the cylinder revolves. This causes the tune to play.

PERIOD: Cylinder music boxes were popular from the mid-1800s to 1890.

ORIGIN: Cylinder music boxes originated in 18th-century Switzerland.

COMMENTS: With the advent of the disc music box and other forms of home entertainment, cylinder music boxes lost some of their popularity. Today such music boxes are quite collectible.

☐ **B. A. Bremond cylinder music box,** Swiss, c. 1870, Serial No. 12788, 13″ cylinder plays 10 airs listed on the original tune sheet, with stop/start and change levers, contained in a rosewood-veneer case with a central medallion of musical and floral motifs (restored), 22″ wide	800.00	1200.00
☐ **German 22″ coin-operated disc music box,** probably by Monopol, c. 1900, the peripheral-driven movement with double combs, crank-wound with coin		

Price Range

slot at side, contained in a glazed-oak case with discs, 42″ high 1500.00 2000.00

☐ **Lecoutre key-wound cylinder music box,** Swiss, late 19th century, 13″ cylinder plays eight airs, replaced blank tune sheet with stop/start, change and instant stop lever, contained in a maple case with fruitwood banding, comb stamped LF Geneve (four teeth replaced, one replaced tip, needs some redampering), 20″ wide 780.00 980.00

☐ **M. Bolivillier key-wound music box,** Swiss, Serial No. 5441, the 10¾″ cylinder plays six airs as indicated on the original tune sheet, with stop/start, change and instant stop levers, contained in a maple case with floral inlay on lid, stamped M. Bolivillier, 5441, 18″ wide 780.00 980.00

☐ **Nicole Freres cylinder "Mandoline" music box,** Swiss, c. 1850, Serial No. 44285, the 13″ cylinder plays eight airs as indicated on the original tune sheet, lever-wound at the side with stop/start and change/repeat levers, contained in a rosewood box with a central medallion, stamped Nicole Freres Geneva, 44285, 21½″ wide 1500.00 1800.00

☐ **Nicole Freres "Mandoline Expressive" cylinder music box,** Swiss, late 19th century, Serial No. 57558, the 11″ cylinder plays six airs including Wagner, Weber, and Verdi, as indicated on original tune sheet, lever wound at the right with double-spring barrel, stop/start and change/repeat

Price Range

levers, contained in a burr walnut and rosewood case with a central floral motif, comb stamped Nicole Freres, 21½″ wide 1500.00   2000.00

☐ **Nicole Freres "Overture" interchangeable music box,** Swiss, late 19th century, Serial No. 43631, each of the 12 16″ cylinders playing 48 overtures by such composers as Handel, Haydn, Mozart, Rossini, Mendelssohn, Strauss, and Mattei, as indicated on the brass engraved tune sheet, lever-wound with stop/start and change/repeat levers, stamped Nicole Freres, Geneve, 43631, contained in a rosewood case with classical inlaid decorative motif on the lid, with mother-of-pearl flowers at the corners, the 12 cylinders contained in a separate mahogany, walnut, and ebonized cabinet with two doors revealing four drawers and two side storage areas (set of 17 replaced teeth), 46″ high 12,600.00 13,800.00

☐ **Regina 11″ disc music box,** American, early 1900s, Serial No. 10651, the center-driven movement with stop/start switches, single comb, and crank-wound at the top, oak box with 13 discs, 13″ wide 800.00   960.00

☐ **Regina "Sublima" style 25, 20″ disc music box,** American, c. 1900, coin-operated musical box with a peripheral driven movement, double comb, crank-wound at side, glazed mahogany case with storage cabinet below with 11 discs, 70″ high 6000.00   7200.00

Price Range

☐ **Swiss "Drum and Bells in Sight" music box,** c. 1875, No. 26428, 13″ cylinder playing 12 airs as listed on the original tune sheet, accompanied by drum and six bells applicable at will, mahogany case with fruitwood banding and foliate inlay (needs redampering, some rust on comb and cylinder), 28″ long. 1500.00   2000.00

☐ **Swiss interchangeable music box,** late 19th century, each of the three 13″ cylinders plays eight airs, lever-wound with double spring barrel, stop/start and change/repeat levers, tune indicator and a temp regulator, rosewood case above a storage drawer, 34″ long 3000.00   4000.00

☐ **Swiss key-wound cylinder music box,** c. 1840, 11¾″ cylinder plays eight airs, key-wound at right with stop/start, change and emergency stop levers, plain case (one tooth missing, dampers need repair), 19″ wide 500.00   600.00

☐ **Swiss "Mandoline Expressive" cylinder music box,** late 19th century, Serial No. 19169, 17″ cylinder plays eight airs (replaced blank tune sheet), lever-wound with double-spring barrel, zither attachment applicable at will, stop/start and change/repeat levers, walnut case with brass and mother-of-pearl inlay, 31″ long. 2000.00   2500.00

☐ **Swiss "Organ" cylinder music box,** Heller, late 19th century, 12½″ cylinder plays eight airs as indicated on the original tune sheet, lever-wound with stop/start

Price Range

and change/repeat levers, rosewood case with fruitwood banding (lacks one tooth, needs new
governor), 23″ wide 300.00   360.00

☐ **Swiss Sublime Harmony cylinder music box,** Allard & San-
doz, late 19th century, Serial No.
3544, 11″ cylinder plays eight
tunes as indicated on the original
tune sheet, with stop/start and
change/repeat levers, burr walnut
case with fruitwood banding (one
broken tip, needs some damper
repair), 20½″ wide 850.00   1050.00

☐ **Symphonion 12″ disc music
box,** German, c. 1900, Serial No.
345361, center-driven movement
with Sublime Harmony comb arrangement, wound to the side,
oak and walnut case with fruitwood floral motif, stamped
345361, with 10 discs, 19″
wide 1000.00   1400.00

☐ **Symphonion, 10¾″ disc music box,** German, early 1900s,
center-driven movement with
Sublime Harmony comb arrangement, stop/start lever, crank-
wound at the center, contained in
an ebonized box with 13 discs,
12½″ wide 500.00   600.00

NICKELODEONS

☐ **Engelhardt Nickelodeon,** American, early 1900s, three rectangular panels of leaded art glass above
the keyboard, electric mechanism
below, oak cabinet, with rolls,
60″ long 2000.00   2800.00

Price Range

☐ **Nickelodeon, Seeburg Model C,** c. 1911, five arched panels of leaded art glass above the keyboard, electric mechanism below, oak cabinet, with rolls, 63″ long 2800.00   3600.00

PLAYER ORGANS

☐ **Empire-style mahogany barrel organ,** 2nd quarter 19th century, hand-cranked at the front, two pinned wood barrels playing 10 tunes as indicated on the original tune sheet, 19 keys and two ranks totaling 36 pipes, mahogany case flanked by columns, 37″ high 800.00   1200.00

☐ **Orchestrian,** German, coin-operated, c. 1900, weight-driven movement with 33″ wooden barrel on piano, two drums, cymbals, two bells, mahogany case with screen doors, winding handle arbor and start/stop lever at the side, 78″ high 2500.00   3500.00

☐ **Paper roll organette,** Canadian, W. E. Abbott & Co., late 19th century, the mahogany case with gold stenciled decoration with two feeding reels and a central flap, with four paper music sheets, 27″ long 500.00   700.00

Metalware

TYPES COVERED: Brass, bronzes, cast-iron, wrought-iron, chrome, copper, pewter, and silver.

Note: The single values shown below are the actual auction-realized prices.

BRASS

DESCRIPTION: Brass is an alloy of copper and zinc and has been used since antiquity. Because of its malleable nature it can be fashioned into a wide variety of utensils, tools, and decorative objects.

COMMENTS: Decorative brassware has been imported from the Orient since the turn of the century. These wares feature very intricate engraving and tooling. Brass is very durable, and although it tarnishes quickly, it can be polished and restored to its lovely golden color very easily. Brassware can often be found in garage sales very cheaply, as many people are unwilling to polish it regularly.

Andirons, pair, c. 1820, by John Hunneman, Boston, marked "Hunneman Boston," 14″ high, 24″ long, $1400. (*Photo courtesy of Phillips, New York*)

	Price Range
☐ **Andirons,** pair, c. 1820, by John Hunneman, Boston, marked "Hunneman Boston," 14″ high, 24″ long	1400.00
☐ **Andirons,** pair, Queen Anne style, ball finial on baluster stem and cabriole leg, 18″ high	40.00
☐ **Cachepot,** Russian, turn-of-the-century, of circular bulbous form, three lion-mask and loose ring handles, raised on scroll legs, 6¾″ high	30.00
☐ **Fireplace screen,** French style, fan type, 26½″ high	40.00
☐ **Letter slots,** two, Victorian, with door handle decoration, variously sized	35.00
☐ **Pot,** 19th century, Persian, circular bulbous flaring form with	

Price Range

straight neck, incised calligraphy
and geometric decoration overall,
8 ½ " high 75.00

☐ **Powder horn,** 19th century,
Middle Eastern, of curved tapering form, with applied cut card
decoration incised on one side
and suspended from two swivel-
ing rings, 13 " long 65.00

BRONZES (See also Art Nouveau/Art Deco)

DESCRIPTION: Sculptures and other decorative objects
were cast in bronze and usually made in limited numbers.

TYPES: Bronze statues were often made in classical styles,
such as gods and goddesses, animals and warriors; also vases,
urns, bookends, and similar items.

PERIOD: Though bronze sculpture is of ancient origin, most
of the collectible specimens on the market are Victorian to
early twentieth century.

CARE AND CONDITION: Clean and polish bronze with a
good bronze polish. This will guard against corrosion.

Price Range

☐ **Candelabra,** by Tiffany Studios,
six-arm candelabra branching
from central bud-finial standard,
each bobeche held in a tripod
crutch, stamped "TIFFANY STU-
DIOS/NEW YORK/1920," 17 ½ "
high 1540.00

☐ **Candlesticks,** pair, by Tiffany ...   1045.00

☐ **Desk Set,** six pieces, by Tiffany,
"Chinese" pattern 1045.00

☐ **Door knocker,** German, satyr
mask and ring handle, signed
"Gesetzlich," 7 " high 70.00

☐ **Lamp base,** rare, made by Tiffany Studios for Tiffany & Company, New York, circular base

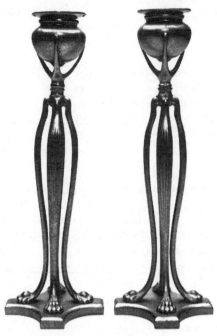

Candlesticks, pair, by Tiffany, $1045. (*Photo courtesy of Butterfield & Butterfield, San Francisco*)

	Price Range
with egg and dart, fitted for three-light fixture, numbered "15023 Tiffany & Co.," 25″ high	2310.00
☐ **Orpheus,** after Edmond Julien Noel, French, 19th century	4675.00
☐ **"Standing Horse Near a Fence with a Flared Tail,"** after P. J. Mene, 15½″ long	230.00
☐ **Tray,** by Paul Manship, depicting Diana and a hound, 3½″ diameter, bearing the foundry mark for Roman Bronze Works	1200.00
☐ **Urns,** pair, French marble and ormolu, Neoclassical style, wine-color marble set with laurel leaf,	

Orpheus, after Edmond Julien Noel, French, 19th century, $4675. (*Photo courtesy of Phillips, New York*)

	Price Range
acanthus, and geometric doré bronze mounts, 27½″ high	1300.00
☐ **Vases,** pair, Continental, 20th century, gilt-bronze, patina rubbed, 12″ high	467.50

CAST AND WROUGHT IRON

DESCRIPTION: Nineteenth-century kitchenware and other household items were often made of iron because of its durability.

COMMENTS: Ironware usually can be found for fairly low prices. Marked pieces are of greater value and importance. Dates on ironware do not always stand for the year made; some dates stand for the year the patent was issued.

Oiling or polishing old ironware decreases its value.

	Price Range	
☐ **Balustrade,** from the Paris Metro, designed by Hector Guimard, c. 1900, cast with an ornate openwork floral and whiplash motif and M, green patina, unsigned, 29″ high		440.00
☐ **Bench,** extremely rare Gothic cast iron, c. 1830, minor repairs, well cast, 57″ long	600.00	1000.00
☐ **Boot scraper,** Classical cast iron, early 19th century	250.00	350.00
☐ **Dachshund boot scraper,** 21″ long	35.00	45.00
☐ **Door knocker,** Classical cast iron, mid-19th century	25.00	50.00
☐ **Garden settee,** c. 1850, grapevine pattern with fretwork seat, 33″ high, 43″ long, 15″ deep ...		800.00
☐ **Infant bath,** 19th century, end-mounted handles, 21″ long		100.00
☐ **Planter,** Victorian, cast-iron, 19th century, bombé form, short whorl feet	125.00	220.00
☐ **Settee,** American, rococo cast-iron, mid-19th century, 45″ long	500.00	700.00
☐ **Urn,** American cast-iron, mid-19th century	400.00	600.00
☐ **Wrought-iron gates,** pair, designed by Eliel Saarinen for the Cranbrook Academy of Arts Museum, c. 1928, the interior with stepped skyscraper device surmounted by a foliate motif, 48″ high, 37″ wide		5500.00
☐ **Wrought-iron corner sconce,** by Raymond Subes, c. 1930,		

Garden settee, c. 1850, the grapevine pattern with fretwork seat, 33″ high, 43″ long, 15″ deep, $800. (*Photo courtesy of Phillips, New York*)

	Price Range
inverted dome with Martele finish, unsigned, 14″ high	550.00

CHROME

☐ **Cocktail shaker set,** by Chase, unmarked, 8 pieces	110.00
☐ **Desk lamp,** American, c. 1930, copper base, unmarked, 14″ high	550.00
☐ **Blanket chest,** polychrome and giltwood, by Max Kuehne, c. 1930, incised to depict Indian or Persian scenes in polychrome,	

Price Range

silver, and giltwood, interior
likewise decorated, 44 1/2 " wide,
19 3/8 " deep, 21 " high 4180.00

COPPER

DESCRIPTION: This versatile metal has been used extensively by mankind in every conceivable way. Copper is an excellent conductor of heat and electricity and is also very malleable. It has been made into wire, cooking utensils, coins, decorative objects, and countless other useful items.

Price Range

☐ **Bookends,** by Roycroft, L-form
with attached ring, in a hammered finish, marked 132.00

☐ **Desk set,** by Roycroft, comprising: a circular inkwell, a pen tray,
letter opener, desk calendar and
four corner blotter-mounts, with
hammered finish, decorative incised borders and star motif,
marked 165.00

☐ **Pan,** large, hammered copper,
mid-19th century, with a large
wrought-iron rear handle and a
brass front handle, 12 " high, 32 "
long, 14 1/2 " diameter 225.00

☐ **Milk pan,** early 19th century,
with double handles, rolled rim,
and dovetail and seamed bottom,
19 " diameter 185.00

☐ **Caldron,** early 19th century,
with wrought-iron swinging handle, and dovetail and seamed
bottom, 21 1/2 " high, including
handle, 14 1/2 " diameter 250.00

☐ **Smoking set,** comprising a cylindrical, covered humidor with
lucite ball knop, matching strike,

Left to right. Pan, large, hammered copper, mid-19th century, with a large, wrought iron rear handle and a brass front handle, 12″ high, 32″ long, 14½″ diameter, $225. Milk pan, early 19th century, with double handles, rolled rim, and dovetail and seamed bottom, 19″ diameter, $185. Caldron, early 19th century, with wrought iron swinging handle, and dovetail and seamed bottom, height including handle—21½″, 14½″ diameter, $250. (*Photo courtesy of Phillips, New York*)

                                                    Price Range

and two cups with saucers on matching circular tray, all in copper with decorative silver applications and copper brads, stamped "STERLING SILVER & OTHER METALS, 9″, tray 13″ diameter 264.00

PEWTER

DESCRIPTION: Pewter is an alloy composed principally of tin. To measure the quality of pewter, a number of criteria can be applied. Among the determining factors are proportion, clarity of outline, vigor of ornament, and the success with which the ornament is integrated into the form of the object. Of course, personal taste and current fashion among collectors may also affect the value of a particular object.

Price Range

☐ **Vase and dish,** vase by Kayser-zinn, design by Hugo Leven, swelled cylindrical body with scalloped rim, upper body molded on each side with a drag-onfly, base with pond lilies, marked, 16″ high; Liberty & Co. dish with curvilinear and cut-out design of leaves and vines, marked, 5″ diameter 220.00

☐ **Inkwell,** silvered pewter, by Kayserzinn, oval, center back rim, squared inkwell with cover formed as a sphinx's head, stamped "KAYSERZINN 4333," 11¾″ long 440.00

☐ **Tudric pewter tray,** large, by Liberty & Co., hammered oval with stepped curved border in-corporating openwork handles, impressed "TUDRIC 0232," 24″ long 220.00

SILVER

DESCRIPTION: Silver is always alloyed with base metal, usually copper, in manufacturing. This is done to provide durability, as silver in its pure state is soft and vulnerable. The grade of silver is determined by the amount or per-centage of alloy material contained. Sterling silver, the tra-ditional American grade for silverware, is .925 fine.

TYPES: American silverware includes both factory mer-chandise and items made by individual craftsmen. Some chief manufacturers include Gorham, Reed and Barton, Towle, Wallace, Rogers, Oneida, Reliance, Kirk, and Inter-national. All types of items are made from silver, including tableware, household ornaments, artwork, and jewelry.

Aesthetic Movement silver centerpiece compote, by Ball, Black & Co., New York, late 19th century, stamped "Ball, Black & Co, New York, English, Sterling 166," 12¾" high, 10¼" diameter, 40.7 oz total weight, $2300. (*Photo courtesy of Phillips, New York*)

Price Range

☐ **Aesthetic Movement silver centerpiece compote,** by Ball, Black & Co., New York, late 19th century, stamped "Ball, Black & Co, New York, English, Sterling 166," 12¾" high, 10¼" diameter, 40.7 oz total weight 2300.00

American silver flatware set, by Wilcox & Evertson, Conn., 135 pieces, 143 oz total weight excluding knives, $3400. (*Photo courtesy of Phillips, New York*)

Price Range

☐ **American silver tankard,** New York, c. 1730, by Adrian Bancker, engraved with monogram "J.H.E.M.," marked below rim on either side of handle "AB" in oval, 7″ high, 36 oz total weight 3700.00

☐ **American silver flatware set,** by Wilcox & Evertson, Conn., 135 pieces, 143 oz total weight excluding knives 3400.00

☐ **Art Deco four-piece silver tea and coffee set,** American, c. 1930, stamped "Sterling 102," 48.1 oz total weight including handles 1200.00

Art Deco four-piece silver tea and coffee set, American, c. 1930, stamped "Sterling 102," 48.1 oz total weight including handles, $1200. (*Photo courtesy of Phillips, New York*)

English silver-plate chambersticks, late 18th century, by Matthew Boulton, stamped with two suns, 4″ high, $600. (*Photo courtesy of Phillips, New York*)

George III silver-gilt centerpiece basket, London, 1779, by Thos Powell, 7 ½ " high, 10 ½ " long, 29.1 oz total weight, $2500. (*Photo courtesy of Phillips, New York*)

	Price Range
☐ **Continental luncheon plates,** five, 10 " diameter	770.00
☐ **Empire silver coffee jug,** Paris, c. 1809–1819, 13 " high, 33 oz total weight	1600.00
☐ **English silver-plate chambersticks,** late 18th century, by Matthew Boulton, stamped with two suns, 4 " high	600.00
☐ **George III silver-gilt centerpiece basket,** London, 1779, by Thos Powell, 7 ½ " high, 10 ½ " long, 29.1 oz total weight	2500.00

German eight-piece tea and coffee service, by Friedlander, 13″ high, $4950. (*Photo courtesy of Christie's East, New York*)

	Price Range
☐ **German silver two-handled tray,** engraved at center with coat-of-arms, length over handles 37″	3740.00
☐ **German eight-piece tea and coffee service,** by Friedlander, 13″ high	4950.00
☐ **German plated two-light wall sconces,** set of four, 19th century, fitted for electricity, 19″ long	2090.00
☐ **Italian silver large standing cup, cover, and tray,** Renaissance style, late 19th century, 18″ high, 14″ diameter, 92.2 oz total weight	3700.00
☐ **Mexican three-handled centerpiece stand,** 16″ high, 121.5 oz weight	1210.00
☐ **Mexican dinner service,** monogrammed, 55 pieces, 630 oz weight	5500.00

Italian silver, large standing cup, cover and tray, Renaissance style, late 19th century, 18″ high, 14″ diameter, 92.2 oz total weight, $3700. (*Photo courtesy of Phillips, New York*)

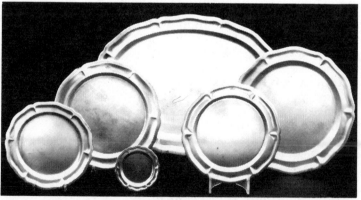

Mexican dinner service, monogrammed, 55 pieces, 630 oz weight, $5500. (*Photo courtesy of Christie's East, New York*)

Movie
Collectibles

DESCRIPTION: Cinemabilia is everything from Dixie ice cream lids, featuring photos of yesterday's movie favorites, to actual costumes or movie props. Malcolm Willits' Hollywood-based, mail-order auctions, called Collectors' Showcase (1708 N. Vine St., Hollywood, CA 90028), has consistently led the pack by smashing record after glamorous record as he scours the attics of Tinseltown.

TYPES COVERED: Ad press kits, autographs, lobby cards, and photographs.

AD PRESS KITS

BACKGROUND: These are packages of black-and-white ads used by the theaters to advertise films, as well as suggestions to help boost customers, like staging a James Dean or Marilyn Monroe look-alike contest.

1950s

	Price Range	
☐ *A Bullet for Joey,* A. Trotter, Edward G. Robinson, George Raft ..	8.00	12.00
☐ *The Bad and the Beautiful,* Lana Turner, Kirk Douglas, Walter Pidgeon, Dick Powell	10.00	15.00
☐ *Blowing Wind,* Gary Cooper, Barbara Stanwyck	10.00	15.00
☐ *Dangerous When Wet,* Esther Williams, Fernando Lamas	8.00	12.00
☐ *Dragnet,* Jack Webb, Bev Alexander	10.00	15.00
☐ *Executive Suite,* William Holden, Barbara Stanwyck, Shelley Winters, Nina Foch, Paul Douglas	10.00	15.00
☐ *The Far Country,* James Stewart	10.00	15.00
☐ *The Homesteaders,* Wild Bill Elliott	8.00	12.00
☐ *The Indian Fighter,* Kirk Douglas	10.00	15.00
☐ *Island in the Sky,* John Wayne	10.00	15.00
☐ *It Could Happen to You,* J. Holliday, Peter Lawford	10.00	15.00
☐ *Johnny Guitar,* Joan Crawford .	10.00	15.00
☐ *Jupiter's Darling,* Esther Williams, Howard Keel	8.00	12.00
☐ *The Left Hand of God,* Gene Tierney, Humphrey Bogart	10.00	15.00
☐ *Man with the Gun,* Robert Mitchum	8.00	12.00
☐ *The Moonlighter,* Fred MacMurray, Barbara Stanwyck	10.00	15.00
☐ *The Naked Spur,* James Stewart, Janet Leigh	10.00	15.00
☐ *Never Let Me Go,* Clark Gable, Gene Tierney	10.00	15.00
☐ *The Man from Laramie,* James Stewart	10.00	15.00

	Price Range	
☐ *Roman Holiday,* Audrey Hepburn, Gregory Peck	10.00	15.00
☐ *Sabrina,* Audrey Hepburn, Humphrey Bogart	10.00	15.00
☐ *Sadie Thompson,* Rita Hayward	10.00	15.00
☐ *Shane,* Van Heflin, Alan Ladd, Jean Arthur	10.00	15.00
☐ *Six Bridges to Cross,* Tony Curtis	8.00	12.00
☐ *Solid Gold Cadillac,* Judy Holliday, Paul Douglas	10.00	15.00
☐ *Summertime,* Katharine Hepburn	10.00	15.00
☐ *Ten Wanted Men,* Randolph Scott, Richard Boone	8.00	12.00
☐ *Texas Lady,* Claudette Colbert	8.00	12.00
☐ *Topeka,* Wild Bill Elliott	8.00	12.00
☐ *Vera Cruz,* Gary Cooper, Burt Lancaster	10.00	15.00
☐ *Violent Men,* Glenn Ford, Barbara Stanwyck	10.00	15.00

1960s

☐ *A Man Called Dagger,* Terry Moore, 1967	4.00	6.00
☐ *Bonnie and Clyde,* Warren Beatty, 1967	15.00	25.00
☐ *Counterpoint,* Charlton Heston, 1967	4.00	6.00
☐ *Custer of the West,* Robert Shaw, 1968	4.00	6.00
☐ 1964	10.00	20.00

CELEBRITY AUTOGRAPHS

☐ **Abbott and Costello,** rare early 8″ × 10″ photo, signed by both	250.00	350.00

	Price Range	
☐ **Bette Davis,** early-1940s, 8″ × 10″ photo, inscribed	50.00	100.00
☐ **Clark Gable,** signed check, matted and framed with 8″ × 10″ color portrait	200.00	300.00
☐ **Greta Garbo,** autographed studio portrait, by MGM photographer Ruth Harriet Louise, with message and signature in lower right corner above photographer's blind stamp, 10¼″ × 13¼″		550.00

LOBBY CARDS

Individual 11″ × 14″

☐ *African Queen,* Humphrey Bogart, 1952, No. 2	40.00	50.00
☐ *Bride of Frankenstein,* 1935, Colin Clive, Ernest Thesiger	1000.00	1300.00
☐ *Bus Stop,* 1956, 20th Century-Fox, Marilyn Monroe, Don Murray, scene card, No. 5	25.00	65.00
☐ *China Seas,* 1935, Wallace Beery, Clark Gable, Jean Harlow	300.00	400.00
☐ *The Harvey Girls,* 1945, MGM, Judy Garland	40.00	60.00
☐ *Holiday,* 1938, Columbia Pictures, Cary Grant, Doris Nolan ...	60.00	80.00
☐ *How to Marry a Millionaire,* Marilyn Monroe, 1953	40.00	50.00
☐ *Libeled Lady,* 1936, William Powell, Jean Harlow, Spencer Tracy	350.00	450.00
☐ *The Misfits,* 1961, United Artists, Clark Gable, Marilyn Monroe	40.00	60.00
☐ *On the Waterfront,* 1954, Columbia Pictures, Marlon Brando, Karl Malden, Eva Marie Saint	40.00	60.00

	Price Range	
☐ *Phantom of the Opera,* 1943, Claude Rains, title card	250.00	350.00
☐ *The Razor's Edge,* 1946, 20th Century-Fox, Tyrone Power, Gene Tierney, John Payne, Herbert Marshall	50.00	100.00
☐ *Saratoga,* 1937, Walter Pigeon, Jean Harlow, Clark Gable	200.00	400.00
☐ *The Seven Year Itch,* 1955, 20th Century-Fox, Marilyn Monroe, Tom Ewell	30.00	60.00
☐ *Woman of the Year,* 1942, MGM, Katharine Hepburn, Spencer Tracy	50.00	70.00

Sets of 8

☐ *Asphalt Jungle,* 1950, MGM	100.00	150.00
☐ *Bridge on the River Kwai,* 1958, Columbia Pictures	50.00	100.00
☐ *Breakfast at Tiffany's,* 1961, Paramount Pictures	30.00	50.00
☐ *Bullitt,* Steve McQueen, 1968 ...	50.00	100.00
☐ *Casino Royale,* Peter Sellers, 1967	35.00	45.00
☐ *Circus World,* John Wayne, 1965	35.00	45.00
☐ *Country Girl,* 1954, Paramount Pictures	50.00	100.00
☐ *Critic's Choice,* Lucille Ball, Bob Hope, 1963	30.00	40.00
☐ *Daniel Boone, Frontier Trail Rider,* Fess Parker, 1968	25.00	35.00
☐ *Donovan's Reef,* John Wayne, 1953	45.00	55.00
☐ *Girls, Girls, Girls,* Elvis Presley, 1962	50.00	70.00
☐ *Grapes of Wrath,* 1956, 20th Century-Fox	100.00	200.00

	Price Range	
☐ *Great Escape,* 1963, United Artists	75.00	125.00
☐ *Hamlet,* 1949, Universal Pictures	100.00	200.00
☐ *Jailhouse Rock,* 1957, MGM	100.00	150.00
☐ *Legend of the Lost,* 1957, United Artists	50.00	100.00
☐ *The Misleading Lady,* 1932, Paramount Pictures, Claudette Colbert, Edmund Lowe	350.00	500.00
☐ *North to Alaska,* John Wayne, 1960	50.00	70.00

PHOTOGRAPHS

☐ **Diana Ross,** color, facial photo .		60.00
☐ **Donna Reed,** portrait with James Stewart from *It's a Wonderful Life*, signed by both		85.00
☐ **Ethel Barrymore,** typed letter dated April 19, 1923		100.00
☐ **Fanny Brice,** early portrait, 8 ″ × 10 ″, b/w		125.00
☐ **Grace Kelly,** official Monaco wedding picture with Crown Prince Rainier, signed by both, matted and framed	1000.00	1500.00
☐ **Jean Arthur,** scene portrait, 8 ″ × 10 ″, b/w, signed by Joel McCrea and Jean Arthur		100.00
☐ **Johnny Weissmuller,** portrait in swimsuit, signed, 1930, Chicago		85.00
☐ **Katharine Hepburn,** signature on 3 ″ × 5 ″ card		55.00
☐ **Laurel and Hardy,** autographed check; Laurel lost $25 to Hardy during a poker game the two were playing between takes at the Hal Roach studio	600.00	700.00

Price Range

☐ **Marilyn Monroe,** magazine photo attached to black paper, signed in red ink 650.00

☐ **Marlene Dietrich,** motion picture still, *The Blue Angel,* signed and inscribed 65.00   80.00

☐ **Ronald Reagan,** 5½″ × 8½″, color postcard from Chicago's O'Hare Airport, signed, dated October 1959 .... 150.00   200.00

☐ **Richard Burton,** theater poster, *Hamlet,* signed 250.00   300.00

☐ **Tom Selleck,** color 8″ × 10″ portrait 25.00

☐ **Victor McLaglen,** full portrait, 8″ × 10″, b/w, in soldier's uniform 250.00

☐ **Vivien Leigh,** rare 6″ × 9″ 1963 theater playbill with her on the cover 80.00   120.00

☐ **Lauren Bacall,** color 8″ × 10″ portrait 28.00

Newspapers

DESCRIPTION: Newspapers are daily or weekly publications that contain news events, features, and advertising.

TYPES: The types of newspapers that are valuable are those with major events headlining their pages. One of the most valuable 20th-century newspapers is that carrying the premature "Dewey Defeats Truman" headline.

	Price Range
☐ **_Relation,_** Paris, April 3, 1635, a rare, very early paper, in French, decorative initial letter, much coverage of fighting in the Thirty Years War	30.00
☐ **_The Observator,_** London, May 3, 1682, one sheet printed front and back, consists of a discussion in dialogue form of current political and religious affairs	12.00
☐ **_The Observator,_** London, July 22, 1682	12.00
☐ **_Minutes of the Proceedings in Parliament,_** Edinburgh, May 30, 1693, one sheet printed front	

Price Range

only, consists of a list of laws passed the previous day 15.00

☐ *The Rehearsal,* London, February 23, 1706, one sheet printed front and back, consists of a discussion of current topics in dialogue form similar to that of *The Observator* 10.00

☐ *The Vision of Sir Heister Ryley: with Other Entertainments,* London, January 10, 1710, lasted only 80 issues, intended to compete with *The Spectator* and *The Tatler* but came to be regarded as too disreputable .. 15.00

☐ *The London Magazine,* January 1776, back-page report of a skirmish between the British and colonists in Boston in November 1775; inside, 2-page answer by the American Congress to a British threat to punish rebellious colonists 15.00

☐ *The Edinburgh Advertiser,* March 5–9, 1779, brief page-2 Revolutionary War report 7.00

☐ *The Independent Gazetteer; or the Chronicle of Freedom,* Philadelphia, August 8, 1789, page-2 proceedings of the House of Representatives, meeting in Philadelphia, page-2 listing of presidential appointments to revenue posts 8.00

☐ *Columbian Centinel,* Boston, September 1, 1790, page-2 report on a meeting between members of the Society of the Cincinnati and President Washington, with brief remarks by both 8.00

Price Range

☐ *New York Evening Post,* November 30, 1802, a very early issue of a paper founded by
Alexander Hamilton, who was
writing some of its editorials at
this time, page-1 illustrated ship-
ping ads and an ad for the sale of
household goods by future mil-
lionaire John Jacob Astor 12.00

☐ *Niles' Weekly Register,* Baltimore, January 7, 1815, inside-
page War of 1812 news, including
a report from New Orleans 5.00

☐ *Washington Gazette,* Washington, DC, August 2–4, 1823, a
scarce paper with an unusual format: news for the 4th on pages 1
and 4, news for the 2nd on pages
2 and 3; lengthy page-3 account
of an Indian attack on an American trading and hunting party on
the Missouri River 250 miles
above Council Bluffs 10.00

☐ *United States Telegraph,*
Washington, DC, October 4,
1828, a campaign paper with numerous articles supporting An-
drew Jackson's candidacy 5.00

☐ *Niles' Weekly Register,* May 27,
1837, long inside-page letter by
General Santa Ana describing his
courteous treatment as a captive
of General Houston and explaining why he visited Washington,
DC, after his release 5.00

☐ *Niles' Weekly Register,* July 1,
1837, page-1 report from Florida
on the current situation in the
Seminole Indian war 5.00

☐ *Niles' Weekly Register,* July 8,
1837, page-1 column-long report

Price Range

of skirmishes, with the Seminoles and an outbreak of cholera at Ft. Mellon 7.00

☐ *The Emancipator,* New York, February 8, 1838, an Abolitionist paper, page-1 account of the murder of Abolitionist editor Elijah Lovejoy by a Missouri mob 7.00

☐ *The Daily Picayune,* New Orleans, August 30, 1840, good page-2 account of a battle between Texans and Comanche Indians, page-3 slave ads, some ads marked in old pen 12.00

☐ *Emancipator and Free American,* Boston, August 3, 1843, an Abolitionist paper consisting of antislavery articles 5.00

☐ *Emancipator and Weekly Chronicle,* Boston, January 15, 1845, an Abolitionist paper, "James G. Birney" appears in old ink at upper right; this copy was delivered to Birney, who twice was the Abolitionist candidate for President, once winning New York State, includes debate over admission of Texas to the Union   7.00

☐ *Emancipator and Weekly Chronicle,* January 22, 1845, Birney's name appears at upper right as in previous lot, page-1 account of a duel between two Congressmen 7.00

☐ *New York Daily Tribune,* a bound run of 13 issues, November 15–December 1, 1849, four issues have lengthy page-1 reports on California and the gold rush ..   30.00

☐ *Daily National Intelligencer,* Washington, DC, January 15,

Price Range

1853, "J. Buchanan" appears in old pen in upper right margin; paper was delivered to future President James Buchanan at his home near Lancaster; page-3 ad for sale of *Uncle Tom's Cabin,* brief page-3 report on an expedition to the Behring Straits 15.00

☐ *Household Words,* London, November 29, 1856, a weekly journal published by Charles Dickens, includes commentary on political and social affairs 7.00

☐ *Harper's Weekly,* New York, May 1, 1858, full-page scene of Indians on horseback raiding a pioneer home, another page divided between two Western scenes, one of Indians hunting buffalo 15.00

☐ *The New York Herald,* April 8, 1861, page-1 heads and all of page 1 on Union mobilization, and a report that Ft. Sumter is to be evacuated the next day 5.00

☐ *Harper's Weekly,* New York, August 5, 1876, page-1 Thomas Nast political cartoon and another inside, full-page Nast cartoon based on the Custer massacre 12.00

☐ *Daily New Mexican,* Santa Fe, January 8, 1881, scarce Territorial paper, "Escaped a Rope"— page-1 account of an incident 20 years earlier when a cattle herder accused of stealing escaped lynching through an emotional appeal to his captors, a group of Texas rangers, interesting ads 10.00

Price Range

☐ *Deseret Evening News,* Salt Lake City, Utah Territory, April 18, 1890, brief page-1 report on General Sherman's birthday and a party at which he was present, good news coverage throughout 10.00

☐ *The Patriot,* Harrisburg, PA, August 36, 1892, "Lizzie Borden Is Given a Hearing—The Young Lady Charged with Killing Her Aged Father with an Axe"—page-1, 1-column heads and a 1½-column report on the trial, including a detailed description of the victim's wounds 15.00

☐ *The Mafeking Mail,* special siege issue, South Africa, April 3, 1900, one sheet printed both sides, published by a British garrison under siege by Dutch settlers during the Boer War; a line in masthead reads: "Issued Daily, Shells Permitting," page-1 report on skirmishing outside the besieged town 25.00

☐ *Canal Record,* Ancon, Canal Zone, March 11, 1908, reports on construction work, social life, and health problems in the Canal Zone, page-3 order signed by the Secretary of War sets fines and/or jail sentences for anyone driving a car over 15 miles per hour in the Zone 12.00

☐ *Olympic Games 1936,* Berlin, 1936, official publication of the XI Olympic Games, 40-page magazine with color cover, written in English, illustrated articles on the upcoming games with photos of many German athletes, plus an

Price Range

article on the 1912 Games with a
photo of Jim Thorpe 15.00

☐ *Guernsey Evening Press,* England, February 4, 1941, fascinating German occupation paper, in
English; Guernsey was a British
Channel Island captured by the
Germans; page 1 includes pro-
German war reports, a lesson in
elementary German appears on
page 4 .... 12.00

Ocean Liner Collectibles

COMMENTS: Current trends of ocean liner memorabilia have items that come from Europe much higher priced due to the falling dollar. This often makes the items out of the range of many collectors, but it also makes the items in the United States more valuable to collectors overseas. Our 20 to 40 percent increase in price is the same as theirs but at a discount.

An auction held in London on the 75th anniversary of the sinking of the *Titanic* featured items from the ship but proved of mixed success. Postcards fetched a high price, almost $4000 for one card. But other items, like plans from the investigation, a card case, and a wooden picture frame from a cabin did not sell because of a too-high reserve. This just shows that often greed places a higher value on an item than it is worth. But sometimes the item that is priced too high today could be worth that amount in the future. Or, quite possibly, when the *Titanic* fever goes down, the items could be worth a lot less.

Several *Titanic* postcard designs had a printing of possibly a million. A couple of years ago they could be bought for $5 to $10 in excellent condition. The recent discovery of the

Titanic caused quite a frenzy, and these cards then had an asking price of $20 and more. Often they go unbought. Obviously, you should know your material before you rush the boats to make a purchase. You may be adrift without a paddle.

Better early ocean liner postcards have become scarce, as have posters (1900–1920s). Cards and posters signed by the artist increase their value, if the artist is important. Condition and design are keys to the value. Bright colors and dramatic images make a poster or card stand out from the more common views. Let your eye give you a feeling of the picture.

Price Range

☐ *Adriatic,* unusual color-coded deck plan with photo interiors/ exteriors for the 1930 Mediterranean cruises of both the *Adriatic* and the *Laurentic,* one plan on each side 45.00

☐ *Adriatic,* menu for Washington's Birthday, February 22, 1929, Art Deco color cover, in a large White Star mailing envelope with house flag, unused, both 15.00

☐ *Adriatic,* silver-plated teaspoon with chain link handle surmounted by enameled portrait of the *Adriatic* at sea and tied with a silver bow, 4″ long 65.00

☐ *Albert Ballin,* rare, fine china demitasse cup and saucer, by Thomas of Bavaria, with a full-color portrait of the *Ballin* on the side, gold trim 100.00

☐ *Allan Line,* passenger list for the *Scotian,* September 26, 1912 ..... 15.00

☐ *Alaunia,* rare enameled pin in the shape of the ship's wheel with crossed British and Canadian flags in the center and ship's name on the rim 35.00

Price Range

☐ *Alaunia,* postcard, highly graphic, color, unused 15.00

☐ *Amerika,* rare, silk lady's handbag with a brass frame and chain, with *S.S. Amerika* and the year 1906 in gold on one side amid tiny brass laurel leaves each individually sewn on, 6″ × 5″ 250.00

☐ *Amerika,* embroidered silk gala night ribbon, black with gold lettering and a full color HAPAG house flag, 3′ long 65.00

☐ *Amerika,* menu, November 16, 1908 .... 15.00

☐ *America II,* copy of the New Testament given to passengers on her maiden voyage, August 10, 1940 .... 65.00

☐ *America II,* menu for her dog kennels, rare, never seen for any other vessel 25.00

☐ **American Line,** color poster of the *Philadelphia* fancifully passing the *Mayflower* for her return to service in 1920, extremely rare 250.00

☐ **Anchor Line,** sterling silver demitasse teaspoon with a full portrait of the *Caledonia* at sea, 3 ½″ long, rare 100.00

☐ *Andrea Doria,* pre-maiden voyage color poster by Patrone, dated 1951 and created for her launch, in original frame with brass nameplate with names of both *Andrea Doria* and *Colombo,* 33″ × 23″ 350.00

☐ *Andrea Doria,* silver-plated ashtray with raised fleur-de-lis in center over the name of the *Doria,* 3″ diameter 125.00

Price Range

☐ *Andrea Doria,* rare booklet of photo interiors showing "Art on board the *Andrea Doria,*" 20 pp · · · 100.00

☐ *Aquitania,* oil painting, canvas, by C. E. Hales, 1922, 21″ × 17″ · · · 1000.00

☐ *Aquitania,* lithograph on tin poster of the famous painting by Bishop of the *Aquitania* fancifully passing the *Britannia* at sea, with brass Cunard nameplate, 44″ × 33″ 800.00

☐ *Berlin I,* deck plan, extremely rare, tissue color-coded, all classes 100.00

☐ *Bremen IV,* booklet, photo interiors/exteriors for all three classes, 14 pp, November 6, 1929 · · · 100.00

☐ *Brittanic,* booklet, pre-maiden voyage, of full-color renderings for first class, 32 pp 165.00

☐ *Cedric,* paperweight, 4″ × 2¼″ × 1″, glass with full-color portrait with mother-of-pearl inserts of ship racing along at sea over her name in water 85.00

☐ **Cunard,** silver-plated serving tray, pre-World War I, the Cunard lion in the center, 10″ diameter, 1″ high 200.00

☐ **Cunard,** deck plan for the *China,* very rare 200.00

☐ **Cunard,** crew sailor hat with woven silk hat band, c. 1930s 125.00

☐ **Fabre Line,** tissue deck plan for the *Asia,* rare 65.00

☐ **Fabre Line,** baggage label, c. 1920s, unused 10.00

☐ *France II,* postcard, unused 15.00

☐ *France III,* chrome sign from the door of the Auvergne Suite, 8″ × 1½″, one of a kind 125.00

Price Range

☐ *Franconia III,* official company half-model, by Art Model Studio of Mt. Vernon, NY, "Cunard's Newest Cruise Liner *R.M.S. Franconia*" on the base, lights up, 40" × 15" × 7" 1500.00

☐ **French Line,** colored poster of *La Provence* greeted by a lady in peasant costume, by F. LeQuejne, behind the vessel the New York skyline and the Statue of Liberty, c. 1890s 1500.00

☐ **Hamburg American Line,** silver-plated egg cup, with enameled HAPAG crest raised out on the side, pre-World War I 125.00

☐ **Holland-America Line,** postcard (Panama-Pacific International Exposition, 1915), extremely rare, unused 45.00

☐ *Ile de France,* bronze medallion, designed by Marcel Renard and executed by French Mint, to dedicate her conversion and entrance into service in 1949, 2 1/4" diameter 100.00

☐ **Italian Line,** pre-maiden voyage booklet of full-color interior/exterior renderings for the *Ansonia,* 1928, 28 pp 200.00

☐ **Italian Line,** postcard of the *Principessa Mafalda* next to the *Cap Polonio* at Rio, unused 20.00

☐ **Leland Line,** china pitcher, by Royal Doulton, Victorian style, white with green design and house logo, 9" high 250.00

☐ *Leviathan,* menu for a private dinner aboard, April 16, 1925, unusual parrot cover 10.00

Price Range

☐ *Leonardo da Vinci,* metal model, 9 1/4 " × 1 1/4 " × 2 1/2 ", name in blue on base, rare 65.00

☐ *Lusitania,* silver-plated bon-bon dish, filagreed sides and the name of the *Lusitania* engraved in the center, 4 " × 1 1/2 " 100.00

☐ *Lusitania,* glass paperweight, with ship's full-color portrait racing along at sea, over her name, 4 " × 3 " × 1 " 75.00

☐ *Mauretania I,* silver-plated three-handled cup, with ship's portrait in a brass frame filling the entire side 75.00

☐ *Mauretania II,* maiden voyage passenger list, June 17, 1939, 3rd class 35.00

☐ *Michelangelo,* color poster of passing the *Raffaello* at sea, by Stor, in original frame with brass nameplate, 26 " × 18 " 100.00

☐ *Moro Castle,* aluminum ashtray, 9 " × 4 1/2 " with a 4 " high funnel for cigarettes and two 1 " high air vents rising out of it, "T.E.L. MORO CASTLE" engraved on rim of tray, on the bottom a label taped "Honeymoon—June, 1934" 200.00

☐ *Nieuw Amsterdam,* wooden model, highly detailed, on a wooden base with clay waves, 11 " × 2 " × 2 " 250.00

☐ **North German Lloyd,** photo portrait menu for the *General Von Steuben*, August 8, 1933 ..... 20.00

☐ **Orient Line,** sterling silver match safe, enameled logo on the lid over the name of the *Orontes,* fully hallmarked, 2 1/4 " × 1 3/4 " × 1/4 " 100.00

Price Range

☐ *Queen Elizabeth I,* china dish, swirled rim, by Staffordshire, with a full-color portrait of the queen in the bowl, racing along at sea, gold trim, 4″ × 3″ × ¾″ 35.00

☐ *Queen Mary,* chrome thermos with the Cunard name on the bottom, 7″ high 65.00

☐ **Red Star Line,** paper folding fan, highly graphic, one side covered with American flags and the other with a harbor scene for the *Vaderland,* in a display case, 16″ × 9″ × 1½″ 100.00

☐ **Red Star Line,** postcard menu for the *Marwuette,* June 21, 1912, folded 20.00

☐ **Swedish American Line,** poster, Art Deco style, 1930s, linen-backed, 39″ × 25″ 300.00

☐ *Titanic,* china plate, by Bauscher, white with gray trim and house logo, 8¼″ diameter ..   30.00

☐ *Titanic,* marble wall plaque, elaborately carved, inscribed " 'The S.S. Titanic' sunk by iceberg on her maiden trip off Halifax, April 15, 1912–1500 people drowned" and under this "S.S. Carpathia rescuing 705 survivors of the SS. Titanic," signed D. Giumettisc, 11½″ × 9½″ × ¾″ 2500.00

☐ **White Star Line,** passenger list for the *Majestic,* for September 12, 1900 ....   35.00

Oriental Collectibles

DESCRIPTION: Of all the objects hobbyists collect, none has more universal reputation and appeal than Chinese porcelain. The Chinese invented porcelain. There is no place in the world that fine Chinese porcelain is not recognized and respected. While specimens of the best T'ang and Ming ware are indeed costly, there are reasonable works of the Ch'ing dynasty on the market. There are huge amounts of Chinese porcelain available. Each dynasty has its porcelains in a rainbow-like assortment of colors and patterns. Because of the enormous variety that exists, it is impossible for Orientalia dealers to have a representative stock of all types of Oriental porcelain. Even the best museums cannot make such a claim. Most dealers have Ch'ing ware and some post-Ch'ing, not because this is the best Chinese porcelain but because it is the most widely affordable for the average collector. The value of a ceramic article will depend on style, time period, scarcity, originality, quality of shaping, quality of decoration, size, and ultimately physical preservation. Whatever you buy and wherever you buy, it is certainly wise to make a careful examination before committing yourself to the purchase. The specialist Orientalia shops try to offer something

Chinese export armorial bowl, $300. (*Photo courtesy of Phillips, New York*)

for nearly everyone interested in Far Eastern artworks. They purposely strive to carry a diverse stock in terms of the types of items offered and in their price ranges.

CHINESE

Ceramics

	Price Range	
☐ **Bowl,** Ch'ing Dynasty, porcelain, blue on white, circular flaring form, geometric decoration, 9″ diameter	70.00	90.00
☐ **Bowl,** armorial, Chinese export, 18th century, porcelain, decorated gilt rim and coat of arms on obverse and reverse, 9½″ diameter		300.00
☐ **Brushwasher,** T'ung-Ch'in period, porcelain, oxblood glaze, wafer form, 4″ diameter	150.00	200.00
☐ **Dish,** footed, porcelain, 19th century, octagonal, polychrome glazed decoration depicting birds,		

	Price Range	
deer, monkeys, and wasps in a landscape, 8½″ diameter	200.00	300.00
☐ **Ginger jar,** multicolored figural decoration on off-white ground, 20th century, 4½″ high	60.00	80.00
☐ **Tankard,** blue and white porcelain, decorated with a painted seascape and a decorated interlaced strap handle, 6″ high, 4¾″ diameter	400.00	600.00
☐ **Figure,** depicting a reclining dog, Chinese blanc de chine, 7″ long, c.1800	200.00	250.00

Furniture

☐ **Panel,** crudely carved wood, depicting the heat of battle in low and high relief, 14½″ × 37″, 20th century, 1950 earliest	200.00	300.00

Textiles

☐ **Rug,** Northern Chinese, 20th-century copy of earlier rug, heavy weave, multicolored geometric decoration on gray-brown background, approximately 2′ × 3′11″	150.00	200.00
☐ **Saddle cover,** wool, Northern Chinese Xizang, upper part rectangular shape, lower part geometric form with animal and bird decoration in predominately blue tones, approximately 1′10″ × 4′1″, c. 1890	100.00	150.00

Price Range

JAPANESE

Bronze and Other Metals

☐ **Ceremonial tea kettle,** pure
gold, by Hirata Sodo (1893–1978) 30,000.00 50,000.00

☐ **Ikebana vessel,** bronze, cylindrical, waisted foot and neck, incised architectural and landscape
decoration, raised on a trefoil
base, 9 3/4 " high, 20th century 200.00 300.00

Ceramics

HISTORY: Throughout history, until the twentieth century, the arts, crafts, and culture of China exerted a strong
influence on corresponding arts in Japan. Most craft trades
followed in Japan had their origins in China, such as the
making of hardpaste porcelain. Imari ware is named for the
Japanese port town where most of it was produced. It is
characterized by elaborate decorations of flowers and figures with intricate borders. Imari underglaze colors are usually black and dark blue with overglazes of gold, green,
orange, and red enamel.

DESCRIPTION: Satsuma pottery features a fine crackled
glaze and was first produced in the early seventeenth century with colored enamel ornamentation. Later Satsuma was
decorated with figures—demons and processionals; such extensive decoration characterizes the Satsuma we know today.

Price Range

☐ **Imari wine cup,** circular, traditional bird and geometric decoration on off-white ground, 3 1/2 "
diameter, early 20th century 80.00 120.00

☐ **Satsuma bowl,** porcelain, with
gilt and painted scalloped edge,
central interior decorated with a
processional scene of nobility,

	Price Range	
outer surface decorated with a painted landscape, 3¾″ high, 19th century	200.00	300.00

Miscellaneous

☐ **Mask,** Noh Theater, lacquer, depicting a smiling male face, 10¾″ high, 19th century	200.00	300.00
☐ **Vases,** pair, cloisonne enamel, by Ando Jibei	4000.00	6000.00

Nippon

DESCRIPTION: Nippon backstamps designate items imported from Japan between 1891 and 1921. Although every exported item during this period was marked, for the collector Nippon has come to mean porcelain. Produced in great quantities, twenty years ago it was abundant in supply, ordinary, and reasonable in cost. However, as more and more people began to collect Nippon, it slowly gained a reputation. Today it is considered a legitimate collectible. When determining value and price, first consider workmanship and condition; second, rarity and current popularity. Look for cobalt and floral items, painted scenics, and items with beadwork and heavy gold trim. The best prices are realized for pieces in mint condition.

	Price Range	
☐ **Basket dish,** floral decoration, gold handles, 9″ long	140.00	165.00
☐ **Bowl,** three-footed, melon-ribbed, heavy gold beading and scrolls, swags of small pink roses and green leaves, magenta "M" in wreath mark, 8″ long, 4″ tall	90.00	120.00
☐ **Bowl,** pale green with white and yellow flowers, gold beading,		

	Price Range	
green "M" in wreath mark, 10″ wide	100.00	130.00
☐ **Chocolate set,** pot with four cups and saucers, gold background with design of red roses, green "M" in wreath mark	250.00	300.00
☐ **Coaster set,** six pieces, scenic decoration, green "M" in wreath mark	90.00	120.00
☐ **Cologne bottle,** small floral design outlined in gold, green "M" in wreath mark, 5″ tall	90.00	120.00
☐ **Cookie jar,** melon shape, decorated profusely with red and pink roses, green "M" in wreath mark	300.00	375.00
☐ **Humidor,** yellow tulips, green leaves on beige matte background, green "M" in wreath mark, 6″ tall	350.00	425.00
☐ **Lemonade set,** pitcher and four cups, white background with large pink and red roses, pagoda mark	125.00	150.00
☐ **Stickpin holder,** with attached tray, scenic, green "M" in wreath mark, 2½″ tall	95.00	130.00
☐ **Sugar and creamer set,** dark green geometric design at top and bottom of bowls and on lids, green "M" in wreath mark	65.00	90.00
☐ **Sugar and creamer set,** Art Deco pattern, green "M" in wreath mark	65.00	90.00
☐ **Vase,** molded basketweave pattern, green "M" in wreath mark, 8¾″ tall, 5″ diameter	400.00	500.00
☐ **Vase,** country scene, jeweling, lots of gold trim, green "M" in wreath mark, 10″ tall	225.00	275.00
☐ **Vase,** melon-ribbed, bottle neck with three ring handles, plushy		

Covered urn, 10″ tall, portrait of Queen Louise, blue maple leaf mark, $700–$900. (*Photo courtesy of Joan Van Patten, Nippon Collectors International*)

	Price Range	
roses, pink jeweling, gold scrolls and beading, green maple leaf mark, 11″ tall	250.00	300.00
☐ **Vase,** muscleman shape, plushy pink and yellow roses, overlay of aquamarine blue with heavy gold beading and scrolls, green "M" in wreath mark, 11″ tall	250.00	300.00
☐ **Scenic and Wedgwood ferner,** 5½″ tall	375.00	500.00
☐ **Covered urn,** portrait of Queen Louise, blue maple leaf mark, 10″ tall	700.00	900.00
☐ **Serving platter,** part of a game set, heavy gold decoration, blue maple leaf mark, 17½″ long	600.00	800.00

Serving platter, 17 ½″ long, part of a game set, heavy gold decoration, blue maple leaf mark, $600–$800. (*Photo courtesy of Joan
Van Patten, Nippon Collectors International*)

	Price Range	
☐ **Vase,** floral and cobalt, blue maple leaf mark, 7 ¾″ tall	250.00	300.00

TIBET

	Price Range	
☐ **Bronze figure,** of a standing Vishnu, raised on a square bronze plinth, 14 ¼″ high, 18th century	700.00	900.00
☐ **Copper horn,** mouth in the shape of a dragon's head, applied coral and turquoise beads, 17″ long, mid-19th century	100.00	150.00

Paper Collectibles

COMMENTS: The paper collectibles scene is a very active one, with many areas reporting escalating prices as collector interest continues to climb. Naturally, because this area is so broad, some items will experience more movement than others. The entire paper collectible market seems to be dominated by the question of condition and rarity. Of course, these two factors are important in other collectible areas, but they are especially significant in the paper-collectible market. Therefore, when purchasing an item from a dealer, investor, or another collector, carefully examine the item for tears, holes, poor restoration, and general condition.

TYPES: Cards, documents, maps and charts.

CARDS

Price Range

☐ **Dance card,** very old, farewell ball, Ulman's Opera House, Thursday, October 10, 1889, inside shows all dances and what gentleman was danced with, on the back written "Good night,

	Price Range	

Good night, Parting is such sweet sorrow, That I shall say good night, 'Till it be morrow'' 8.00 15.00

☐ **Dance card,** c. 1880s, has a picture of a young lady dressed up on the cover, the card inside is filled out, also has the original pencil used to fill it out still attached by its ribbon 15.00 20.00

☐ **Gentleman's greeting card,** small, 3½" × 4½" card and envelope, superb calligraphy, envelope reads, "Miss Nellie Parsons, Greeting,'' card has embossed roses in upper left corner and reads, "Miss Nellie, May I have the pleasure to call on you this evening. Your Friend, John Reider,'' dated May 6, 1884, in lower left corner 15.00 20.00

DOCUMENTS

☐ **Baltimore city check,** signed by the city commissioner and the mayor, November 2, 1868, to pay for repairs at "Eastern Spring'' ... 10.00 15.00

☐ **Last will and testament,** of Adam Keller, 1863 .... 15.00 17.00

☐ **Ledger account book,** of Josiah Frost, neat manuscript entries dating from 1886 to 1903, approximately 50 pp, from the Brookfield, MA, area 25.00 30.00

☐ **New York City document,** August 17, 1819, affidavit of rent due, W. Cox complains that Isaac Marshall hasn't paid the rent 14.00 16.00

☐ **New York City document,** Summons for Money Demand

	Price Range	
against Ben Vandermark, hand-written, dated October 18, 1869	5.00	10.00
☐ **New York City mortgage,** dated December 8, 1826, between Joel Bishop and Simeon Strong, Lansing, NY	10.00	15.00
☐ **U.S. Internal Revenue tax stamp,** unused, yellow, for display in the place of business, it has a beautiful engraving of the nation's Capitol and is boldly dated 1882	10.00	20.00
☐ **1842 Tax collector's receipt,** from Prince George's County, MD, "State Tax on $2986 at 20¢ Per $100 . . . $5.58," signed by both collector and debtor	8.00	15.00
☐ **State of Maryland,** commission for Justice of the Peace, large document with big red state seal, signed by Governor William T. Hamilton in 1880	15.00	20.00
☐ **Talbot County, Maryland, deed,** 1891, 21″ × 15″, beautifully printed and easily readable, has county seal, dollar figures, description of land and much more	12.00	18.00

MAPS AND CHARTS

DESCRIPTION: Maps showing the layout of the land were printed as early as the mid-1400s. From an artistic and historical perspective, maps from the 1600s are the most desirable. However, for the purposes of the average collector, specimens that date from the 1800s are most affordable and easily found. While maps can be quite beautiful, they also chronicle an interesting part of history. Their progression and growth are fascinating. Earlier maps reflect the misconceptions people had about distance and the relationship between land forms. More modern maps not only cover greater areas with more accurate details but also feature landmarks, altitudes, and territorial boundaries.

	Price Range	
☐ **Blaeu, William,** *Americae nova tabula,* engraved map, old hand-coloring, depictions of tribes and places around three of the margins, cartouche of Greenland along upper margin, text on verso in French, foxing, taped down to mat, 16½″ × 22″, Amsterdam, c. 1650	800.00	1000.00
☐ **Chart, Delawar Bay,** composed and published for the use of Pilotage, engraved map with aquatint, showing the bay from Bombay Hook to Cape May, title panel in upper corner, some browning, margins, 30¾″ × 22¼″, London, June 1, 1779	1400.00	1800.00
☐ **Hondius, Jodocus,** America, engraved map, old hand-coloring, inset of natives in lower corner, slight wear down centerfold, foxing, margins, 15″ × 20″, Amsterdam, c. 1609	1800.00	2000.00
☐ **Mercator, Gerard,** *America sive india nova,* engraved map, old hand-coloring, three small inset maps in the corners depicting Haiti, Gulf of Mexico, and Cuba, text on verso in French, some browning and staining (mainly in the margins), torn with loss in upper corner, 14¾″ × 18½″, Duisburg, c. 1600	1000.00	1500.00
☐ **Muenster, Sebastian,** *Tabula novarum insularum—Die Nuw Welt,* woodcut map, hand-coloring, depicts the complete American continent, title and description on verso in Latin, four		

Price Range

worm holes in image, slight fox-
ing around margins, taped to mat,
$10\frac{1}{2}''$ × $13\frac{1}{2}''$, Basel, c. 1550 ..   500.00   700.00

☐ **"Plan of Fort Montgomery and
Fort Clinton,** taken by His Majes-
ty's Forces under the Command
of Maj. Gen.l Sir Henry Clinton . . .—Part of Hudson's River,
showing the position of Fort
Montgomery and Fort Clinton
with the . . . cables, chains, etc.
to obstruct the Passage of His Maj-
esty's Forces up the River . . .
1777,'' engraved map with etching and aquatint, inset panel of
"Part of Hudson's River,'' partly
hand-colored and with wash,
some slight browning, very faint
central crease, $21\frac{1}{2}''$ × $31''$,
London, January 1779 ....   800.00   1200.00

Paper Dolls

HISTORY: For over 150 years, paper dolls have been played with as toys and collected as an art form. Publishers of early paper dolls such as Raphael Tuck produced gorgeous lithographic work in Bavaria, Germany. The history of paper dolls very closely follows the growth of the printing and publishing industries. The styles and techniques have changed throughout the years. By the 1890s American advertising was making full use of printed trade cards and paper doll sets to merchandise household products. In the 1920s, children's book publishers began to make paper dolls. Likenesses of movie stars of the 1930s and 1940s were created as paper dolls. In the 1980s celebrated artists such as Bill Woggon, Tom Tierney, and Joan Anglund are drawing paper dolls again. Interest in paper dolls is enjoying a new resurgence.

COMMENTS: Prices fluctuate widely depending on age, condition, and whether or not the set has been cut. They can range from several dollars to several thousand dollars for a boxed Victorian set. Uncut sets are the most valuable, selling for twice the price of cut versions. Even though they have not reached what is considered a vintage age, modern paper dolls are highly collectible. Collectors are eager for the sheets drawn for magazines like *Good Housekeeping* by

Joan Anglund, for paper doll books by Tom Tierney, and for new comic book creations, including Misty and Vicki Valentine.

	Price Range	
☐ **Raphael Tuck and Sons' Courtly Beatrice,** c. 1894, doll, all four dresses, three of four hats, in folder, good condition	65.00	70.00
☐ **Taglioni, C.** 1827–1832, original box, doll and clothing, six outfits, three headdresses, all are back and front, box 10½″ × 7½″ and unbroken, doll is 9″ tall with her head turned to left, rare and hard to find	2,000	2,500.00
☐ **J. F. Spear's original character dolls,** c. 1895, Bavaria, 11″ doll, five heads, five costumes with hats, mends and creases on pieces, no box, very scarce	110.00	130.00
☐ **W. H. Baker's Chocolate and Cocoa series,** six dolls, each with extended skirt to form into a circle for standing, small size	.50	2.00
☐ **Williamantic Star Thread,** "Our Star Circus," envelope with set of animals and performers as paper toy stand-ups; set	25.00	50.00
☐ *Ladies' Home Journal* **magazine sheet,** October 1908 to September 1918, Lettie Lane and Betty Bonnet series by Shelia Young		
☐ **Uncut sheet**	5.00	15.00
☐ **Cut set from single sheet**	3.00	8.00
☐ *McCall's,* 1906–1936, Betsy McCall, uncut	3.00	8.00
☐ *Woman's Home Companion,* 1906–1933, uncut	4.00	20.00
☐ **Hedy Lamarr dolls and clothes,** 1942, No. 3482, favorite of all the movie star sets, except		

Price Range

for Shirley Temple, for the gorgeous art, unsigned

☐ **Uncut set**		200.00
☐ **Cut set**		65.00
☐ *Gone with the Wind,* 1940, No. 3405, five dolls.		
☐ **Uncut set**	225.00	300.00
☐ **Cut set**	85.00	110.00
☐ **New Shirley Temple in Paper Dolls,** 1942, No. 2425, teen pair with costumes form her personal wardrobe, film *Kathleen*, boxed (the clothes were reissued twice with non-Shirley dolls).		
☐ **Uncut #2425 set**	90.00	100.00
☐ **Cut set**	50.00	60.00
☐ **Kewpie Dolls,** 1963, No. 6088, boxed version of several reissued books		
☐ **Uncut boxed set**	20.00	30.00
☐ **Uncut book**	18.00	30.00
☐ **Hedy Lamarr,** 1951, No. 2600, uncut set	65.00	85.00
☐ *Nancy and Sluggo Coloring Book,* 1972, No. 1053, one paper doll on back cover with costumes inside among items to be colored, unused book		4.50
☐ **Pinocchio Push-out Stick-on and Color,** 1962 and 1971, No. 1683, unused set in box		14.00
☐ **Blondie,** 1938, paper doll square with outfits.		
☐ **Uncut set**		6.00
☐ **Cut set**		4.00
☐ **Boots,** 1938–1939, ¼ of large page, uncut	6.00	10.00
☐ **Katy Keene,** by Bill Woggon, appearing in various comic books and then in her own *Katy Keene Comics,* annual, "Pin-Up Pa-		

	Price Range	
rade,'' all with adventure stories and paper dolls with costume designs sent in by readers.		
☐ **Uncut annual**	15.00	60.00
☐ **Single sheet uncut paper doll**	4.00	9.00
☐ **Tom Tierney Paper Doll Books,** Dover Publications, Inc.: *Gone with the Wind*, Princess Grace, Nancy and Ronald Reagan, Gibson Girls, John Wayne, Pope John II; uncut book		3.95

Paper Money

DESCRIPTION: Currency notes issued by the federal government, as a medium of exchange ("legal tender").

MAKER: Since 1861 all U.S. paper money is produced by the U.S. Bureau of Printing and Engraving (BP&E) at Washington, DC. The first U.S. notes are known as Demand Notes. Earlier specimens were contracted for with private firms. From its origin to the present time, all U.S. paper money has been engraved. This process is considered the most difficult to counterfeit.

MATERIALS: A special quality of paper issued for U.S. paper money with tiny blue and red threads running through the fabric of the note.

NEW DESIGN: The currency redesign plan of the 1980s was necessitated by the growing ability of sophisticated copy machines to effectively reproduce currency and to stifle other counterfeiting methods. Two subtle but significant alterations were made to the face of the note. The addition of a clear polyester thread woven into the surface of the paper will appear vertically across the face of each note between the seal and the portrait on the $1 note and between the seal and the left edge of the note on all other denominations. The thread will act as a watermark which will be visible when held to a light source and will have "U.S.A." and the denomination repeated along its length in microprinted letters visible by a 7-power magnification but small enough not to be reproduced. The other change has the "United States of America" microprinted repeatedly and continuously around the top and sides of the portrait on the note.

MARKS: Various standard markings appear on U.S. paper money, including the Treasury Seal, district number, district, control number, and serial number. Serial numbers appear in different colors on various types of notes and appear twice on most notes. National Bank Notes have bold charter numbers appearing on each note. Paper money that has a star appearing in the serial number denotes that this is a replacement note for a damaged note and commands an additional premium price. When the numbers on a note are not alike or the Treasury Seal or district numbers are missing or wrongly positioned, it is regarded as an error note and commands a premium price.

GRADING: There are nine basic levels of grading conditions, with Uncirculated being split into four levels, for a total of twelve grading categories. The highest possible grade is Superb Gem Crisp Uncirculated (CU-67), followed by Gem Crisp Uncirculated (CU-65), Choice Crisp Uncirculated (CU-63) and uncirculated (CU-60). The circulated grades comprise About Uncirculated (AU-55), Extremely Fine (EF-45), Very Fine (VF-35), Fine (F-25), Very Good (VG-15), Good (G-10), Fair (F-3), and Poor (P-0).

PAPER: Paper money deteriorates in circulation very rapidly. When a note is said to be uncirculated, it has no creases, wrinkles, fading, or signs of fatigue; the paper is crisp and the printing fresh and bright. Notes in very deteriorated condition, with holes or corners missing, etc., are not deemed collectible unless the type is very rare.

Early U.S. paper money is often found with tiny pinholes, even when the condition is otherwise excellent. This is due to the common practice among oldtime storekeepers of impaling notes on nails before the use of cash registers. Since the defect is so commonplace, it does not cause a great reduction in values unless the hole occurs on the portrait.

VALUATIONS: The valuations given here are offered as a guide to collectors; prices were most carefully prepared and are based on recent sales records, supply and demand, rarity, and a thorough analytical study of the market. The prices represent an average at or about which the notes would be obtainable from a numismatic dealer.

COMMENTS: Traditionally, collectors/investors were interested only in the early types or "large size" currency. In 1929 the government reduced the physical size of notes to their present proportions. Today all paper money is collectible; however, common specimens must be in strictly uncirculated condition in order to be classified as a collectible.

MARKET TRENDS: The long awaited upturn in the currency market finally arrived in 1987. A positive change in attitude was apparent, for both the collector and dealer are actively searching for and puchasing in all grade levels. For the first time in about two years a significant amount of choice material has become available. I am very optimistic about the long-term future of the market and see 1988 as the year of opportunity for the collector/investor.

LARGE-SIZE NOTES: This is one of the primary areas in which collectors and dealers are having problems in locating suitable merchandise. There is an abundance of common issues, but the more elusive issues are difficult to find. Major activity is in the higher circulated grades. Top-quality notes are becoming difficult to obtain and now command substantial increases in price.

SMALL-SIZE NOTES: Small-size notes represent about the most sluggish portion of the current market, and yet here too there are some bright spots. Early Federal Reserve Notes and Star notes remain popular and in demand. The rarer notes are also proving quite salable, especially in higher grades. Error notes, on the other hand, are at bargain levels.

FRACTIONAL CURRENCY: The fractional currencies too seem to be coming out of the doldrums. The rarer issues and top-quality notes are seeing quite a bit of activity. Even specimens seem to be enjoying a bit of renewed interest.

NATIONAL BANK NOTES: Nationals remain very popular, with activity limited only by the amount of new material entering the currency market. Type Nationals remain very popular in the large size, with collectors, investors, and dealers seeking the higher circulated and uncirculated grades.

CLASSIFICATION NUMBERS: The classification numbers (FR-) used in this section are attributed to *Robert Friedberg's Paper Money of the United States.*

REFERENCES: The data sources listed below offer to the collector/investor a real resource of paper money information related to market trends, valuations, grading, and specific or general research materials.

Bank Note Reporter, 700 E. State St., Iola, WI 54990 ($18.00)

Currency Dealer Newsletter, P.O. Box 11099, Torrance, CA 90510 ($35.00)

U.S. Paper Money Grading Standard, H. J. Kwart, P.O. Box 2172, Ridgecrest, CA 93555 ($9.25)

Paper Money of the United States, 11th ed., Robert Friedberg, The Coins & Currency Institute, Inc., P.O. Box 1057, Clifton, NJ 07014 ($24.00)

Standard Catalog of U.S. Paper Money, Krause & Lemke, 4th ed., 700 E. State St., Iola, WI 54990 ($21.00)

ORGANIZATIONS: The paper money organizations listed below offer to their membership a quarterly publication or newsletter and auction. They also maintain an extensive library of paper money publications, which is offered through the mail to their membership.

Society of Paper Money Collectors, P.O. Box 6011, St. Louis, MO 63139 ($15)

International Banknote Society, P.O. Box 1642, Racine, WI 53401 ($17.50)

World Paper Money Collectors, P.O. Box 2172, Ridgecrest, CA 93555 ($6.00)

LARGE-SIZE NOTES

Demand Notes—Five Dollars

No.	Yr. Issued	Payable at	VG	VF	XF
☐ 1	1861	New York	800.	910.	2300.
☐ 2	1861	Philadelphia	800.	910.	2550.
☐ 3	1861	Boston	325.	900.	2300.

Legal Tender Notes—Ten Dollars

No.	Series	Signatures	Seal	VF	CU	Gem CU
☐ 114	1901	Lyons-Roberts	small Red	225.	850.	1200.
☐ 119	1901	Parker-Burke	small Red	225.	850.	1000.
☐ 122	1901	Spellman-White	small Red	200.	700.	975.

Silver Certificates—One Dollar

No.	Series	Signatures	Seal	VF	CU	Gem CU
☐ 215	1886	Rosecrans-Jordan	small Red	155.	650.	1000.
☐ 221	1886	Tillman-Morgan	small Red-Sep	200.	550.	1000.
☐ 224	1896	Tillman-Morgan	small Red-Rays	250.	750.	900.
☐ 226	1899	Lyons-Roberts	Blue	80.00	150.	180.
☐ 236	1899	Spellman-White	Blue	75.00	140.	110.
☐ 237	1923	Spellman-White	Blue	15.00	35.00	43.00
☐ 239	1923	Woods-Tate	Blue	14.00	35.00	38.00

Silver Certificates—Two Dollars

No.	Series	Signatures	Seal	VF	CU	Gem CU
☐ 247	1896	Tillman-Morgan	small Red	350.	2000.	2400.
☐ 248	1896	Bruce-Roberts	small Red	350.	2000.	2400.

Silver Certificates—Five Dollars

No.	Series	Signatures	Seal	VF	CU	Gem CU
☐ 282	1923	Spellman-White	Blue	225.	1000.	1050.

Treasury or Coin Notes—One Dollar

No.	Series	Signatures	Seal	VF	CU	Gem CU
□ 347	..1890	..Rosencrans- Huston	large Brown ..	235.	1000.	1300.
□ 348	..1890	..Rosencrans- Nebeker.......	large Brown ..	225.	1000.	1200.
□ 349	..1890	..Rosencrans- Nebeker	small Red	220.	1000.	1350.

(First Charter Period) National Bank Notes— Two Dollars

No.	Series	Signatures	Seal	VF	CU	Gem CU
□ 387	..Orig- inal	Colby- Spinner	Red/ Rays	500.	2000.	2500.
□ 390	..1875	..Allison- New	Red/ Scallops	430.	1500.	2000.
□ 392	..1875	..Allison- Gilfillan.......	Red/ Scallops	430.	1500.	1900.
□ 393	..1875	..Scofield- Gilfillan.......	Red/ Scallops	400.	1500.	1800.

(Second Charter Period) National Bank Notes— Ten Dollars

No.	Series	Signatures	Seal	VF	CU	Gem CU
□ 479	..1882	..Bruce- Gilfillan.......	Brown ..	150.	425.	600.
□ 481	..1882	..Bruce- Jordan	Brown ..	150.	420.	575.
□ 483	..1882	..Rosencrans- Hyatt	Brown ..	150.	425.	550.
□ 485	..1882	..Rosenkrans- Nebeker	Brown ..	150.	425.	540.

(Third Charter Period) National Bank Notes— Twenty Dollars

No.	Series	Signatures	Seal	VF	CU	Gem CU
□ 642	..1902– 1908	..Lyons- Robert	Blue	75.00	450.	450.

No.	Series	Signatures	Seal	VF	CU	Gem CU

☐ 644 ..1902– Vernon-
   1908 ..Taeat ....Blue ..... 70.00   200.   400.
☐ 646 ..1902– Napier-
   1908 ..McClung .....Blue ..... 70.00   175.   390.

Federal Reserve Note—Two Dollars

☐ 747 ..1918 ..Teehee-
   Burke ....Blue .....   135.   335.   520.
☐ 750 ..1918 ..Teehee-
   Burke ....Blue .....   125.   325.   500.
☐ 759 ..1918 ..Teehee-
   Burke ....Blue .....   120.   320.   485.
☐ 780 ..1918 ..Elliott-
   Burke ....Blue .....   120.   320.   485.

National Gold Bank Notes—Five Dollars

☐ 1136 1800 ..Allison-
   Spinner(SF)..Red ......   500. 1500.   5500.
☐ 1139 1870 ..Allison-
   Spinner(SB) .Red ......   450. 1450.   5000.
☐ 1140 1870 ..Allison-
   Spinner(ST) .Red ......   450. 1450.   5000.
☐ 1141 1870 ..Allison-
   Spinner(SJ) ..Red ......   450. 1450.   5000.

Gold Certificates—Twenty Dollars

☐ 1179 1905 ..Lyons-   small
   Roberts ....Red ......   500. 6500.   7500.
☐ 1182 1906 ..Vernon-
   McClung .....Gold..... 95.00   500.   800.
☐ 1185 1906 ..Parker-Berk .Gold..... 70.00   500.   700.
☐ 1187 1922 ..Spellman-
   White ....Gold..... 65.00   520.   610.

FRACTIONAL CURRENCY

3-Cent Notes

No.	Issue	Variety	VG	CU	Gem CU
☐ 1226	Third	Dark background	10.00	55.00	95.00

5-Cent Notes

No.	Issue	Variety	VG	CU	Gem CU
☐ 1228	First	perforated/ABCO	15.00	75.00	200.
☐ 1232	Second	small surcharge fig	10.00	125.	270.
☐ 1236	Third	Red reverse	15.00	90.00	185.

10-Cent Notes

No.	Issue	Variety	VG	CU	Gem CU
☐ 1240	First	perforated/ABCO	12.00	100.	200.
☐ 1244	Second	small surch/figs	10.00	30.00	97.00
☐ 1251	Third	Red reverse	12.00	70.00	210.
☐ 1256	Fourth	Large red seal	9.00	40.00	75.00
☐ 1264	Fifth	Green seal	7.00	35.00	65.00

15-Cent Notes

No.	Issue	Variety	VG	CU	Gem CU
☐ 1267	Fourth	Large red seal	17.00	80.00	170.

25-Cent Notes

No.	Issue	Variety	VG	CU	Gem CU
☐ 1279	First	perforated/ABCO	19.00	100.	210.
☐ 1291	Third	Red reverse	13.00	50.00	180.
☐ 1308	Fifth	Long thin Treas. key	6.00	20.00	40.00

50-Cent Notes

No.	Issue	Variety	VG	CU	Gem CU
☐ 1310	First	perforated/ABCO	22.00	155.	350.
☐ 1324	Third	no design figs on back	27.00	140.	310.

No.	Issue	Variety	VG	CU	Gem CU
☐ 1374	.Fourth	..Large seal/ watermark............	45.00	175.	500.
☐ 1380	.Fifth	.....Red seal	13.00	39.00	55.00

SMALL-SIZE NOTES

1-Dollar Notes

No.	Series	Signatures	VF	CU	Gem CU
☐ 1500	.1928	.....Woods-Woodlin ...	4.00	12.50	80.00

Legal Tender Notes—2-Dollar Notes

☐ 1501	.1928	.....Tate-Mellon..........	12.50	35.00	30.00
☐ 1504	.1928-C	..Julian-Morgenthau.	7.50	40.00	47.00
☐ 1508	.1928-G	.Clark-Snyder	6.00	12.50	9.00

5-Dollar Notes

☐ 1525	.1928	.....Woods-Mellon	8.00	20.00	27.00
☐ 1532	.1953	.....Priest-Humphrey...	7.50	12.50	15.00
☐ 1536	.1963	.....Granahan-Dillon ...	7.50	10.00	10.00

100-Dollar Notes

☐ 1550	.1966	.....Granahan-Fowler ..	115.	175.	215.
☐ 1551	.1966-A	..Elston-Kennedy	120.	300.	375.

1-Dollar Notes—Silver Certificates

☐ 1600	.1928	.....Tate-Mellon..........	5.00	13.00	18.00
☐ 1605	.1928-E	..Julian-Morganthau.	300.	1300.	1800.
☐ 1609	.1935-A	..Julian-Morganthau.	—	4.00	250.

5-Dollar Notes

No.	Series	Signatures	VG	CU	Gem CU
☐ 1650	.1934	.....Julian-Morganthau.	13.00	35.00	55.00
☐ 1654	.1934-D	.Clark-Snyder	8.00	14.00	12.00
☐ 1657	.1935-B	..Smith-Dillion........	—	12.50	12.00

10-Dollar Notes

No.	Series	Signatures	VG	CU	Gem CU
☐ 1700	.1933	.....Julian-Morganthau.	370.	2800.	4200.
☐ 1705	.1934-D	.Clark-Snyder	12.00	19.00	29.00
☐ 1707	.1953-A	..Priest-Anderson	16.00	100.	180.

National Bank Notes—5 Dollar Notes

No.	Type	VF	CU	Gem CU
☐ 1800–1	.........1	15.00	40.00	75.00
☐ 1800–2	.........2	17.00	49.00	85.00

10 Dollars

No.	Type	VF	CU	Gem CU
☐ 1801–1	.........1	16.00	59.00	100.
☐ 1801–2	.........2	19.00	55.00	130.

20 Dollars

☐ 1802–1	.........1	37.00	65.00	140.
☐ 1802–1	.........2	42.00	70.00	130.

50 Dollars

☐ 1803–1	.........1	75.00	105.	155.
☐ 1803–2	.........2	85.00	130.	295.

100 Dollars

☐ 1804–1	.........1	135.	170.	250.
☐ 1804–2	.........1	145.	180.	400.

Federal Reserve Bank Notes—5 Dollars

No.	Type	VF	CU	Gem CU
☐ 1850-A	Boston	8.00	25.00	40.00
☐ 1850-F	Atlanta	8.00	25.00	40.00

10 Dollars

☐ 1860-A	Boston	13.00	25.00	35.00
☐ 1860-E	Richmond	12.00	20.00	33.00

20 Dollars

☐ 1870-B	New York	22.00	33.00	55.00
☐ 1870-D	Cleveland	23.00	33.00	49.00

50 Dollars

☐ 1880-B	New York	60.00	85.00	130.
☐ 1880-L	San Francisco	60.00	95.00	130.

100 Dollars

☐ 1890-G	Chicago	115.	150.	175.
☐ 1890-K	Dallas	115.	150.	175.

Federal Reserve Notes—1-Dollar Series 1969D

☐ 1907-A	Boston	—	2.15	2.75

2-Dollar Series 1976

☐ 1935-F	Atlanta	—	2.50	3.00

5-Dollar Series 1950

No.	Type	VF	CU	Gem CU
☐ 1961-C..........Philadelphia		—	14.00	28.00

10-Dollar Series 1928

☐ 2000-A..........Boston..................		—	15.00	31.00

20-Dollar Series 1934-C

☐ 2057-B..........New York		—	23.00	35.00

50-Dollar Series 1950E

☐ 2112-L ....San Francisco		—	65.00	95.00

100-Dollar Series 1969A

☐ 2165-J...........Kansas City		—	130.	150.

EMERGENCY NOTES

1 Dollar—Silver Certificate—Hawaii

No.	Series	No. Printed	VF	CU	Gem CU
☐ 2300..1935-A..35,052,000..........			6.00	30.00	39.00

5 Dollar—Federal Reserve Note—Hawaii

☐ 2301..1934.....9,416,000............			25.00	100.	135.

10 Dollar—Federal Reserve Note—Hawaii

No.	Series	No. Printed	VF	CU	Gem CU
☐ 2303	1934-A	10,424,000	25.00	235.	255.

20 Dollar—Federal Reserve Note—Hawaii

☐ 2304	1934	11,246,000	70.00	775.	1020.

GOLD CERTIFICATES

10 Dollars

☐ 2400	1928	130,812,000	50.00	300.	400.

20 Dollars

☐ 2402	1928	66,209,000	70.00	350.	450.

50 Dollars

☐ 2404	1928	5,520,000	125.	1000.	1525.

100 Dollars

☐ 2405	1928	3,240,000	225.	1400.	1960.

MISCELLANEOUS NOTES

	Price Range	
☐ FR-248, two dollars, silver educational note, 1896	100.00	2400.00
☐ FR-434, twenty dollars, national banknote, 1875	125.00	4000.00
☐ FR-752, two dollars, federal reserve note, 1918	60.00	700.00

FR-248, two dollars, silver educational note, 1896, $100–$2400.

FR-434, twenty dollars, national banknote, 1875, $125–$4000.

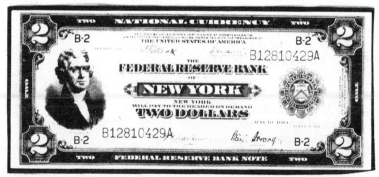

FR-752, two dollars, federal reserve note, 1918, $60–$700.

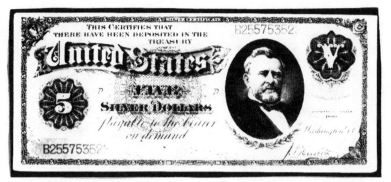

FR-263, five dollars, silver dollar back, 1886, $150–$3000.

☐ FR-263, five dollars, silver dollar
  back, 1886 ....   150.00   3000.00
☐ FR-161, fifty dollars, legal tender
  note, 1880 ....   200.00   3700.00
☐ FR-217, one dollar, silver certifi-
  cate, 1886 ....   50.00   960.00

FR-161, fifty dollars, legal tender note, 1880, $200–$3700.

FR-217, one dollar, silver certificate, 1886, $50–$960.

Paperweights

TYPES: Millefiori weights contain arrays of small ornamental glass beads or stems arranged in a striking pattern. They are quite colorful. Sulfides are ceramic relief plaques encased in glass. Many other artistic types of paperweights were made, and souvenir paperweights featuring some company or place are also common, though not as desirable.

PERIOD: Paperweights were not seen before the 1700s; they are a recent item. The most important paperweights were made in the 1800s.

MAKERS: Clichy, Baccarat, and St. Louis are all important producers of artistic glass paperweights. Prices for famous makers like these are high, although lesser-known craftsmen can also produce exquisite items.

MATERIALS: For the most part, glass is the medium used for artistic paperweights. Functional weights are rarely made of metal.

COMMENTS: The weight of the specimen is not an indication of quality. Rather, the name of the maker and the level of artistry evident determine the value of a paperweight.

ADDITIONAL TIPS: Famous makers like Clichy, Baccarat, and St. Louis sometimes put their initials on one of the canes in a millefiori weight. This makes certain specimens easy to identify.

	Price Range	
☐ **Bridgeton Studio,** geometric, yellow stylized floral and geometric decoration on pale green ground, 2½″ diameter	40.00	60.00
☐ **Bridgeton Studio,** sea horse, orange-on-white decoration next to stylized underwater flora on lavender ground, 2½″ diameter	50.00	90.00
☐ **Bridgeton Studio,** stylized white flower surrounded by orange ribbon on white ground, 2½″ diameter	10.00	20.00
☐ **Egyptian,** bronze, depicting the figure of a seated Egyptian man, 2½″ high	30.00	50.00
☐ **John Lotton,** art glass, internal geometric swirl decoration in blue tones, signed John Lotton, 1986, 2½″ diameter	80.00	120.00
☐ **Lead crystal,** egg form with etched carnation decoration, 3″ long	24.00	28.00
☐ **Mercury bubble,** central bubble raised on eight multicolor ribbons terminating in smaller bubbles, supported by a scrambled glass pillow, 2½″ diameter	5.00	15.00
☐ **Moser,** automobile, containing a milk-glass wafer with transfer decoration depicting the 1895 Lanchester, raised on a red, white, and blue scrambled ground, 2¾″ diameter	25.00	35.00
☐ **Murano,** multicolor concentric canes on aventurine ground, seven printies, 2½″ diameter	5.00	15.00
☐ **Murano,** white-petaled flower with cane center, stem with two leaves on a blue transparent ground, 3″ diameter	10.00	15.00

Price Range

☐ **Swedish crystal,** hollow-blown, orange ribbon flash decoration with five printies, 3″ diameter ...   60.00   80.00

☐ **Scrambled glass,** red, white, and blue internal swirl decoration, 2½″ diameter 10.00   15.00

☐ **Warna Murano,** crown, multicolor rose garland separated by blue and orange latticino, 3″ diameter 15.00   25.00

☐ **Warna Murano,** checkered, orange, white, and blue canes separated by white and blue latticino rods, 3″ diameter 75.00   95.00

☐ **Warna Murano,** checkered, rose canes separated by white and red latticino rods, 3″ diameter 20.00   30.00

☐ **Warna Murano,** crown, central orange and blue cane supported by rose garlands separated by white and blue latticino, 3″ diameter 40.00   60.00

☐ **Warna Murano,** crown, central rose supported by S-curve rose garlands separated by blue and white latticino, 3″ diameter 50.00   70.00

☐ **Warna Murano,** seven surface canes surrounded by maroon ribbon decoration over a bubble glass ground, 3″ diameter 15.00   25.00

Pens and Pencils

TYPES: Pens can be either dip pens, the earliest type, fountain pens, or ballpoint pens. Dip pens are the style of modern calligraphy pens: A pointed nib is dipped in ink and used quickly. Fountain pens contain their own ink supply, as do ballpoints. Pencils are either traditional or mechanical.

PERIOD: The fountain pen, which is the most collectible type, experienced its heyday in the 1920s and 1930s.

ORIGIN: The fountain pen was invented in the 1880s by Lewis Waterman.

MAKERS: The big names in pen and pencil production are Waterman, Parker, Conklin, Sheaffer, and Wahl-Eversharp. All of these companies produced fine pens that are currently in great demand by collectors.

COMMENTS: As mentioned before, few ballpoint or dip pens are collected by modern enthusiasts. Also, collectors focus on post-1880 specimens.

ADDITIONAL TIPS: Rarity and condition are very important; the second more so than the first. Historical importance may also play a part, though only in isolated instances.

502

DESCRIPTION ABBREVIATION CODE:

BHR—black hard rubber
BCHR—black chased hard rubber
RHR—red hard rubber
RCHR—red chased hard rubber
STR—striped
MBL—marbled
GFM—gold-filled metal
SPM—silver-plated metal
GFT—gold-filled trim
CPT—chrome-plated trim
NPT—nickel-plated trim
ED—eyedropper filled
BF—button filler
VF—Vacumatic filler
CR—Crescent filler
CF—coin filler
AF—aerometric filler
TD—Touchdown filler
PF—plunger filler
I—initialed
M—mint condition
E—excellent condition
G—good condition
A—average condition

PARKER

	Price Range
☐ **1913,** ''Black Giant'' Lucky Curve pen in BHR, ED, CPT, rare, E	1500.00
☐ **1912,** No. 18 Lucky Curve pen in BHR, ED, E	129.00
☐ **1917,** No. 24½ Jackknife Lucky Curve pen in BCHR, ED, slightly worn BBL imprint, otherwise E ..	139.00
☐ **1920,** No. 20 Jackknife Safety Lucky Curve pen in BCHR, BF, G (faded)	25.00

Price Range

☐ **1922,** Duofold Sr. "Big Red" pen RHR, rare bandless model with large BBL imprint, BF, E 695.00

☐ **1928,** Duofold Sr. "Big Red" pen, BF, E 175.00

☐ **1929,** Duofold Sr. "Prototype" pen in Mandarin yellow with black cap bands, BF, M 750.00

☐ **1931,** Duofold Jr. pen in lapis blue MBL, BF, E 89.00

☐ **1931,** Duofold pen in lapis blue MBL, BF, E 79.00

☐ **1931,** Duofold Deluxe pencil in Moderne pearl and black MBL, E 79.00

☐ **1932,** True Blue pen (blue-cream MBL), BF, G 39.00

☐ **1931,** Duofold Deluxe pencil in Moderne pearl and black MBL, E 125.00

☐ **1934,** Duofold Deluxe pen in emerald pearl MBL, BF, rare, slight plating wear on bands, otherwise E 175.00

☐ **1936,** Vacumatic in emerald pearl STR, VF, G (discoloration) 69.00

☐ **1937,** Challenger in silver-black MBL, NPT, BF, E 29.00

☐ **1940,** Challenger in black, NPT, BF, E 39.00

☐ **1941,** Debutante Vacumatic in emerald pearl STR, VF, E 35.00

☐ **1941,** Blue Diamond Duofold in blue-silver pearl STR, VF 85.00

☐ **1941,** Blue Diamond "51" in blue with sterling cap, VF, rare, E 120.00

☐ **1945,** Blue Diamond "51" in light brown with GF cap, VF, I, cap has a few minor dents, otherwise E 75.00

☐ **1960,** "51" pen in black with GF cap, AF, E 69.00

	Price Range
☐ **1956,** "Victory" pen in blue, made in England, AF, E	69.00
☐ **1958,** "41" pen in aqua with chrome cap, CPT, AF, M	65.00
☐ **1957,** "61" pen in red with Lustraloy cap, GF clip, CF, E	65.00
☐ **1955,** "61" Experimental "Prototype" pen in black with Lustraloy cap, GF clip, "61" impressed in end of barrel, M	295.00
☐ **1957,** "61" Heirloom pen in red with 2-tone pink-gold-filled cap, CF, E	189.00
☐ **1957,** "61" Legacy pen with silver Rainbow cap, CPT, CF, E	189.00
☐ **1960,** "61" pen in black with Lustraloy cap, CPT, CF, E	52.00
☐ **1960,** "61" Flighter pen in stainless steel, CPT, CF, E	155.00
☐ **1970,** "75" Flighter pen in stainless steel, GF clip, AF, stub nib, E	159.00
☐ **1970,** "75" pen in vermeil (14K gold over sterling), AF, M	185.00

SHEAFFER'S

☐ **1919,** No. 2 ladies' pen in black-lined HR, E	45.00
☐ **1926,** LIfetime pen in black, G ..	29.00
☐ **1926,** Lifetime pen in green jade MBL, G	59.00
☐ **1930,** White Dot Balance pen in pearl and black MBL, G	35.00
☐ **1931,** golf pencil in pearl and black MBL, Mint	59.00
☐ **1939,** Lifetime Balance pen in black, E	175.00
☐ **1946,** Lifetime Triumph "1000" pen in red pearl STR, PF, E	59.00

	Price Range
☐ **1949,** White Dot Triumph pen in maroon, TD, G	35.00
☐ **1948,** White Dot Triumph "1250" pen in brown, I, PF, E ...	75.00
☐ **1947,** Lifetime Triumph "875" pen in gold pearl STR, E	89.00

MISCELLANEOUS

☐ **1926,** Wahl No. 2 pen in GFM, E	25.00
☐ **1937,** Coronet pen in GFM with red pearl pyralin insets, safety ink shut-off valve, I, Rare, E	395.00
☐ **1945,** $64 pen and repeater pencil set in green with sold 14K-gold caps, clips, and derbies, E	450.00
☐ **1945,** $64 pen in black with solid 14K-gold cap, clip, and derby, E	259.00
☐ **1931,** Waterman Ideal No. 92 pen in red-gold MBL, E	85.00
☐ **1932,** Waterman Ideal No. 5 pen in black with purple nib, minor wear on top of cap but otherwise E	99.00
☐ **1936,** Waterman Ideal Emerald Ray Ink-Vue pen (emerald-black MBL), E	395.00
☐ **1947,** Waterman Supersize Emblem pen in black, E	350.00
☐ **1926,** Aiken Lambert "Mercantile" pen in green jade MBL, E ...	45.00
☐ **1926,** Carter No. 3313 pen in black-lined HR with red band on top of cap, NPT, E	149.00
☐ **1926,** Conklin Endura pen in sapphire blue, E	195.00
☐ **1923,** Conklin No. 4 NL Crescent Filler pen in BCHR, E	225.00

Price Range

☐ **1929,** Swan "Fyne Point" pencil in black with green jade MBL bands, G 69.00

☐ **1977,** Mont Blanc Diplomat pen in black, twist filler, plating wear on bands but otherwise E 119.00

☐ **1977,** Mont Blanc Classic in black, twist filler, E 69.00

☐ **1903,** Fairchild's "Unique" pen in BCHR, overfeed, ED, E 75.00

☐ **1982,** Pilot pen in sterling, unusual pattern, 18K nib, BF, M 165.00

☐ **1917,** Salz "Army & Navy" Bullet pen in BHR, ED, E 99.00

☐ **1925,** Century Duropoint No. 65C pen in black-lined HR, top-of-the-line model, M 250.00

Photography

COMMENTS: Photographs are usually one of four varieties: daguerreotypes, ambrotypes, tintypes, or modern paper prints. Ambrotypes and tintypes are less valuable but are often collected. Three varieties of pictures made from negatives are original prints, later prints, or reproductions. Original prints are those made by the photographer, or someone in his employ, shortly after taking the negative. Later prints are made from the original negative at a later date, sometimes fifty or more years later. Reproductions are made by making a new negative from the photo print. In most instances, original prints taken during the 1800s are most in demand by collectors. Early 1900s scenes, especially of the outdoor environment, are becoming more popular.

ADDITIONAL TIPS: Value is determined by age and subject matter. Of course, the quality of the print is important; it must be in good condition to merit its full value. Works by famous photographers, such as Edward Curtis, Mathew Brady, Alfred Stieglitz, or Carlton Watkins all command high prices in the collector market.

Note: The single values shown below are the actual auction-realized prices.

Price Range

☐ **Abbott, Berenice,** Columbia Heights, Brooklyn, NY, May 22, 1936, silver gelatin print, 10″ × 8″, titled, stamped by the photographer and with Federal Art Project stamp on verso 400.00

☐ **Abbott, Berenice,** Fortieth Street, between Sixth and Seventh Avenues, September 8, 1938, view taken from Salmon Tower, silver gelatin print, 10″ × 8″, titled, stamped by the photographer and with Federal Art Project stamp on verso 700.00

☐ **Abbott, Berenice,** "New York by Night," 1936, silver gelatin print, 10″ × 8″, signed below image, lower right, on mount board, stamped on verso 1000.00

☐ **Albok, John,** 6 New York City street portraits, c. 1940, ferrotyped silver gelatin prints, various sizes, approximately 9½″ × 7½″, most have stamped signature below image line lower right and stamped on verso 350.00

☐ **Barnard, George,** "Battleground of Resaca," Georgia, No. 1, 1866, albumen print, 11¼″ × 14½″, incorrectly titled "Battlefield of Chattanooga" lower left on mount 130.00

☐ **Bell, Hugh,** "Hot Jazz," 1952, silver gelatin print, 10¼″ × 13½″, signed, titled, and dated on the verso 300.00

Price Range

☐ **Besse, Lotte,** circle of heads, c. 1929, silver gelatin print, 3¼″ diameter, tipped to 5½″ square black paper, cover photo of Issue No. 4 of *Bauhaus* magazine 2000.00

☐ **Bravo, Manuel Alvarez,** untitled, c. 1940, silver gelatin print, 7¼″ × 9¼″, signed, lower right, on verso 525.00

☐ **Bull, Clarence Sinclair,** Greta Garbo, c. 1940, silver gelatin print, 12¼″ × 9¼″, blind-stamped, lower right, and stamped on verso, printed on buff paper, head and shoulders portrait with feathered hat 275.00

☐ **Cartier-Bresson, Henry,** "Behind the Gare St. Lazare," Paris, 1932, silver gelatin print, 14″ × 10″, signed, lower right in ink and blindstamped, lower left, below image 800.00

☐ **Cartier-Bresson, Henry,** Mexico, c. 1950, silver gelatin print, 14¼″ × 9½″, signed, lower right below image, a young girl carrying an old photographic portrait of a woman 600.00

☐ **Cartier-Bresson,** Henry, New York, c. 1960, signed, lower right below image, the foot of a secretary entering her boss's office before a glass window 600.00

☐ **Jacobi, Lotte,** Alfred Stieglitz at an American Place, c. 1940, silver gelatin print, 9¾″ × 8″, signed lower right, on print, Stieglitz is pictured on his cot before a pair

Price Range

of Marin watercolors, he has a newspaper open to a hosiery ad reminiscent of his photograph of Dorothy Norman's leg 650.00

☐ **Kertesz, Andre,** Martinique, January 1, 1972, silver gelatin print, 10 1/2 ″ × 13 3/4 ″, signed, titled, and dated on verso 1100.00

☐ **Kertesz, Andre,** Washington Square, 1954, silver gelatin print, 13 3/4 ″ × 10 1/4 ″, signed, titled, and dated on verso 800.00

☐ **O'Sullivan, Timothy H.,** canyon of the Colorado River near mouth of San Juan River, Arizona, No. 14, 1873, albumen print, 7 3/4 ″ × 10 3/4 ″, titled, numbered, and photographer identified on mount board, from the Wheeler Expedition of 1873, view of textural layering of terrain with river in the distance 950.00

☐ **Outerbridge, Paul Jr.,** self-portrait, c. 1930, silver gelatin print, 6 ″ × 4 ″ 1400.00

☐ **Steichen, Edward,** Martha Graham, New York, 1931, silver gelatin print, 10 ″ × 8 ″, numbered in the negative, pencil notations on verso 1200.00

☐ **Stieglitz, Alfred,** Camera Work Number 42/43, April/July 1913, photogravure and four-color halftone, devoted to the photographs and printings of Edward Steichen, complete and uncut 1200.00

☐ **Stieglitz, Alfred,** woman with a boat, c. 1895, platinum print, 3 1/4 ″ × 4 1/2 ″, mounted to board 2000.00

Price Range

☐ **Van der See, James,** Black
woman leaning on piano before
tropical sunset, 1932, silver gelatin print, 9 ½″ × 7 ½″, signed
and dated in the negative, G. G.
C. Studio stamp on verso 300.00

☐ **Watkins, Carlton E.,** Yosemite
Falls from Glacier Point, c. 1866,
albumen print, 20 ½″ × 15 ½″ .   1200.00

☐ **Weegee,** victims of a fire, 1942,
ferrotyped silver gelatin print,
10 ¼″ × 13″, early print 425.00

Van Der See, James, black woman leaning on piano before tropical
sunset, 1932, silver gelatin print, 9 ½″ × 7 ½″, signed and dated
in the negative, G.G.C. Studio stamp on verso, $300. (*Photo cour-
tesy of Phillips, New York*)

Pipes

THE TOBACCO PIPE: Smoking tobacco through a pipe is native to the Americas. History records the practice originated from the religious ceremonies of ancient priests in Mexico. Farther north, in the mounds of the Mississippi Valley, archaeologists have uncovered elaborate carved pipes of bone, wood, and clay that may have been smoked a thousand years before any European set foot in North America.

Pipe collecting itself enters historical records in the mid-1880s. Several collections are noted from that time in England. Today major collections of antique and classic pipes from estates and private individuals enter the market each year through auctions such as those held by Christie's in New York.

MATERIALS: Early pipes were made from wood, bone, metal, glass, porcelain, gourds, corncobs, and clay. Clays were most popular in England. The first pipe to challenge the popularity of the clay pipe was the meerschaum, a mineral material found mainly in Turkey. It usually has a mouthpiece of amber.

Briar as a pipe material was introduced in the nineteenth century. It is a superior material for pipe bowls because the

513

roots of the heath tree (a species of heather found in Mediterranean countries) are tougher, lighter, and more resistant to heat than most other materials.

TIPS: Old pipes in their original condition are usually the most valuable. Parts that have been replaced lower the value of the pipe. Original boxes, instruction booklets, and sales receipts increase the value.

The bowl of the pipe, its workmanship, and decoration generally determine the price of the pipe. Overall, the worth of a pipe, as with any antique or collectible object, depends on its age and condition, the pipe's maker or manufacturer, the quality of workmanship, the scarcity of the particular type, and the current demand. Actually, the price paid for a pipe is usually based on the buyer's desire and the price he is willing to pay. In this way, many prices are set by buyers at auctions.

TRENDS: Most pipe smokers have a collection of pipes. The favorite small collection is a seven-day set (a pipe for each day of the week). Many smoker-collectors have hundreds of pipes. Today, growing numbers of nonsmokers are also collecting pipes.

Many commemorative and limited-edition pipes are made for the collector market. Collectors treasure these pipes as works of art. Indeed, craftsmen have produced lavishly carved and decorated pipes, such as the elaborately carved meerschaum pipes, that were only meant to be admired, never smoked.

CLUBS AND ASSOCIATIONS: The serious collector will want to join a local club and/or a national organization. Both of the following associations have publications for members. For more information write:

The Universal Coterie of Pipe Smokers
20–37 120th Street
College Point, NY 11356

Pipe Collectors International
P. O. Box 22085
Chattanooga, TN 37422.

Price Range

☐ **Dunhill (English),** gold umbrella, all-weather pipe, one of 12 made, umbrella and bowl rim are 14K gold, excellent condition,

Price Range

never smoked, has own locked glass custom display case, very rare* 7000.00   8000.00

☐ **Dunhill (English),** c. 1954, billiard ball bit, Dublin shape, rich mahogany-color bowl, smoked, slight wear 350.00   400.00

☐ **Dunhill (English),** c. 1979, shell original, near-black bowl of medium size with grain in bold relief, standard taper mouthpiece .. 120.00   160.00

☐ **Dunhill (English),** c. 1978, root original apple shape, tan polished bowl, slight wear 175.00   190.00

☐ **Dunhill (English),** 1982, Christmas pipe, No. 131 of 500, original box, never smoked 250.00   275.00

☐ **Dunhill (English),** large bowl, root tan, bulldog shape, with spare bit 180.00   200.00

☐ **Castello (Italian),** black "sea rock," marked "KK 34" and "Carlo Scotti," billiard bowl, dark green pearl stem with slight bend, some light aging to finish 100.00   130.00

☐ **Caminetto (Italian),** marked "Business 175 KS," full bent, tan with very dark wine-color pearl stem, only slightly used, finish still somewhat bright 75.00   85.00

☐ **Caminetto (Italian),** marked "New Dear" and "118," bears all three makers' names, billiard bowl with tan finish and straight pearl stem, very heavy carving from the early 1970s, light use and aging 125.00   140.00

☐ **Barling (English),** make No. 4804, Oliphant, well-grained,

*Umbrella pipe only (no case), $5000–$6000.

	Price Range	

medium-size bowl, smoked, slight wear 40.00 50.00

☐ **Charatan (English),** relief, No. 391, tan, tall large Dublin shape with taper bit, smoked but in pristine condition 30.00 40.00

☐ **GBD (English),** Super Flame "Anniversary," 1850–1980, pipe like new, unsmoked, quarter bent, short rectangular shanked billiard, with original commemorative box 60.00 75.00

☐ **GBD (English),** bronze velvet No. 357, Prince, medium-size bowl, taper bit, smoked, excellent condition 20.00 35.00

☐ **Charatan (English),** Relief No. 461X, black pitch, Dublin with saddle bit, new condition 50.00 60.00

☐ **Ashton,** c. 1985, XXX PG billiard, African rubber stem 100.00 125.00

☐ **Ashton,** c. 1985, XXX PG sterling silver spigot, Dublin with African rubber stem (rare) 215.00 245.00

☐ **Barling (English),** Ye Old Wood, 53 Fossil, TVF, Liverpool (pretrans.) 110.00 130.00

☐ **Barling (English),** 4185 Liverpool shape with smooth finish (Isle of Man) 40.00 65.00

☐ **Charatan (English),** tan Relief, quarter bent, bell Dublin 75.00 90.00

☐ **Comoy's (English),** 225 tawny calabash, saddle mouthpiece 35.00 45.00

☐ **Comoy's (English),** 1982 Christmas pipe, slight wear 35.00 55.00

☐ **Castello (Italian),** KKK 15 Old Sea Rock, brown billiard with military push bit 120.00 140.00

☐ **Castello (Italian),** KKK 15 natural virgin billiard 130.00 160.00

Price Range

☐ **Ascorti (Italian),** Business KS, dark carved apple 50.00   60.00

☐ **GBD (English),** Irvin's Conquest, Canadian with sterling silver band, fair condition 25.00   35.00

☐ **Peterson (Irish),** Kildare full-bent pot, OIS with special patented lip 15.00   30.00

☐ **Peterson (Irish),** sterling silver spigot, straight pot F/T 606S 125.00   150.00

☐ **George Jensen North Dane (Danish),** "Amber" bent billiard, 34 .... 20.00   30.00

☐ **Stanwell (Danish),** bench made, smooth pear shape 25.00   35.00

☐ **Ben Wade (Danish),** "Majestic," designer series, sandblast, large full bent 25.00   35.00

☐ **Weber (American),** straight grain, smooth Lovat with saddle bit 25.00   35.00

☐ **Chacom (French),** Super Flame, smooth Dublin shape, has spare stem, good condition 40.00   55.00

☐ **Ascorti (Italian),** "New Dear," tan, KS, Canadian 65.00   75.00

☐ **Ascorti (Italian),** Business KS, billiard with square shank, tan ... 50.00   65.00

☐ **Savinelli (Italian),** autograph, smooth "O," full bent 195.00   225.00

☐ **Savinelli (Italian),** Giubiled D'oro, walnut, billiard 75.00   95.00

☐ **Prattware (clay),** in the form of a sailor smoking a pipe, c. 1800, 6 ½ " long 500.00   550.00

☐ **Prattware pipe,** shaped as a hand holding a pipe, c. 1810 ..... 300.00   350.00

☐ **Meerschaum,** carved and signed by Bekler for CAO, full profiles of the great musicians Strauss and Brahms on one pipe, 1984 limited

	Price Range	
edition, No. 57 of 100, complete with original certificate of authenticity by CAO, never smoked	300.00	350.00
☐ **Meerschaum,** smooth bowl and stem, carved as a gartered woman's leg, 4 ½ ″ long, has own case	90.00	110.00
☐ **Meerschaum,** carved as sailing ship, amber mouthpiece, with fitted case, c. 19th century, 7 ″ long	130.00	150.00
☐ **Porcelain,** German, hand-painted mountain scene on bowl, cherry wood and horn stem, c. 1890, 12 ″ long, slightly used	200.00	250.00
☐ **Peace pipe,** Western Plains Indian red catlinite antique peace pipe, 4 ″ with 2 ″-high bowl, original 11 ″ wooden stem almost fully carved in twisted shape and with original decoration of hot file markings on edge of twist and lower section, all showing genuine aging and use	450.00	500.00
☐ **Peace pipe,** Eastern Plains, wood and decorated stone pipe in L-shape, bowl 2 ½ ″ high, oval wood stem decorated with strip of leather, 24 ″ long overall	750.00	800.00
☐ **Clay (Holland),** fancy clay pipe with bowl molded in form of a Negro head, early 1900s, not smoked, pristine, "Bon Fumeur" in raised letters on right side of stem, "Tobago" on left	40.00	50.00
☐ **Clay (English),** c. 1901, Coronation Cutty, showing Edward VII on left side of bowl and Imperial State Crown on right side, believed to be a product of John Pollock, original, smoked	35.00	50.00
☐ **Clay (English),** dating 1915, very fine finish, 7 ½ ″ long, text		

Price Range

embossed on left side of stem, "Original 1715–Revived 1915," text on right side, "The Bi-Centenary Pipe" 40.00   55.00

☐ **Pipe case (Dutch),** 19th century ebony and brass-mounted pipe case, fancy, 9″ long 260.00   300.00

☐ **Pipe bowl (Swedish),** c. 1840, parcel gilt silver, 4¾″ high, bowl has hinged cover, very ornate work by Johan Wilhelm Ohlsson, fitted with a contemporary turned wood stem, 24″ long 450.00   500.00

☐ **Glass pipe,** made of opaque white glass with a waved design in red and blue, slightly curved stem, 18″ long 130.00   160.00

Political Memorabilia

TYPES: Though political memorabilia is associated primarily with banners, buttons, and posters, the actual range of material is vast. Toy banks, curios, automotive accessories, games, and other novelties make this a fascinating field of collecting.

COMMENTS: Every four years, the United States goes through a political maelstrom, as the nation experiences the electoral process at work. Part of this barrage—the barnstorming, the old whistle-stop tours, the baby kissing, and the hand shaking—includes a slew of objects intended to show one's affinity for one candidate or one's dislike for another. Particularly since the time of McKinley, the nation has been showered with pinbacks and paper as characters of varied repute seek to fill our highest office.

What to collect from the '88 campaign? A hard call, particularly this year when there have been so many prominent fallen candidates even before any ballots were cast. Gary Hart dropped out early, but amid much publicity, for reasons that had as much to do with the fixations of the media as with the matter of the national trust.* Joe Biden was up-ended by opponents within his own party. Whether these and other also-rans became collectible in the future depends on what happens to them in times to come and whether they will be able to prevail.

DESCRIPTION: This section covers only the most popular presidents and their jugates/pinbacks, undoubtedly the hottest form of political memorabilia.

Note: The following list includes jugates (buttons featuring the heads of two candidates, usually framed in a design) and other pinbacks from the twentieth century.

COX–ROOSEVELT JUGATE PINBACKS

Indisputably the rarest, most fervently pursued jugates in the hobby, Cox–Roosevelt received perhaps more notoriety than deserved when a unique, 1¼" black and white specimen set a record at $30,000 during the New England Rare Coin Auction of the Don Warner Collection of Political Americana in 1981.

Of the 10 or 12 (depending on whom you talk to) varieties known, there are but five 1¼" Cox–Roosevelt jugate pinbacks that have surfaced publicly. Dave Frent, cataloger of the Warner collection, estimated that in total, only 70 of these elusive jugates have come to light.

	Price Range	
☐ "**Americanize America. Vote for Cox and Roosevelt**" (Hake 2011), ⅞" black, white	4500.00	5000.00
☐ "**Cox–Roosevelt Club,**" conjoining portraits (Hake 1) 1"; bluetone, white, red lettering	4000.00	4500.00
☐ **Cox–Roosevelt conjoining portraits** (Hake 2010, Warner 715) ⅞"; black, white, also exists in 1¼", only three known	3000.00	4000.00

*During the production of this book, Gary Hart reentered the race.

Price Range

☐ **"Cox and Roosevelt,"** conjoining portraits (Hake 2008) 1 ¼", black and white. 4000.00 4500.00

☐ **"Sunburst Eagle,"** eagle from which emanate an ever widening array of stripes, plus flag waving below, background for circular insets of Cox–Roosevelt (Hake 20009; Warner 359), ⅞", black, white; also exists in 1 ¼"; only one known 4000.00 5000.00

JOHN DAVIS JUGATE PINBACKS–1924

☐ **Davis and Bryan (Charles) conjoined portraits** (Hake 2002, Warner 371), 1 ¼" black, white, key item rarity, mate to La-Follette–Coolidge jugates 4000.00 4200.00

☐ **Davis and Bryan conjoining portraits,** head-on view (Hake 2003), 1 ¼", black, white 3500.00 4000.00

☐ **"Davis and Bryan Club. St. Joseph, Mo.,"** oval pinback, circular jugate portraits (Hake 2004), 1 ¼" long, ¾" high, black, white 3000.00 3500.00

☐ **"Davis and Bryan–Nebraska,"** oval pinback, circular jugate portraits (Hake 2005), 1 ¼" long, ¾" high, black, white 2700.00 2900.00

HARDING–COOLIDGE JUGATE PINBACKS

☐ **"Harding & Coolidge Junior Booster. America First,"** portraits with four stars reversed out of blue and red, white stripes surrounding (Hake 28), ¾", red, white, blue, and black, white lettering reversed out of red border 1500.00 1700.00

Price Range

HARDING TRIGATE PINBACKS

☐ **Harding, Coolidge, and un-
identified coat-tail candidate,** "Republican Candidates,"
"1920," and draped U.S. flags below (Hake 25), 1 ¼ ", red, white,
blue, black .... | 1300.00 | 1500.00

JOHN F. KENNEDY JUGATE PINBACKS—1960

☐ **"America's Men for the '60s,"**
canted silhouetted portraits Kennedy–Johnson (Hake 2007) 4 ",
red, white, blue .... | 20.00 | 25.00

☐ **"For America. For President.
Pull That First Lever. Vote
Straight Democratic,"** conjoining portraits (Hake 6, Warner
828), 3 ½ ", white, bluetone,
black, red, Philadelphia item ...... | 80.00 | 90.00

☐ **"For America. For President.
Vote Straight Democratic,"**
conjoining portraits, as above
(Hake 2008), 3 ¾ ", red, white,
blue .... | 35.00 | 45.00

☐ **"Kennedy/Johnson,"** silhouetted bust portraits (Hake 3), ⅞ ",
red, black, white .... | 55.00 | 65.00

☐ **"Kennedy/Johnson,"** rectangular shape, circular portraits under
winged eagle, starred border
(Hake 2001), 2 ¾ " wide, 1 ¾ "
high, red, white, blue, black, sil-
ver .... | 175.00 | 200.00

☐ **"Leadership for the '60s/Ken-
nedy/Johnson,"** rectangle, silhouetted busts, stars (Hake 2) 3 "
wide, 2 " high, red, white, blue,
black .... | 20.00 | 25.00

Price Range

McKINLEY JUGATES

☐ **McKinley–Lincoln,** "Maintain the Flag. For Lincoln. For McKinley," oval portraits of both separated by furled flag (Hake 291), 1 1/4 ", black on white 100.00   110.00

McKINLEY TRIGATES AND MULTIGATES

☐ **McKinley – Hobart – Roscoe Conkling,** New York item (unlisted), 1 1/4 ", black on white 125.00   135.00
☐ **McKinley – Frink – Roosevelt** (Hake 127), 1 1/4 ", black with names reversed in white 35.00   45.00
☐ **McKinley – Roosevelt – Van Sant–Morris,** Minnesota State Republican League multigate (Hake 128), 1 1/4 ", red, white, blue, black with gold background 80.00   90.00
☐ **McKinley–Washington–Grant–Lincoln,** "The Right Men In The Right Place" (unlisted), 2 ", multicolor 150.00   175.00
☐ **McKinley and his cabinet,** President McKinley in center surrounded by all seven members of his cabinet in 1900, including John Hay and Elihu Root (Hake 3211, Warner 514), a unique motif, 3 ", red, white, cream 100.00   125.00

Price Range

RONALD REAGAN–GEORGE BUSH PINBACK JUGATES—1980, 1984

Inaugurals

☐ **"50th Inauguration,"** Ronald Reagan raising hand to be sworn in, 2″ wide, 1½″ high, red, white, blue, black	1.00	2.00
☐ **"50th Presidential Inauguration,"** Reagan–Bush jugate, crossed flags, "Jan. 21, 1985"	1.00	2.00

Jugates

☐ **"America Loves Reagan–Bush/ 1984,"** conjoining portraits in heart-shape pinback, 2″ high, 1½″ wide, red, white, blue	2.00	3.00
☐ **"Bringing America Back/Reagan–Bush,"** 2″ wide, 1½″ high, red, white, blue, black	2.00	3.00
☐ **"Help Keep America Great/Reelect Ronald Reagan–Bush/ '84,** 1¼″, flag background, red, white, blue, black	2.00	3.00
☐ **"Reagan–Bush,"** eagle over oval portraits separated by flag, shield, 1″, red, white, blue, black	1.00	2.00
☐ **Reagan – Bush "no-name,"** striped shield between paired ovals, 1″, red, white, blue, black	1.00	2.00
☐ **"Reagan / Bush / One More Time,"** circle portraits on flag background, oval, 1½″ wide, 1″ high, red, white, blue, black, 1984	2.00	3.00

FRANKLIN D. ROOSEVELT– LOCAL CANDIDATES JUGATES

☐ "**Me and Roosevelt For John-son,**" oval portraits of FDR and Lyndon Johnson, from Johnson's 1941 Senate race in Texas (Hake unlisted, Warner 785), 2¼", red, white, blue 550.00   600.00

FRANKLIN D. ROOSEVELT– MISCELLANEOUS JUGATES

☐ "**Victory Parade,**" oval jugate of FDR and James Michael Curley, New York Democrat leader, "July 4, 1932" (Hake 2153), 2¾" wide, 2⅛" high, black, white 350.00   375.00

FDR–WARTIME LEADERS JUGATES

☐ "**Casablanca. Unconditional Sur-render,**" oval portraits of Winston Churchill and FDR with flags of their respective nations flying above (Hake unlisted, Warner 786), 1¾", red, white, blue; celebrated World War II meeting of two leaders in 1943 .... 125.00   150.00

Pottery and Porcelain

POTTERY

Redware

HISTORY: Early settlers, and the American natives before them, worked with the red clay which was available throughout most of the country. Most probably, the first successful potters were those in New England, Pennsylvania, and along the Atlantic coast, in Virginia and North Carolina, who worked on a wheel. The redware pottery, thrown by hand, was fragile and crude. By 1850, it had all but disappeared because people preferred the sturdier stoneware and yellow earthenware. Remaining redware potteries confined themselves to flowerpots and drain tiles, with the exception of some portions of the South where redware was used for many household items until the late 1800s. Most of the pieces were utilitarian—crocks, jugs, jars, plates and mugs—intended for everyday use.

SHENANDOAH VALLEY POTTERY (c. 1800–1880)

The most noted potters from this region in Virginia and Maryland were undoubtedly the Bell family—father Peter and his sons John, Samuel, and Solomon. Their wares, in the bright colors and varied styles associated with the Valley, range from the utilitarian to the decorative. The colorful glaze, intricacy of design, and relative age make these wares highly collectible.

	Price Range	
☐ **Bowl,** 15″, white, handled, marked S. Bell & Son, Strasburg, c. 1870	500.00	525.00
☐ **Dish,** 10″, circular, green, orange, and cream, marked S. Bell & Son, Strasburg, c. 1875	650.00	680.00
☐ **Figurine,** 3½″, lamb, sleeping, cream, green and brown, unmarked, c. 1850	2100.00	2200.00
☐ **Pitcher,** 9″, handled, gray and green, angels and grapevine motif, marked John Bell, Waynesboro, Pennsylvania, c. 1860	1000.00	1050.00
☐ **Pitcher,** 10¼″, bulbous green body, tall brown neck, marked John Bell, Waynesboro, Pennsylvania, c. 1860	650.00	680.00

FULPER POTTERY (1805–1929)

The firm, of Flemington, New Jersey, did both industrial and farm ceramics as well as the utilitarian figurewear for which the company is best known by collectors. While the early domestic wares are valued for their scarcity, the later work, reflecting the concerns and style of the Arts and Crafts movement, is particularly prized. Before the factory burned down in 1929, after employing five generations of the Flemington townspeople, Fulper was attempting to enter the porcelain field as well. These pieces are also quite collectible.

Price Range

☐ **Bowl,** 4″ high × 4″ dia., deep
purple over rose, "Fulper"
stamped on bottom, c. 1905 ......   60.00   80.00

☐ **Lamp** (electric), mushroom, with
a flaring ceramic base and a ceramic shade with 64 pieces of colored, leaded glass, glazed in a light
cucumber   green,   crystalline
flambé.   Early   rectangular   ink
stamp, c. 1910, and "Patent
Pending United States, Canada,"
18″ high × 19″ dia. 4200.00   5400.00

☐ **Urn,** large and bulbous, with two-
looped ("riveted") handles and
glazed in a very fine, silvery-green
flambé, c. 1918, 12″ × 9″ 540.00   800.00

☐ **Bowl,** 9″, rolled-in edge, thick,
brilliantly mottled rim, green and
brown fades on outside to mottled blues, inside to mottled blues
and purples, vertical impressed
mark, c. 1900 ....   130.00   140.00

Stoneware

HISTORY: Stoneware potters were located in the Northeast
until the middle 1800s, when stoneware clay was discovered near East Liverpool, Ohio. In 1850, Ohio surfaced as a
major center. Stoneware was produced on a potter's wheel,
a salt glaze was applied, and often it was decorated with
cobalt-blue. Stoneware was generally produced until 1900
(in parts of the South and Southwest until the 1920s).

COMMENTS: Highly prized items come primarily from the
areas of upstate and central New York and Pennsylvania, as
these pieces tend to be older. Personalization, as well as the
quality and complexity of design, also enhance the value of
a piece.

	Price Range	
☐ **Crock,** Haxstan, Ottman & Co., Fort Edward, New York, 24-quart, floral basket design (in blue), mid-19th century	690.00	750.00
☐ **Jug,** Hull & Bach Co., Buffalo, New York, bulbous waist, with handle from collar to spout, 14″ high by 11″ dia., single flower design, c. 1838	275.00	340.00
☐ **Jug,** Nathan Clark & Co., Mount Morris, New York, without handle, bulbous waist, incised design featuring sailing ship, c. 1840	5500.00	6800.00

Yellowware and Rockinghamware

HISTORY: New Jersey and Ohio were the primary locations of the clay used in yellowware pottery. Taylor & Specler was the first Trenton Company to manufacture pottery on a full-scale commercial basis, and their success was responsible for the huge pottery industry in Trenton that followed. In Bennington, Vermont, the U.S. Pottery Company, the first U.S. factory to gain an international reputation, and whose wares had become established as collectors' items as early as 1890, also produced yellowware. Most pieces were cast in molds and shaped as bowls, rolling pins, pitchers, coffeepots, and teapots. Covered with clear glaze, they were sometimes decorated with bands of color. Rockingham-glazed yellowware, with a mottled brown finish, was popular into the 1870s. Plain yellowware was made until the 1930s.

BENNINGTON

☐ **Basin,** 12″, mottled brown Rockingham glaze	70.00	90.00
☐ **Bowl,** 6″, Rockingham glaze, bell-shaped	90.00	100.00

	Price Range	
☐ **Crock,** 4 gal., yellow-brown with 4″ impressed with cobalt blue ...	315.00	355.00
☐ **Flower pot,** 6″, Rockingham glaze, eagles in relief on sides	35.00	45.00
☐ **Pie plate,** 10½″, mottled brown Rockingham glaze	125.00	150.00
☐ **Pitcher,** 5½″, tulip and sunflower motif	60.00	70.00
☐ **Teapot,** 2 qt., mottled brown glaze	130.00	145.00

Art Pottery

HISTORY: Art pottery had its beginning around 1880, co-inciding with the development of the Arts and Crafts movement in this country. The Philadelphia Centennial Exposition of 1876 also had a great influence on potters, since it provided them with their first opportunity to view Oriental and continental wares. Rookwood, in Cincinnati, is perhaps the most important art pottery manufacturer. Other major producers included Grueby, in Massachusetts, and Weller and Roseville in Ohio. Using molds, most art pottery was produced by individual studios until 1930 when it became factory-produced.

ROOKWOOD

A Cincinnati art pottery firm that produced exclusive wares for over 60 years, Rookwood was founded in 1879 and survived in name until 1967 (the original firm filed for bankruptcy in 1941). Most highly prized are the pieces produced before 1937, when the Depression finally forced the firm to lay off its staff of artists. Particularly sought after are Rookwood vases, with their extraordinary underglaze paintings.

☐ **Ashtray,** 7″, owl perched on the side, light green, high glaze, dated 1944	80.00	110.00

	Price Range	
☐ **Bookends,** 7″, item #2998, cream, in the shape of hounds, dated 1953	110.00	160.00
☐ **Bowl,** 5½″, yellow shades to chartreuse, glazed finish, dated 1917	40.00	50.00
☐ **Candlesticks,** 6″, item #2199, embossed columns, dated 1922 ..	55.00	65.00
☐ **Vase,** 5″, brown glaze, rust and yellow pansies, by L. Lincoln, dated 1896	260.00	320.00
☐ **Vase,** 5″, item #2718, pink, matte finish, dated 1924	40.00	50.00

GRUEBY

Founded by William H. Grueby in 1891, the Grueby Faience and Tile Company was intended to reach what we would call today the "upscale" market. With an enviable reputation for creativity and quality, the firm's products were noted for their warm, satin finish and their brilliant use of color. In 1907, after having taken a firm lead in the art pottery field, Grueby was bought out by Tiffany, and all the pieces produced were thereafter marked "Tiffany."

☐ **Tile,** 4″, windmill design	125.00	140.00
☐ **Tile,** 6″, grape motif	60.00	70.00
☐ **Vase,** bulbous base, purple glaze	300.00	310.00

WELLER

Another Ohio firm, this one was founded in 1873 by Sam Weller, and is very popular among collectors. Though it survived until 1948, Weller's strongest years were undoubtedly at the turn of the century, when the company was producing a wide variety of lines under seven different marks, including Aurelian, Dickensware, Auroro, Eocean, and so on. Regardless of the line, however, each piece was hand-designed, reflecting the individual style of the artist.

Price Range

☐ **Lamp,** 11″, brown background,
  yellow and floral motif, marked
  Aurelian 920.00   940.00
☐ **Vase,** 7″, black with dark brown
  and olive toning, bulbous form
  with narrow neck, decorated with
  painting of speckled leaves, hand-
  inked factory mark, and the ar-
  tist's initials E.A. 190.00   220.00

ROSEVILLE

If Rookwood represented the top of the line, Roseville
was intended for those who aspired to have Rookwood but
who couldn't afford the cost. In the hierarchy of the art
pottery movement, Rookwood competed with Grueby, and
Roseville with Weller. Founded in Roseville, Ohio, in 1885,
the company began first in stoneware, then in 1902, opened
an art pottery factory in Zanesville, Ohio. Their artware
bears the name ROZANE. Among the various lines produced
by Roseville were "Egypto," "Mongol," "Woodland," and
"Mara." Particularly prized are the special items made for
individuals and organizations.

☐ **Basket,** shape #311, 12″, blue,
  stylistic V shape, with handle
  curving under one side, marked
  Roseville in relief 90.00   110.00
☐ **Bowl,** shape #300, 4″, pink 35.00   38.00
☐ **Bowl,** shape #328, 8″, green 35.00   40.00
☐ **Jardiniere,** shape #342, 6″,
  green 40.00   42.00

PORCELAIN

HISTORY: Porcelain was more expensive to produce, and
had great difficulty displacing the indigenous clays that inspired the production of red-, stone-, and yellowware in the
Northeast and Ohio. Therefore, it was not until the late 18th

century that factories specializing in porcelain began to appear in this country, and it was not until the late 19th century that porcelain was produced in America on anything like a mass scale. Fine quality porcelain tableware did not became readily available until the early 1900s.

Lenox

HISTORY: Founded in 1889 by Coxon and Lenox, employees of Ott & Brewer, the company produced both decorated and undecorated wares and emphasized giftware instead of dinnerware. The partnership dissolved and Lenox, Inc. was formed in 1906. Dinnerware was greatly expanded. President Wilson ordered Lenox for the White House, which helped to establish the fine reputation for dinnerware the company still enjoys.

	Price Range	
☐ **Ashtray,** coat of arms shape and decoration, gold trim	35.00	40.00
☐ **Ashtray,** green with gold trim ...	20.00	25.00
☐ **Butter pat,** item #176, 3″, gold trim, C.A.C. lavendar palette mark	25.00	30.00
☐ **Cigarette holder,** shape #2614, 3″ high, blue, Lenox wreath mark	20.00	25.00
☐ **Salt shaker,** shape #584, 2³/₈″ high, undecorated and unmarked, pair	45.00	50.00
☐ **Tray,** shape #15, 6½″ square, ruffled rim, plain, white Lenox palette mark	30.00	35.00

American Art China Works

HISTORY: Formed in 1891, the American Art China Works produced a Belleek-type ware which was sold both decorated and undecorated. The company was not in business very long and its items are rare.

☐ **Bon-bon dish,** 6″ round, ruffled top, pearlized pink interior, gold

Price Range

trim on rim, factory decorated,
mark B 160.00   180.00
☐ **Vase,** 13″ high, handles, gold
paste and hand painting, mark A   400.00   470.00

Ott & Brewer

HISTORY: Beginning around 1876, the company made a ware known as ivory porcelain. Although its color, styling, and type of decoration resembles Irish Belleek, it is not the same composition and not quite as fine. O & B is generally considered to be the finest china ever made in the United States, and is certainly the most expensive of the Trenton chinas. The company closed in 1893.

☐ **Basket,** 6″, rustic handle, raised,
gold paste trim in thistle pattern
on beige, matte finish, mark 1 ....   600.00   700.00
☐ **Cup and saucer,** Tridacna pat-
tern, teacup size, pearlized yellow
interior, gold trim on handle and
rims, mark k 175.00   200.00
☐ **Shell,** raised on coral and seashell
base, pearlized pink interior to
shell, gold trim on rim and on
base, one of the small shells that
form the base has been broken off,
mark 1 ....   410.00   475.00
☐ **Shoe,** 5″, hand-painted small
flowers in scatter pattern, gold
trim, marks 1 and J 410.00   475.00
☐ **Sugar and creamer,** ruffled top
sugar, creamer fits inside of sugar,
raised, gold paste trim in oak leaf
pattern on beige, matte finish,
mark k 315.00   410.00
☐ **Vase,** 7″, beautiful hand-painted
orchid, raised, gold paste work,
openwork handles, raised on

Price Range

small openwork feet, one of
which is damaged, probably had a
lid at one time which is no longer
present, mark k 415.00 475.00

☐ **Vase,** 10″, bulbous bottom with
long neck, hand-painted yellow
and brown flowers, raised, gold
trim, mark 1 .... 530.00 630.00

Radios

INTRODUCTION: Radio collecting is one of those not too well-publicized hobbies. Although the number of radio collectors is small compared to other collecting fields, the hobby has steadily gained popularity over the years. It is now estimated that there are over 5,000 collectors in the United States who in some way have an interest in collecting certain types of pre-1940 radios. Perhaps the technical aspect of the hobby is the reason most of the collectors of radios are those professionally engaged in some aspect of the radio or electronics field.

HOBBY SUPPORT: As in most collecting hobbies there are publications and clubs to help unite the individual collector with others who have the same interest. The radio collecting hobby is privileged to have over twelve radio clubs and four independent publications serving the needs of collectors all over the country. With over forty-five radio conventions and flea markets per year, the active radio collector has no major problem in acquiring new items for his collection.

THE RADIO COLLECTOR: Radio collectors basically fall into three categories: First there are those who collect the really early radios, well before the advent of commercial broadcasting in 1921. Known as ''wireless collectors,'' they collect items from the 1905-to-1920 period. The second group are the "battery set collectors," those who collect radios from the years 1921 to 1928. It was during this period that almost all of the radios made worked on batteries (they did not plug into the electric wall socket). The last group of collectors concentrate on radios that were electrically operated (AC sets), covering the years 1928 to the early 1940s.

With the thousands and thousands of different radios manufactured during this time span, collectors soon find they start to specialize in a certain aspect of the hobby. Some will collect certain manufacturers such as Atwater Kent, Crosley, RCA, Philco, Zenith, Scott, etc., while others will concentrate on specific types or styles of radios such as crystal sets, early wireless sets, superhets, regenerative sets, cathedral radios, console radios, novelty radios, and a host of other specialties.

In addition to collecting radios, most collectors will be in search of related items to complement their collection. This may include items like vacuum tubes, speakers, parts, radio magazines and books, service manuals, catalogs, and advertising signs. With so many items to collect, radio collectors are in a never-ending search to find new items for their collections.

VALUES: Placing values on old radios is perhaps one of the most difficult aspects of the hobby. With the bewildering amount of radios manufactured during the early days of radio, pricing a radio is at times almost an impossible task. It is usually collector demand that ultimately determines the price. During certain periods collector "fads" may drive certain types of radios up in price, only to fall again to a stable level. The current phase at present has swung to the electric sets of the 1930s, causing some prices of 1920s radios to fall dramatically.

With so many variables affecting price—age, rarity, manufacturer, condition, completeness, working condition, desirability, country—prices can range from next to nothing to the absurd. With many collectors specializing, the value of a radio may be greater to one collector than another, even though in broad terms they both have the same general interest in old radios.

The bottom line to values is, as in all old things, whatever a person is willing to pay for it, or in some cases what the collector market has established as a price through much buying, selling, and trading over the years. The prices listed here are just a general guide—with all the variables taken into account the prices could vary greatly.

Note: Values shown below are the actual auction-realized prices.

	Price Range
☐ **Bakelite radio,** by Fada, of bullet form in amber bakelite, 10½″ long	440.00
☐ **Bakelite radio,** by DeWald, lyre form with horizontal dial above vertical grillwork and two knobs in a swirled tortoiseshell Bakelite, 6½″ high	440.00
☐ **Bakelite radio,** by DeWald, rectangular with stepped top, horizontal dial above horizontal bright yellow grill over two yellow knobs, 6¾″ high	440.00
☐ **Blue/green Bakelite radio,** by Fada, Model 711, marked, 7¾″ high	495.00
☐ **Amber Bakelite radio,** by Fada, Model 1000, marked, 7″ high	770.00
☐ **Marbleized Bakelite radio,** by Addison, cathedral shape in black and green marbleized ground, marked, 9″ high	880.00
☐ **Amber Bakelite radio,** by Emerson, marked, 9″ high	495.00
☐ **Amber and green Bakelite radio,** by Fada, with decal "Fada," 5¼″ high	550.00
☐ **Ivorene Bakelite radio,** by Fada, Model 845, marked, 6″ high	330.00
☐ **Celluloid two-tone radio,** by Fada, Art Deco style, shaped rectangular form, circular dial, 10½″ long	475.00

Price Range

☐ **Glass, nickel-plated metal, and wood radio,** designed by Walter Dorwin Teague, executed by Spartan, face printed "SPARTAN JACKSON, MICHIGAN MADE IN U.S.A.," 15″ high 1210.00

Railroad Memorabilia

DESCRIPTION: Any items that pertain to the railroad make up railroadiana. This includes items from the steam-powered, diesel, and electric eras.

TYPES: Paper and hardware are the two basic types of railroadiana. The most collected paper item is the timetable, while uniforms are an especially sought after hardware item. The major areas of collecting are paper, hardware, china, and silver.

ADDITIONAL TIPS: Some collectors obtain any object of railroadiana, while others specialize in such areas as dining car items, ashtrays, or keys.

Price Range

☐ **Advertising brochure,** Monroe
hydraulic shock absorbers proved
for railroad freight cars, 6 pp,
cover showing large railroad yard,
c. 1950s 3.00

☐ **Blueprints,** railroad cars from
General Steel Industries, Inc., c.
1950s 10.00

Cable car painted wooden front, Presidio Avenue, California, and Market Streets, 6′4″ long, $1320. (*Photo courtesy of Butterfield & Butterfield, San Francisco*)

	Price Range
☐ **Cable car painted wooden front,** Presidio Avenue, California, and Market Streets, 6′4″ long	1320.00
☐ **Document,** Mississippi Central Railroad Company, dated May 18, 1865, concerns the transfer of stock for bonds that were purchased to help rebuild the railroad	16.00
☐ **Johnson fare boxes,** two, together with a Cleveland lock box and 22 former Oakland 10-cent fare box labels	330.00
☐ **Headlights,** four, Kraw Heinz Imperial, from Bay Area Interurban systems, with prismatic lenses	660.00
☐ **Headlights,** six, golden glow, from San Mateo Line and Market Street Railway, together with parts	330.00
☐ **Letters,** two, Northern Pacific Railroad, typed on special stationery, 1897 and 1899	8.00

Johnson fare boxes, two; together with a Cleveland lock box and 22 former Oakland ten-cent fare box labels, $330. *(Photo courtesy of Butterfield & Butterfield, San Francisco)*

	Price Range
☐ **Magazine,** Norfolk and Western Railway magazine, 2 issues, August 1957 and November 1961 ..	5.00
☐ **Photo,** old, B & W, of trolley car on street scene, looks down the street showing horse carriages, many old buildings	4.00

Signs, enameled metal, comprising San Mateo Depot, 2nd and Market Street, San Francisco, L line at West Portal and Express in San Francisco, $825. (*Photo courtesy of Butterfield & Butterfield, San Francisco*)

	Price Range
☐ **Signs,** enameled metal, comprising San Mateo Depot, 2nd and Market Street, San Francisco, L line at West Portal and Express in San Francisco	825.00
☐ **Sign,** enameled, Western Pacific Feather River Route, 21½″ × 26″, together with a Feather River Route booklet	247.50
☐ **Receipt,** The South Western Rail Road Company, for purchase of shares of stock, State of Georgia, January 5, 1874	26.00
☐ **Ticket,** used, August 30, 1870, Reading & Columbia Railroad, one seat, Petersburg to Sinking Spring, with depot station stamp on back	6.00

Sign, enameled, Western Pacific Feather River route, 21½″ × 26″; together with a Feather River Route booklet, $247.50. (*Photo courtesy of Butterfield & Butterfield, San Francisco*)

	Price Range
☐ **Traffic signal,** San Francisco, electric, by the Wiley Signal Company, painted yellow, with a pineapple finial, 4′8″ high	3300.00
☐ **San Francisco Municipal Railway,** circular enameled emblem, 30″ diameter	125.00
☐ **Munsing Wear enameled advertising sign,** of rectangular form with central vertical panel depicting a young man clad in underclothing being gestured at by two fashionably dressed young men, 27¼″ high	150.00

San Francisco traffic signal, electric, $3300. (*Photo courtesy of Butterfield & Butterfield, San Francisco*)

Records

COMMENTS: Between 1948 and 1950 the major format in records started changing from the 78-rpm disc to the forms we know today—the 33-rpm LP and the 45-rpm single. This change coincided with the birth of rock and roll. Well into the 1960s, the 7-inch single was the primary means of promoting an artist or group, but toward the end of the decade the LP became the dominant form in the industry.

In what follows, we examine several Top Twenty charts dating back to the early 1950s. What is remarkable about them is the difference between the albums that remained at No. 1 for the longest time and those that remained on the charts for the longest time. The reader might be surprised to see the predominance of soundtracks and original cast recordings on both lists, but this only serves to show the changing tastes of the American market.

We focus on these various (and varying) lists of best-sellers because these are the records people are most likely to have in their collections. What makes records collectible, however, is a combination of the popularity of the artist among a given group of collectors and the uniqueness of the release in question. Thus, though Elvis Presley's *Blue Hawaii* sold in the millions, the first pressing is of greatest importance to collectors. Such differences—sometimes as slight as a misprint or a change in wording—can dramatically upgrade the value of an album or a single.

TIPS: In collecting records, condition is all-important. In the case of albums this extends to include the cover as well—almost to the point where the condition of the album cover is on a par with the condition of the record itself. Beware of anyone trying to present a record as being in "mint" condition! Even if the cellophane wrapping hasn't been broken, the record itself may have been scuffed in the packaging process. For that reason the prices below reflect the standard of the record-collecting field: records valued in "near-mint" condition.

TOP 20 LPs BY LENGTH OF TIME AT NO. 1 ON CHARTS

Note: In those cases where a number of records were at No. 1 for the same number of weeks, the ranking here depended on the total number of weeks in the charts.

54 weeks

	Price Range	
☐ **1. *West Side Story*** (soundtrack)		
☐ **Columbia Mono** OL-5670, 1961	10.00	15.00
☐ **Stereo** OS-2070, 1961	15.00	20.00

37 weeks

☐ **2. *Thriller*** (Michael Jackson), Epic 38112, 1982	5.00	8.00

31 weeks

☐ **3. *South Pacific*** (soundtrack)		
☐ **RCA Mono** LOC-1032, 1957	12.00	15.00
☐ **Stereo** LSO-1032, 1958	15.00	20.00

	Price Range	
☐ **Deluxe edition** LOCD-2000, 1957 (mono only)	20.00	30.00
☐ **4.** *Rumours* (Fleetwood Mac), Warner Brothers 3010, 1977	5.00	8.00
☐ **5.** *Calypso* (Harry Belafonte), RCA Victor LPM 1248, 1956	12.00	20.00

24 weeks

☐ **6.** *Saturday Night Fever* (soundtrack), RSO 2-4001, 1977	8.00	12.00
☐ **7.** *Purple Rain* (Prince), Warner Brothers 25110, 1984	5.00	8.00

20 weeks

☐ **8.** *Blue Hawaii* (Elvis Presley)		
☐ **RCA Victor mono** LPM-2426, 1961	75.00	90.00
☐ **Stereo** LPS-2426, 1961	90.00	100.00

Note: Black label with "Long Play" at bottom distinguishes first release from subsequent releases; on stereo edition, black label with "Living Stereo" at bottom.

18 weeks

☐ **9.** *More of the Monkees,* Colgems 102, 1967	15.00	20.00

17 weeks

☐ **10.** *Synchronicity* (The Police), A&M 3735, 1983	5.00	8.00

	Price Range	
☐ **11.** *Love Me or Leave Me* (Doris Day; soundtrack), Columbia CL-710, 1955	25.00	30.00

16 weeks

	Price Range	
☐ **12.** *Sound of Music* (original cast)		
☐ **Columbia mono** KOL-5450, 1959	15.00	20.00
☐ **Stereo** KOS-2020, 1959	25.00	30.00
☐ **13.** *Days of Wine and Roses* (Andy Williams)		
☐ **Columbia mono** CL-2015, 1963	10.00	15.00
☐ **Stereo** CS-8815, 1963	10.00	15.00

15 weeks

	Price Range	
☐ **14.** *My Fair Lady* (original cast), Columbia mono OL-5090, 1956 ...	25.00	30.00
☐ **15.** *Tapestry* (Carole King), Ode 77009, 1971	8.00	12.00
☐ **16.** *Sgt. Pepper's Lonely Hearts Club Band* (The Beatles):		
☐ **Capitol mono** MAS-2653, 1967 ..	30.00	40.00
☐ **Stereo SMAS**-2653, 1967	20.00	30.00
☐ **17.** *The Kingston Trio at Large*		
☐ **Capitol mono** T-1199, 1959	10.00	15.00
☐ **Stereo** ST-1199, 1959	15.00	20.00
☐ **18.** *The Wall* (Pink Floyd), Columbia 36183, 1979	8.00	12.00
☐ **19.** *High Infidelity* (REO Speedwagon), Epic 36844, 1980	5.00	8.00
☐ **20.** *Business as Usual* (Men at Work), Columbia 37978, 1982	5.00	8.00

Price Range

TOP 20 LPs BY LENGTH OF TIME IN THE TOP 100

700+ weeks (and still counting!)

☐ **1.** *The Dark Side of the Moon*
(Pink Floyd), Harvest 11163, 1973   10.00   15.00

490 weeks

☐ **2.** *Johnny's   Greatest   Hits*
(Johnny Mathis), Columbia mono
1133, 1958 ....   8.00   10.00

480 weeks

☐ **3.** *My Fair Lady* (original cast),
Columbia mono OL-5090, 1956 ...   25.00   30.00

305 weeks

☐ **4.** *Oklahoma!* (soundtrack), Cap-
itol mono WAO-595, 1955 ....   15.00   25.00

302 weeks

☐ **5.** *Tapestry* (Carole King), Ode
77009, 1971 ....   8.00   12.00

295 weeks

☐ **6.** *Heavenly* (Johnny Mathis)
☐ **Columbia mono** 1351, 1959 ......   8.00   10.00
☐ **Stereo** 8152, 1959 ....   8.00   10.00

	Price Range	

277 weeks

☐ **7.** *The Sound of Music* (original cast)
☐ **Columbia mono** KOL-5450, 1959

....	15.00	20.00
☐ **Stereo** KOS-2020, 1959	25.00	30.00

277 weeks

☐ **8.** *Hymns* (Tennessee Ernie Ford),

Capitol 756, 1956	5.00	10.00

274 weeks

☐ **9.** *The King and I* (soundtrack),

Capitol 740, 1956	15.00	25.00

265 weeks

☐ **10.** *Camelot* (original cast)

☐ **Columbia mono** OL-5620, 1960	20.00	30.00
☐ **Stereo** OS-2031, 1960	30.00	40.00

262 weeks

☐ **11.** *South Pacific* (soundtrack)

☐ **RCA mono** LOC-1032, 1957	12.00	15.00
☐ **Stereo** LSO-1032, 1958	15.00	20.00
☐ **Deluxe edition** LOCD-2000, 1957, mono only	20.00	30.00

Price Range

245 weeks

☐ **12.** *The Music Man* (original cast)
☐ **Capitol mono** WAO-990, 1957 ...   15.00   20.00
☐ **Stereo** SWAO-990, 1957 ....   25.00   30.00

NOTE: Original issue featured fold-out cover in both mono and stereo.

234 weeks

☐ **13.** *Led Zeppelin IV,* Atlantic
7208, 1971 ....   8.00   10.00

233 weeks

☐ **14.** *Sound of Music* (soundtrack)
☐ **RCA mono** LOCD-2005, 1965 ....   15.00   20.00
☐ **Stereo** LSOD-2005, 1965 ....   25.00   30.00

233 weeks

☐ **15.** *Hot Rocks 1964–1971* (Roll-
ing Stones), London 606–7, 1971 .   10.00   12.00

231 weeks

☐ **16.** *Film Encores* (Mantovani),
London 1700, 1957 ....   5.00   10.00

206 weeks

☐ **17.** *Fiddler on the Roof* (original cast)

☐**RCA mono** LOC-1093, 1964	10.00	20.00
☐**Stereo** LSO-1093, 1964	10.00	20.00

204 weeks

☐ **18.** *Sing Along with Mitch* (Mitch Miller and the Gang), Columbia mono 1160, 1958 .... · · · · · 5.00 · · · · · 10.00

198 weeks

☐ **19.** *West Side Story* (soundtrack)

☐ **Columbia mono** OL-5670, 1961	10.00	15.00
☐ **Stereo** OS-2070, 1961	15.00	20.00

195 weeks

☐ **20.** *The Kingston Trio,* Capitol mono 996, 1958 .... · · · · 10.00 · · · · · 20.00

TOP 20 SINGLES BY LONGEVITY IN CHARTS

43 weeks

☐ **"Tainted Love"** (Soft Cell), Sire 49855, 1982 .... · · · · · 1.00 · · · · · 3.00

Price Range

40 weeks

☐ **"I Go Crazy"** (Paul Davis), Bang
733, 1977 .... 2.00   3.00

39 weeks

☐ **"The Twist"** (Chubby Checker),
Parkway 811 (white label), 1960   5.00   8.00
☐ **"Honky Tonk"** (Bill Doggett),
King 4950, 1956 .... 4.00   6.00
☐ **"Wonderful!   Wonderful!"**
(Johnny Mathis), Columbia 40784,
1957 .... 3.00   5.00

38 weeks

☐ **"So Rare"** (Jimmy Dorsey), Fra-
ternity 755, 1957 .... 3.00   5.00
☐ **"Rock Around the Clock"** (Bill
Haley and His Comets), Decca
29124, 1955 .... 10.00   15.00
☐ **"Why Me"** (Kris Kristofferson),
Monument 85, 1973 .... 2.00   3.00

37 weeks

☐ **"The Wayward Wind"** (Gogi
Grant), Era 1013, 1956 .... 3.00   5.00
☐ **"The Monster Mash"** (Bobby
Boris Pickett)
☐ **Garpax** 1, 1962 .... 8.00   10.00
☐ **Garpax** 44167, 1962 .... 3.00   6.00

	Price Range	

36 weeks

☐ **"Gloria"** (Laura Branigan), Atlantic 4048, 1982 .... 1.00 3.00

34 weeks

☐ **"Love Letters in the Sand"** (Pat Boone), Dot 15570, 1957 .... 3.00 5.00
☐ **"It's Not for Me to Say"** (Johnny Mathis), Columbia 40851, 1957 .... 3.00 5.00
☐ **"Around the World in 80 Days"** (Victor Young), Decca 30262, 1957 .... 2.00 4.00

33 weeks

☐ **"How Deep Is Your Love"** (the Bee Gees), RSO 882, 1977 .... 2.00 3.00

32 weeks

☐ **"Feelings"** (Morris Albert), RCA Victor 10279, 1975 .... 2.00 3.00
☐ **"Baby, Come to Me"** (Patti Austin and James Ingram), Qwest 50036, 1982 .... 1.00 3.00
☐ **"Around the World in 80 Days"** (Mantovani), London 1746, 1957 .... 2.00 4.00
☐ **"Baby Come Back"** (Player), RSO 879, 1977 .... 2.00 3.00
☐ **"Jessie's Girl"** (Rick Springfield), RCA Victor 12201, 1981 .. 1.00 3.00

Rock 'n' Roll Memorabilia

THE BEATLES

VARIATIONS: There is an unlimited variety of Beatles memorabilia. Records are quite collectible as well as buttons, posters, and other souvenir items.

ORIGIN: The Beatles were formed in Liverpool, England, in the late 1950s. Band members included Paul McCartney, John Lennon, Ringo Starr, and George Harrison. They took America by storm in 1964 when they appeared on the Ed Sullivan show. Credited with starting the musical British invasion, the Beatles contributed much to the development of rock and roll.

COMMENTS: The Beatles, along with Elvis Presley, are more collected than other recording artists. From the start of Beatlemania, anything Beatle-related has become collectible.

ADDITIONAL TIPS: The listings in this section include memorabilia and records.

Price Range

☐ **Beatles,** *Yesterday and Today* album, featuring the rejected "Butcher" version, stereo, c. 1966 ....   495.00

☐ **Beatles,** autographed color portrait, in group posed in front of an American flag, signed by all four with message in Harrison's hand, "To Joanne, lots of love from the Beatles xxx," c. 1966, 10″ × 13″   605.00

Beatles and Carl Perkins, autographs, on Carl Perkins Fan Club stationery, signed in EMI Studios, London, on the occasion of the Beatles recording of Perkins' song, "Matchbox," 1964, $880. (*Photo courtesy of Christie's East, New York*)

Five early Beatles tailoring sessions photos, the publicity photos showing the Beatles with Dougie Millings, whose family business made the Beatles' clothing for "Hard Day's Night" and "Help," and who appeared as the tailor in the former, framed together with a 1964 Dow color lithograph of the Beatles in their collarless suits, $330. (*Photo courtesy of Christie's East, New York*)

	Price Range
☐ **Beatles and Carl Perkins,** autographs, on Carl Perkins Fan Club stationery, signed in EMI Studios, London, on the occasion of the Beatles recording of Perkins's song "Matchbox," 1964 ...	880.00
☐ **Beatles,** five early tailoring sessions photos, publicity photos showing the Beatles with Dougie Millings, whose family business made the Beatles' clothing for *Hard Day's Night* and *Help* and who appeared as the tailor in the former, framed together with a 1964 Dow color lithograph of the Beatles in their collarless suits	330.00

Left. Beatles signed color portraits, taken from the "Sgt. Pepper" album cover, signed 1979–1982, $440. *Right.* Early Beatles autograph, including signature of original drummer Pete Best, ink on white paper, 1961, $330. (*Photo courtesy of Christie's East, New York*)

	Price Range
☐ **Beatles gold LP,** for *The Beatles 1962–66*	2860.00
☐ **Beatles signed color portraits,** taken from the *Sgt. Pepper* album cover, signed 1979–82	440.00
☐ **Early Beatles autograph,** including signature of original drummer Pete Best, ink on white paper, 1961	330.00
☐ **Beatles autographed album cover,** *Beatles for Sale,* signed by all four, c. 1978–80; a British fan sent the album to Lennon at the Dakota, who wrote, "Thanks, love, John Lennon from NYC— the USA!!!"	550.00

Beatles autographed album cover, "Beatles For Sale," signed by all four, c. 1978–1980; a British fan sent the album to Lennon at the Dakota, who wrote, "Thanks, love, John Lennon from NYC–the USA!!!," $550. (*Photo courtesy of Christie's East, New York*)

Price Range

☐ **John Lennon caricature,** of himself and Yoko, black marker on white paper, signed John Lennon 1969, obtained in the Apple offices by a journalist following Lennon and Ono's first bed-in, 8½" × 11½" 1320.00

ELVIS PRESLEY

DESCRIPTION: Elvis Presley, a rock-and-roll legend, was one of the greatest influences on music. His twenty-year

Elvis Presley, autographed LP, "Elvis' Christmas Album,"
RCA British version, c. 1958, with copy of letter explaining how autograph was obtained at the Lido Club in Paris,
1959, $990. (*Photo courtesy of Christie's East, New York*)

career lasted from 1956 until his untimely death in 1977.
Because of the millions of Elvis Presley fans throughout the
world, any items belonging to the "King of Rock and Roll"
are valuable among collectors.

TYPES: There are all kinds of Elvis memorabilia, from
clothes, cars, and contracts to autographed photos and
school items. One of the largest collecting areas is his records.

COMMENTS: Some Elvis fans collect only his records, while
others collect all types of his memorabilia.

Price Range

☐ **Elvis Presley,** autographed LP,
Elvis' Christmas Album, RCA
British version, c. 1958, with

Price Range

copy of letter explaining how autograph was obtained at the Lido
Club in Paris, 1959 ....   990.00
☐ **Autographed display,** including
signature, photograph, and a
"Blue Suede Shoes" 45 in com-
memoration of Elvis's 50 anniver-
sary, 14″ × 18″ 300.00   500.00
☐ **Autographed album,** *Rock 'n'*
Roll, RCA British version, c. 1958,
with letter explaining how the
signature was obtained at the Lido
Club in Paris 800.00   900.00
☐ **Elvis Presley Commemorative**
50th Birthday Award, a framed
gold 45 "Elvis' Greatest Hits,
Golden Singles, Vol. 1" above inscribed plaque, 1955–85, one of a
series of 12 presented to RCA ex-
ecutives 800.00   1000.00

MISCELLANEOUS

☐ **Billy Joel,** autographed sheet
music, "Honesty," 1978, signed
"Cheers! Billy Joel" next to his
picture on the cover 100.00   200.00
☐ **Bob Dylan,** autographed album,
Street-Legal, Columbia, 1978 .....   200.00   250.00
☐ **Bruce Springsteen,** auto-
graphed poster, promoting his
concert at The Bottom Line, c.
1974, also autographed by three
band members 1000.00   1200.00
☐ **Bruce Springsteen,** platinum
record, for *The River,* Columbia
Records in-house award, with in-
scribed plaque 300.00   350.00
☐ **Frank Zappa,** "200 Motels,"
color celluloid, depicting Zappa,

	Price Range	
numbered 486 17 J115, 10 ½″ × 12 ½″	100.00	200.00
☐ **Jimi Hendrix,** experimental color photograph, by Nona Hatay, "Purple Haze," 1986	300.00	400.00
☐ **Jimi Hendrix,** platinum record, for *Electric Ladyland,* Warner Bros. in-house award, with inscribed plaque	800.00	900.00
☐ **Journey,** platinum record, for *Frontiers,* Columbia in-house award, with inscribed plaque	200.00	250.00
☐ **Kiss,** gold record, for *Destroyer,* Casablanca in-house award, with inscribed plaque	300.00	400.00

Led Zeppelin, autographed LP, "Led Zeppelin," Atlantic, 1971, front cover signed by Robert Plant and Jimmy Page backstage at Madison Square Garden in 1977, $550. (*Photo courtesy of Christie's East, New York*)

Price Range

☐ **Led Zeppelin,** autographed LP, *Led Zeppelin,* Atlantic, 1971, front cover signed by Robert Plant and Jimmy Page backstage at Madison Square Garden in 1977 ....   550.00

☐ **Little Richard,** gold LP, for *Little Richard's Grooviest 17 Original Hits!* with inscription 1000.00   1500.00

☐ **Pete Townshend,** store display poster, printed in shades of blue with full-figure rendering of Townshend with halo, produced to promote *Empty Glass* album, 44″ × 26″, c. 1980 ....   88.00

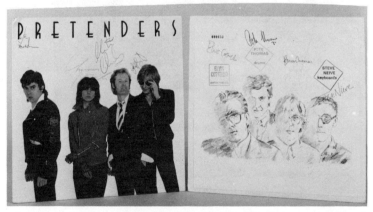

Left. Pretenders, autographed LP, "Pretenders," the cover signed by Chrissie Hynde, Pete Farndon, Martin Chambers, and James Honeyman Scott, 1979, $165. *Right.* Elvis Costello, autographed LP, promotional copy entitled "Elvis Costello Introduces . . . The Tracks from His New Album 'Almost Blue,' " 1981, the cover signed by Costello, Pete Thomas, Bruce Thomas and Steve Neive, $132. (*Photo courtesy of Christie's East, New York*)

Prince, gold 45 award, for "When Doves Cry," with inscribed plaque, $1320. (*Photo courtesy of Christie's East, New York*)

Price Range

☐ **Poster,** Woodstock color poster, large, depicting a white dove perched on a blue and green guitar neck with orange, black, and white lettering, signed by the artist (Skolnick) in black ink 190.00

☐ **Pretenders,** autographed LP, *Pretenders,* cover signed by Chrissie Hynde, Pete Farndon, Martin Chambers, and James Honeyman Scott, 1979 .... 165.00

☐ **Elvis Costello,** autographed LP, promotional copy entitled *Elvis Costello Introduces . . . the Tracks from His New Album "Almost Blue,"* 1981, cover signed by Costello, Pete Thomas, Bruce Thomas, and Steve Neive 132.00

☐ **Prince,** gold 45 award, for *When Doves Cry,* with inscribed plaque 1320.00

☐ **Stevie Nicks,** autographed sheet music "Stand Back," 1983, signed on cover "Don't Blame it on me' . . . much love, Stevie" in gold ink   200.00   250.00

Scouting
Memorabilia

ORIGIN: Englishman Sir Robert S. S. Baden-Powell is the original founder of Boy Scouts and Girl Scouts in England. The development of scouting in America is due to Daniel Carter Beard, William Boyce, and James E. West for Boy Scouts of America, and Juliette Gordon Low for Girl Scouts of America. The two groups are separate and distinct.

COMMENTS: The 1950 Boy Scout National Jamboree brought a new rage to scouting and the American collecting scene. Scouts were trading everything from patches to rattlesnake skins. Thus began the collecting of boy scout memorabilia. It really never hit the bit time until the 1970s when scout memorabilia trading slowed up, and buying took over. Now the collectors are the men who were scouts in 1950, and trade-o-rees, akin to flea markets, are held to trade and sell memorabilia, with hundreds of people attending. And as in all collectibles, professional dealers have evolved.

FICTION AND MISCELLANEOUS BOOKS

Price Range

☐ *Lone Scout of the Sky,* West, 1928, vg 10.00

☐ *Animal Heroes,* Every Boys Library, some water stains 8.00

☐ *Skyward Ho!* edited by Franklin Mathiews, Chief Scout Librarian, 1930 .... 10.00

☐ *A Boy Scout with Byrd,* Paul Siple, dj, 1931, ex 10.00

☐ *Wild Animals at Home,* Seton, 1925, vg 8.00

☐ *Lone Scout of the Sky,* James E. West, 1928, ex 12.00

☐ *Lucky Boy Scout,* Sherwood, dj, 1916 .... 10.00

☐ *Our Young Aeroplane Scouts in the Balkans,* Porter, vg, no title page 6.00

☐ *Golden Anniversary Book of Scouting,* 1959, g-vg 20.00

☐ *Our Young Aeroplane Scouts in England,* Porter, 1916, ex ... 6.00

☐ *Lucky the Boy Scout,* Sherwood 7.50

☐ *Boy Scout's Life of Lincoln,* Tarbell, 1924, good 10.00

☐ *Boy Scouts for Uncle Sam,* Payson, 1912, jd, vg 5.00

☐ *Boy Scout Aviators,* Durston, ex-mint, 1921 .... 7.50

☐ *A Boy Scout with Byrd,* Siple, dj, 1931 .... 12.00

☐ *Boy Scouts: How a Patrol Leader Made Good,* Douglas, 1913, good 4.00

☐ *Boy Scouts of the Air on the Great Lakes,* Stuart, 1914, dj, ex 6.00

	Price Range
☐ *The Boy Scouts: An American Adventure,* Peterson, 1984	12.95

JAMBOREE

☐ 1973 National Jamboree, leather patch	6.00
☐ 1969 National Jamboree, souvenir, neckerchief	7.00
☐ 1967 National Jamboree, neckerchief	12.00
☐ 1969 National Jamboree, bracelet	4.00
☐ 1973 National Jamboree, decal	1.00
☐ 1969 National Jamboree, coin	5.00
☐ 1973 National Jamboree, neckerchief	4.00
☐ 1953 National Jamboree, souvenir belt buckle	3.00
☐ 1953 National Jamboree, telephone handbook	10.00
☐ 1975 National Jamboree, "Will You Be There?" bumper sticker	3.00
☐ 1973 National Jamboree, *The Spokesman Review,* Spokane, WA, paper	6.00
☐ 1973 National Jamboree, West Journals—1,2,3,4,6,8,9, each ...	1.00
☐ 1969 National Jamboree, Sandpoint, ID News-Bulletin	5.00
☐ 1973 National Jamboree, wide game cards—R,T, each	3.00
☐ 1973 National Jamboree, directions 73 for leaders—1,3, each	1.00
☐ 1960 National Jamboree, neckerchief	20.00
☐ 1969 National Jamboree, neckerchief	12.00

Price Range

☐ **1977 National Jamboree, set of souvenir projector slides**	25.00
☐ **Repro National Jamboree, pocket patch, 64**	2.00
☐ **1973 National Jamboree, East Journals, 8**	1.00
☐ **1957 National Jamboree, pocket patch**	25.00
☐ **1981 National Jamboree, pen** .	1.00
☐ **1973 National Jamboree, commissary and equipment manual,** for trading post managers, in 3-ring binder	10.00
☐ **1969 National Jamboree, book**	8.00

NECKERCHIEFS AND SLIDES

☐ **California Bicentennial,** 1969, slide	2.00
☐ **Scout Fair,** 1965, slide	2.00
☐ **Johnston National Scouting Museum,** neckerchief	8.00
☐ **Pine Hill Scout Reservation,** 50th Anniversary neckerchief	3.00
☐ **Missouri Synod Lowisomo Camper,** neckerchief	3.00
☐ **Four Rivers Council,** neckerchief	3.00
☐ **General Greene Scout Reservation,** neckerchief	3.00
☐ **Region 7 Canoe Base,** neckerchief	10.00
☐ **1961 Scouting Fair,** neckerchief	1.00
☐ **Neckerchief, 1960,** 50th Anniversary, "For God And Country," metal	8.00

	Price Range
☐ **Neckerchief "Safety Good Turn,"** green enamel cross on aluminum, 1950	5.00
☐ **"Philmont Training Center,"** 2-color enamel brass, slide, 1965	8.00
☐ **Neckerchief, "Strengthen the Arm of Liberty,"** bronze, large, both Cubs and BSA versions, 1960s, with Statue of Liberty	16.00

Scrimshaw

DESCRIPTION: Scrimshaw is artwork done on bone. It can be carved, engraved, or painted.

MATERIALS: Whalebone is the most commonly found material, followed by walrus tusks. Least used are ivory and shell. Occasionally, a low-grade ivory such as whale tooth is used.

COMMENTS: The age, size, artistic quality, subject matter, and state of preservation all go into determining the value of scrimshaw. Articles made from whalebone by American whalers in the nineteenth century are widely popular among collectors.

Price Range

☐ **Sperm whale's tooth,** dated 1878, engraved on the obverse with a finely detailed spread-winged American eagle grasping an olive branch and arrows, encircled with the words "Hope, Faith and Charity" and 13 stars, the reverse engraved with a whaling vessel and bearing the initials "TW," 6″ long 1400.00

Sperm whale's tooth, depicting a schooner at sea, signed "LETH," 6″ long, estimated value $700–$900. (*Photo courtesy of Phillips, New York*)

	Price Range	
☐ **Sperm whale's tooth,** depicting a schooner at sea, signed "LETH," 6″ long	700.00	900.00
☐ **Sperm whale's tooth,** American, c. 1840, depicting six whalers in a boat spearing a whale, schooner in the distance, initialed "S.M.," 8″ long		400.00
☐ **Sperm whale's tooth,** American, engraved on the obverse with an American ship at sea and bearing the words "The Ship Niger, N.B.," the reverse depicting figures in fishing boats in a harbor, bearing the words "Fiji Is. Pacific Ocean," 6¼″ high	1000.00	1500.00
☐ **Sperm whale's tooth,** with carving on the obverse side depicting General Ulysses S. Grant, the reverse with engraved Civil War motifs, reading "Shiloh 1862," initialed "H.H.," 5½″ high	1000.00	1500.00

☐ **Justice and Liberty,** engraved walrus tusks, pair, the figure of Liberty in red and blue below a figure of George Washington, Justice in red and blue below two figures depicting her virtues, each with eyelet at the far tip, 22½″ long 700.00

Scripophily

DESCRIPTION: Scripophily (collecting stock certificates and bonds) is the newest and most fascinating hobby in the collectibles world. As early as 1670, stock certificates were being issued. The development of the West, the era of the Gold Rush, and the era of the Iron Horse are examples of important events in our nation's history that are found in scripophily.

The fine engravings appearing on stocks and bonds were designed by the same world-renowned bank note companies that are also known for their excellent stamp and currency engravings. Certificates and bonds are being prominently displayed in homes, offices, banks, hotels, libraries, etc., by decorators as well as collectors because of their attractiveness.

Since rarity and condition as well as many other factors determine the worth of a certificate, it is preferable to receive photocopies so that the highest bid possible can be submitted. The following prices are broad guidelines: railroad (pre-1930), $5 and up; (pre-1900), $10 and up; mining (pre-1930), $5 and up; (pre-1900), $10 and up; general (pre-1930, $5 and up; autographed certificates, $150 and up.

GRADING: UNC, uncirculated (clean and crisp); EF, extremely fine (clean, but perhaps traces of folds); F, fine (very creased or worn, but still clear); Fair, extremely creased and worn. All items are in EF condition unless designated otherwise.

ABBREVIATIONS: B, bond; U, unissued; Cp, coupons; Rn, revenue stamp; Ph, punch holes; states, U.S. Postal Service designations.

	Price Range
☐ **Elmira State Line Railroad Co.,** 1885, train	45.00
☐ **Fort Pitt Traction Co.** (PA), 1895, electric streetcar	30.00
☐ **Franfort, Tacony & Holmesburg Street Railway Co.** (PA), 1910, B, electric trolley	35.00
☐ **Gauley & Meadow River Railroad Co.** (WV), 1912, train	18.00
☐ **Grand Junction Railroad & Depot Co.** (MA), 1852, bond guaranteed by Eastern RR Co.	35.00
☐ **Hartford & Connecticut Western Railroad,** 1881, signed by William L. Gilbert (capitalist), train	25.00
☐ **Hestonville, Mantua & Fairmount Passenger Railroad** (PA), 1894, passenger railroad car, VF	20.00
☐ **Holly, Wayne & Monroe Railroad Co.** (MI), 1871, B, trains, town, imprinted revenue stamps	75.00
☐ **Hot Springs Railroad Co.** (AR), 1892, train	38.00
☐ **Indiana Southern Railway Co.** (IN), 1866, B, 7-car train, Cp	60.00
☐ **International Railroad Co.** (TX), 1871, B, Un, train at busy depot, cowboys	25.00
☐ **Ionia & Lansing Railroad Co.** (MI), 1869, signed by H. P. Baldwin (governor and senator), B, train	45.00

	Price Range
☐ **Ironton Railroad Co.** (PA), 1874, portraits of Henry Clay and Daniel Webster, train	50.00
☐ **Joliet & Chicago Railroad Co.**, 1892, train	30.00
☐ **Kentucky Central Railroad,** 1900, train	25.00
☐ **Kentucky & Great Eastern Railway** (KY), 1872, U, Daniel Boone battling Indians, Cp	60.00
☐ **Lexington & Eastern Railway Co.** (KY), 1894, B, train	75.00
☐ **Iowa Falls & Sioux City Railroad Co.**, 1886, train, factories .	22.00
☐ **City of New York,** 1914, municipal gold bond, portrait	30.00
☐ **Connecticut Fire Insurance Co.**, 1887, state seal	15.00
☐ **County of Shelby** (IL), 1865, train, eagle, allegoricals, seals	20.00
☐ **Fortuna Gold Placer Co.** (Arizona Territory), 1905, mining	15.00
☐ **Game Ridge Mining Co.** (NY), 1887, mine location, Rosita, CO, miners drilling	40.00
☐ **Katonah Silk Co.**, (NY), 1891, farmer, allegorical	20.00
☐ **McClintockville Petroleum Co.** (PA), 1864, detailed vignette of town on river edge, sign on bridge reads "Fine for driving faster than a walk," Rn	95.00
☐ **Merced Gold Mining Co. of Montana,** 1895, mining	35.00
☐ **Newport & Cincinnati Bridge Co.**, 1910, bridge spanning river, sidewheelers, sailboat	25.00
☐ **Nimson Forge & Axle Co.** (PA), 1875, factory	20.00

Price Range

☐ **Phoenix Insurance Co.** (CT), 1865, "The Phoenix" (mythological bird) 20.00

☐ **Portland Copper & Silver Mining Co.** (ME), 1882, mining 30.00

☐ **Sampson Mining Co.** (Utah Territory), 1898, mines at Bingham, UT, mining 30.00

☐ **Sequatchie Coal & Iron Co.** (TN), 1894, miners, VF 15.00

☐ **Taylor Plumas Gold Mining Co.** (NY), 1883, location of mines, Plumas County, CA, mining 40.00

Sewing Collectibles

COMMENTS: The implements or tools used during sewing have always been very important in the antiques and collectibles market. Items such as thimbles, buttons, sewing tables and stands, spinning wheels, yarn winders, and early irons have long been desired by collectors. Recent trends have shown the whole realm of related sewing items commanding a market of their own.

One of the most appealing things about collecting anything related to sewing is that novice collectors can easily begin by simply looking around their own homes. History has proved that every homemaker is involved with some form of sewing. Every home has a sewing box or basket, and there is absolute delight in searching through these to find all that has accumulated over the years. Many sewing tools have changed in form slightly or not at all over the ages, so they will be relatively easy to recognize.

Since sewing has traditionally been the work of women, it can be said that there has been no other tangible art form that has expressed to such a degree their individuality and their creativity. In every form, this expression of ingenuity is very personal and will always carry with it a part of its creator.

BUTTONS

COMMENTS: Dating back to the 13th century, buttons were first used for decoration. Early buttons had very elaborate and exquisite designs and therefore are much sought by collectors. Currently, buttons from the 18th century to the present are the most available and collectible. Most antique and collectible buttons on the market today are American-, French-, or English-made.

	Price Range	
☐ **Caramel-color glass button,** with black and gold highlights, three inset steel facets, $7/16''$ diameter	40.00	50.00
☐ **Gold,** woven hair under swirls, cartwheel design, 19th century		130.00
☐ **Jet faceted buttons** on original card, $11/16''$ diameter		9.00
☐ **18th century,** silver wash over gold with blue enamel background, 32 rose-point diamonds		135.00
☐ **Mother-of-pearl,** Tiffany & Co., 1915, sapphire inset		650.00
☐ **Red glass button,** pressed, with rose design highlighted in gold, black painted rim, self-shank, $7/8''$ long	30.00	40.00

PAPER

☐ **Cards,** Singer Sewing Machine, set of 10 large ($7 1/4'' \times 4 1/2''$) sepiatone photograph cards of Washington historical areas, backs of cards describe the front scene

	Price Range	

and carry Singer advertising, in original envelope, mint condition 10.00 20.00

☐ **Trade card** "Fascimile of Embroidery Done on the Davis Vertical Feed Sewing Machine, Watertown, NY" 3.50

☐ **Trade card,** "For Hand and Machine, Coats Thread" 4.00

☐ **Flier,** fold-out, Empire Sewing Machine, shows engravings of six different machines, printed in German, front marked "Carson Bros., Gen Agents, Pittsburgh, 1867" 15.00 20.00

☐ **Booklet,** "Ribbon and Fabric Trimmings," published by Woman's Institute of Domestic Arts & Sciences, Inc, Scranton, PA, 1925 12.00

☐ **Booklet,** 1916, "Embroidery and Decorative Stitches" 15.00

☐ **Flier,** Empire Sewing Machine, c. 1867, 6″ × 9″, interesting printing 15.00 20.00

☐ **Flier,** thread sales, Clark's Thread, red/white, with advertising and a long list of sewing machine dealers' endorsements of the threads (Wilson's, Grover & Baker, Singer's Florence and Home), 8½″ × 11″, 1870 .... 15.00 25.00

TOOLS

☐ **Advertising combination,** buttonhole cutter, seam ripper, needle threader, green metal case, 3⅝″ long 15.00

☐ **Pincushions,** beaded and needlework, 19th century 50.00 60.00

Price Range

☐ **Darning egg,** ebony, sterling silver handle with raised floral and scroll decoration, 5¾″ long 45.00

☐ **Fluting   iron,**   three-piece, marked on base "Shepard Hardware Company/Buffalo, NY" 75.00

☐ **Fluting iron,** two-piece, cast iron, waffle top handle, "C.W. Whitefield/Syracuse NY" 40.00

☐ **Slug iron,** cast iron, wood turned handle 80.00

☐ **Slug iron,** brass, wood turned handle and brass support 80.00

☐ **Tape measure,** tin case with brass cat head, green glass eyes, German, c. 1910 ....   60.00   80.00

☐ **Thread holder,** Victorian, white metal, holds 6 spools, cat on top center 150.00   180.00

☐ **Spinning wheel,** wool wheel, mixed woods with all parts intact, working condition, circa early 18th century 650.00

☐ **Store cabinet,** Willimantic Silk Thread, walnut, original decals on front and sides, wood pulls, 13″ high, 24¾″ wide 450.00

☐ **Sterling silver thimble,** wide plain band with feathery border, marked "9" 25.00

☐ **Sterling silver thimble,** wide band with paneled medallions 28.00

☐ **Sterling silver thimble,** wide band with feathery engraving in alternate panels 32.00

☐ **Yarn winder,** cherry with evidence of original red paint, all intact and in working order, early 18th century 125.00

Sheet Music

DESCRIPTION: Sheet music is often copyrighted, therefore reproduction is forbidden. The collecting interests of sheet music can be quite varied, from ragtime and blues to Mom, World War II, and roses. Sheet music is known to have existed at least two hundred years ago, and more than a million pieces have been published.

	Price Range	
☐ **"Auntie Skinner's Chicken Dinner,"** black men/women on the cover, 1915	8.00	12.00
☐ **"Casablanca,"** inset Humphrey Bogart, Ingrid Bergman, and Paul Henreid, 1941	5.00	15.00
☐ **"Do Something,"** painting of Uncle Sam pointing, signed James Montgomery Flagg, 1917	10.00	20.00
☐ **The Ethiopian Glee Book,** black dialect songs, 1843	20.00	30.00
☐ **Four Ukulele Song Books,** 1950s	30.00	40.00
☐ **"Get on the Raft with Taft,"** 1908, full-page photo of Taft	20.00	30.00

	Price Range	
☐ **"God Bless America,"** Irvin Berlin, 1939	4.00	6.00
☐ **"Isabella with the Gingham Umbrella,"** 1860s, pictorial border	12.00	16.00
☐ **"I've Got No Strings,"** published by Irving Berlin, Pinocchio song, c. 1939	13.00	15.00
☐ **"I've Got You Under My Skin,"** Cole Porter musical, *Born to Dance,* song for Eleanor Powell .	8.50	10.00
☐ **"Ivory Tower,"** words and music by Jack Fulton and Lois Steele, inset Cathy Carr, publisher Melrose, c. 1956	3.00	5.00
☐ **"Jim Crow Polka,"** as sung by Christy's Minstrels, 1847, vignettes of performers in blackface	35.00	45.00
☐ **"McKinley's Funeral March,"** photo of McKinley, 1901	10.00	14.00
☐ **"My Heart Cries for You,"** by Carl Sigman and Percy Faith, inset Dinah Shore, publisher Massy, c. 1950	4.00	6.00
☐ **"Newsboy Galop,"** photo of newsboy on street corner, 1905 .	10.00	14.00
☐ **"The Naughty Lady of Shady Lane,"** by Sid Tepper and Roy C. Bennet, inset the Ames Bros., publisher Paxton, c. 1954	3.00	5.00
☐ **"Oh, Dem Old Brown Plants,"** 1860s, ethnic lyrics	8.00	12.00
☐ **"Our Gallant Hero,"** Admiral Dewey, photo of Dewey with flags and eagle	8.00	12.00
☐ **Pre-1875 bound book of music,** 39 complete pieces of early sheet music	150.00	160.00
☐ **"Short'nin Bread," "Mammy,"** 1928	12.00	15.00

	Price Range	
☐ **"Teen-Age Wedding,"** 1963, large photo of Annette Funicello in wedding gown	4.00	6.00
☐ **"Thanks for the Memory,"** W. C. Fields' film *The Big Broadcast of 1938,* cover has caricatures of Fields, Bob Hope, and Martha Raye, 1938	12.00	15.00
☐ **"The Midnight Fire Alarm,"** by Harry Lincoln, arranged by E. T. Paul, colored lithograph on cover	30.00	40.00
☐ **"When It's Springtime in the Rockies,"** Rudy Vallee, 1929	6.50	7.50
☐ **"When You Wish Upon a Star,"** published by Irving Berlin, Pinocchio song, c. 1939	13.00	15.00

Silhouettes

BACKGROUND: During the 1700s people of an artistic turn of mind were in the habit of making what were called silhouettes. The sitter was so posed that the light from a lamp threw the profile of his face in sharp shadow against a white screen. It was then easy to obtain a fairly accurate silhouette, by either outlining the profile or cutting it out from the screen. Their popularity did not fall from favor until the middle of the 1880s.

Price Range

☐ **Hunter warding off a bull,** 13″ × 20″ and trotting horse, 10¾″ × 10½″, artist: Wilhelm Hunt Diedrich 900.00

Artist: Wilhelm Hunt Diedrich. *Left*. Hunter warding off a bull, 13″ × 20″. *Right*. Trotting horse, 10¾″ × 10½″, sold at auction for $900. (*Photo courtesy of Phillips, New York*)

	Price Range	
☐ **Alexander Hamilton,** bust portrait wearing frilled smock, signed J. W. Jarvis, dated 1804, 4½″ × 3½″	450.00	650.00
☐ **Double portrait,** gentleman and lady, full-length figures, signed Aug. Edouart, dated 1844, 9″ × 7⅛″	200.00	350.00
☐ **Gentleman, wearing top hat,** landscape setting, signed Aug. Edouart, dated 1829, 8⅞″ × 1¼″	250.00	350.00

Sports Collectibles

COMMENTS: The market for sports collectibles has enjoyed a solid year, with upward trends to be noted in the majority of prices. It is apparent that the growth of the sports collectibles field derives from within the hobby itself. With its present rate of growth, the competition for better, scarcer items has greatly increased. This has become evident through the rising numbers of dealer shows held around the country. The strength of the sports collectibles field becomes clear when one considers that it succeeded in riding out the aftermath of "investment fever" with no ill effects.

As far as categories are concerned, a careful review of the past year's market reveals the continuation of a trend that began several years ago. This is the increased collector awareness and appreciation of items outside the scope of traditional sports collectibles, pointing to a greater sophistication in the hobby and increased willingness on the part of collectors to invest more money for quality items.

COLLECTING TIPS: Sports collecting often bears little resemblance to other collecting fields. In most cases, beauty of manufacture and the quality of the material from which something was produced is not necessarily important. Rather, the age, historical importance, and scarcity are the telling points. As often happens in the realm of sports collectibles, the least costly items end up being worth the most. Athletes never charged for their autographs, yet each time they signed a baseball, photo, or sportscard, they were giving away something that would eventually grow to hundreds of dollars in value.

Note: In each category, unless otherwise noted, all drawings are by Burris Jenkins Jr., American illustrator, 1897–1966, who worked for Hearst Publications.

BASEBALL

	Price Range	
☐ **Babe Ruth,** c. 1927, postcard, photograph by Nickolas Muray ..	20.00	30.00
☐ **Babe Ruth,** in Yankees uniform, portrait by Bruce Stark, signed, oil on canvas board, 18″ × 15¾″ (original artwork for *The Saturday Evening Post* framed with a copy of the article and illustration, p. 55)	1500.00	2500.00
☐ **Baseball,** autographed, representing a mixture of signatures from various teams including Adolfo ("The Pride of Havana") Luque, Ernie Kruger, Curtis Walker, Grover Land, Hugh Critz, and Jake May	150.00	200.00
☐ **Baseball,** 1955 Brooklyn Dodgers, with 27 signatures, including Jackie Robinson, Sandy Koufax, Gil Hodges, Duke Snider, Pee Wee Reese, Carl Furillo (auction price)		550.00
☐ **Belt,** an early Brooklyn "Continentals" baseball team leather belt, c. 1870, finished in white with "Continental" in black		

Casey Stengel Baseball Hall of Fame ring, presented to Mr. Stengel on his induction into the Baseball Hall of Fame in 1966, $17,000. (*Photo courtesy of Phillips, New York*)

	Price Range
letters, together with an early baseball bat of the same period ..	950.00
☐ **Casey Stengel Baseball Hall of Fame ring,** presented to Mr. Stengel on his induction into the Baseball Hall of Fame in 1966	17,000.00
☐ **Drawing,** "Joe D-Day, Contributions for Charity," signed, pencil with ink heightened with white, 22″ × 18″	400.00
☐ **Drawing,** "After a Brief Intermission," (Dodgers vs. Yankees, Oct '53, April '54), signed, pencil with ink, 4½″ × 20″	300.00
☐ **Etching,** The American National Game of Baseball, "Grand Match for the Championship at the Elysian Fields, Hoboken, N.J. 1865," etching and aquatint printed in color, 17¼″ × 23½″	300.00
☐ **Game,** coin-operated "Hit A Homer," 5 balls for 1¢, wooden frame, painted glass front with lithograph diamond and stadium	

Drawing, "Joe D-Day, Contributions for Charity," signed, pencil with ink heightened with white, 22″ × 18″, $400. (*Photo courtesy of Phillips, New York*)

	Price Range
background, 18″ long, 21½″ high	475.00
☐ **Game,** "Inside Baseball," Popular Games Company, tinplate, c. 1911, with spinner, lithographed baseball diamond, 20 tokens, each representing players in the 1911 World Series, New York vs. Philadelphia, 13″ × 13″	375.00

Price Range

☐ **George Herman "Babe" Ruth baseball,** signed by Ruth and other members of the 1943 Yankees, including Joe McCarthey, Red Ruffing, Joe Page, George Stirnweiss, and from Cincinnati, Bucky Walters 1000.00

☐ **George Herman "Babe" Ruth photograph,** cut from a newspaper, signed; and Ty Cobb photograph, cut from magazine, signed 350.00

☐ **Group of 12 lithographed-paper baseball players,** c. 1887, six representing the Chicago White Stockings and six representing the New York Giants, all mounted on small wooden blocks with the names of players on back of blocks 800.00

☐ **Newspaper premium,** New York Giants, color, 1892, features the team posing in the stadium with capacity crowd, included in the photo are Hall of Famers William Ewing, Jim O'Rourke, Amos Rusie, and Mickey Welch, in ornate period frame, 7½″ × 9½″ 200.00

☐ **Poster,** *Roogies Bump,* movie, starring Brooklyn Dodgers Roy Campanella, Billy Loes, Carl Erskine, and Russ Meyer, 36″ × 15″, and two lobby cards from the same movie, 11″ × 15″ 70.00

☐ **Radio,** an unusual official league baseball radio, "Trophy Trademark," oversize baseball houses the radio apparatus and is mounted on a bilevel base, 9″ high 800.00

Radio, an unusual official league baseball radio, "Trophy Trademark," the oversized baseball houses the radio apparatus and is mounted on a bi-level base, 9″ high, $800. (*Photo courtesy of Phillips, New York*)

Baseball Cards

DESCRIPTION: Baseball cards usually have the picture of a baseball player on one side and the player's baseball record on the other. Baseball cards were made in different sizes depending on the era and the company.

ORIGIN: Baseball cards were introduced in the mid-1880s. At first they were made exclusively by tobacco companies for distribution with cigarettes or other tobacco products. From 1900 to 1930 other firms also printed baseball cards but not on a regular basis. The modern era of baseball cards began during the Depression, when gum companies began packaging cards along with bubble gum. At first the motive was simply to boost gum sales, but as the public became more interested in the cards, card issuing developed into a thriving industry.

TYPES: There are basically two types of cards—cards from before the 1930s and the modern cards, after the 1930s.

COMPANIES: Major companies that produced baseball cards in the late 1800s and early 1900s include Goodwin and Company, Allen and Ginter, P. H. Mayo and Brothers Tobacco Company, and D. Buchner.

Since the early 1930s, modern card companies like Goudey Gum Company, Leaf/Donruss, Delong Gum Company, and Frank H. Fleer have been major card producers. The Topps Chewing Gum Company, which began distributing cards in the early 1950s, is the one most people associate with baseball cards.

ADDITIONAL INFORMATION: For more information, consult *The Official Price Guide to Baseball Cards,* published by The House of Collectibles and authored by Dr. James Beckett.

1987 TOPPS

This 792-card set is reminiscent of the 1962 Topps baseball cards with their simulated woodgrain borders. The backs are printed in yellow and blue on gray card stock. The manager cards contain a checklist of the respective team's players on the back. Subsets in the set include Record Breakers (1–7), Turn Back the Clock (311–315), and All-Star selections (595–616). The Team Leader cards typically show players conferring on the mound inside a white cloud. The wax pack wrapper gives details of "Spring Fever Baseball" where a lucky collector can win a trip for four to spring training. Four different sets of two smaller (2 1/8 " by 3 ") cards were printed on the side of the wax pack box; these eight cards are lettered A through H and listed at the end of the checklist below.

			Mint	*VG-E*	*F-G*
		Complete Set	22.00	9.00	2.20
		Common Player	.03	.01	.00
☐	**1**	RB: Roger Clemens..............	.35	.14	.03
		Most strikeouts, 9 inning game			

			Mint	*VG-E*	*F-G*
☐	2	RB: Jim Deshaies .... Most cons. K's, start of game	.10	.04	.01
☐	3	RB: Dwight Evans .... Earliest home run, season	.08	.03	.01
☐	4	RB: Davey Lopes................. Most steals, season 40-year-old	.06	.02	.00
☐	5	RB:Dave Righetti................. Most saves, season	.10	.04	.01
☐	6	RB: Ruben Sierra .... Youngest player to switch-hit homers in game	.15	.06	.01
☐	7	RB: Todd Worrell .... Most saves, season, rookie	.15	.06	.01
☐	8	Terry Pendleton...................	.05	.02	.00
☐	9	Jay Tibbs	.03	.01	.00
☐	10	Cecil Cooper.......................	.09	.04	.01
☐	11	Indians Team .... (mound conference)	.03	.01	.00
☐	12	Jeff Sellers...........................	.12	.05	.01
☐	13	Nick Esasky	.03	.01	.00
☐	14	Dave Stewart	.03	.01	.00
☐	15	Claudell Washington	.05	.02	.00
☐	16	Pat Clements.......................	.05	.02	.00
☐	17	Pete O'Brien	.08	.03	.01
☐	18	Dick Howser MGR .... (checklist back)	.06	.01	.00
☐	19	Matt Young..........................	.03	.01	.00
☐	20	Gary Carter..........................	.25	.10	.02
☐	21	Mark Davis	.03	.01	.00
☐	22	Doug DeCinces	.07	.03	.01
☐	23	Lee Smith	.07	.03	.01
☐	24	Tony Walker........................	.12	.05	.01
☐	25	Bert Blyleven	.09	.04	.01
☐	26	Greg Brock	.05	.02	.00
☐	27	Joe Cowley..........................	.05	.02	.00
☐	28	Rick Dempsey......................	.05	.02	.00
☐	29	Jimmy Key...........................	.07	.03	.01
☐	30	Tim Raines	.25	.10	.02

			Mint	*VG-E*	*F-G*
☐	**31**	Braves Team........................ (Hubbard/Ramirez)	.03	.01	.00
☐	**32**	Tim Leary............................	.03	.01	.00
☐	**33**	Andy Van Slyke....................	.05	.02	.00
☐	**34**	Jose Rijo.............................	.05	.02	.00
☐	**35**	Sid Bream...........................	.05	.02	.00
☐	**36**	Eric King	.25	.10	.02
☐	**37**	Marvell Wynne	.03	.01	.00
☐	**38**	Dennis Leonard....................	.05	.02	.00
☐	**39**	Marty Barrett	.10	.04	.01
☐	**40**	Dave Righetti.......................	.12	.05	.01
☐	**41**	Bo Diaz..............................	.05	.02	.00
☐	**42**	Gary Redus..........................	.05	.02	.00
☐	**43**	Gene Michael MGR.............. (checklist back)	.06	.01	.00
☐	**44**	Greg Harris..........................	.05	.02	.00
☐	**45**	Jim Presley	.20	.08	.02
☐	**46**	Dan Gladden........................	.05	.02	.00
☐	**47**	Dennis Powell......................	.08	.03	.01
☐	**48**	Wally Backman	.07	.03	.01
☐	**49**	Terry Harper	.03	.01	.00
☐	**50**	Dave Smith..........................	.06	.02	.00
☐	**51**	Mel Hall	.07	.03	.01
☐	**52**	Keith Atherton.....................	.03	.01	.00
☐	**53**	Ruppert Jones	.03	.01	.00
☐	**54**	Bill Dawley..........................	.03	.01	.00
☐	**55**	Tim Wallach	.07	.03	.01
☐	**56**	Brewers Team...................... (mound conference)	.03	.01	.00
☐	**57**	Scott Nielsen.......................	.15	.06	.01
☐	**58**	Thad Bosley.........................	.03	.01	.00
☐	**59**	Ken Dayley..........................	.03	.01	.00
☐	**60**	Tony Pena...........................	.10	.04	.01
☐	**61**	Bobby Thigpen	.20	.08	.02
☐	**62**	Bobby Meacham...................	.03	.01	.00
☐	**63**	Fred Toliver	.05	.02	.00
☐	**64**	Harry Spilman......................	.03	.01	.00
☐	**65**	Tom Browning......................	.08	.03	.01
☐	**66**	Marc Sullivan	.03	.01	.00
☐	**67**	Bill Swift	.03	.01	.00

			Mint	VG-E	F-G
☐	68	Tony LaRussa MGR .... (checklist back)	.06	.01	.00
☐	69	Lonnie Smith	.05	.02	.00
☐	70	Charlie Hough.....................	.05	.02	.00
☐	71	Mike Aldrete	.12	.05	.01
☐	72	Walt Terrell........................	.03	.01	.00
☐	73	Dave Anderson	.03	.01	.00
☐	74	Dan Pasqua.........................	.15	.06	.01
☐	75	Ron Darling	.20	.08	.02
☐	76	Rafael Ramirez	.03	.01	.00
☐	77	Bryan Oelkers	.03	.01	.00
☐	78	Tom Foley...........................	.03	.01	.00
☐	79	Juan Nieves........................	.06	.02	.00
☐	80	Wally Joyner.......................	2.00	.80	.20
☐	81	Padres Team .... (Hawkins/Kennedy)	.03	.01	.00
☐	82	Rob Murphy........................	.15	.06	.01
☐	83	Mike Davis..........................	.05	.02	.00
☐	84	Steve Lake	.03	.01	.00
☐	85	Kevin Bass..........................	.07	.03	.01
☐	86	Nate Snell...........................	.03	.01	.00
☐	87	Mark Salas	.03	.01	.00
☐	88	Ed Wojna	.03	.01	.00
☐	89	Ozzie Guillen	.10	.04	.01
☐	90	Dave Stieb	.10	.04	.01
☐	91	Harold Reynolds	.03	.01	.00
☐	92	Urbano Lugo........................	.03	.01	.00
☐	93	Jim Leyland MGR .... (checklist back)	.06	.01	.00
☐	94	Calvin Schiraldi....................	.09	.04	.01
☐	95	Oddibe McDowell	.20	.08	.02
☐	96	Frank Williams.....................	.03	.01	.00
☐	97	Glenn Wilson.......................	.08	.03	.01
☐	98	Bill Scherrer	.03	.01	.00
☐	99	Darryl Motley	.03	.01	.00
☐	100	Steve Garvey	.30	.12	.03
☐	101	Carl Willis	.10	.04	.01
☐	102	Paul Zuvella........................	.03	.01	.00
☐	103	Rick Aguilera	.05	.02	.00
☐	104	Billy Sample........................	.03	.01	.00
☐	105	Floyd Youmans....................	.10	.04	.01

		Mint	VG-E	F-G
☐ 106	Blue Jays Team .... (Bell/Barfield)	.10	.04	.01
☐ 107	John Butcher	.03	.01	.00
☐ 108	Jim Gantner .... (Brewers logo reversed)	.03	.01	.00
☐ 109	R.J. Reynolds	.05	.02	.00
☐ 110	John Tudor	.09	.04	.01
☐ 111	Alfredo Griffin	.05	.02	.00
☐ 112	Alan Ashby	.03	.01	.00
☐ 113	Neil Allen	.05	.02	.00
☐ 114	Billy Beane	.05	.02	.00
☐ 115	Donnie Moore......................	.05	.02	.00
☐ 116	Bill Russell.........................	.05	.02	.00
☐ 117	Jim Beattie.........................	.03	.01	.00
☐ 118	Bobby Valentine MGR .... (checklist back)	.06	.01	.00
☐ 119	Ron Robinson	.05	.02	.00
☐ 120	Eddie Murray	.30	.12	.03
☐ 121	Kevin Romine	.12	.05	.01
☐ 122	Jim Clancy.........................	.03	.01	.00
☐ 123	John Kruk..........................	.25	.10	.02
☐ 124	Ray Fontenot	.03	.01	.00
☐ 125	Bob Brenly	.05	.02	.00
☐ 126	Mike Loynd	.25	.10	.02
☐ 127	Vance Law..........................	.03	.01	.00
☐ 128	Checklist 1–132	.06	.01	.00
☐ 129	Rick Cerone........................	.03	.01	.00
☐ 130	Dwight Gooden	1.00	.40	.10
☐ 131	Pirates Team....................... (Bream/Pena)	.05	.02	.00
☐ 132	Paul Assenmacher................	.10	.04	.01
☐ 133	Jose Oquendo	.03	.01	.00
☐ 134	Rich Yett...........................	.05	.02	.00
☐ 135	Mike Easler	.06	.02	.00
☐ 136	Ron Romanick	.05	.02	.00
☐ 137	Jerry Willard.......................	.03	.01	.00
☐ 138	Roy Lee Jackson..................	.03	.01	.00
☐ 139	Devon White	.30	.12	.03
☐ 140	Bret Sabenhagen.................	.15	.06	.01
☐ 141	Herm Winningham	.03	.01	.00
☐ 142	Rick Sutcliffe	.10	.04	.01

			Mint	VG-E	F-G
☐	143	Steve Boros MGR (checklist back)	.06	.01	.00
☐	144	Mike Scioscia	.05	.02	.00
☐	145	Charlie Kerfeld	.10	.04	.01
☐	146	Tracy Jones	.25	.10	.02
☐	147	Randy Niemann	.03	.01	.00
☐	148	Dave Collins	.05	.02	.00
☐	149	Ray Searage	.03	.01	.00
☐	150	Wade Boggs	1.00	.40	.10
☐	151	Mike LaCoss	.03	.01	.00
☐	152	Toby Harrah	.03	.01	.00
☐	153	Duane Ward	.12	.05	.01
☐	154	Tom O'Malley	.03	.01	.00
☐	155	Eddie Whitson	.05	.02	.00
☐	156	Mariners Team (mound conference)	.03	.01	.00
☐	157	Danny Darwin	.03	.01	.00
☐	158	Tim Teufel	.05	.02	.00
☐	159	Ed Otwine	.12	.05	.01
☐	160	Julio Franco	.09	.04	.01
☐	161	Steve Ontiveros	.03	.01	.00
☐	162	Mike Lavalliere	.09	.04	.01
☐	163	Kevin Gross	.03	.01	.00
☐	164	Sammy Khalifa	.03	.01	.00
☐	165	Jeff Reardon	.06	.02	.00
☐	166	Bob Boone	.05	.02	.00
☐	167	Jim Deshaies	.25	.10	.02
☐	168	Lou Piniella MGR (checklist back)	.07	.01	.00
☐	169	Ron Washington	.03	.01	.00
☐	170	Bo Jackson	1.00	.40	.10
☐	171	Chuck Cary	.15	.06	.01
☐	172	Ron Oester	.03	.01	.00
☐	173	Alex Trevino	.03	.01	.00
☐	174	Henry Cotto	.03	.01	.00
☐	175	Bob Stanley	.05	.02	.00
☐	176	Steve Buechele	.03	.01	.00
☐	177	Keith Moreland	.05	.02	.00
☐	178	Cecil Fielder	.07	.03	.01
☐	179	Bill Wegman	.07	.03	.01
☐	180	Chris Brown	.15	.06	.01

		Mint	VG-E	F-G
☐ **181**	Cardinals Team .... (mound conference)	.03	.01	.00
☐ **182**	Lee Lacy	.03	.01	.00
☐ **183**	Andy Hawkins	.03	.01	.00
☐ **184**	Bobby Bonilla	.15	.06	.01
☐ **185**	Roger McDowell	.10	.04	.01
☐ **186**	Bruce Benedict....................	.03	.01	.00
☐ **187**	Mark Huismann...................	.03	.01	.00
☐ **188**	Tony Phillips	.03	.01	.00
☐ **189**	Joe Hesketh	.05	.02	.00
☐ **190**	Jim Sundberg	.05	.02	.00
☐ **191**	Charles Hudson...................	.05	.02	.00
☐ **192**	Cory Snyder	.60	.24	.06
☐ **193**	Roger Craig MGR .... (checklist back)	.06	.01	.00
☐ **194**	Kirk McCaskill	.10	.04	.01
☐ **195**	Mike Pagliarulo	.15	.06	.01
☐ **196**	Randy O'Neal	.03	.01	.00
☐ **197**	Mark Bailey	.03	.01	.00
☐ **198**	Lee Mazzilli........................	.03	.01	.00
☐ **199**	Mariano Duncan..................	.08	.03	.01
☐ **200**	Pete Rose	.60	.24	.06
☐ **201**	John Cangelosi....................	.25	.10	.02
☐ **202**	Ricky Wright	.03	.01	.00
☐ **203**	Mike Kingery	.20	.08	.02
☐ **204**	Sanny Stewart.....................	.03	.01	.00
☐ **205**	Graig Nettles......................	.10	.04	.01
☐ **206**	Twins Team........................ (mound conference)	.03	.01	.00
☐ **207**	George Frazier	.03	.01	.00
☐ **208**	John Shelby	.03	.01	.00
☐ **209**	Rick Schu	.03	.01	.00
☐ **210**	Lloyd Moseby	.10	.04	.01
☐ **211**	John Morris	.08	.01	.00
☐ **212**	Mike Fitzgerald	.03	.01	.00
☐ **213**	Randy Myers.......................	.45	.18	.04
☐ **214**	Omar Moreno	.03	.01	.00
☐ **215**	Mark Langston	.06	.02	.00
☐ **216**	B.J. Surhoff........................	.50	.20	.05
☐ **217**	Chris Codiroli.....................	.03	.01	.00

			Mint	*VG-E*	*F-G*
☐	**218**	Sparky Anderson MGR......... (checklist back)	.06	.01	.00
☐	**219**	Cecilio Guante	.03	.01	.00
☐	**220**	Joe Carter	.20	.08	.02
☐	**221**	Vern Ruhle	.03	.01	.00
☐	**222**	Denny Walling.....................	.03	.01	.00
☐	**223**	Charlie Leibrandt	.05	.02	.00
☐	**224**	Wayne Tolleson..................	.03	.01	.00
☐	**225**	Mike Smithson	.03	.01	.00
☐	**226**	Max Venable	.03	.01	.00
☐	**227**	Jamie Moyer	.15	.06	.01
☐	**228**	Curt Wilkerson	.03	.01	.00
☐	**229**	Mike Birkbeck.....................	.12	.05	.01
☐	**230**	Don Baylor..........................	.10	.04	.01
☐	**231**	Giants Team .... (mound conference)	.03	.01	.00
☐	**232**	Reggie Williams	.15	.06	.01
☐	**233**	Russ Morman	.20	.08	.02
☐	**234**	Pat Sheridan	.03	.01	.00
☐	**235**	Alvin Davis.........................	.12	.05	.01
☐	**236**	Tommy John........................	.10	.04	.01
☐	**237**	Jim Morrison.......................	.03	.01	.00
☐	**238**	Bill Krueger	.03	.01	.00
☐	**239**	Juan Espino.........................	.03	.01	.00
☐	**240**	Steve Balboni......................	.05	.02	.00
☐	**241**	Danny Heep.........................	.03	.01	.00
☐	**242**	Rick Mahler	.03	.01	.00
☐	**242**	Whitey Herzog MGR............ (checklist back)	.06	.01	.00
☐	**244**	Dickie Noles	.03	.01	.00
☐	**245**	Willie Upshaw	.07	.03	.01
☐	**246**	Jim Dwyer...........................	.03	.01	.00
☐	**247**	Jeff Reed.............................	.03	.01	.00
☐	**248**	Gene Walter	.05	.02	.00
☐	**249**	Jim Pankovits......................	.03	.01	.00
☐	**250**	Teddy Higuera	.15	.06	.01
☐	**251**	Rob Wilfong	.03	.01	.00
☐	**252**	Denny Martinez	.03	.01	.00
☐	**253**	Eddie Milner	.05	.02	.00
☐	**254**	Bob Tweksbury...................	.20	.08	.02
☐	**255**	Juan Samuel	.10	.04	.01

		Mint	VG-E	F-G
☐ 256	Royals Team .... (Brett/F. White)	.10	.04	.01
☐ 257	Bob Forsch	.05	.02	.00
☐ 258	Steve Yeager.......................	.05	.02	.00
☐ 259	Mike Greenwell...................	.15	.06	.01
☐ 260	Vida Blue	.07	.03	.01
☐ 261	Ruben Sierra	1.00	.40	.10
☐ 262	Jim Winn...........................	.03	.01	.00
☐ 263	Stan Javler	.07	.03	.01
☐ 264	Checklist 133–264...............	.06	.01	.00
☐ 265	Darrell Evans	.07	.03	.01
☐ 266	Jeff Hamilton	.15	.06	.01
☐ 267	Howard Johnson	.03	.01	.00
☐ 268	Pat Corrales MGR................ (checklist back)	.06	.01	.00
☐ 269	Cliff Speck.........................	.08	.03	.01
☐ 270	Jody Davis.........................	.07	.03	.01
☐ 271	Mike Brown....................... (Mariners P)	.03	.01	.00
☐ 272	Andres Galarraga.................	.08	.03	.01
☐ 273	Gene Nelson	.03	.01	.00
☐ 274	Jeff Hearron.......................	.10	.04	.01
☐ 275	LaMarr Hoyt	.06	.02	.00
☐ 276	Jackie Gutierrez.................,	.03	.01	.00
☐ 277	Juan Agosto	.03	.01	.00
☐ 278	Gary Pettis.........................	.07	.03	.01
☐ 279	Dan Plesac.........................	.20	.08	.02
☐ 280	Jeff Leonard.......................	.06	.02	.00
☐ 281	Reds Team......:.................. (Rose conference)	.10	.04	.01
☐ 282	Jeff Calhoun.......................	.09	.04	.01
☐ 283	Doug Drabek	.15	.06	.01
☐ 284	John Moses	.15	.06	.01
☐ 285	Dennis Boyd.......................	.08	.03	.01
☐ 286	Mike Woodard	.05	.02	.00
☐ 287	Dave Von Ohlen	.03	.01	.00
☐ 288	Tito Landrum......................	.03	.01	.00
☐ 289	Bob Kipper........................	.03	.01	.00
☐ 290	Leon Durham......................	.07	.03	.01
☐ 291	Mitch Williams....................	.20	.08	.02
☐ 292	Franklin Stubbs	.10	.04	.01

		Mint	VG-E	F-G
☐ 293	Bob Rodgers MGR (checklist back)	.06	.01	.00
☐ 294	Steve Jeltz	.03	.01	.00
☐ 295	Len Dykstra	.20	.08	.02
☐ 296	Andres Thomas	.25	.10	.02
☐ 297	Don Schulze	.03	.01	.00
☐ 298	Larry Hemdon	.03	.01	.00
☐ 299	Joel Davis	.10	.04	.01
☐ 300	Reggie Jackson	.30	.12	.03
☐ 301	Luis Aquino	.09	.04	.01
☐ 302	Bill Schroeder	.03	.01	.00
☐ 303	Juan Berenguer	.03	.01	.00
☐ 304	Phil Gamer	.05	.02	.00
☐ 305	John Franco	.08	.03	.01
☐ 306	Red Sox Team (mound conference)	.05	.02	.00
☐ 307	Lee Guetterman	.12	.05	.01
☐ 308	Don Slaught	.03	.01	.00
☐ 309	Mike Young	.07	.03	.01
☐ 310	Frank Viola	.05	.02	.00
☐ 311	Turn Back 1982 Rickey Henderson	.12	.05	.01
☐ 312	Turn Back 1977 Reggie Jackson	.12	.05	.01
☐ 313	Turn Back 1972 Roberto Clemente	.12	.05	.01
☐ 314	Turn Back 1967 Carl Yastrzemski	.12	.05	.01
☐ 315	Turn Back 1962 Maury Wills	.06	.02	.00
☐ 316	Brian Fisher	.05	.02	.00
☐ 317	Clint Hurdle	.03	.01	.00
☐ 318	Jim Fregosi MGR (checklist back)	.06	.01	.00
☐ 319	Greg Swindell	.45	.18	.04
☐ 320	Barry Bonds	.35	.14	.03
☐ 321	Mike Laga	.03	.01	.00
☐ 322	Chris Bando	.03	.01	.00
☐ 323	Al Newman	.10	.04	.01
☐ 324	Dave Palmer	.05	.02	.00
☐ 325	Garry Templeton	.07	.03	.01

		Mint	VG-E	F-G
☐ 326	Mark Gubicza	.06	.02	.00
☐ 327	Dale Sveum	.15	.06	.01
☐ 328	Bob Welch	.06	.02	.00
☐ 329	Ron Roenicke	.03	.01	.00
☐ 330	Mike Scott	.15	.06	.01
☐ 331	Mets Team (Carter/Strawberry)	.12	.05	.01
☐ 332	Joe Price	.03	.01	.00
☐ 333	Ken Phelps	.03	.01	.00
☐ 334	Ed Correa	.35	.14	.03
☐ 335	Candy Maldoriado	.08	.03	.01
☐ 336	Allan Anderson	.15	.06	.01
☐ 337	Darrell Miller	.03	.01	.00
☐ 338	Tim Conroy	.03	.01	.00
☐ 339	Donnie Hill	.03	.01	.00
☐ 340	Roger Clemens	1.00	.40	.10
☐ 341	Mike Brown (Pirates OF)	.03	.01	.00
☐ 342	Bob James	.03	.01	.00
☐ 343	Hal Lanier MGR (checklist back)	.06	.01	.00
☐ 344	Joe Niekro	.07	.03	.01
☐ 345	Andre Dawson	.16	.07	.01
☐ 346	Shawon Dunston	.10	.04	.01
☐ 347	Mickey Brantley	.10	.04	.01
☐ 348	Carmelo Martinez	.05	.02	.00
☐ 349	Storm Davis	.07	.03	.01
☐ 350	Keith Hernandez	.20	.08	.02
☐ 351	Gene Garber	.03	.01	.00
☐ 352	Mike Felder	.10	.04	.01
☐ 353	Ernie Camacho	.03	.01	.00
☐ 354	Jamie Quirk	.03	.01	.00
☐ 355	Don Carman	.05	.02	.00
☐ 356	White Sox Team (mound conference)	.03	.01	.00
☐ 357	Steve Fireovid	.10	.04	.01
☐ 358	Sal Butera	.03	.01	.00
☐ 359	Doug Corbett	.03	.01	.00
☐ 360	Pedro Guerrero	.20	.08	.02
☐ 361	Mark Thurmond	.03	.01	.00
☐ 362	Luis Quinones	.10	.04	.01

	Mint	VG-E	F-G
☐ 363 Jose Guzman	.10	.04	.01
☐ 364 Randy Bush	.03	.01	.00
☐ 365 Rick Rhoden	.05	.02	.00
☐ 366 Mark McGwire	.10	.04	.01
☐ 367 Jeff Lahti	.03	.01	.00
☐ 368 John McNamara MGR (checklist back)	.06	.01	.00
☐ 369 Brian Dayett	.03	.01	.00
☐ 370 Fred Lynn	.15	.06	.01
☐ 371 Mark Eichhorn	.35	.14	.03
☐ 372 Jerry Mumphrey	.05	.02	.00
☐ 373 Jeff Dedmon	.03	.01	.00
☐ 374 Glenn Hoffman	.03	.01	.00
☐ 375 Ron Guidry	.15	.06	.01
☐ 376 Scott Bradley	.05	.02	.00
☐ 377 John Henry Johnson	.03	.01	.00
☐ 378 Rafael Santana	.03	.01	.00
☐ 379 John Russell	.03	.01	.00
☐ 380 Rich Gossage	.12	.05	.01
☐ 381 Expos Team (mound conference)	.03	.01	.00
☐ 382 Rudy Law	.03	.01	.00
☐ 383 Ron Davis	.03	.01	.00
☐ 384 Johnny Grubb	.03	.01	.00
☐ 385 Orel Hershiser	.15	.06	.01
☐ 386 Dickie Thon	.05	.02	.00
☐ 387 T.R. Bryden	.12	.05	.01
☐ 388 Geno Petralli	.03	.01	.00
☐ 389 Jeff Robinson	.03	.01	.00
☐ 390 Gary Matthews	.05	.02	.00
☐ 391 Jay Howell	.05	.02	.00
☐ 392 Checklist 265–396	.06	.01	.00
☐ 393 Pete Rose MGR (checklist back)	.35	.10	.02
☐ 394 Mike Bielecki	.06	.02	.00
☐ 395 Damaso Garcia	.07	.03	.01
☐ 396 Tim Lollar	.03	.01	.00
☐ 397 Greg Walker	.10	.04	.01
☐ 398 Brad Havens	.03	.01	.00
☐ 399 Curt Ford	.20	.08	.02
☐ 400 George Brett	.30	.12	.03

		Mint	*VG-E*	*F-G*
☐ 401	Billy Jo Robidoux	.10	.04	.01
☐ 402	Mike Trujillo	.03	.01	.00
☐ 403	Jerry Royster	.03	.01	.00
☐ 404	Doug Sisk	.03	.01	.00
☐ 405	Brook Jacoby	.09	.04	.01
☐ 406	Yankees Team	.25	.10	.02
	(Henderson/Mattingly)			
☐ 407	Jim Acker	.03	.01	.00
☐ 408	John Mizerock	.03	.01	.00
☐ 409	Milt Thompson	.03	.01	.00
☐ 410	Fernando Valenzuela	.25	.10	.02
☐ 411	Darnell Coles	.09	.04	.01
☐ 412	Eric Davis	.50	.20	.05
☐ 413	Moose Haas	.05	.02	.00
☐ 414	Joe Orsulak	.05	.02	.00
☐ 415	Bobby Witt	.40	.16	.04
☐ 416	Tom Nieto	.03	.01	.00
☐ 417	Pat Perry	.07	.03	.01
☐ 418	Dick Williams MGR	.06	.01	.00
	(checklist back)			
☐ 419	Mark Portugal	.10	.04	.01
☐ 420	Will Clark	.60	.24	.06
☐ 421	Jose DeLeon	.05	.02	.00
☐ 422	Jack Howell	.05	.02	.00
☐ 423	Jaime Cocanower	.03	.01	.00
☐ 424	Chris Speier	.03	.01	.00
☐ 425	Tom Seaver	.25	.10	.02
☐ 426	Floyd Rayford	.03	.01	.00
☐ 427	Ed Nunez	.03	.01	.00
☐ 428	Bruce Bochy	.03	.01	.00
☐ 429	Tim Pyznarski	.15	.06	.01
☐ 430	Mike Schmidt	.30	.12	.03
☐ 431	Dodgers Team	.05	.02	.00
	(mound conference)			
☐ 432	Jim Slaton	.03	.01	.00
☐ 433	Ed Hearn	.10	.04	.01
☐ 434	Mike Fischlin	.03	.01	.00
☐ 435	Bruce Sutter	.12	.05	.01
☐ 436	Andy Allanson	.15	.06	.01
☐ 437	Ted Power	.06	.02	.00
☐ 438	Kelly Downs	.12	.05	.01

	Mint	VG-E	F-G
☐ **439** Karl Best	.03	.01	.00
☐ **440** Willie McGee	.15	.06	.01
☐ **441** Dave Leiper	.10	.04	.01
☐ **442** Mitch Webster	.09	.04	.01
☐ **443** John Felske MGR (checklist back)	.06	.01	.00
☐ **444** Jeff Russell	.03	.01	.00
☐ **445** Dave Lopes	.06	.02	.00
☐ **446** Chuck Finley	.12	.05	.01
☐ **447** Bill Almon	.03	.01	.00
☐ **448** Chris Bosio	.10	.04	.01
☐ **449** Pat Dodson	.20	.06	.02
☐ **450** Kirby Puckett	.30	.12	.03
☐ **451** Joe Sambito	.05	.02	.00
☐ **452** Dave Henderson	.05	.02	.00
☐ **453** Scott Terry	.10	.04	.01
☐ **454** Luis Salazar	.03	.01	.00
☐ **455** Mike Boddicker	.07	.03	.01
☐ **456** A's Team (mound conference)	.03	.01	.00
☐ **457** Len Matuszek	.03	.01	.00
☐ **458** Kelly Gruber	.03	.01	.00
☐ **459** Dennis Eckersley	.05	.02	.00
☐ **460** Darryl Strawberry	.30	.12	.03
☐ **461** Craig McMurtry	.03	.01	.00
☐ **462** Scott Fletcher	.05	.02	.00
☐ **463** Tom Candiotti	.05	.02	.00
☐ **464** Butch Wynegar	.05	.02	.00
☐ **465** Todd Worrell	.35	.14	.03
☐ **466** Kal Daniels	.15	.06	.01
☐ **467** Randy St. Claire	.03	.01	.00
☐ **468** George Bamberger MGR (checklist back)	.06	.01	.00
☐ **469** Mike Diaz	.20	.08	.02
☐ **470** Dave Dravecky	.06	.02	.00
☐ **471** Ronn Reynolds	.03	.01	.00
☐ **472** Bill Doran	.09	.04	.01
☐ **473** Steve Farr	.03	.01	.00
☐ **474** Jerry Narron	.03	.01	.00
☐ **475** Scott Garrelts	.05	.02	.00
☐ **476** Danny Tartabull	.25	.10	.02

		Mint	*VG-E*	*F-G*
☐ **477**	Ken Howell	.05	.02	.00
☐ **478**	Tim Laudner	.03	.01	.00
☐ **479**	Bob Sebra	.10	.04	.01
☐ **480**	Jim Rice	.25	.10	.02
☐ **481**	Phillies Team	.05	.02	.00
	(cage conference)			
☐ **482**	Daryl Boston	.05	.02	.00
☐ **483**	Dwight Lowry	.15	.06	.01
☐ **484**	Jim Traber	.09	.04	.01
☐ **485**	Tony Fernandez	.09	.04	.01
☐ **486**	Otis Nixon	.15	.06	.01
☐ **487**	Dave Gumpert	.03	.01	.00
☐ **488**	Ray Knight	.07	.03	.01
☐ **489**	Bill Gullickson	.05	.02	.00
☐ **490**	Dale Murphy	.35	.14	.03
☐ **491**	Ron Karkovice	.25	.10	.02
☐ **492**	Mike Heath	.03	.01	.00
☐ **493**	Tom Lasorda MGR	.07	.01	.00
	(checklist back)			
☐ **494**	Barry Jones	.10	.04	.01
☐ **495**	Gorman Thomas	.08	.03	.01
☐ **496**	Bruce Bochte	.05	.02	.00
☐ **497**	Dale Mohorcic	.15	.06	.01
☐ **498**	Bob Kearney	.03	.01	.00
☐ **499**	Bruce Ruffin	.30	.12	.03
☐ **500**	Don Mattingly	2.00	.80	.20
☐ **501**	Craig Lefferts	.03	.01	.00
☐ **502**	Dick Schofield	.05	.02	.00
☐ **503**	Larry Andersen	.03	.01	.00
☐ **504**	Mickey Hatcher	.03	.01	.00
☐ **505**	Bryn Smith	.03	.01	.00
☐ **506**	Orioles Team	.05	.02	.00
	(mound conference)			
☐ **507**	Dave Stapleton	.03	.01	.00
☐ **508**	Scott Bankhead	.05	.02	.00
☐ **509**	Enos Cabell	.03	.01	.00
☐ **510**	Tom Henke	.06	.02	.00
☐ **511**	Steve Lyons	.03	.01	.00
☐ **512**	Dave Magadan	.60	.24	.06
☐ **513**	Carmen Castillo	.03	.01	.00
☐ **514**	Orlando Mercado	.03	.01	.00

		Mint	VG-E	F-G
☐	515 Willie Hernandez	.09	.04	.01
☐	516 Ted Simmons	.09	.04	.01
☐	517 Mario Soto	.07	.03	.01
☐	518 Gene Mauch MGR (checklist back)	.06	.01	.00
☐	519 Curt Young	.03	.01	.00
☐	520 Jack Clark	.10	.04	.01
☐	521 Rick Reuschel	.05	.02	.00
☐	522 Checklist 397–528	.06	.01	.00
☐	523 Earnie Riles	.07	.03	.01
☐	524 Bob Shirley	.03	.01	.00
☐	525 Phil Bradley	.18	.08	.01
☐	526 Roger Mason	.07	.03	.01
☐	527 Jim Wohlford	.03	.01	.00
☐	528 Ken Dixon	.05	.02	.00
☐	529 Alvaro Espinoza	.09	.04	.01
☐	530 Tony Gwynn	.30	.12	.03
☐	531 Astros Team (Y.Berra conference)	.07	.03	.01
☐	532 Jeff Stone	.05	.02	.00
☐	533 Argenis Salazar	.03	.01	.00
☐	534 Scott Sanderson	.03	.01	.00
☐	535 Tony Armas	.09	.04	.01
☐	536 Terry Mulholland	.10	.04	.01
☐	537 Rance Mulliniks	.03	.01	.00
☐	538 Tom Niedenfuer	.06	.02	.00
☐	539 Reid Nichols	.03	.01	.00
☐	540 Terry Kennedy	.06	.02	.00
☐	541 Rafael Belliard	.10	.04	.01
☐	542 Ricky Horton	.03	.01	.00
☐	543 Dave Johnson MGR (checklist back)	.08	.01	.00
☐	544 Zane Smith	.03	.01	.00
☐	545 Buddy Bell	.09	.04	.01
☐	546 Mike Morgan	.03	.01	.00
☐	547 Rob Deer	.15	.06	.01
☐	548 Bill Mooneyham	.10	.04	.01
☐	549 Bob Melvin	.03	.01	.00
☐	550 Pete Incaviglia	1.00	.40	.10
☐	551 Frank Wills	.03	.01	.00
☐	552 Larry Sheets	.05	.02	.00

		Mint	*VG-E*	*F-G*
☐ 553	Mike Maddux	.10	.04	.01
☐ 554	Buddy Biancalana	.03	.01	.00
☐ 555	Dennis Rasmussen	.06	.02	.00
☐ 556	Angels Team (mound conference)	.05	.02	.00
☐ 557	John Cerutti	.20	.08	.02
☐ 558	Greg Gagne	.05	.02	.00
☐ 559	Lance McCullers	.05	.02	.00
☐ 560	Glenn Davis	.30	.12	.03
☐ 561	Rey Quinones	.10	.04	.01
☐ 562	Bryan Clutterbuck	.10	.04	.01
☐ 563	John Stefero	.03	.01	.00
☐ 564	Larry McWilliams	.03	.01	.00
☐ 565	Dusty Baker	.06	.02	.00
☐ 566	Tim Hulett	.05	.02	.00
☐ 567	Greg Mathews	.25	.10	.02
☐ 568	Earl Weaver MGR (checklist back)	.08	.01	.00
☐ 569	Wade Rowdon	.10	.04	.01
☐ 570	Sid Fernandez	.20	.08	.02
☐ 571	Ozzie Virgil	.05	.02	.00
☐ 572	Pete Ladd	.03	.01	.00
☐ 573	Hal McRae	.05	.02	.00
☐ 574	Manny Lee	.05	.02	.00
☐ 575	Pat Tabler	.07	.03	.01
☐ 576	Frank Pastore	.03	.01	.00
☐ 577	Dann Bilardello	.03	.01	.00
☐ 578	Billy Hatcher	.05	.02	.00
☐ 579	Rick Burleson	.06	.02	.00
☐ 580	Mike Krukow	.07	.03	.01
☐ 581	Cubs Team (Cey/Trout)	.05	.02	.00
☐ 582	Bruce Berenyi	.03	.01	.00
☐ 583	Junior Ortiz	.03	.01	.00
☐ 584	Ron Kittle	.09	.04	.01
☐ 585	Scott Bailes	.10	.04	.01
☐ 586	Ben Oglivie	.06	.02	.00
☐ 587	Eric Plunk	.08	.03	.01
☐ 588	Wallace Johnson	.03	.01	.00
☐ 589	Steve Crawford	.03	.01	.00
☐ 590	Vince Coleman	.35	.14	.03

		Mint	*VG-E*	*F-G*
☐ **591**	Spike Owen	.05	.02	.00
☐ **592**	Chris Welsh	.03	.01	.00
☐ **593**	Chuck Tanner MGR (checklist back)	.06	.01	.00
☐ **594**	Rick Anderson	.03	.01	.00
☐ **595**	Keith Hernandez AS	.10	.04	.01
☐ **596**	Steve Sax AS	.07	.03	.01
☐ **597**	Mike Schmidt AS	.20	.08	.02
☐ **598**	Ozzie Smith AS	.07	.03	.01
☐ **599**	Tony Gwynn AS	.12	.05	.01
☐ **600**	Dave Parker AS	.09	.04	.01
☐ **601**	Darryl Strawberry AS	.15	.06	.01
☐ **602**	Gary Carter AS	.12	.05	.01
☐ **603**	Dwight Gooden AS	.25	.10	.02
☐ **604**	Fern. Valenzuela AS	.12	.05	.01
☐ **605**	Todd Worrell AS	.09	.04	.01
☐ **606**	Don Mattingly AS	.35	.14	.03
☐ **607**	Tony Bernazard AS	.05	.02	.00
☐ **608**	Wade Boggs AS	.25	.10	.02
☐ **609**	Cal Ripken AS	.12	.05	.01
☐ **610**	Jim Rice AS	.12	.05	.01
☐ **611**	Kirby Puckett AS	.12	.05	.01
☐ **612**	George Bell AS	.08	.03	.01
☐ **613**	Lance Parrish AS	.08	.03	.01
☐ **614**	Roger Clemens AS	.25	.10	.02
☐ **615**	Teddy Higuera AS	.07	.03	.01
☐ **616**	Dave Righetti AS	.07	.03	.01
☐ **617**	Al Nipper	.03	.01	.00
☐ **618**	Tom Kelly MGR (checklist back)	.06	.01	.00
☐ **619**	Jerry Reed	.03	.01	.00
☐ **620**	Jose Canseco	2.00	.80	.20
☐ **621**	Danny Cox	.05	.02	.00
☐ **622**	Glenn Braggs	.40	.16	.04
☐ **623**	Kurt Stillwell	.15	.06	.01
☐ **624**	Tim Burke	.05	.02	.00
☐ **625**	Mookie Wilson	.05	.02	.00
☐ **626**	Joel Skinner	.05	.02	.00
☐ **627**	Ken Oberkfell	.03	.01	.00
☐ **628**	Bob Walk	.03	.01	.00
☐ **629**	Larry Parrish	.05	.02	.00

	Mint	VG-E	F-G
☐ **630** John Candelaria....................	.07	.03	.01
☐ **631** Tigers Team......................... (mound conference)	.05	.02	.00
☐ **632** Rob Woodward...................	.10	.04	.01
☐ **633** Jose Uribe...........................	.03	.01	.00
☐ **634** Rafael Palmeiro...................	.30	.12	.03
☐ **635** Ken Schrom........................	.05	.02	.00
☐ **636** Darren Daulton...................	.03	.01	.00
☐ **637** Bip Roberts.........................	.09	.04	.01
☐ **638** Rich Bordi...........................	.03	.01	.00
☐ **639** Gerald Perry.......................	.03	.01	.00
☐ **640** Mark Clear..........................	.03	.01	.00
☐ **641** Domingo Ramos..................	.03	.01	.00
☐ **642** Al Pulido............................	.03	.01	.00
☐ **643** Ron Shepherd......................	.05	.02	.00
☐ **644** John Denny.........................	.06	.02	.00
☐ **645** Dwight Evans......................	.09	.04	.01
☐ **646** Mike Mason........................	.03	.01	.00
☐ **647** Tom Lawless.......................	.03	.01	.00
☐ **648** Barry Larkin.......................	.45	.18	.04
☐ **649** Mickey Tettleton.................	.03	.01	.00
☐ **650** Hubie Brooks......................	.09	.04	.01
☐ **651** Benny Distefano..................	.05	.02	.00
☐ **652** Terry Forster......................	.05	.02	.00
☐ **653** Kevin Michell......................	.35	.14	.03
☐ **654** Checklist 529–660..............	.06	.01	.00
☐ **655** Jesse Barfield......................	.15	.06	.01
☐ **656** Rangers Team..................... (Valentine/R.Wright)	.05	.02	.00
☐ **657** Tom Waddell.......................	.03	.01	.00
☐ **658** Robby Thompson................	.30	.12	.03
☐ **659** Aurelio Lopez......................	.03	.01	.00
☐ **660** Bob Horner.........................	.15	.06	.01
☐ **661** Lou Whitaker......................	.10	.04	.01
☐ **662** Frank DiPino......................	.03	.01	.00
☐ **663** Cliff Johnson......................	.03	.01	.00
☐ **664** Mike Marshall.....................	.10	.04	.01
☐ **665** Rod Scurry.........................	.03	.01	.00
☐ **666** Von Hayes..........................	.12	.05	.01
☐ **667** Ron Hassey........................	.03	.01	.00
☐ **668** Juan Bonilla.......................	.03	.01	.00

		Mint	VG-E	F-G
☐ **669**	Bud Black	.03	.01	.00
☐ **670**	Jose Cruz	.09	.04	.01
☐ **671**	Ray Soff	.09	.04	.01
☐ **672**	Chili Davis	.07	.03	.01
☐ **673**	Don Sutton	.12	.05	.01
☐ **674**	Bill Campbell	.03	.01	.00
☐ **675**	Ed Romero	.03	.01	.00
☐ **676**	Charlie Moore	.03	.01	.00
☐ **677**	Bob Grich	.05	.02	.00
☐ **678**	Camey Lansford	.07	.03	.01
☐ **679**	Kent Hrbek	.15	.06	.01
☐ **680**	Ryne Sandberg	.25	.10	.02
☐ **681**	George Bell	.15	.06	.01
☐ **682**	Jerry Reuss	.05	.02	.00
☐ **683**	Gary Roenicke	.05	.02	.00
☐ **684**	Kent Tekulve	.05	.02	.00
☐ **685**	Jerry Hairston	.03	.01	.00
☐ **686**	Doyle Alexander	.05	.02	.00
☐ **687**	Alan Trammell	.12	.05	.01
☐ **688**	Juan Beniquez	.05	.02	.00
☐ **689**	Darrell Porter	.05	.02	.00
☐ **690**	Dane Iorg	.03	.01	.00
☐ **691**	Dave Parker	.15	.06	.01
☐ **692**	Frank White	.06	.02	.00
☐ **693**	Terry Puhl	.05	.02	.00
☐ **694**	Phil Niekro	.15	.06	.01
☐ **695**	Chico Walker	.15	.06	.01
☐ **696**	Gary Lucas	.03	.01	.00
☐ **697**	Ed Lynch	.03	.01	.00
☐ **698**	Arnie Whitt	.03	.01	.00
☐ **699**	Ken Landreaux	.05	.02	.00
☐ **700**	Dave Bergman	.03	.01	.00
☐ **701**	Willie Randolph	.06	.02	.00
☐ **702**	Greg Gross	.03	.01	.00
☐ **703**	Dave Schmidt	.03	.01	.00
☐ **704**	Jesse Orosco	.05	.02	.00
☐ **705**	Bruce Hurst	.07	.03	.01
☐ **706**	Rick Manning	.03	.01	.00
☐ **707**	Bob McClure	.03	.01	.00
☐ **708**	Scott McGregor	.07	.03	.01
☐ **709**	Dave Kingman	.10	.04	.01

		Mint	*VG-E*	*F-G*
☐ 710	Gary Gaetti	.09	.04	.01
☐ 711	Ken Griffey	.06	.02	.00
☐ 712	Don Robinson	.03	.01	.00
☐ 713	Tom Brookens	.03	.01	.00
☐ 714	Dan Quisenberry	.10	.04	.01
☐ 715	Bob Dernier	.05	.02	00
☐ 716	Rick Leach	.03	.01	.00
☐ 717	Ed VandeBerg	.03	.01	.00
☐ 718	Steve Carlton	.25	.10	.02
☐ 719	Tom Hume	.03	.01	.00
☐ 720	Richard Dotson	.05	.02	.00
☐ 721	Tom Herr	.07	.03	.01
☐ 722	Bob Knepper	.07	.03	.01
☐ 723	Brett Butler	.08	.03	.01
☐ 724	Greg Minton	.05	.02	.00
☐ 725	George Hendrick	.05	.02	.00
☐ 726	Frank Tanana	.05	.02	.00
☐ 727	Mike Moore	.05	.02	.00
☐ 728	Tippy Martinez	.03	.01	.00
☐ 729	Tom Paciorek	.03	.01	.00
☐ 730	Eric Show	.03	.01	.00
☐ 731	Dave Concepcion	.08	.03	.01
☐ 732	Manny Trillo	.05	.02	.00
☐ 733	Bill Caudill	.05	.02	.00
☐ 734	Bill Madlock	.10	.04	.01
☐ 735	Rickey Henderson	.30	.12	.03
☐ 736	Steve Bedrosian	.05	.02	.00
☐ 737	Floyd Bannister	.05	.02	.00
☐ 738	Jorge Orta	.03	.01	.00
☐ 739	Chet Lemon	.05	.02	.00
☐ 740	Rich Gedman	.08	.03	.01
☐ 741	Paul Molitor	.08	.03	.01
☐ 742	Andy McGaffigan	.03	.01	.00
☐ 743	Dwayne Murphy	.05	.02	.00
☐ 744	Roy Smalley	.05	.02	.00
☐ 745	Glenn Hubbard	.03	.01	.00
☐ 746	Bob Ojeda	.08	.03	.01
☐ 747	Johnny Ray	.08	.03	.01
☐ 748	Mike Flanagan	.07	.03	.01
☐ 749	Ozzie Smith	.12	.05	.01
☐ 750	Steve Trout	.05	.02	.00

		Mint	VG-E	F-G
☐ 751	Garth Iorg	.03	.01	.00
☐ 752	Dan Petry	.09	.04	.01
☐ 753	Rick Honeycutt	.05	.02	.00
☐ 754	Dave LaPoint	.03	.01	.00
☐ 755	Luis Aguayo	.03	.01	.00
☐ 756	Carlton Fisk	.12	.05	.01
☐ 757	Nolan Ryan	.30	.12	.03
☐ 758	Tony Bernazard	.05	.02	.00
☐ 759	Joel Youngblood	.03	.01	.00
☐ 760	Mike Witt	.10	.04	.01
☐ 761	Greg Pryor	.03	.01	.00
☐ 762	Gary Ward	.05	.02	.00
☐ 763	Tim Flannery	.03	.01	.00
☐ 764	Bill Buckner	.08	.03	.01
☐ 765	Kirk Gibson	.20	.08	.02
☐ 766	Don Aase	.05	.02	.00
☐ 767	Ron Cey	.07	.03	.01
☐ 768	Dennis Lamp	.03	.01	.00
☐ 769	Steve Sax	.12	.05	.01
☐ 770	Dave Winfield	.25	.10	.02
☐ 771	Shane Rawley	.07	.03	.01
☐ 772	Harold Baines	.15	.06	.01
☐ 773	Robin Yount	.25	.10	.02
☐ 774	Wayne Krenchicki	.03	.01	.00
☐ 775	Joaquin Andujar	.08	.03	.01
☐ 776	Tom Brunansky	.09	.04	.01
☐ 777	Chris Chambliss	.05	.02	.00
☐ 778	Jack Morris	.15	.06	.01
☐ 779	Craig Reynolds	.03	.01	.00
☐ 780	Andre Thornton	.05	.02	.00
☐ 781	Atlee Hammaker	.05	.02	.00
☐ 782	Brian Downing	.05	.02	.00
☐ 783	Willie Wilson	.12	.05	.01
☐ 784	Cal Ripken	.25	.10	.02
☐ 785	Terry Francona	.03	.01	.00
☐ 786	Jimy Williams MGR (checklist back)	.06	.01	.00
☐ 787	Alejandro Pena	.05	.02	.00
☐ 788	Tim Stoddard	.03	.01	.00
☐ 789	Dan Schatzeder	.03	.01	.00
☐ 790	Julio Cruz	.03	.01	.00

		Mint	*VG-E*	*F-G*
☐ **791**	Lance Parrish	.20	.08	.02
☐ **792**	Checklist 661–792	.06	.01	.00
☐ **A**	Don Baylor			
	(wax pack box card)	.15	.06	.01
☐ **B**	Steve Carlton			
	(wax pack box card)	.30	.12	.03
☐ **C**	Ron Cey			
	(wax pack box card)	.10	.04	.01
☐ **D**	Cecil Cooper			
	(wax pack box card)	.10	.04	.01
☐ **E**	Rickey Henderson			
	(wax pack box card)	.50	.20	.05
☐ **F**	Jim Rice			
	(wax pack box card)	.30	.12	.03
☐ **G**	Don Sutton			
	(wax pack box card)	.20	.08	.02

BASKETBALL

	Price Range	
☐ **Drawing,** "Dolph Schayes, Rebound Artist," signed, pencil, 12″ x 18″	100.00	200.00
☐ **Hank Luisetti,** photograph, signed and inscribed, 10″ x 8″— George Mikan; and one with his brother Ed, signed and inscribed*	150.00	250.00

BOWLING AND BILLIARDS

☐ **Trophies,** two, bowling, one with three crossed pins on a wooden base, the other a single pin and ball on wooden base, 7½″ and 6″ high	40.00

*Luisetti, of Stanford University, revolutionized basketball with his one-hand jump shot and his passing.

	Price Range	

☐ **Cup,** double-handled American Bowling League, classic trophy cup form on circular base, inscribed "American Bowling League Cup, Team Championship William Nelson Cromwell Donor," and under "1932 Fall Season," "American Express Co." .. 100.00 150.00

☐ **Drawings,** "Billiards Champs," two, one of Jimmy Caras and Ralph Greenleaf and another of "The Fastest Growing Sport Bowling," signed, pencil and ink, 15″ x 19″ 250.00 350.00

BOXING

☐ **Cartoon,** Bill Gallo, original pen-and-ink carton, boxing and hockey, one half depicts the WBC facing the WBA with a punch-happy boxer in between, the other side shows Smith, No. 31, catching a puck, signed "To the Heart Fund, Bill Gallo," 14½″ x 11½″ 150.00 250.00

☐ **Drawings,** two, "Tonight's Fight, Burman vs. Maurillo," and "Primo Carnera New Champion," signed, pencil with ink heightened with white, 12″ x 15″ 250.00 350.00

☐ **Drawings,** two, "Louis Angel Firpo vs. Dempsey," and "Champions," signed, pencil, 11″ x 8½″ 300.00 400.00

☐ **Photograph,** Jack Dempsey, signed and inscribed, "To Evelyn McLean, Hang on—the worst is over, Sincerely, Jack Dempsey,"

Price Range

9 1/4 ″ x 7 1/4 ″, with a printed note of thanks from Dempsey's family at the time of his death (Evelyn Walsh McLean was the owner of the Hope diamond and used this as collateral to help raise the ransom money needed for the release of the Lindbergh baby) 275.00

☐ **Toys,** two, keywind, tinplate, slugger champion boxing, together with a composition mouse boxer, a porcelain Olympic bear boxer, and a tinplate duck on skis (5) 100.00

FOOTBALL

☐ **Bookends,** pair, plated, Knute Rockne, in the shape of the face of the legendary coach over Notre Dame Stadium with dates of his undefeated seasons 1924, 1930, 1929, 7 3/4 ″ high 90.00

☐ **Charles Dana Gibson,** "The leading features of a liberal education," signed, pen and ink, 10 3/4 ″ x 16 3/4 ″ (Princeton vs. Yale at Football) 400.00

☐ **Drawing,** "Signals, College Football," signed, pencil, 16 1/2 ″ x 19 1/2 ″ 200.00 300.00

☐ **Drawing,** "Fordham Football," signed, pencil, 12 1/2 ″ x 9 3/4 ″ (Crowley, Cavanaugh, Klanowski, and Frisch) 200.00 250.00

☐ **Photographs of football's All-Americans,** including Otto Graham (Cleveland Browns), signed and inscribed; "Jarrin' Jaw" Kimbrough (New York Yankees),

Price Range

signed and inscribed; Harry
Gilmer (Alabama), signed and in-
scribed; Bill Daley (Brooklyn
Dodgers), signed and inscribed;
Felix "Doc" Blanchard and Glenn
Davis, signed by both 200.00   300.00

☐ **Ring,** 1973 Liberty Bowl ring,
10KT gold inset with a football-
shaped red stone marked "NSC,"
top of ring marked in raised letters "A.C.C. Champions Football
1973," one side has raised "N.C.
State" "Wolf Pack 600" and
"pride," which surrounds a raised
football; opposite side has raised
letters "Libery Bowl N.C. 31 Kansas 18 Champs 1973" and "re-
spect" surrounding a raised
Liberty Bell, each side inset with
three small red stones, weight
18.7 dwt 300.00

Football Cards

1986 TOPPS

The 1986 Topps football set contains 396 cards featuring
players of the NFL. Cards are standard size, 2½″ by 3½″.
The set is distinguished by the green border on the fronts of
the cards. The first seven cards in the set recognize record-
breaking (RB) achievements during the previous season. Sta-
tistical league leaders are featured on cards 225–229. Team
cards feature a distinctive yellow border on the front with
the team's results and leaders (from the previous season)
listed on the back. The set numbering is again ordered by
teams, i.e., Chicago Bears (9–28), New England Patriots (29–
43), Miami Dolphins (44–59), Los Angeles Raiders (60–75),
Los Angeles Rams (76–93), New York Jets (94–110), Denver
Broncos (111–123), Dallas Cowboys (124–136), New York
Giants (137–154), San Francisco 49ers (155–169), Washington Redskins (170–184), Cleveland Browns (185–199), Se-

attle Seahawks (200–212), Green Bay Packers (213–224), San Diego Chargers (230–241), Detroit Lions (242–253), Cincinnati Bengals (224–267), Philadelphia Eagles (268–279), Pittsburgh Steelers (280–291), Minnesota Vikings (292–302), Kansas City Chiefs (303–313), Indianapolis Colts (314–325), St. Louis Cardinals (326–337), New Orleans Saints (338–348), Houston Oilers (349–359), Atlanta Falcons (360–371), Tampa Bay Buccaneers (372–382), and Buffalo Bills (383–393). The last three cards in the set (394–396) are checklist cards.

			Mint	*VG-E*	*F-G*
		Complete Set	11.00	5.50	1.10
		Common Player (1-396)	.03	.01	.00
☐	1	RB: Marcus Allen, Los Angeles Raiders, most yards from scrimmage, season...............	.20	.05	.01
☐	2	RB: Eric Dickerson, Los Angeles Rams, most yards rushing, playoff game	.20	.10	.02
☐	3	RB: Lionel James, San Diego Chargers, most all-purpose yards, season	.05	.02	.00
☐	4	RB: Steve Largent, Seattle Seahawks, most seasons, 50 or more receptions..............	.06	.03	.00
☐	5	RB: George Martin, New York Giants, most touchdowns, def. lineman, career .	.06	.03	.00
☐	6	RB: Stephone Paige, Kansas City Chiefs, most yards receiving, game......................	.05	.02	.00
☐	7	RB: Walter Payton, Chicago Bears, most consecutive games, 100 or more yards rushing...............................	.20	.10	.02
☐	8	Super Bowl XX, Bears 46, Patriots 10 (McMahon handing off)...............................	.15	.07	.01
☐	9	Chicago Bears, Team Card (Payton in motion)..............	.20	.10	.02
☐	10	Jim McMahon......................	.20	.10	.02
☐	11	Walter Payton AP..............	.50	.25	.05
☐	12	Matt Suhey	.03	.01	.00

			Mint	VG-E	F-G
☐	13	Willie Gault	.07	.03	.01
☐	14	Dennis McKinnon	.03	.01	.00
☐	15	Emery Moorehead	.03	.01	.00
☐	16	Jim Covert AP	.12	.06	.01
☐	17	Jay Hilgenberg AP	.10	.05	.01
☐	18	Kevin Butler	.20	.10	.02
☐	19	Richard Dent AP	.15	.07	.01
☐	20	William Perry	1.25	.60	.12
☐	21	Steve McMichael	.03	.01	.00
☐	22	Dan Hampton	.08	.04	.01
☐	23	Otis Wilson	.06	.03	.00
☐	24	Mike Singletary	.12	.06	.01
☐	25	Wilber Marshall	.15	.07	.01
☐	26	Leslie Frazier	.03	.01	.00
☐	27	Dave Duerson	.12	.06	.01
☐	28	Gary Fencik	.03	.01	.00
☐	29	New England Patriots, Team Card (James on the run)	.07	.03	.01
☐	30	Tony Eason	.15	.07	.01
☐	31	Steve Grogan	.07	.03	.01
☐	32	Craig James	.10	.05	.01
☐	33	Tony Collins	.06	.03	.00
☐	34	Irving Fryar	.09	.04	.01
☐	35	Brian Holloway AP	.06	.03	.00
☐	36	John Hannah AP	.07	.03	.01
☐	37	Tony Franklin	.03	.01	.00
☐	38	Garin Veris	.06	.03	.00
☐	39	Andre Tippett AP	.08	.04	.01
☐	40	Steve Nelson	.03	.01	.00
☐	41	Raymond Clayborn	.06	.03	.00
☐	42	Fred Marion	.03	.01	.00
☐	43	Rich Camarillo	.03	.01	.00
☐	44	Miami Dolphins, Team Card (Marino sets up)	.07	.03	.01
☐	45	Dan Marino AP	.40	.20	.04
☐	46	Tony Nathan	.05	.02	.00
☐	47	Ron Davenport	.08	.04	.01
☐	48	Mark Duper	.09	.04	.01
☐	49	Mark Clayton	.09	.04	.01
☐	50	Nat Moore	.05	.02	.00
☐	51	Bruce Hardy	.03	.01	.00

			Mint	*VG-E*	*F-G*
☐	**52**	Roy Foster	.03	.01	.00
☐	**53**	Dwight Stephenson	.07	.03	.01
☐	**54**	Fuad Reveiz	.03	.01	.00
☐	**55**	Bob Baumhower	.06	.03	.00
☐	**56**	Mike Charles	.03	.01	.00
☐	**57**	Hugh Green	.07	.03	.01
☐	**58**	Glenn Blackwood	.03	.01	.00
☐	**59**	Reggie Roby	.05	.02	.00
☐	**60**	Los Angeles Raiders, Team Card (Allen cuts upfield)	.07	.03	.01
☐	**61**	Marc Wilson	.09	.04	.01
☐	**62**	Marcus Allen AP	.30	.15	.03
☐	**63**	Dokie Williams	.06	.03	.00
☐	**64**	Todd Christensen	.05	.02	.00
☐	**65**	Chris Bahr	.05	.02	.00
☐	**66**	Fulton Walker	.03	.01	.00
☐	**67**	Howie Long	.09	.04	.01
☐	**68**	Bill Pickel	.03	.01	.00
☐	**69**	Ray Guy	.06	.03	.00
☐	**70**	Greg Townsend	.03	.01	.00
☐	**71**	Rod Martin	.03	.01	.00
☐	**72**	Matt Millen	.03	.01	.00
☐	**73**	Mike Haynes AP	.08	.04	.01
☐	**74**	Lester Hayes	.06	.03	.00
☐	**75**	Vann McElroy	.03	.01	.00
☐	**76**	Los Angeles Rams, Team Card (Dickerson stiff-arm)	.07	.03	.01
☐	**77**	Dieter Brock	.10	.05	.01
☐	**78**	Eric Dickerson	.40	.20	.04
☐	**79**	Henry Ellard	.06	.03	.00
☐	**80**	Ron Brown	.25	.12	.02
☐	**81**	Tony Hunter	.05	.02	.00
☐	**82**	Kent Hill AP	.03	.01	.00
☐	**83**	Doug Smith	.03	.01	.00
☐	**84**	Dennis Harrah	.03	.01	.00
☐	**85**	Jackie Slater	.03	.01	.00
☐	**86**	Mike Lansford	.03	.01	.00
☐	**87**	Gary Jeter	.03	.01	.00
☐	**88**	Mike Wilcher	.03	.01	.00
☐	**89**	Jim Collins	.03	.01	.00
☐	**90**	LeRoy Irvin	.03	.01	.00

			Mint	VG-E	F-G
☐	**91**	Gary Green	.03	.01	.00
☐	**92**	Nolan Cromwell	.06	.03	.00
☐	**93**	Dale Hatcher	.12	.06	.01
☐	**94**	New York Jets, Team Card (McNeil Powers)	.07	.03	.01
☐	**95**	Ken O'Brien	.20	.10	.02
☐	**96**	Freeman McNeil	.12	.06	.01
☐	**97**	Tony Paige	.03	.01	.00
☐	**98**	Johnny "Lam" Jones	.05	.02	.00
☐	**99**	Wesley Walker	.06	.03	.00
☐	**100**	Kurt Sohn	.03	.01	.00
☐	**101**	Al Toon	.40	.20	.04
☐	**102**	Mickey Shuler	.03	.01	.00
☐	**103**	Marvin Powell	.05	.02	.00
☐	**104**	Pat Leahy	.03	.01	.00
☐	**105**	Mark Gastineau	.12	.06	.01
☐	**106**	Joe Klecko AP	.07	.03	.01
☐	**107**	Marty Lyons	.06	.03	.00
☐	**108**	Lance Mehl	.05	.02	.00
☐	**109**	Bobby Jackson	.03	.01	.00
☐	**110**	Dave Jennings	.03	.01	.00
☐	**111**	Denver Broncos, Team Card (Winder up middle)	.07	.03	.01
☐	**112**	John Elway	.25	.12	.02
☐	**113**	Sammy Winder	.07	.03	.01
☐	**114**	Gerald Willhite	.06	.03	.00
☐	**115**	Steve Watson	.05	.02	.00
☐	**116**	Vance Johnson	.10	.05	.01
☐	**117**	Rick Karlis	.03	.01	.00
☐	**118**	Rulon Jones	.05	.02	.00
☐	**119**	Karl Mecklenburg AP	.25	.12	.02
☐	**120**	Louis Wright	.05	.02	.00
☐	**121**	Mike Harden	.03	.01	.00
☐	**122**	Dennis Smith	.03	.01	.00
☐	**123**	Steve Foley	.03	.01	.00
☐	**124**	Dallas Cowboys, Team Card (Hill evades defender)	.08	.04	.01
☐	**125**	Danny White	.15	.07	.01
☐	**126**	Tony Dorsett	.30	.15	.03
☐	**127**	Timmy Newsome	.03	.01	.00
☐	**128**	Mike Renfro	.03	.01	.00

		Mint	VG-E	F-G
☐ **129**	Tony Hill..............................	.06	.03	.00
☐ **130**	Doug Cosbie AP	.06	.03	.00
☐ **131**	Rafael Septien	.06	.03	.00
☐ **132**	Ed "Too Tall" Jones............	.10	.05	.01
☐ **133**	Randy White.......................	.12	.06	.01
☐ **134**	Jim Jeffcoat	.05	.02	.00
☐ **135**	Everson Walls AP	.06	.03	.00
☐ **136**	Dennis Thurman	.03	.01	.00
☐ **137**	New York Giants, Team Card (Morris opening)..........	.07	.03	.01
☐ **138**	Phil Simms..........................	.15	.07	.01
☐ **139**	Joe Morris...........................	.25	.12	.02
☐ **140**	George Adams......................	.10	.05	.01
☐ **141**	Lionel Manuel	.07	.03	.01
☐ **142**	Bobby Johnson.....................	.03	.01	.00
☐ **143**	Phil McConkey.....................	.06	.03	.00
☐ **144**	Mark Bavaro	.15	.07	.01
☐ **145**	Zeke Mowatt........................	.03	.01	.00
☐ **146**	Brad Benson	.06	.03	.00
☐ **147**	Bart Oates	.05	.02	.00
☐ **148**	Leonard Marshall AP............	.25	.12	.02
☐ **149**	Jim Burt	.05	.02	.00
☐ **150**	George Martin......................	.06	.03	.00
☐ **151**	Lawrence Taylor AP	.25	.12	.02
☐ **152**	Harry Carson AP	.10	.05	.01
☐ **153**	Elvis Patterson	.03	.01	.00
☐ **154**	Sean Landeta.......................	.10	.05	.01
☐ **155**	San Francisco 49ers, Team Card (Craig scampers)..........	.07	.03	.01
☐ **156**	Joe Montana........................	.30	.15	.03
☐ **157**	Roger Craig	.10	.05	.01
☐ **158**	Wendell Tyler......................	.05	.02	.00
☐ **159**	Carl Monroe	.03	.01	.00
☐ **160**	Dwight Clark	.06	.03	.00
☐ **161**	Jerry Rice	.45	.22	.04
☐ **162**	Randy Cross	.03	.01	.00
☐ **163**	Keith Fahnhorst	.03	.01	.00
☐ **164**	Jeff Stover..........................	.03	.01	.00
☐ **165**	Michael Carter	.20	.10	.02
☐ **166**	Dwaine Board......................	.03	.01	.00
☐ **167**	Eric Wright.........................	.03	.01	.00

		Mint	*VG-E*	*F-G*
☐ **168**	Ronnie Lott	.06	.03	.00
☐ **169**	Carlton Williamson	.03	.01	.00
☐ **170**	Washington Redskins, Team Card (Butz gets his man)	.07	.03	.01
☐ **171**	Joe Theismann	.20	.10	.02
☐ **172**	Jay Schroeder	.30	.15	.03
☐ **173**	George Rogers	.10	.05	.01
☐ **174**	Ken Jenkins	.03	.01	.00
☐ **175**	Art Monk AP	.08	.04	.01
☐ **176**	Gary Clark	.15	.07	.01
☐ **177**	Joe Jacoby	.05	.02	.00
☐ **178**	Russ Grimm	.05	.02	.00
☐ **179**	Mark Moseley	.06	.03	.00
☐ **180**	Dexter Manley	.06	.03	.00
☐ **181**	Charles Mann	.03	.01	.00
☐ **182**	Vernon Dean	.03	.01	.00
☐ **183**	Raphel Cherry	.06	.03	.00
☐ **184**	Curtis Jordan	.03	.01	.00
☐ **185**	Cleveland Browns, Team Card (Kosar fakes handoff)	.07	.03	.01
☐ **186**	Gary Danielson	.07	.03	.01
☐ **187**	Bernie Kosar	.50	.25	.05
☐ **188**	Kevin Mack	.25	.12	.02
☐ **189**	Earnest Byner	.15	.07	.01
☐ **190**	Glen Young	.03	.01	.00
☐ **191**	Ozzie Newsome	.07	.03	.01
☐ **192**	Mike Baab	.03	.01	.00
☐ **193**	Cody Risien	.03	.01	.00
☐ **194**	Bob Golic	.05	.02	.00
☐ **195**	Reggie Camp	.03	.01	.00
☐ **196**	Chip Banks	.07	.03	.01
☐ **197**	Tom Cousineau	.07	.03	.01
☐ **198**	Frank Minnifield	.06	.03	.00
☐ **199**	Al Gross	.03	.01	.00
☐ **200**	Seattle Seahawks, Team Card (Warner breaks free)	.07	.03	.01
☐ **201**	Dave Krieg	.12	.06	.01
☐ **202**	Curt Warner	.12	.06	.01
☐ **203**	Steve Largent AP	.09	.04	.01
☐ **204**	Norm Johnson	.03	.01	.00
☐ **205**	Daryl Turner	.03	.01	.00

		Mint	VG-E	F-G
☐ **206**	Jacob Green	.06	.03	.00
☐ **207**	Joe Nash	.05	.02	.00
☐ **208**	Jeff Bryant	.03	.01	.00
☐ **209**	Randy Edwards	.03	.01	.00
☐ **210**	Fredd Young	.06	.03	.00
☐ **211**	Kenny Easley	.07	.03	.01
☐ **212**	John Harris	.03	.01	.00
☐ **213**	Green Bay Packers, Team Card (Coffman conquers)	.07	.03	.01
☐ **214**	Lynn Dickey	.08	.04	.01
☐ **215**	Gerry Ellis	.03	.01	.00
☐ **216**	Eddie Lee Ivery	.06	.03	.00
☐ **217**	Jessie Clark	.03	.01	.00
☐ **218**	James Lofton	.08	.04	.01
☐ **219**	Paul Coffman	.03	.01	.00
☐ **220**	Alphonso Carreker	.03	.01	.00
☐ **221**	Ezra Johnson	.03	.01	.00
☐ **222**	Mike Douglass	.03	.01	.00
☐ **223**	Tim Lewis	.06	.03	.00
☐ **224**	Mark Murphy	.03	.01	.00
☐ **225**	Passing leaders: Ken O'Brien AFC, New York Jets; Joe Montana NFC, San Francisco 49ers	.12	.06	.01
☐ **226**	Receiving leaders: Lionel James AFC, San Diego Chargers; Roger Craig, NFC, San Francisco 49ers	.06	.03	.00
☐ **227**	Rushing leaders: Marcus Allen AFC, Los Angeles Raiders; Gerald Riggs NFC, Atlanta Falcons	.12	.06	.01
☐ **228**	Scoring leaders: Gary Anderson AFC, Pittsburgh Steelers; Kevin Butler NFC, Chicago Bears	.06	.03	.00
☐ **229**	Interception leaders: Eugene Daniel AFC, Indianapolis Colts; Albert Lewis AFC, Kansas City Chiefs; Everson Walls NFC, Dallas Cowboys	.05	.02	.00

		Mint	*VG-E*	*F-G*
☐ **230**	San Diego Chargers, Team Card (Fouts over top)	.07	.03	.01
☐ **231**	Dan Fouts............................	.20	.10	.02
☐ **232**	Lionel James	.08	.04	.01
☐ **233**	Gary Anderson....................	.25	.12	.02
☐ **234**	Tim Spencer	.07	.03	.01
☐ **235**	Wes Chandler	.07	.03	.01
☐ **236**	Charlie Joiner.....................	.08	.04	.01
☐ **237**	Kellen Winslow	.08	.04	.01
☐ **238**	Jim Lachey..........................	.03	.01	.00
☐ **239**	Bob Thomas	.03	.01	.00
☐ **240**	Jeffery Dale.........................	.03	.01	.00
☐ **241**	Ralf Mojsiejenko...................	.03	.01	.00
☐ **242**	Detroit Lions, Team Card (Hipple spots receiver).........	.07	.03	.01
☐ **243**	Eric Hipple	.08	.04	.01
☐ **244**	Billy Sims	.10	.05	.01
☐ **245**	James Jones........................	.06	.03	.00
☐ **246**	Pete Mandley	.03	.01	.00
☐ **247**	Leonard Thompson	.03	.01	.00
☐ **248**	Lomas Brown	.10	.05	.01
☐ **249**	Ed Murray	.03	.01	.00
☐ **250**	Curtis Green	.03	.01	.00
☐ **251**	William Gay........................	.03	.01	.00
☐ **252**	Jimmy Williams...................	.03	.01	.00
☐ **253**	Bobby Watkins....................	.03	.01	.00
☐ **254**	Cincinnati Bengals, Team Card (Esiason zeroes in).......	.07	.03	.01
☐ **255**	Boomer Esiason	.50	.25	.05
☐ **256**	James Brooks	.06	.03	.00
☐ **257**	Larry Kinnebrew	.05	.02	.00
☐ **258**	Cris Collinsworth	.07	.03	.01
☐ **259**	Mike Martin	.03	.01	.00
☐ **260**	Eddie Brown.......................	.25	.12	.02
☐ **261**	Anthony Munoz	.06	.03	.00
☐ **261**	Jim Breech..........................	.03	.01	.00
☐ **263**	Ross Browner	.05	.02	.00
☐ **264**	Carl Zander	.03	.01	.00
☐ **265**	James Griffin......................	.03	.01	.00
☐ **266**	Robert Jackson....................	.03	.01	.00
☐ **267**	Pat McInally........................	.05	.02	.00

		Mint	VG-E	F-G
☐ 268	Philadelphia Eagles, Team Card (Jaworski surveys)	.07	.03	.01
☐ 269	Ron Jaworski	.09	.04	.01
☐ 270	Earnest Jackson	.06	.03	.00
☐ 271	Mike Quick	.07	.03	.01
☐ 272	John Spagnola	.03	.01	.00
☐ 273	Mark Dennard.....................	.03	.01	.00
☐ 274	Paul McFadden....................	.03	.01	.00
☐ 275	Reggie White	.12	.06	.01
☐ 276	Greg Brown........................	.03	.01	.00
☐ 277	Herman Edwards.................	.03	.01	.00
☐ 278	Roynell Young....................	.03	.01	.00
☐ 279	Wes Hopkins AP	.06	.03	.00
☐ 280	Pittsburgh Steelers, Team Card (Abercrombie inches)...	.07	.03	.01
☐ 281	Mark Malone......................	.08	.04	.01
☐ 282	Frank Pollard.....................	.03	.01	.00
☐ 283	Walter Abercrombie	.06	.03	.00
☐ 284	Louis Lipps	.12	.06	.01
☐ 285	John Stallworth..................	.07	.03	.01
☐ 286	Mike Webster.....................	.06	.03	.00
☐ 287	Gary Anderson AP...............	.03	.01	.00
☐ 288	Keith Willis	.03	.01	.00
☐ 289	Mike Merriweather	.06	.03	.00
☐ 290	Dwayne Woodruff...............	.03	.01	.00
☐ 291	Donnie Shell......................	.05	.02	.00
☐ 292	Minnesota Vikings, Team Card (Kramer audible)	.07	.03	.01
☐ 293	Tommy Kramer...................	.10	.05	.01
☐ 294	Darrin Nelson	.06	.03	.00
☐ 295	Ted Brown	.05	.02	.00
☐ 296	Buster Rhymes	.15	.07	.01
☐ 297	Anthony Carter	.20	.10	.02
☐ 298	Steve Jordan	.03	.01	.00
☐ 299	Keith Millard......................	.03	.01	.00
☐ 300	Joey Browner......................	.03	.01	.00
☐ 301	John Turner.......................	.03	.01	.00
☐ 302	Greg Coleman.....................	.03	.01	.00
☐ 303	Kansas City Chiefs, Team Card (Blackledge)	.07	.03	.01
☐ 304	Bill Kenney........................	.09	.04	.01

			Mint	VG-E	F-G
☐	305	Herman Heard	.03	.01	.00
☐	306	Stephone Paige....................	.07	.03	.01
☐	307	Carlos Carson	.05	.02	.00
☐	308	Nick Lowery........................	.03	.01	.00
☐	309	Mike Bell...........................	.05	.02	.00
☐	310	Bill Maas............................	.06	.03	.00
☐	311	Art Still	.05	.02	.00
☐	312	Albert Lewis	.06	.03	.00
☐	313	Deron Cherry AP	.06	.03	.00
☐	314	Indianapolis Colts, Team Card (Stark booms it)...........	.07	.03	.01
☐	315	Mike Pagel.........................	.07	.03	.01
☐	316	Randy McMillan	.05	.02	.00
☐	317	Albert Bentley.....................	.06	.03	.00
☐	318	George Wonsley..................	.10	.05	.01
☐	319	Robbie Martin	.03	.01	.00
☐	320	Pat Beach	.03	.01	.00
☐	321	Chris Hinton......................	.05	.02	.00
☐	322	Duane Bickett	.20	.10	.02
☐	323	Eugene Daniel.....................	.03	.01	.00
☐	324	Cliff Odom	.03	.01	.00
☐	325	Rohn Stark AP	.03	.01	.00
☐	326	St. Louis Cardinals, Team Card (Mitchell outside)	.07	.03	.01
☐	327	Neil Lomax.........................	.10	.05	.01
☐	328	Stump Mitchell....................	.06	.03	.00
☐	329	Ottis Anderson....................	.12	.06	.01
☐	330	J.T. Smith..........................	.03	.01	.00
☐	331	Pat Tilley...........................	.05	.02	.00
☐	332	Roy Green	.06	.03	.00
☐	333	Lance Smith.......................	.03	.01	.00
☐	334	Curtis Greer.......................	.05	.02	.00
☐	335	Freddie Joe Nunn	.10	.05	.01
☐	336	E.J. Junior.........................	.07	.03	.01
☐	337	Lonnie Young......................	.03	.01	.00
☐	338	New Orleans Saints, Team Card (W. Wilson running)....	.07	.03	.01
☐	339	Bobby Hebert......................	.15	.07	.01
☐	340	Dave Wilson	.07	.03	.01
☐	341	Wayne Wilson	.03	.01	.00
☐	342	Hoby Brenner	.03	.01	.00

		Mint	*VG-E*	*F-G*
☐ 343	Stan Brock	.03	.01	.00
☐ 344	Morten Andersen	.03	.01	.00
☐ 345	Bruce Clark	.05	.02	.00
☐ 346	Rickey Jackson	.03	.01	.00
☐ 347	Dave Waymer	.03	.01	.00
☐ 348	Brian Hansen	.05	.02	.00
☐ 349	Houston Oilers, Team Card (Moon throws bomb)	.07	.03	.01
☐ 350	Warren Moon	.15	.07	.01
☐ 351	Mike Rozier	.15	.07	.01
☐ 352	Butch Woolfolk	.05	.02	.00
☐ 353	Drew Hill	.06	.03	.00
☐ 354	Willie Drewrey	.05	.02	.00
☐ 355	Tim Smith	.05	.02	.00
☐ 356	Mike Munchak	.06	.03	.00
☐ 357	Ray Childress	.15	.07	.01
☐ 358	Frank Bush	.03	.01	.00
☐ 359	Steve Brown	.03	.01	.00
☐ 360	Atlanta Falcons, Team Card (Riggs around end)	.07	.03	.01
☐ 361	Dave Archer	.25	.12	.02
☐ 362	Gerald Riggs	.10	.05	.01
☐ 363	William Andrews	.07	.03	.01
☐ 364	Billy Johnson	.06	.03	.00
☐ 365	Arthur Cox	.03	.01	.00
☐ 366	Mike Kenn	.05	.02	.00
☐ 367	Bill Fralic	.25	.12	.02
☐ 368	Mike Luckhurst	.03	.01	.00
☐ 369	Rick Bryan	.07	.03	.01
☐ 370	Bobby Butler	.03	.01	.00
☐ 371	Rick Donnelly	.15	.07	.01
☐ 372	Tampa Bay Buccaneers, Team Card (Wilder sweeps left)	.07	.03	.01
☐ 373	Steve DeBerg	.07	.03	.01
☐ 374	Steve Young	.12	.06	.01
☐ 375	James Wilder	.10	.05	.01
☐ 376	Kevin House	.05	.02	.00
☐ 377	Gerald Carter	.03	.01	.00
☐ 378	Jimmie Giles	.06	.03	.00
☐ 379	Sean Farrell	.03	.01	.00

	Mint	VG-E	F-G
☐ **380** Donald Igwebulke	.03	.01	.00
☐ **381** David Logan	.03	.01	.00
☐ **382** Jeremiah Castille	.06	.03	.00
☐ **383** Buffalo Bills, Team Card (Bell sees daylight)	.07	.03	.01
☐ **384** Bruce Mathison....................	.06	.03	.00
☐ **385** Joe Cribbs...........................	.07	.03	.01
☐ **386** Greg Bell............................	.08	.04	.01
☐ **387** Jerry Butler........................	.07	.03	.01
☐ **388** Andre Reed.........................	.03	.01	.00
☐ **389** Bruce Smith........................	.20	.10	.02
☐ **390** Fred Smerlas	.05	.02	.00
☐ **391** Darryl Talley	.05	.02	.00
☐ **392** Jim Haslett..........................	.03	.01	.00
☐ **393** Charles Romes	.03	.01	.00
☐ **394** Checklist 1-132....................	.06	.01	.00
☐ **395** Checklist 133-264	.06	.01	.00
☐ **396** Checklist 265-396	.06	.01	.00

GOLF

	Price Range	
☐ **Trophy,** plated trumpet form, with five figural woods encircling the base, linked by swags inscribed "Strawberry Cup, May 1927, won by J.G. Hancock," 17″ high	200.00	300.00
☐ **Trophy,** flare form, plated, with single club-shape handle and figure of a golfer following through his swing, inscribed "H. Holt Trophy, B.A. & B.C. Spring Tournament 1929 winner J. McCall," 11½″ high	200.00	250.00

Price Range

HOCKEY AND SKATING

☐ **Drawings,** "Five Straight Defeats," two, New York's, Vanishing Americans and "Looks like the last scene, Rangers to the Playoffs," signed and inscribed "with apologies to Fraser," pencil heightened with white, 15″ x 19½″ 250.00   350.00

☐ **Drawings,** "Fancy Figures," two, Barbara Ann Scott and Sonja Henie on " 'giving the Main Stem a whirl', Roller Derby," signed, pencil with ink heightened with white, 13½″ x 18″ 250.00   350.00

POLO

☐ **Drawing,** "The Thirty Years Warrior," depicting Dev Milburn riding against the English, signed, pencil with ink heightened with white, 18″ x 19½″ 300.00

☐ **Drawing,** "Pardon My Eastern Accent," depicting polo east and west, signed, pencil and ink heightened with blue crayon, 17½″ x 19½″ 300.00   400.00

SOCCER

☐ **Musical automaton,** "The Soccer Players," features three bisque head figures on soccer field with goal and goalie kicking ball upfield, 15″ long, 8½″ wide, 19″ high 400.00

Musical automaton, "The Soccer Players," features three bisque head figures on soccer field with goal and goalie kicking ball upfield, 15″ long, 8½″ wide, 19″ high, $400. (*Photo courtesy of Phillips, New York*)

	Price Range	

TENNIS

	Price Range	
☐ **Ashtray,** plated, circular form with tennis racket and ball cigarette holder, 3″ high	80.00	120.00
☐ **Book,** Wallis A. Myers, *Lawn Tennis at Home and Abroad,* illustrations, cloth, New York, 1903	10.00	15.00
☐ **Drawing,** "Althea Gibson," signed, pencil, 9″ x 7½″	150.00	250.00
☐ **Drawing,** "Just Like A Woman," Helen Wills Moody, a superchamp, signed, pencil with ink		

Drawing, "Too Big To Budge," Don Budge at Flushing Meadow, signed, pencil with ink, 15 ½ " × 19 ½ ", estimated value $300–$500. (*Photo courtesy of Phillips, New York*)

	Price Range	
heightened with white, 18 " x 19 ½ "	250.00	350.00
□ **Drawing,** "Too Big To Budge," Don Budge at Flushing Meadow, signed, pencil with ink, 15 ½ " x 19 ½ ", estimated value	300.00	500.00
□ **Trophy,** plated, formed by a wooden and metal base with three rackets supporting a cup, 6 " high	80.00	120.00
□ **Racket,** Wilson, "Family Player," oak frame, center of throat in elongated triangle form	200.00	300.00
□ **Racket,** unusual Spaulding baseball handle, bears Spaulding label on center of inset convex throat	200.00	300.00
□ **Racket,** "Beeckman" model,		

	Price Range	
Peck and Snyder, with V-incised grip and walnut throat center, and original decal	100.00	150.00
☐ **Racket,** F. and J. Bancroft, "Pawtucket Rhode Island, Premier," model, with original decal		50.00

YACHTING

	Price Range	
☐ **Drawing,** "Well It's A New Angle," signed, pencil, 13½" x 19"	150.00	180.00
☐ **Drawing,** "Chasing Rainbows," America's Cup, Sopwith and Lipton, signed, pencil with ink heightened with white, 17" x 19½"	250.00	300.00

Steins

COMMENTS: A new area of particular interest is character steins, made of stoneware, porcelain, and occasionally pewter in the shapes of animals, famous people, humorous characters, towers, footballs, bowling pins, and even vegetables—rather than in the cylindrical shape of the ordinary beer stein. Usually the body of the stein is the body of the character, and the head forms the hinged lid. Such steins are valued at anywhere between $200 for the more common and often-seen steins to $2,000 and up for fine porcelain steins with lithophanes, such as those manufactured by the Dresden-area firm of Schierholz & Sons (usually marked with a ''#'' mark and the word *Musterschutz*, meaning ''protected design,'' i.e., design patent). Other character stein manufacturers were Ernst Bohne & Sons, Merkelbach & Wick, Albert Jac. Thewalt, Marzi & Remy. Munich child character steins are often marked ''Joseph Mayer'' or ''Joseph Reinemann,'' but we don't know whether these gentlemen were manufacturers or distributors/wholesalers.

Also, older steins—17th and 18th centuries—are becoming more appreciated, and their prices are rising. Steins from Creussen, Saxony, Bunzlau, and the Westerwald are showing up at auctions, and prices can range into the tens of thousands of dollars, as, for example, for a genuine 17th-century Creussen ''Apostle'' stein.

A final category of stein for which there currently seems to be a greater awareness is glass steins encased in a filigreed pewter covering. They are usually of clear, green, or amber glass, and it is the pewter surface covering that forms the design. At one time these steins were overlooked, but now they fetch prices of $300 to $500 for the half-liter sizes!

	Price Range	
☐ **Art Nouveau,** copper and brass, 14″	110.00	130.00
☐ **Bacchus,** silver, Sheffield, 11½″	580.00	675.00
☐ **Beer stein,** Germany, porcelain with pewter lid, decorated with trio of merrymakers in relief, c. 1900s	175.00	250.00
☐ **Character,** drunken monkey, Musterschutz, 1/2 liter	400.00	465.00
☐ **Crying radish,** Musterschutz, 3/10 liter	340.00	400.00
☐ **Firefighting scene,** pewter lid, 1/2 liter	340.00	390.00
☐ **Ivory,** battle scene, carved, 13¾″	2375.00	2950.00
☐ **Lithophanes,** clown, 1/2 liter	400.00	430.00
☐ **Lithophanes,** German scene, 6½″	110.00	130.00
☐ **Mettlach,** No. 202, 1 liter	355.00	375.00
☐ **Mettlach,** No. 1395, 1/2 liter	375.00	500.00
☐ **Mettlach,** No. 1403, 1/2 liter	300.00	475.00
☐ **Mettlach,** No. 1527, 1/2 liter	300.00	550.00
☐ **Mettlach,** No. 1675, Heidelberg, 1/2 liter	400.00	485.00
☐ **Mettlach,** No. 1934, soldiers, inlaid lid	650.00	850.00
☐ **Mettlach,** No. 2002, Munich, 1/2 liter	300.00	400.00
☐ **Mettlach,** No. 2007, Lot No. 90, black cat on pewter handle, signed F. Stuck	400.00	500.00
☐ **Mettlach,** No. 2038, Black Forest, 3.8 liter	3500.00	3800.00

	Price Range	
☐ **Mettlach,** No. 2082, 1/2 liter (comes in three sizes), inlaid lid, featuring Robin Hood character firing crossbow	1250.00	1450.00
☐ **Mettlach,** No. 2136, brewmaster, 1/2 liter	2000.00	2500.00
☐ **Mettlach,** No. 2181, pug, 1/2 liter	300.00	350.00
☐ **Mettlach,** No. 2277, 1/2 liter, inlaid lid, castle and clock tower ...	450.00	550.00
☐ **Mettlach,** No. 2277, 3/10 liter, inlaid lid, castle and clock tower	275.00	330.00
☐ **Mettlach,** No. 2333, dancing gnomes, pewter lid	135.00	155.00
☐ **Mettlach,** No. 2388, pretzel, 1/2 liter	330.00	385.00
☐ **Mettlach,** No. 2832, 1/2 liter	400.00	450.00
☐ **Mettlach,** No. 2833F, inlaid lid, tavern scene of men toasting, brick wall motif around base	385.00	500.00
☐ **Mettlach,** No. 2931, 1/2 liter	350.00	400.00
☐ **Mettlach,** No. 2958, bowling, 16″	775.00	975.00
☐ **Pewter,** Kayserzinn, 10″	190.00	220.00
☐ **Porcelain,** pewter lid, Roman soldier on sides	150.00	180.00
☐ **Porcelain,** figural top, blacksmith crest	180.00	220.00
☐ **Pottery,** Marzi & Remi, tavern scene	35.00	45.00
☐ **Pottery,** pewter lid, border of grapes on top edge, seated men and women talking	55.00	75.00
☐ **Pottery,** pewter lid, eagle crest in oval medallion	85.00	125.00

Stoves

PERIOD: Collectible stoves are those made from the 18th century to the mid-1930s.

ORIGIN: Cooking stoves with ovens were first made in the early 19th century. Before that time most cooking was done over an open fire. Heating stoves date from Benjamin Franklin's 1742 invention. In 1850 the first gas cookers appeared on the market. Electric cookers were introduced in 1894, and stoves didn't come with thermostats until 1923.

ADDITIONAL TIPS: The listings include a description of each stove and the price range. For more complete information, refer to *The Official Price Guide to Kitchen Collectibles,* published by the House of Collectibles.

COMMENT: An antique stove's value is composed of two parts: its basic utilitarian value and its decorative/artistic value. The "antique" premium added to the utilitarian value depends hardly at all on sheer age and very largely on the stove's artistic merits. A spectacular base burner from 1909 is worth much more than a plain laundry stove from 1870.

Price Range

☐ **Base burner,** Favorite No. 30, c. 1897, ornate black iron with lots of nickel trim and many paned

Price Range

mica doors on 3 sides, magazine feed, fully restored 1500.00 1700.00

☐ **Box stove,** BF 7 M Co., No. 1, c. 1850, black iron, plain, fully restored 80.00 120.00

☐ **Laundry stove,** No. 14, 1883, plain black iron, with flatirons, unusually nice for a laundry stove, fully restored 350.00 450.00

☐ **Oak stove,** Signal Oak No. 1, Sears & Roebuck, c. 1915, small, black iron, plain, fully restored .. 100.00 120.00

☐ **Oak stove,** Glenwood Base Heater No. 18, 1909, black iron with nickel trim, reversible flue heats base, large, fully restored .. 650.00 750.00

☐ **Oval air-tight heater,** Peerless, c. 1845, sheet metal body, vertical, between black cast iron base and top, top and end feed 80.00 100.00

☐ **Four-column parlor heater,** No. 4, c. 1845, side and end doors, ornate black iron, fully restored 1100.00 1300.00

☐ **Four-column heater,** signed only "Albany, N.Y." 1000.00 1300.00

☐ **Range,** Glenwood Co., C. 1910, plain black iron with nickel trim, with high shelf and reservoir, fully restored 800.00 900.00

☐ **Range,** Imperial Clarion 8-20, 1898, ornate black iron with nickel trim and high closet, fully restored 1400.00 1600.00

☐ **Stove,** Franklin, no name, c. 1830, ornate black, open front, fully restored 200.00 300.00

☐ **Surface burner,** double-cased, Moore's Air-Tight Heater 402-B, c. 1915, ornate black cast-iron

	Price Range	
outer jacket with nickel trim, one mica door, fully restored	700.00	800.00
☐ **Wood parlor heater,** Sylvan Red Cross No. 31, 1889, ornate black iron with four decorative tiles, side and end doors, fully restored	200.00	250.00

TOYS

☐ **Buck's Junior 4,** toy range, 22″ high, 15 1/2″ long, Buck's Stove & Range Co, St. Louis, MO	800.00	900.00
☐ **Charter Oak,** toy cookstove, 14″ high, 21 1/2″ long, G. F. Filley, St. Louis	700.00	750.00
☐ **Dainty,** toy range, 11″ high, 11 1/2″ long, Reading Stove Works, Reading, PA	250.00	300.00
☐ **Midget,** toy range, 27 1/2″ high, 16″ long, Belleville Stove Works, Belleville, IL	1000.00	1300.00
☐ **The Pet,** toy heater, 10″ high, 8 1/2″ long, Young & Bro., Albany	150.00	180.00
☐ **Toy range,** "Star," c. 1910, 16″ long, ornate cast iron with oxidized finish, made by toy manufacturer, barely functional for child's cooking	450.00	550.00
☐ **Qualified,** toy range, 21″ high, 13″ long, blue porcelain, Qualified Range Co., Belleville, IL	1500.00	2000.00

Teddy Bears

HISTORY: Teddy bears are stuffed animals said to have first been created simultaneously in the United States and Germany early in this century. The American origin began after a couple from Brooklyn created a bear in honor of a publicized incident involving President Teddy Roosevelt and a bear during a hunting trip in 1906. The European Teddy was created by the Steiff Company of Germany about the same time.

COMMENTS: Bears are being produced in various sizes by Steiff, Gund, Alresford, Hermann, and others. The Teddy Bear was catapulted back into the public eye largely through the publicity accorded the release of *The Teddy Bear Catalog*, authored by Peggy and Alan Bialosky and published by Workman Publishing in 1980. Bears that imitate living personalities are becoming very popular.

	Price Range
☐ **American,** homemade, large, of soft black plush with glass button eyes and brown velvet snout, 23″ high, 1920–1930s	150.00

Back row, left to right. Gold mohair, with amber eyes and swivel neck, 20″ height, c. 1920, $176. Steiff, of creamy white mohair with black shoe-button eyes, 16″ height, c. 1910, $3520. Mechanical "Yes-No," gold mohair with brown glass eyes, bear moves head up and down or from side to side when tail lever is operated, 17″ height, probably Schuco, c. 1920, $418. *Front row, left to right.* Steiff, tan mohair with black shoe button eyes, 13″ height, c. 1910, $550. Two tiny teddy bears, Steiff, one with button and tag, $200–$300. Steiff, small, of apricot-gold mohair with black shoe-button eyes, 10″ height, c. 1910, $770. (*Photo courtesy of Christie's East, New York*)

	Price Range
☐ **Electric standing,** dark blue mohair with glass-bulb eyes operating from knobbed cord in chin, c. 1918	165.00
☐ **German,** blonde/gold mohair with brown glass eyes, 13″ high, probably Steiff, c. 1915	385.00
☐ **Gold mohair,** with amber eyes and swivel neck, 20″ high, c. 1920	176.00

Price Range

☐ **Steiff,** of creamy white mohair with black shoe-button eyes, 16″ high, c. 1910 .... 3520.00

☐ **Mechanical "Yes-No,"** gold mohair with brown glass eyes, bear moves head up and down or from side to side when tail lever is operated, 17″ high, probably Schuco, c. 1920 .... 418.00

☐ **Steiff,** tan mohair with black shoe-button eyes, 13″ high, c. 1910 .... 550.00

☐ **Two tiny Teddy Bears,** Steiff, one with button and tag 200.00 300.00

☐ **Steiff,** small, of apricot-gold mohair with black shoe-button eyes, 10″ high, c. 1910 .... 770.00

☐ **Hermann,** large, blonde mohair with brown glass eyes and kid pads, 30″ high, c. 1920 .... 880.00

☐ **"Shirley Temple" type,** large cinnamon, with dark brown glass eyes, long plush snout and hump at base of neck, 30″ high, c. 1930 .... 220.00

Telephones

BACKGROUND: On March 10, 1876, Alexander Graham Bell, standing in a little attic at 5 Exeter Place, Boston, sent through his crude telephone the first spoken words ever carried over a wire to his associate Thomas A. Watson. The first telephone line was less than one hundred feet long.

	Price Range	
☐ **1900 Ericsson Swedish Magneto Wall Set,** walnut and metal case known as the fiddleback style	150.00	200.00
☐ **1896 Ericsson Swedish desk set**	75.00	100.00
☐ **1905 Swedish-American Telephone Mfg. Co.,** wall mount switchboard, quarter-sawed oak .	325.00	400.00
☐ **1899 Manhattan Electrical Supply Co.,** compact magneto wall set, walnut or oak	100.00	150.00
☐ **Stromberg-Carlson magneto wall set,** style known as "two-boxer," oak or walnut	165.00	200.00
☐ **1916 Couch inter-com phone,** oak	65.00	115.00

	Price Range	
☐ **1935 automatic electric mag-neto wall set,** with handset, oak	65.00	100.00
☐ **1913 Western Electric mag-neto wall set,** oak	165.00	200.00
☐ **1920 Western Electric dial metal wall set,** add $35 to value if phone can be used	65.00	100.00
☐ **1920 Western Electric candle-stick phone,** black painted brass or steel, earlier phones are made of brass	65.00	95.00

PORCELAIN TELEPHONE SIGNS

TYPES: All signs are two-sided and have a flange.

☐ **1895 Bell Telephone sign,** 17″ x 18″	100.00	135.00
☐ **1921 AT&T booth sign,** 18″ x 20″	150.00	200.00
☐ **1921 Bell Telephone of Penn-sylvania sign,** 11″ x 11″	75.00	125.00
☐ **1921 New England T&T busi-ness office sign,** 24″ x 36″, add $35+ for hanging bracket for sign	250.00	300.00
☐ **1939 Bell System public tele-phone,** 11″ x 11″	25.00	45.00
☐ **1939 Bell System public tele-phone,** 8″ round, known as "hubcap" sign due to shape	25.00	45.00
☐ **1920 independent telephone,** 17″ x 18″	135.00	175.00

Sign, 1921, Bell Telephone of Pennsylvania, 11″ × 11″, $75–$125. (*Photo courtesy of Tom Vaugn*)

Sign, 1920, Independent Telephone, $135–$175. (*Photo courtesy of Tom Vaugn*)

Textiles

DESCRIPTION: Textiles are cloth products, including curtains, seat covers, bed linens, samplers, towels, clothing, quilts, pillows, and coverlets.

COMMENTS: Printed or embroidered textile items appeared on America's shores as early as the beginning of the 1600s. Generally, the design of the textile will provide insight into the work's approximate age.

Note: The single values shown are the actual auction-realized prices.

BEDCOVERS

Price Range

☐ **Applique bedcover,** worked in orange, red, and green printed and solid cottons, with a central flower basket and scattered flowerheads against a cream ground, the orange border cut in points, c. 1850 .... 121.00

	Price Range
☐ **Eau de nil silk,** tambour-embroidered in a delicate floral pattern, with matching pillow cover, together with two ecru embroidered net single bedcovers and an embroidered chaise spread trimmed with ribbon and rosettes	605.00
☐ **Irish lace,** set of two, backed with quilted pale rose silk	308.00
☐ **Mixed ivory lace,** backed with rose satin	880.00

COVERLETS

DESCRIPTION: Coverlets are bedspreads that have been woven on a loom.

VARIATIONS: The many types of designs produced by weavers fall into two categories: geometrics and jacquards. The geometrics are the earliest coverlets made, and they have small simple designs such as the star, diamond, or snowball. The jacquards, produced using a loom device made by Frenchman Joseph Jacquard, having curving, ornate designs such as flowers, birds, and trees.

PERIOD: Coverlets were made from the eighteenth to the twentieth centuries in the East, South, and Midwest. Some are still made today in isolated areas.

MAKER: The early geometric coverlets were woven at home, usually by women. The jacquards were more often made by professional male weavers. The jacquard device enabled the weaver to put his name on his work; the simple loom didn't.

MATERIALS: Two threads are used in weaving. The warp threads, which are vertical, are usually cotton, and the weft threads are horizontal and usually wool. All-cotton or all-wool coverlets are fairly rare. Red and blue dyes were primarily used until the middle of the nineteenth century, when synthetic dyes brought a greater color variety.

Price Range

☐ **American,** 19th century, blue and white jacquard, floral, geometric, architectural, animal, and bird decoration, including eight American Eagles, signed ''R. C. H.,'' measuring approximately 6′10″ x 7′7″ 500.00

☐ **Double-woven,** of indigo wool and cream cotton, worked in a snowflake pattern with pine tree border, c. 1830 .... 495.00

☐ **Jacquard,** worked in red wool and cream cotton with a central medallion and elaborate floral borders, dated 1843 .... 660.00

EMBROIDERY

☐ **Eastern Indian embroidery,** four pieces, consisting of two long decorative panels, one with scalloped rim, one without, each with floral, animal, and figural decoration set with mirrors, together with two contemporary floral- and animal-decorated square pieces 15.00   25.00

☐ **European brocade table scarf,** early 19th century, multicolor floral- and bird-embroidered decoration on pale blue ground, silver-banded outer edges, measuring approx. 3′4″ x 5′8″ 45.00   55.00

☐ **Sunbonnet Babies,** red embroidery on natural linen 10.00

HOOKED RUGS

☐ **Rectangular,** worked with a large reclining lion, a smaller lion, and palm trees in the background, the colors predominantly tan and pale green, with dark green and red striped border 308.00

LACE

☐ **Milanese lace banquet cloth,** worked with wide band insertions of cutwork and embroidered linen, with 12 matching napkins, Swiss 320.00

LINENS

☐ **Tablecloth,** eyelet-embroidered, worked with needlepoint lace insertions and border 440.00

☐ **Table set,** embroidered linen tablecloth, lace-trimmed, with 12 napkins, together with two similar luncheon cloths with napkins 495.00

QUILTS

☐ **Applique quilt,** worked with a serpentine floral rounded in pastel cottons surrounded by blue lattice strips and scattered flowers against a white ground quilted with flower heads, c. 1930 .... 242.00

☐ **Amish pieced,** diamond design, worked in muted red, forest

Price Range

green, and chocolate brown
wools, quilted with a central star
within a feather wreath, with serpentine and scrolling feather bor-
ders, c. 1920 ....   385.00

☐ **Baskets,** pieced quilt, worked in
rose-red and dark blue calicos and
solid orange cotton, the triangle-
pieced baskets on white ground
set with diagonal triple bands
with nine-patch joinings, bound
with dark blue, third quarter 19th
century 440.00

☐ **Eastern Star,** pieced quilt,
worked in red, mustard, and
green calicos against a sprigged
mustard ground and set with narrow bands of red and green, c.
1870 ....   352.00

☐ **Irish chain,** pieced quilt, worked
in red calico and solid red and
white cottons, the border applique with oak leaf motif in the
same fabrics, 1870–1880s 330.00

☐ **Mariner's Compass,** pieced
quilt, the pattern worked in multicolor circular cotton "blocks"
against a rust-red calico ground,
c. 1850 ....   330.00

☐ **North Carolina Lily,** pieced
quilt, worked in turkey red, yellow, and pale green solid cottons
against a white ground with tri-
ple-band border and red binding,
c. 1880 ....   198.00

☐ **Pieced silk,** nine-patch design,
worked in multicolor against a
cream ground, together with a
pieced quilt worked in green and
white bands 77.00

Afshar Soumac rug, the ivory ground covered by two rows of brick red and navy blue botehs with small star-filled octagons, birds and quadrupeds, surrounded by eleven borders and midnight blue skirts, 4′1″ × 2′8″, $1100. (*Photo courtesy of Christie's East, New York*)

Price Range

☐ **Puss in the Corner,** pieced quilt, worked mainly in blue and white cottons, printed with cats, dogs and horses, c. 1900 .... 154.00

RUGS

☐ **Afshar Soumac rug,** the ivory ground covered by two rows of brick-red and navy blue botehs with small star-filled octagons,

Bakshaish carpet, the midnight blue ground covered by a light brick-red petal-form medallion and various floral sprays with brick-red spandrels and three guard borders, 10′10″ × 8′4″, $2800. (*Photo courtesy of Christie's East, New York*)

Price Range

birds, and quadrupeds, surrounded by 11 borders and midnight-blue skirts, 4′1″ x 2′8″ 1100.00

☐ **Bakshaish carpet,** the midnight-blue ground covered by a light brick-red petal-form medallion and various floral sprays with brick-red spandrels and three guard borders, 10′10″ x 8′4″ ...   2800.00

☐ **Kashan pictorial prayer rug,** cream ground covered by a circular central medallion containing a

Kuba rug, the tomato ground covered by three hexagonal inter-connecting medallions with birds and quadrupeds, surrounded by three decorative guard borders, 7'3" × 3'10", $1000. (*Photo courtesy of Christie's East, New York*)

Price Range

seated figure, probably a shah, with various floral sprays and columns leading to the prayer arch, surrounded by six borders, the central border with Farsi inscription and animals, 6'10" x 4'6" 4000.00   5000.00

☐ **Kuba rug,** tomato ground covered by three hexagonal interconnecting medallions with birds and

Price Range

quadrupeds, surrounded by three decorative guard borders, 7'3" x 3'10" 1000.00

☐ **Zeichur rug,** fine, last quarer 19th century, ivory ground covered by 2½ navy blue Georgian crosses and various geometric devices, surrounded by three guard borders, 6'4" x 4'3" .... 3500.00　4500.00

SAMPLERS

☐ **American,** needlework, Westtown School, Chester, PA, worked in blue, green, cream, and black silks on linen, with a short pious verse above a rendering of the school building, deep lawn surrounded by birds, trees, animals, and carnation bouquets, a scrolling monogram "ABC" below, dated 1812 .... 6050.00

☐ **American,** needlework, in blue, green, yellow, cream, and brown silks on linen with a central house and trees, three sheep and a lady in contemporary dress standing beside a gate on the front lawn, the deep floral border with flower baskets, cornucopias, and central signature, "Eliza. Robert's work, A.D. 1829," reframed and glazed 2200.00

☐ **Continental,** worked in green, yellow, black, and brown silks with a central house surrounded by flowers, fruit, birds, animals, and a heraldic lion below, "A. De Vroe. Anno 1793," probably Dutch, framed and glazed 330.00

American needlework, in blue, green, yellow, cream and brown silks on linen with a central house and trees, three sheep and a lady in contemporary dress standing beside a gate on the front lawn, the deep floral border with flower baskets, cornucopias, and central signature, "Eliza. Robert's work, A.D. 1829," reframed and glazed, $2200. (*Photo courtesy of Christie's East, New York*)

Price Range

☐ **English,** small, worked in colored silks on linen with alphabets, numerals, a verse, and birds, "Frances Manning Nov'r 9th, 1791" 550.00

☐ **English,** long, 17th century, worked in bright-colored silks on linen with bands of acorns, strawberries, mixed flowers, and vines, an alphabet above the signature "Elizabeth Cole, 1661" 2420.00

English sampler, long, 17th century, worked in bright colored silks on linen with bands of acorns, strawberries, mixed flowers and vines, an alphabet above the signature "Elizabeth Cole, 1661," $2420. (*Photo courtesy of Christie's East, New York*)

Price Range

☐ **English,** long, worked in red, green, blue, and brown silks on linen with alphabets, numerals, and pious verses separated by carnation, strawberry, and mixed floral bands, Elizabeth Richards, probably late 18th century, framed and glazed 275.00

Franco-Flemish tapestry, late 17th/early 18th century, worked in fresh colors, depicting a mailed Saracen knight conversing with his commander, before a tent, in a wooded river landscape, within applied borders of birds, fruit and flowers, 116″ high, 71″ wide, $4620. (*Photo courtesy of Christie's East, New York*)

Price Range

TAPESTRY

☐ **Franco-Flemish tapestry,** late 17th/early 18th century, worked in fresh colors, depicting a mailed Saracen knight conversing with his commander, before a tent, in a wooded river landscape, within

Price Range

applied borders of birds, fruit, and
flowers, 116″ high, 71″ wide 4620.00

☐ **Franco-Flemish verdure tapestry,** late 17th century, signed
"RAET," worked in fresh colors,
depicting animals in a wooded
river landscape with a bird of prey
attacking a rabbit in the fore-
ground, within borders classical
figures hold baskets of fruit in architectural niches, fruited garlands, and woodland scenes,
approximately 152″ high, 172″
wide 8800.00

Toys and Games

BACKGROUND: Lithography on the board games from the 1800s and turn of the century have long proved a fascination for collectors, the art of lithography having been phased out many years ago. Toys that hold collector fascination are mechanical gems like a "Hoppy on a Horse" produced for about four or five years during the '50s or an Olive Oyl with pop-up squeaker by Linemar Toys (a subsidiary of Marx).

BOOKS: *Character Toys and Collectibles,* David Longest, Collector Books, 1984; *The Knopf Collectors' Guides to American Antiques—Toys,* Blair Whitton, Alfred Knopf, 1984; *The Illustrated Encyclopedia of Metal Toys,* Gordon Gardiner and Alistair Morris, Harmony Books, 1984; *Modern Toys, American Toys 1930-1980,* Linda Baker, Collector Books, 1985.

Extremely rare French wood and metal mechanical rowboat, "L'Auto-Rameur," c. 1910, windup, the rower leans forward on the oars to actually row the boat in the water, 22″ long, $2200. (*Photo courtesy of Phillips, New York*)

TOYS

Boats

	Price Range
☐ **Bing tinplate ferryboat,** key-wind, finished in maroon, gray, and yellow with two sidewheels, 16″ long	1400.00
☐ **Ives tinplate mechanical rowboat,** pat. 1869, figure dressed in original cloth clothes and tin hat, 11″ long	900.00
☐ **"L'Auto-Rameur,"** extremely rare French wood and metal mechanical rowboat, c. 1910, windup, the rower leans forward on the oars to actually row the boat in the water, 22″ long	2200.00

Cars and Trucks

☐ **American coach and four,** tinplate, late 19th century, coach finished in deep red with a yellow roof, 36″ long	18,700.00

American coach and four, tinplate, late 19th century, the coach is finished in deep red with a yellow roof, 36″ length, $18,700. (*Photo courtesy of Phillips, New York*)

	Price Range
☐ **Fire engine ladder truck,** German, c. 1930, keywind, tinplate, lithographed in red with yellow and black piping with driver and two firemen, 9½″ long	425.00
☐ **Metalcraft Coca-Cola delivery truck,** finished in red and yellow, 12″ long	425.00
☐ **Metalcraft "Heinz Pickle" truck,** finished in white with Heinz pickle decal and battery-operated headlights, complete with side tie, 12″ long	425.00
☐ **Delivery truck,** Distler, keywind tinplate, canvas-back, c. 1922, lithographed in green with gold and light green piping, 12½″ long	400.00
☐ **Limousine,** Brimtoy, tinplate, lithographed in red with black roof and white wheels, 10½″ long	600.00

1927 Packard sedan, Hubley, cast iron, finished in green and black, 11″ length, $6500. (*Photo courtesy of Phillips, New York*)

	Price Range
☐ **1927 Packard sedan,** Hubley, cast iron, finished in green and black, 11″ long	6500.00

Comic Character Toys

☐ **Dandy Jim Dancer,** lithographed tin, keywind, clown with cymbals dances on the Big Top's roof, 9½″ high	350.00
☐ **Davy Crockett pocket watch,** the face lithographed with a scene of Davy standing in front of the Alamo and two crossed pistols on the second dial, back is engraved with a scroll, crossed pistols, "DAVY CROCKETT," and "REMEMBER THE ALAMO," with chain, in original box	275.00
☐ **Popeye overhead punching bag,** Chein, keywind, colorfully lithographed, features Popeye working out, 9½″ high	1650.00

Price Range

☐ **Popeye on rollerskates,** Linemar, lithographed tin, with original cloth pants, keywind mechanism, Popeye has plate with can of spinach in right hand, 6 ½ " high 325.00

☐ **Popeye Express,** Marx, c. 1935, keywind, the base lithographed with various scenes and characters, having small train, two tunnels, a bridge, and Popeye flying above the crowd, in original box with instructions, 5 ½ " high 750.00

☐ **Charlie McCarthy Crazy Car,** Marx, with keywind mechanism, 7 " long, lithographed tin 400.00

☐ **Popeye the Champ** (The Big Fight Toy), Marx, c. 1935, features Popeye slugging it out with archrival Bluto, 7 " long, 7 " wide, 7 " high 2000.00

☐ **Mickey Mouse ashtray,** features Mickey seated on the blue porcelain tray, playing a drum 100.00

☐ **Bubble-blowing Popeye,** Linemar, battery-operated, 12 " high . 500.00

☐ **Popeye in a rowboat,** c. 1935, with clockwork mechanism, 15 " long, rare 3000.00

☐ **Popeye,** chalkware figure, incised "1933" and "K.E.S. INC.," 10 " high 80.00

☐ **Popeye Knockout Bank,** features unpainted Popeye and Bluto on a lithographed base, 4 ½ " high 190.00

☐ **Stuffed Mickey Mouse,** Steiff, with sharp snout, oversize yellow hands, red pants, and orange shoes, 5 " high 180.00

Britains, set #40, 1st (The Royal) Dragons mounted in review order, 15 pieces, $2090. (*Photo courtesy of Phillips, New York*)

Price Range

Lead Soldiers and Militaria Toys

☐ **American sailors,** c. 1900, Heyde, in white uniforms and tropical service hats, set of 20 ...   225.00

☐ **Britains,** set No. 36, The Royal Sussex Regiment marching at the slope in review order with mounted officer, seven pieces 140.00

☐ **Britains,** set No. 40, 1st (The Royal) Dragons mounted in review order, 15 pieces 2090.00

☐ **Britains,** set No. 2014, U.S. Marine Corps Band, in original box, 21 pieces 2800.00

☐ **Britains,** set No. 2096, Drum and Pipe Band of the Irish Guards marching in review order with six pipes, bass and side drummers, cymbalist, and drum major, 12 pieces 500.00

Britains, rare, set #2110, U. S. Military band marching in yellow-and-black dress uniforms with complete instrumentation, 25 pieces, $2800. (*Photo courtesy of Phillips, New York*)

	Price Range
☐ **Britains,** rare, set No. 2110, U.S. Military band marching in yellow-and-black dress uniforms with complete instrumentation, 25 pieces	2800.00
☐ **Britains,** set No. 9402, state open road landau, drawn by six Windsor Greys, with three postilions, two footmen, and Queen Elizabeth II and Prince Phillip, 10 pieces	450.00
☐ **Britains,** extremely rare "Walking Elephant," c. 1890, on spinning the parasol, which the rider carries, and placing the elephant on a smooth table, it will walk along, legs moving in a most natural manner	2300.00
☐ **French cuirassiers,** 1890–1914, Heyde, mounted at the walk with sabers, set of 24	350.00
☐ **Horch staff car,** No. 733, battery-operated headlights, re-	

Police wagon "Happy Hooligan," Kenton, horse drawn, cast iron, hand painted in yellow, with red piping and wheels, 17½″ length, $2800. (*Photo courtesy of Phillips, New York*)

	Price Range
tractable canvas top, with saluting general officer, two seated men and driver	475.00
☐ **Police wagon,** "Happy Hooligan," Kenton, horse-drawn, cast iron, hand-painted in yellow, with red piping and wheels, 17½″ long	2800.00
☐ **Six-wheel armored car,** Lineol, camouflage colors, Panzer officer in turret, 10″ long	650.00
☐ **U.S. Cavalry,** c. 1900, Heinrich, rare, hollow-cast, movable arms, in khaki campaign dress, with officer and trumpeter, set of 14	950.00
☐ **U.S. Navy recognition models,** British, complete set in carrying case, models made by Franburg & Co., include seven battleships and battle cruisers, three carriers, several cruiser and destroyer classes, set of 29	650.00

Price Range

Ships

☐ **Ocean liner,** Bing, tinplate, three stacks, four lifeboats, finished in red, blue, and white, keywind, 20″ long 2200.00

☐ **Ocean liner,** Bing, hand-painted tinplate, with two masts and two stacks over white superstructure, flag, and two lifeboats, clockwork mechanism, 12½″ long 700.00

☐ **Ocean liner,** *Mauretania,* Carette, tinplate, wind-up, with four funnels, two lifeboats, mast ladder, rigging, anchor, aft wheel, and full railing, painted red, black, and cream, with red and gold piping, 19½″ long 2800.00

Miscellaneous

☐ **Doll on velocipede,** clockwork, France, c. 1870, the bisque-head boy in blue jacket appears to pedal the front single wheel powered by the clockwork mechanism, partial original box, 8½″ high, 7½″ long 1800.00

☐ **Musical automaton,** of a peasant and a pig, French, Vichy, c. 1870, peasant seated on the back of a ladder-back chair turns and nods his head and blinks his eyes, the right hand bottle-feeds the pig on his lap, whose head moves and tongue darts out, 30″ high 14,000.00

Musical automaton of a peasant and a pig, French, Vichy, c. 1870, the peasant seated on the back of a ladder-back chair, turns and nods his head and blinks his eyes, the right hand bottle-feeds the pig on his lap whose head moves and tongue darts out, 30″ high, $14,000. (*Photo courtesy of Phillips, New York*)

Price Range

GAMES—COMIC STRIPS

☐ **Andy Gump, His Game,** licensed by Sidney Smith Corp., 1924	75.00	100.00
☐ **Beetle Bailey, The Old Army Game,** Milton Bradley, 1963	25.00	35.00
☐ **Charlie McCarthy Topper Game,** Whitman Publishing, 1938	35.00	40.00
☐ **Charlie McCarthy Question and Answer Game,** Whitman Publishing, 1938	25.00	35.00

	Price Range	
☐ **Dick Tracy Detective Game,** Whitman Publishing, 1937	35.00	50.00
☐ **Dick Tracy Playing Card Game,** Whitman Publishing, 1937	25.00	35.00
☐ **Donald Duck's Party Game for Young Folks,** Parker Bros.	50.00	75.00
☐ **Eddie Cantor's Tell It to The Judge,** Parker Bros., 1938	35.00	50.00
☐ **Ed Wynn, The Fire Chief,** Selchow & Righter, 1937	25.00	35.00
☐ **Fibber McGee and the Wistful Vista Mystery Game,** Milton Bradley	25.00	35.00
☐ **Hi-way Henry Cross Country Auto Race,** c. late 1920s	250.00	300.00
☐ **High Spirits, with Calvin and the Colonial,** Milton Bradley, 1920s .	25.00	35.00
☐ **Little Orphan Annie Game,** Milton Bradley, 1927	50.00	75.00
☐ **The Nebbs,** Adventures of, Milton Bradley, 1925–1927	35.00	50.00
☐ **Oh Blondie,** 1940, Whitman Publishing (played like bingo)	25.00	35.00
☐ **Popeye Playing Card Game,** c. 1934, Whitman Publishing	15.00	25.00
☐ **Smitty Game,** Milton Bradley, c. 1930	50.00	75.00
☐ **Snow White and the Seven Dwarfs,** Milton Bradley, 1937 ...	75.00	100.00
☐ **Toonerville Trolley Game,** Milton Bradley, 1927	75.00	100.00
☐ **Uncle Remus Game,** Zip, Parker Bros., c. 1930	50.00	75.00
☐ **Uncle Wiggily,** Milton Bradley, 1918	35.00	50.00
☐ **Walt and Skeezix Gasoline Alley Game,** Milton Bradley, c. 1920	50.00	75.00
☐ **Yellow Kid,** maker unknown, late 1890s	100.00	125.00

Typewriters

PERIOD: The first commercially successful typewriter was manufactured in the sewing machine factory of E. Remington & Sons, Ilion, NY, in 1874. There being no other typewriter at the time, it was simply called "The Type Writer," and because it was patented by Christopher L. Sholes and Carlos Glidden, it is referred to by collectors as the Sholes & Glidden.

Beginning with the 1880s, a great many other typewriters followed, in many different designs, to avoid infringing on the original Sholes & Glidden patents. By the 1920s the design of typewriters became rather standardized, and with some exceptions, typewriters after 1920 are less sought after by collectors.

DESCRIPTION: There are two basic kinds of collectible early typewriters: keyboard machines and index machines. Keyboard machines, which type by the depression of keys, came in three kinds: (1) full-keyboard models with a separate key for each character printed; capital and lowercase letters were on separate keys, so there were as many as eight rows of keys; (2) single-shift machines, in which each key could print a capital and small letter or a numeral and punctuation mark by use of a shift key; these typewriters usually had four rows; (3) double-shift machines, which printed three characters to a key with two shifts, one for capital letters and another for numerals and symbols; these usually had three rows.

Toward the end of the 1880s index machines appeared on the market. These were cheap and simple machines in which a pointer was used to select the desired character from a dial (the index), and a lever was depressed to print the selected character. Index machines, which sold for only a few dollars, met the need for inexpensive typewriters until there were enough secondhand and rebuilt keyboard typewriters available. By the early 1900s the index machines pretty well disappeared.

COMMENTS: How much are early typewriters worth? There is no simple answer. Unlike other, more popular collectibles, such as Carnival glass or postage stamps, typewriters harvest very few collectors. There is no big, active market to establish "standard" or "market" values. It pretty much comes down to how much a buyer is willing to pay and how much a seller is willing to accept.

Also, condition is very important, A typewriter can vary in condition from a rust bucket to mint and everything between. And much of the value of an early typewriter comes from the time, skill, and effort of a collector who restores it. So it is impossible to set an arbitrary value on a machine. However, some general statements can be made about value. Machines such as L. C. Smith, Underwood, Royal, and most Remingtons have, believe it or not, little or no value. Most portables are not of much value since all but one were made after about 1920; that one is the folding Corona, and even it is only worth $10 to $25. Exceptions among post-1920 portables are the Gar-Bell, the Rem-Blick, and the MassPro.

A machine does not have to look odd to be valuable. The very unusual-looking Blickensderfers are generally valued at under $75 (except for the Blickensderfer Electric, which is worth hundreds). The unusual-looking Oliver Nos. 3 through 11 are worth under $50. Most Hammonds are worth under $100 ("most," not "all," because within a make that is otherwise not valuable there can be models that are valued).

On the other hand, collectors will leap at such keyboard machines as the Sholes & Glidden, Sholes Visible, Hartford, Chicago, McCool, Shimer, Munson, Caligraph, Commercial Visible, Postal, and many more. Most index machines are of interest, such as the Odell, World, Hall, Morris, Index Visible, American, and Edison. There are many early typewriters that are of middling interest, and if a collector does not already have it, he will be interested in making a fair offer. There are also many early foreign-made typewriters that are of limited interest to Americans but are bought by collectors overseas.

Also of interest to typewriter collectors are items related to typewriters, such as advertising, catalogs, typing magazines and books, accessories, postcards showing typewriters, and so on. It is particularly important that pages of advertising from magazines include the date of the publication.

	Price Range	
☐ **American Typewriter**	50.00	75.00
☐ **The Caligraph,** depending on model	125.00	250.00
☐ **The Crandall**	400.00	450.00
☐ **The Densmore**	75.00	100.00
☐ **Franklin Typewriter**	100.00	200.00
☐ **Hall Type-Writer**	100.00	150.00
☐ **Hammond**	150.00	250.00
☐ **National Type Writer**		400.00
☐ **Remington,** Model No. 6	40.00	50.00
☐ **The Smith Premier Typewriter,** Model No. 1	75.00	100.00
☐ **The Smith Premier Typewriter,** Model No. 2	35.00	50.00
☐ **The Smith Premier Typewriter,** Model No. 4	50.00	75.00
☐ **World Typewriter**	100.00	150.00
☐ **Yost,** Model No. 4		150.00 and up

Watches

TYPES: Collectible watches include both the pocket and wrist styles. Fobs that attach to pocket watches are also valuable. All types of watches are collectible, including 1930s Walt Disney character children's wristwatches, 1920s men's and women's wristwatches, and European pocket watches. Watches are available from antique dealers, pawnshops, and flea markets. Even inoperative watches can be quite valuable after repair.

COMMENTS: Age, manufacturer, movement's complexity and accuracy, design, and material are all factors that determine the value of a watch.

GENTLEMEN'S

	Price Range	
☐ **Precision,** Rolex, 18k gold, white mat dial with gold batons and hands, sweep hand for the seconds	75.00	850.00
☐ **Patek Philippe,** gold, plain white dial, gold baton chapters and hands, subsidiary seconds		

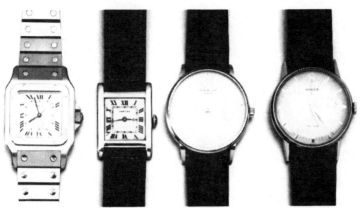

Left to right. Cartier, stainless steel Santos wristwatch, the square bezel with 18k gold rim, the stainless bracelet with gold screw heads, automatic lever movement with septagonal winder set with synthetic blue sapphire, weight of gold 4.08 grams, $900–$1000. Cartier, gold tank watch, ivory dial with full, black Roman chapters, the movement case bearing both English 18k gold assay marks and French poincons, $1500–$2500. Patek Philippe, gold, plain, white dial, gold baton chapters and hands, subsidiary seconds dial, 18-jewel movement, Serial No. 731486, adjusted to heat, cold, and isochronism, and five positions, case bears "Swiss 18k" gold assay marks, $1000–$1500. Precision, Rolex, 18k gold, white mat dial with gold batons and hands, with sweep hand for the seconds, $75–$850. (*Photo courtesy of Phillips, New York*)

	Price Range	
dial, 18-jewel movement, Serial No. 731486, adjusted to heat, cold, and isochronism and five positions, case bears "Swiss 18K" gold assay marks	1000.00	1500.00
☐ **Cartier,** gold tank watch, ivory dial with full black Roman chapters, the movement case bearing both English 18k-gold assay marks and French poincons	1500.00	2500.00
☐ **Cartier,** stainless steel Santos wristwatch, square bezel with 18 k-gold rim, stainless bracelet with gold screw heads, automatic		

Left to right. Gold circular wristwatch, c. 1920, the 15-jewel, bar lever movement in 18k gold, Swiss-made case with gold cuvette, monogrammed case back, $300–$400. Le Coultre, circular, 14k gold wristwatch, black dial with gilt baton hands, subsidiary seconds, 17-jewel movement, on brown lizard strap, c. 1950s, $200–$300. Hamilton Masterpiece, 14k gold, circular wristwatch, silvered dial, gilt baton hands and special fluted, water-resistant case, c. 1950s, $250–$300. (*Photo courtesy of Phillips, New York*)

	Price Range	
lever movement with septagonal winder set with synthetic blue sapphire, weight of gold 4.08 grams	900.00	1000.00
☐ **Hamilton Masterpiece,** 14k-gold circular wristwatch, silvered dial, gilt batons, hands, and special fluted water-resistant case, c. 1950s	250.00	300.00
☐ **Helbros,** 14k rose gold, rectangular wristwatch, mat-finish white dial with gilt chapters and hands, subsidiary hands, 17-jewel movement, c. 1950s	200.00	300.00
☐ **Le Coultre,** circular 14k-gold wristwatch, black dial with gilt batons, hands, subsidiary seconds, 17-jewel movement, on brown lizard strap, c. 1950s	200.00	300.00
☐ **Gold circular wristwatch,** c. 1920, the 15-jewel bar lever		

Price Range

movement in 18k-gold Swiss-made case with gold cuvette, monogrammed case back	300.00	400.00
☐ **Paul Breguette,** square, 14k-gold dress wristwatch, the silver dial with white stud chapters, the three principal points diamond set, subsidiary seconds, flint crystal, gold-filled bracelet, c. 1950 ..	200.00	300.00
☐ **Helbros,** rectangular 14k rose gold, mat-finish white dial with gilt chapters and hands, 17-jewel movement, c. 1950s	200.00	300.00
☐ **Granada,** square, gold wristwatch, white dial with black Arabic figures, hands, subsidiary seconds, 17-jewel movement, flint crystal, 14k Stonewall case with dedication, c. 1945	150.00	200.00
☐ **Rolex,** gold circular calendar wristwatch, c. 1960, the white dial with gold Arabic numerals and hands, with 17-jewel Precision movement, plated winder, English hallmarked case, Fixoflex expanding plated bracelet	300.00	500.00
☐ **Rolex,** perpetual moon phase chronometer wristwatch, c. 1965, stainless-steel circular wristwatch with day and month apertures, silvered dial with batons and luminous spots	400.00	600.00
☐ **Rolex,** 18k-gold wristwatch, officially certified chronometer, heavy case, black enamel dial with gold batons and hands, gold sweep hand for the seconds	850.00	950.00
☐ **Seamaster de Ville,** 18k-gold Omega automatic calendar wristwatch, circular case with white mat dial, gold batons and hands,		

Left to right. Vacheron & Constantin, platinum, c. 1935, silvered dial, bold, black Arabic numerals and hands, 17-jewel movement adjusted for temperature and three positions with overcoil balance, Serial No. 414874, $2500–$3500. Vacheron & Constantin, square, gold wristwatch, in massive case on heavy Florentine gold, mesh bracelet, said to have been owned by the late Ernie Kovacs, $2000–$3000. Vacheron & Constantin, 18k gold, circular wristwatch with a leather strap, silvered dial with gold batons and hands, sweep seconds, c. 1955, $700–$1000. Vacheron & Constantin, gold dress wristwatch, the plain, silvered dial with gold batons and hands, strap, c. 1960, $800–$1000. (*Photo courtesy of Phillips, New York*)

	Price Range	
gold sweep hand, joined with an open and tapered 18k-gold hinged bracelet	750.00	850.00
☐ **Vacheron & Constantin,** gold dress wristwatch, plain silvered dial with gold batons and hands, strap, c. 1960	800.00	1000.00
☐ **Vacheron & Constantin,** 18k-gold circular wristwatch with leather strap, silvered dial with gold batons and hands, sweep seconds, c. 1955	700.00	1000.00
☐ **Vacheron & Constantin,** square gold wristwatch, in massive case on heavy Florentine gold-mesh		

Price Range

bracelet, said to have been owned by the late Ernie Kovacs 2000.00 3000.00

☐ **Vacheron & Constantin,** platinum, c. 1935, silvered dial, bold, black Arabic numerals and hands, 17-jewel movement adjusted for temperature and three positions with overcoil balance, Serial No. 414874 .... 2500.00 3500.00

LADIES'

☐ **Cartier,** France, No. 06135, platinum and diamond bracelet wristwatch, the "snakelike" flexible bracelet with pavé-set diamonds, baguette, and bullet-cut diamonds, back wind, c. 1940 .... 6000.00 8000.00

☐ **Ogival Watch Co.,** 17 jewels, Art Deco style, diamond and onyx bracelet wristwatch, rectangular case flanked with stylized acanthus motif, set with numerous small round diamonds, and French-cut onyx 3400.00 3800.00

☐ **Rolex,** an unusual fob watch in the design of a lantern, inverted textured white dial with gold batons and hands, gold bow brooch fob and connections, English hallmarked 18k gold 800.00 1000.00

POCKET WATCHES

☐ **Swiss taille-douce engraved pocket watch,** by H. Peregaux, Locle, mid-19th century, raised gold Roman numerals and troi-co-

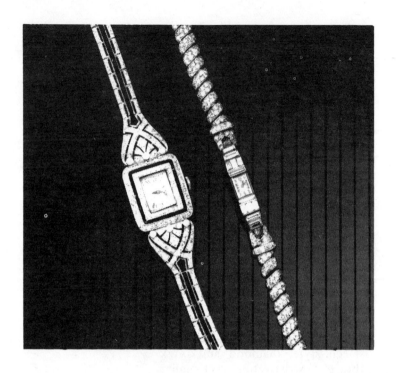

Left. Ogival Watch Co., 17 jewels, Art Deco style, diamond and onyx bracelet wristwatch, the rectangular case flanked with stylized acanthus motif, set with numerous, small round diamonds, and French-cut onyx, $3400–$3800. *Right.* Cartier, France, No. 06135, platinum and diamond bracelet wristwatch, the "snakelike" flexible bracelet pavé-set diamonds, baguette and bullet-cut diamonds, back wind, c. 1940, $6000–$8000. (*Photo courtesy of Phillips, New York*)

	Price Range
leur decorated border, 1⅞″ diameter	300.00

☐ **Elgin gold hunter pocket watch,** 14k-gold hunter case, back cover engraved with a scene depicting two dogs and a stag, signed, black Roman numerals, No. 1462213, case No. 29844

Left. Swiss Taille-Douce engraved pocket watch, by H. Peregaux, Locle, mid-19th century, raised gold Roman numerals and troicoleur decorated border, 1⅞″ diameter, $300. *Right*. Elgin gold hunter pocket watch, 14k gold hunter case, the back cover engraved with a scene depicting two dogs and a stag, signed, black Roman numerals, No. 1462213, the case No. 29844 with U.S. assay marks, 1½″ diameter, $300. (*Photo courtesy of Phillips, New York*)

Left. Gold-cased quarter repeating pocket watch, 18k-gold open face with plain cover, Swiss assay marks, 2″ diameter, $950. *Right*. Hexagonal fob watch, 14k gold open-faced case, with triangular pendant, the hinged damascened keyless movement signed "A.W.W. Co., Waltham, Mass.," 17 jewels, No. 22604316, 1¾″ diameter, $350-$400. (*Photo courtesy of Phillips, New York*)

Left. Gold hunter-cased gentleman's dress watch, Gruen, c. 1915, 14k-gold case, the back engraved with foliage, the white enamel dial signed "Diener Unos, Mexico–Gruen Precision," the keyless nickel movement, signed and numbered 138396, the case marked "Gruen, No. 17226," 1¼" diameter, $550. *Right.* Swiss dress fob watch, Elhero, chronometer, steel open face cased with engraved pendant, keyless movement with 17 jewels, 1¾" diameter, $30. (*Photo courtesy of Phillips, New York*)

	Price Range	
with U.S. assay marks, 1½" diameter	300.00	
☐ **Gold-cased quarter repeating pocket watch,** 18k-gold openface with plain cover, Swiss assay marks, 2" diameter	950.00	
☐ **Hexagonal fob watch,** 14k-gold openfaced case, with triangular pendant, the hinged damascened keyless movement signed "A.W.W. Co., Waltham, Mass.," 17 jewels, No. 22604316, 1¾" diameter	350.00	400.00
☐ **Gold hunter-cased gentleman's dress watch,** Gruen, c. 1915, 14k-gold case, the back engraved with foliage, the white en-		

Price Range

amel dial signed "Diener Unos, Mexico—Gruen Precision," keyless nickel movement, signed and numbered 138396, case marked "Gruen, No. 17226," 1¼″ diameter 550.00

☐ **Swiss dress fob watch,** Elhero, chronometer, steel openface cased with engraved pendant, keyless movement with 17 jewels, 1¾″ diameter 30.00

☐ **Gold hunter-cased quarter repeater,** by Invicta, 18k-gold hunter-cased quarter repeating keyless lever watch, 2″ diameter   1100.00

☐ **Minute repeating watch,** by Longines, 18k-gold hunter cased, silvered dial, black Arabic chapters, 2″ diameter 1700.00

☐ **Quarter repeating watch,** early 19th century, the cuvette inscribed "breguet No. 3033," c. 1830, 2″ diameter 1300.00

☐ **Minute repeating open-faced pocket watch,** by Cartier, nickeled movement, mat silvered dial signed Cartier, 1¾″ diameter 1700.00

☐ **Gold-cased quarter repeater,** early 19th century, 18k-gold-open faced verge watch, the back cover engine turned with a circular ray design, the case marked "Pts 1737/1360," 2⅛″ diameter 550.00

☐ **Gold-cased quarter repeating verge watch,** early 19th century, French, inside back cover stamped "2295 P&S," 2″ diameter 660.00

Top Left. Gold hunter-cased quarter repeater, by Invicta, 18k-gold hunter-cased quarter repeating keyless lever watch, 2″ diameter, $1100. *Right.* Minute repeating watch, by Longines, 18k-gold hunter cased, silvered dial, black Arabic chapters, 2″ diameter, $1700. (*Photo courtesy of Phillips, New York*) *Middle Left.* Quarter repeating watch, early 19th century, the cuvette inscribed "breguet No. 3033," c. 1830, 2″ diameter, $1300. *Right.* Minute repeating open-faced pocket watch, by Cartier, nickeled movement, mat silvered dial signed Cartier, 1¾″ diameter, $1700. (*Photo courtesy of Phillips, New York*) *Bottom Left.* Gold-cased quarter repeater, early 19th century, 18k-gold, open faced verge watch, the back cover engine turned with a circular ray design, the case marked "Pts 1737/1360," 2⅛″ diameter, $550. *Right.* Gold-cased quarter repeating verge watch, early 19th century, French, the inside back cover stamped "2295 P&S," 2″ diameter, $660. (*Photo courtesy of Phillips, New York*)

Wicker

DESCRIPTION: Wicker is the general term for pieces made of woven rattan, cane, dried grasses, willow, reed, or other pliable material.

HISTORY: Wicker can be dated to about 4000 B.C., when the Egyptians used it. Interest in wicker in the United States began in the 1850s. Cyrus Wakefield and the Heywood Brothers were the best-known wicker manufacturers. They later joined to become the Heywood–Wakefield Company. Other companies include the American Rattan Company and Paines Manufacturing Company.

COMMENTS: While nineteenth-century wicker is more valuable, pieces from the 1920s and 1930s are also very collectible and easier to find. Natural-finish wicker is most desirable, and less common pieces are the most sought after.

	Price Range	
☐ **Daybed,** painted, c. 1900, having a shaped woven skirt, on six capped feet, joined by stretchers, 72″ long	300.00	500.00
☐ **Gentleman's rocker,** c. 1890, rolled serpentine back enclosing a woven center panel surrounded		

Left to right. Natural wicker lady's reception chair, by Heywood–Wakefield, partial paper label, Model 6499a, $180. Natural wicker occasional table, 29″ high, 22″ wide, 18″ deep, estimated value $400–$500. Natural wicker "fancy" reception chairs (pair), one bearing partial paper label, $400. (*Photo courtesy of Phillips, New York*)

	Price Range	
by a floral border above a woven seat with a scrolled skirt, 42″ high	1400.00	1600.00
☐ **Natural wicker lady's reception chair,** by Heywood–Wakefield, partial paper label, Model 6499a		180.00
☐ **Natural wicker occasional table,** 29″ high, 22″ wide, 18″ deep, estimated value	400.00	500.00
☐ **Natural wicker "fancy" reception chairs,** pair, one bearing partial paper label		400.00
☐ **Lady's rocking chair,** painted, c. 1895, possibly Heywood–Wakefield, the open-work back		

Painted tall armchairs, by Heywood–Wakefield, Model No. 6213c, $1000. (*Photo courtesy of Phillips, New York*)

	Price Range	
with woven fan motif above a caned seat, 34 ½ ″ high	3600.00	4000.00
☐ **Painted tall armchairs,** by Heywood–Wakefield, Model No. 6213c		1000.00
☐ **Painted reception chairs,** pair, attributed to Heywood–Wakefield, estimated value	800.00	1200.00
☐ **Painted platform rocker**		325.00
☐ **Platform rocker,** painted, attributed to Ordway Co., c. 1890, latticework and basketweave backrest surrounded by scrolling decoration and flanked by continuous rolled arm rests, 48″ high ..	300.00	500.00
☐ **Platform rocker,** attributed to Ordway Co., c. 1890, shaped and		

Left. Painted reception chairs (pair), attributed to Heywood–Wakefield, estimated value $800–$1200. *Right.* Painted platform rocker, $325. (*Photo courtesy of Phillips, New York*)

	Price Range	
rolled frame encasing an openwork back with woven lyre motif, surmounted by a latticework headrest, 42″ high	300.00	400.00

THE 1980s—
COLLECTIBLES
FOR THE FUTURE

The 1980s— Collectibles for the Future

The majority of items listed in this section are still currently available at their original retail prices. In these instances, the majority of prices listed do not represent estimates but rather the latest price the item sells for on the primary market.

COMIC BOOKS

The comic book is one collectible that people never seem to grow tired of collecting. An integral part of America's pop culture, the comic book has been the subject of thousands of books and articles, has served as the inspiration for countless movies and toys, and each year hundreds of comic book conventions are held nationwide. The fun of collecting these colorful, often action-packed animations is frequently sweetened by the monetary value a great deal of comics now have. While most extremely valuable comics hail from 30 to

40 years ago, certain comics of the 1980s are already on their way up the ladder of full collectible status.

TYPES: Super-hero comics, including the extensive list produced by Marvel and DC comics, remain a staple among the more serious collectors. Other popular comic figures range from Disney's Mickey Mouse to Archie Andrews.

COMMENTS: One of the notable developments in collecting comics of the 1980s was the resurgence of Batman. The industry, experiencing something of a lull, was greatly revived by the four-part Batman series, published by DC, entitled *The Dark Knight.* Written and drawn by Frank Miller, the series, available in multiformat fashion, created desirability and headaches for the industry simultaneously. According to noted comic book expert Bob Overstreet, in his *Official Overstreet Comic Book Price Guide,* the series turned out to be the hottest of the decade. Published at first in a deluxe format, with the help of DC publicity the four single issues were soon in far more demand than their actual supply. Prices, according to Overstreet's guide, were up to $10 and more on the first-run issues almost immediately. When repackaged in a hard-bound edition, the books once again went for premium prices. A trade publication jointly released by DC and Warner Books and issued with two different covers went as rapidly. Indeed, Miller's ''Dark Knight'' is one of the greatest comic book success stories of the 1980s.

Another hot comic book was the newly revised *Superman.* Totally revamped, right down to the issue number, these comics became a desired item right out of the gate, as was anticipated by collectors. In fact, the series became one of DC's most popular titles, reports Overstreet.

The 1980s saw the return en masse of the small-scale publisher, whose black and white issues of first-run pressings now command high prices. The initial publication of the cult favorite, *Teenage Mutant Ninja Turtles,* by Eastman and Laird, can currently go for as much as $150, according to Overstreet. The First Comics Graphic Novel editions of such titles as *Time Beavers* can go for $6, and titles such as *Elric of Melnibone* now sell for $14.95.

	Price Range	

☐ *Batman: The Dark Knight Returns,* initially published in March 1986 by DC comics, Vol. 1, No. 1, in paperback, the Miller story and pencils sell for top dollars these days 4.15   25.00

☐ *Batman: The Dark Knight Returns,* hardcover, trade edition . 7.00   40.00

☐ *Batman: The Dark Knight Returns,* hardcover, signed limited edition of 4,000 copies, originally sold for $40 .... 40.00   400.00

☐ *The Life of Pope John Paul II,* published in January 1983 by the Marvel Comics Group .... .25   1.50

☐ *The Transformers,* published September 1984 by Marvel Comics Group based on the Hasbro toy, Vol. 1, No. 1, introducing the toy company heroes to the comic world 1.10   6.50

☐ *Uncle Scrooge Goes to Disneyland,* August 1985, reprint, Dell Giant with new cover art by Mel Crawford, published by Gladstone press .... .40   2.50

☐ *The Watchmen,* publication date, September 1986, 12-issue mid-series with Alan Moore scripts in all, No. 1 issue .... .40   3.00

GOLDEN GATE BRIDGE

It was the bridge many claimed could never be built—the majestic, arched bridge that has become San Francisco's trademark, such like the Statue of Liberty has become synonymous with New York City's port of entry. Construction began on the suspension bridge in 1933 and was completed in 1937. On May 27, 1987, the bridge celebrated its fiftieth anniversary. A gala celebration was held, and as a result, a rush of commemorative items was marketed before, during, and after the event. Many of these items are currently climbing in value.

TYPES: Banners, photographs, buttons, newspapers, and magazines.

COMMENTS: Although there are collectors of all sorts of landmark memorabilia, it is undoubtedly the commemorative items pertaining to anniversaries of the leading landmarks that will reap the largest profit in this field. Best bets on gathering a collection of such memorabilia would be to save travel souvenirs—maps with drawings or vintage photographs on them, brochures, etc.—as well as the purchased items that are clearly indicative of a certain historical spot such as Mt. Rushmore, the Lincoln Monument, and the Statue of Liberty.

	Price Range
☐ **Golden Gate Bridge cable,** manufactured in the mid-1980s by retired restaurateur Bob Smith, 3 lbs of authentic cable that was replaced beginning in 1973, painted orange, delivered to the purchaser with a wooden display stand and a certificate of authenticity; thousands were initially sold	12.95
☐ **Commemorative coin,** sterling silver, with the anniversary logo on front reading "50 Golden Years, 1937–1987," and "Light the Bridge, Live the Dream" on reverse	19.50
☐ **Ashtray,** rainbow painted over bridge, on a white background, with the skyline of San Francisco	2.25
☐ **T-shirts,** white, anniversary logo, by local district artist	8.50
☐ **Hooded sweat shirt,** gray and white, anniversary logo, by local district artists	21.99

MT. ST. HELENS

Natural disasters have always piqued people's curiosity, and therefore it comes as no surprise that memorabilia is of interest. (Witness the prices now associated with items recalling the San Francisco earthquake.) Into this category falls one of the most spectacular natural disasters of the past fifty years—the eruption of Mt. St. Helens, an 8,364-foot volcano in Washington state. Among the more interesting pieces of memorabilia created from that day (May 18, 1980) when the volcano erupted in full force are the ceramic creations of former professional ceramic teacher Marti Studhalter from Morton, Washington. "Marti's Ceramics" products consist of a literal treasure trove of ceramic, ashware, and porcelain artifacts, actually made with some of the volcanic ash the explosion left around the vicinity of the Studhalter's home. Marti's creations are becoming so popular that the artisan is adding complete new lines, with different deposits of ash she collected from all over the state included in her wares. With a new mountain road being built to replace the one that was destroyed, Marti's souvenir shop has become a tourist attraction in the seven-plus years since the eruption, with many people eagerly snatching up her unique pieces of the mountain. Once a mold is broken, these pieces can never be redone. And with the popularity of these artifacts, volcanic ceramics are indeed a true collectible from the 1980s.

TYPES: T-shirts, ceramics, hats, books, and general memorabilia on the mountain, particularly items manufactured *before* the eruption.

	Price Range	
☐ **Mt. St. Helens T-shirt,** several variations of design and quality ..	7.95	9.95
☐ ***Mount St. Helens: The Story Behind the Scenery,*** 1985, by Thom Corcoran, KC Publications, Inc., color soft-bound book, 48 pp		5.50
☐ **Adjustable Mt. St. Helens caps**	5.50	6.25
☐ **Stoneware-ashware coffee mugs,** pair, Marti Studhalter's ceramic creations		8.95
☐ **Porcelain-with-ash figurines,** approx. 3″ high, mold of "Little		

Price Range

Ash Babies," 1987, Marti Studhalter's ceramic creations 10.98

☐ **Porcelain-with-ash figurines,** approx. 5″ high, porcelain pig with little piglet peeping over its back, 1987, Marti Studhalter's ceramic creations 12.95

OLYMPICS

Collecting Olympic memorabilia has become a great international hobby. Olympic collecting in this country received quite a boost in America when the XXIII Olympics were held in Los Angeles, the first summer games to be held in the United States in more than half a century.

TYPES: Some of the more popular forms of Olympic memorabilia are the pins from various participating countries, particularly mascot pins from specific games. Materials printed originally for the spectator, such as programs, special passes, and ticket stubs, are highly prized. A limited-edition gold coin (the first to be produced in the United States in fifty years) commemorating the Los Angeles summer games is of considerable value to collectors already.

COMMENTS: Due to the U.S. 1980 boycott of the Moscow Olympics, very few items depicting the official mascot of the games, Misha the bear, found their way into this country. Therefore, these items are of considerable value. Limited-edition items, as in all fields of collecting, are of the most value.

Price Range

☐ **"Tribute" collector plate,** keystone of an eight-plate series produced by Rudy Escalera (selected by the L.A. Organizing Committee as Official Commemorative Plate Artist of the XXIII Olympiad), features a collage of athletes in action, highlighting a woman torch bearer 50.00

Price Range

☐ **Limited-edition poster,** 24″ x 34″, featuring a Robert Rauschenberg design using the 1984 Oylmpic Games official symbol, "The Stars in Motion," pictures a panorama of people, places, and events that reflect the contemporary world, produced by Knapp Communications Corporation, unsigned 30.00

☐ **Limited-edition poster,** same as the above but signed by Rauschenberg as part of a limited series of 750 .... 250.00

☐ **XXIII Olympiad $10 gold coin,** issued in 1984, the first gold coin issued by the United States Mint in fifty years, depicts male and female runners carrying the Olympic torch 353.00

☐ **Official gold and silver coins of the XXIV Olympiad,** Seoul, Korea, summer 1988, minted in .925 gold and .925 sterling silver, the low mintage of uncirculated coins available in the United States solely through the American Express Co. The first set was issued in the fall of 1987 (there will be four series in the complete set). Each series will consist of five coins: one ½-oz gold coin, two 1-oz silver coins, and two ½-oz silver coins. The fluctuating prices of gold and silver make these coins and the yet unminted sets highly desirable, as prices on these future series cannot even be established yet.

☐ **Uncirculated sets,** direct retail . 549.00

Price Range

☐ **Proof sets,** all five in each of these series encased in a clear acrylic case to protect the flawless finish; as with other series, they will come with a letter of authenticity 570.00

POLITICS

One of the more popular forms of collecting, presidential memorabilia receives a boost of publicity every four years due to the campaign and mass media. Political memorabilia from the 1980, 1984, and 1988 campaigns are already being scrutinized by the ever-growing legion of political collectors.

TYPES: Buttons generate the greatest interest in political memorabilia. Bumper stickers, autographs, and banners are all coming into their own.

COMMENTS: Memorabilia from the first Carter campaign (1976) remains far more commonplace than that of his uneventful 1980 campaign, when his popularity had waned greatly. By the same token, Reagan memorabilia from the 1980 campaign is much easier to obtain simply because, as in 1984, he was the overwhelming choice of the electorate and consequently a great amount of mass-produced items were circulated.

Price Range

☐ **"America Loves Reagan" pinback,** N. G. Slater Corp., New York, heart-shaped, shows Reagan, and carries the year 1984 twice, 2 3/4 " across with a red, white, and blue banner design ... 5.00

☐ **Anti-Mondale button,** "Fritzbusters," modeled after buttons made for the film *Ghostbusters,* which depicted a cartoon ghost-like figure with a void symbol superimposed on it; Mondale button

Price Range

has a cartoon of a ghost resembling Mondale on it and a similar void symbol over the Democrat ... 10.00

☐ **Jimmy Carter knife,** medium-size, white knife, depicts a donkey and reads "Carter 1980," Case Knife Company 30.00   40.00

☐ *Geraldine Ferraro: My Story,* book by Geraldine Ferraro with Linda Bird, published by Bantam Books, 1985, 340 pp 17.95

☐ **First Lady Nancy Teddy Bear,** produced by Wes Soderstrom, features a lifelike face of the First Lady, made of soft vinyl with furry body 49.50

ELVIS PRESLEY

During his celebrated lifetime (1935–1977), Elvis Aaron Presley was known as "The King of Rock 'n' Roll." His popularity has continued, even after his death, as evidenced by the wide assortment of memorabilia produced posthumously. In fact, the 1980s have proved to be a very big decade for Presley collectors: in 1985 the fiftieth anniversary celebration of his birth and in 1987 wide-scale observances of the tenth anniversary of his death. On both occasions a large assortment of commemorative items—some tasteful, most carnival-like—were produced. There are over ninety active Presley fan clubs in existence around the globe today. Most of these are geared toward original Presley fans, now in their early to mid-40s, a prime, expendable-income age bracket. Consequently, the value of Presley memorabilia can be expected to peak over the next five to ten years.

TYPES: RCA Victor released several promotional records during the 1980s that saw limited circulation. Limited-edition collector's items, including collector plates, statues, and watches, were among the assortment of articles produced in conjunction with those two anniversary dates.

Price Range

☐ **Elvis commemorative gold watch,** issued to mark Presley's 50th birthday by Bradley Time of New York in 1985, timepiece accentuated with a relief portrait of Elvis cast on gilt-finish "coin" set in 18k-gold case, available in either men's or ladies' models, produced in limited editions 1985.00

☐ **Elvis doll,** made by World Doll, Inc., of New York, all-porcelain figure, 17″ high, costumed in an "Aloha Hawaii" outfit studded with rhinestones, a diamond in the belt buckle, and scarf from Presley's personal wardrobe; only 750 numbered pieces produced, each with an authentic ticket from Elvis Presley's last concert 2500.00

☐ **10th anniversary jacket,** silver satin jacket with "10 Years Is Forever" printed on the front and an embroidered portrait of Elvis Presley (c. 1950s) emerging from the gates of Graceland 119.95

☐ **Commemorative plate,** shows Elvis on the front and words "Ten Years Is Forever" in gold, approx. 14,000 marketed through Graceland 12.95

☐ **Hat pin,** "Because We Care" written in gold on a black cloisonne pin, decorated with a red rose 3.99

☐ **Commemorative T-shirts,** black, number 10 in hot pink on the front, with black and white portrait of Presley within the 0, date printed on bottom, also marketed by Graceland 9.00

THE ROYAL FAMILY

There can be no doubt that Britain's Royal Family has held the attention of the world for the last decade. Not since the Duke of Windsor gave up his throne in the 1930s for the woman he loved has the ruling monarchy of England attracted as much attention as it has since the July 1981 wedding of Prince Charles (the heir apparent to the throne) and Lady Diana Spencer. Prince Charles and Lady Diana memorabilia include items dating from their courtship, wedding, and the birth of their children. (Headlines from London tabloids intent on revealing matrimonial turmoil in the six-year marriage are currently increasingly popular in 1987.) The newest line of Royal Family memorabilia is that pertaining to the wedding of Prince Andrew and Miss Sarah Ferguson, known affectionately worldwide as "Fergie." Their July 1986 wedding produced yet another line of royalty memorabilia. A member of the Wedgwood china group, Coalport, has issued six commemorative items to form the newest royal wedding collection. Some of the items include a round box, a classic beaker, and a table bell. The British Commonwealth also issued 12 and 17 denominations of postage stamps for the event, depicting the couple in an informal pose.

TYPES: Other memorabilia manufactured included teacups and saucers, royal wedding scrapbooks, limited-edition stamp sets, paper doll books.

COMMENTS: True Royal Family collectors often find it a timely and expensive hobby. More often than not it is regarded as an investment, since royalty memorabilia can be traced back as far as the Windsor family tree. Recent memorabilia can be found much more easily in Britain than in the United States, where items were not so easily marketed. Experts on the Royal Family tend to agree that the items of a humorous vein and the more elaborate British quality items will be the objects to look for in the future.

Price Range

☐ **Goblet,** issued by Franklin Mint in 1981, limited edition of 950, identifiable by the three-feathers symbol from the coat of arms of

Price Range

the Prince of Wales incorporated
into its stem 1950.00

☐ **Plate,** 10¾″ diameter, bone
china, commemorating the wedding of Prince Andrew and Miss
Sarah Ferguson, full-color portrait
of both with gold trim, made in
England, mint condition 25.00

☐ **Plate,** 10⅛″ diameter, bone
china, Royal Family Series, full-
color portrait of Queen Elizabeth,
Prince Charles, Lady Diana, with
their two children, Prince William and Prince Henry, made in
England, mint condition 30.00

☐ **Mug,** 3¾″ tall, 3¼″ diameter,
bone china, for the wedding of
Prince Andrew and Miss Sarah
Ferguson, color portraits of both
with inscription and gold trim,
made by Colclough, England,
mint condition 18.00

☐ **Mug,** 4⅜″ tall, for the wedding
of Prince Andrew and Miss Sarah
Ferguson, color portraits with
gold trim and inscription, mint
condition, made by F. R. Gray &
Sons, Staffordshire, England 18.00

☐ **Mug, plate, and bowl set,** to
commemorate the wedding of
HRH Prince Charles and Lady Diana Spencer, July 29, 1981. Each
of the three pieces has colored
center portraits of both with
heart-shaped ribbon surrounding
them together with lion/unicorn
motif and crown, blue trim, excellent condition, made by Mid-
winter–Staffordshire, England 45.00

SPORTS

The sports collecting field has often been considered third, only behind stamps and coins, as a popular form of collecting. The average number of sports collectors (the majority of whom were once considered to be male and in their early thirties) has expanded. Today's collectors hail from all strata of society and all age groups, and sports collecting is no longer predominantly a male-oriented field.

TYPES: Of all forms of sports memorabilia, there is no artifact as popular as the bubble gum card, although other forms of sports collectibles, such as tickets, game programs, and sports periodicals, show up in vast quantities at sports collectors' shows. The 1980s saw a whole new line of sports collectibles gain popularity—the porcelain limited-edition plate. These plates, autographed and portraying leading players, have become as desirable as the rare baseball card. Items pertaining to the baseball strike of 1985 or the NFL strike of 1987 are to be sought out. Cards and other memorabilia of specific celebrities and personalities such as Joe Montana, Doug Flutie, Pete Rose, or Larry Bird are also quite in demand.

	Price Range	
☐ **T-shirt,** "I Survived the 49 Day Baseball Strike," white with red letters, the words "49 Day" within a baseball	10.00	12.00
☐ **MacDonald's Falcons football cards,** issued by the fast-food franchise around Atlanta, GA, over a four-week period: blue tabs the first week, black (or gray) tabs the second week, gold (or orange) tabs the third week, and green the fourth week; approx. $3\,1/16''$ x $4\,11/16''$ with the tab intact, cards are numbered by units.		
☐ **Mint,** black		150.00
☐ **Good,** black		15.00
☐ **Topps football card,** 1984, Miami Dolphins No. 123, Dan		

<table>
<tr><td></td><td align="right">**Price Range**</td></tr>
</table>

Marino (one card out of the 396-card set that featured players of the NFL).

☐ **Mint**	2.50
☐ **Fair**	.25

☐ **Topps football card,** 1984, USFL series, New Jersey Generals No. 74, Herschel Walker (this 1984 set contained 132 cards, all in full color and all prepackaged in their own specially made box).

☐ **Mint**	4.00
☐ **Fair**	.40

☐ **Sportflics baseball card,** 1986, Don Mattingly.

☐ **Mint**	4.00
☐ **Fair**	.40

☐ **Sportflics baseball card,** 1986, Wade Boggs.

☐ **Mint**	2.50
☐ **Fair**	.25

The Sportsflics cards were produced as 200 cards that were marketed with small trivia cards. This initial set contained 139 single-player "magic motion" cards (which could be tilted to give the viewer three different views of the player) and 50 "Tri-Stars" cards, which gave the collector three players on one card.

<table>
<tr><td></td><td align="right">**Price Range**</td></tr>
</table>

☐ **Topps card,** 1987, Jose Canseco. The Topps card is similar to the 1962 series with its simulated wood grain border.

☐ **Mint**	2.00
☐ **Fair**	.25

☐ **Reggie Jackson collector plate,** 1982, art by Christopher Paluso, manufactured by Hackett American of Huntington Beach, CA,

Price Range

10,000 individually numbered plates were issued (Jackson autographed 464 plates for the special "Home Run" series, the first baseball player on a collector plate).

☐ **Signed** 100.00
☐ **Unsigned** 60.00

STATUE OF LIBERTY

The Statue of Liberty has become our nation's most powerful symbol, the lighted torch standing for freedom and opportunity for millions of immigrants in the early part of this century. Lady Liberty—originally called "Liberty Enlightening the World"—was the subject of a large-scale refurbishing for the two years leading up to her centennial. The centennial bash, held in July 1986, was a gala celebration in which dignitaries, movie stars, common folk, and various celebrities rallied around, with the president dedicating the relighting of the torch.

TYPES: Always a popular souvenir, models of the Statue of Liberty took on new dimensions during her centennial year, with a reproduction offered for every size wallet. One of those offered was made from the actual portions of cement and metal discarded during renovation.

COMMENTS: The Statue of Liberty is a universally recognized symbol. Collectibles produced in its image are sure to appreciate in value.

Price Range

☐ **Lithograph of Liberty centennial U.S. postage stamp,** red, blue, and metallic silver colors, 12′ x 18′, issued in edition of 5,000, International Stamp Art ...   250.00
☐ **Statue of Liberty model,** 15″ high, made of materials removed from the actual statue during renovations, marketed by Mader's

	Price Range	
Tower Gallery of Milwaukee during the centennial	139.50	
☐ **Statue of Liberty model,** 26″ high, cast of 30 lbs of solid American bronze, sculpted and signed by Bonita Thien Knickmeyer, produced in a limited edition of 5,000 by Liberty Bronze, Inc., of St. Louis.		
☐ **Brown**	595.00	
☐ **Green**	645.00	
☐ **Statue of Liberty flashlights,** Time Products, regular length with a green body, actual flashlight head resembles a torch (head section is clear, amber toned)	5.00	7.00
☐ **Harley Davidson limited-edition motorcycle,** special Liberty/Harley edition with the Liberty logo	9000.00	10,000.00
☐ **Sculpted reliefs,** Fine Art Ltd., Chesterfield, MO, cast in three different mediums, 15″ x 21″ with frame, one of 15 different reliefs representing 15 of the thousands of different ethnic groups that came to America via Ellis Island.		
☐ **Liberty relief,** upper torso cast in stainless steel	7000.00	
☐ **Liberty relief,** in bronze	4000.00	
☐ **Liberty relief,** in paper	800.00	

THE VOYAGER

The Voyager aircraft was a technological dream. Piloted by Dick Rutan and Jeana Yeager, it became the first aircraft to fly around the world without a refueling stop, taking off on December 14, 1986, and landing December 23, 1986. According to the authorized Voyager Fact Sheet, it took over two years and 22,000 man-hours to construct the craft. A selective amount of memorabilia was marketed for the trip, and due to the limited quantity, a great many of these items are extremely scarce. The Voyager Aircraft Co., Inc., manufactured or distributed items pertaining to the aircraft and the flight, novelty items (such as milkshakes) being of the more desirable collectibles.

	Price Range
☐ **Photo poster,** "Voyager over the Mojave Desert," 16″ x 20″	10.00
☐ **Postcards,** 3 styles, D.1., D.2., D.3, each	.35
☐ all three	1.00
☐ **Voyager patch,** round, 1987	5.00
☐ **Voyager patch,** blue border/yellow border, 1987	7.50
☐ **Cap,** adjustable, in navy blue with direct embroidery	12.00
☐ **Cap,** adjustable, with Voyager patch in navy blue	10.00
☐ **Visor,** 1987, light blue and white	10.00
☐ **Sweat shirt,** "Voyager" in navy blue	20.00
☐ **Shacklee "Voyager Shake"**	1.25
☐ **Shacklee "Voyager Soup"**	1.75
☐ **Button**	1.50
☐ **Limited-edition Voyager special covers,** single covers, signed, "flown around the world" marked in red on front cover	750.00
☐ **Limited-edition Voyager special covers,** signed, "flown around the world" marked in red on front cover, on special lightweight paper, sold as a set of two, includes a 16″ x 20″ photograph framed with a certificate of authenticity and material from aircraft	1250.00
☐ **Voyager covers,** signed, marked in indelible ink on front or back "NOT flown"	20.00

Credit Listings

We'd like to thank the following contributors for supplying information to this year's edition of *The Official Price Guide to Antiques and Collectibles.*

American Indian Artifacts (pp. 49–53), Frank H. Boos Gallery, Bloomfield, MI; Butterfield & Butterfield, San Francisco, CA; Phillips, New York, NY.

Animals (pp. 54–58), Marilyn Dipboye, president of the Cat Collectors' Club, Warren, MI; Richard W. Massiglia, National Elephant Collectors' Society, Boston, MA.

Animated Cels (pp. 59–64), Phillips, New York, NY.

Arcade Machines (pp. 65–66), Butterfield & Butterfield, San Francisco, CA.

Arms and Armor (pp. 67–73), Christie's East, New York, NY.

Art Deco (pp. 74–83), Tony Fusco, Director of Fusco & Four, Brighton, MA.

Art Graphics (pp. 84–100), Christie's East, New York, NY; Christie's, New York, NY; Phillips, New York, NY; Butterfield & Butterfield, San Francisco, CA.

Art Nouveau (pp. 101–107), Christie's East, New York, NY; Phillips, New York, NY.

Arts and Crafts (pp. 108–114), Bruce E. Johnson, *Craftsman Antiques,* Knock On Wood Publications, Durham, NC.

Autographs (pp. 115–127), Phillips, New York, NY.

Aviation Memorabilia (pp. 128–130), John William Aldrich, Pine Mtn. Lake Airport, Groveland, CA.

Banks (pp. 131–139), Richard Friz, author of *The Official Price Guide to Collectible Toys,* 4th ed., published by House of Collectibles, New York, NY.

Baskets (pp. 140–144), Frank H. Boos Gallery, Bloomfield, MI; Butterfield & Butterfield, San Francisco, CA.

Bells (pp. 145–146), Frank H. Boos Gallery, Bloomfield, MI; Phillips, New York, NY; Christie's East, New York, NY.

Belt Buckles (pp. 147–149), Phillips, New York, NY.

Books (pp. 154–161), Christie's East, New York, NY; Frank H. Boos Gallery, Bloomfield, MI; Phillips, New York, NY; Reverend Lewie Miller, Jr., Greenville, SC.

Bottles (pp. 162–170), Western World Publishing, publishers of *Avon-8;* Phillips, New York, NY.

Boxes (pp. 171–175), Frank H. Boos Gallery, Bloomfield, MI; Christie's East, New York, NY; Phillips, New York, NY.

Breweriana (pp. 176–177), Robert Jaeger, National Association of Breweriana Advertising, Wauwatosa, WI.

British Royalty (pp. 178–179), Daisy F. Banks, North Swansey, NH.

Cameras (pp. 180–184), Warren S. Patrick, Jamaica, VT.

Carousel Animals (pp. 185–192), Phillips, New York, NY.

Cartoon Art (Original) (pp. 204–208), Maggie Thompson, *Comic Buyer's Guide,* Krause Publications, Iola, WI; Phillips, New York, NY.

Cash Registers (pp. 209–211), Frank H. Boos Gallery, Bloomfield, MI; Butterfield & Butterfield, San Francisco, CA.

Circus Memorabilia (pp. 212–215), Christie's East, New

York, NY; Phillips, New York, NY; Richard Friz, author of *The Official Price Guide to Collectible Toys,* 4th ed., published by House of Collectibles, New York, NY.

Clocks (pp. 219–223), Christie's East, New York, NY; Phillips, New York, NY; Frank H. Boos Gallery, Bloomfield, MI.

Clothing (pp. 224–228), Christie's East, New York, NY.

Coins (pp. 233–257), Herbert Kwart, contributing editor, *Private Coin Collector* and *Currency Market Review,* Ridgecrest, CA.

Comic Books (pp. 258–260), Robert Overstreet, author of *The Official Overstreet Comic Book Price Guide,* 18th ed., published by *House of Collectibles,* New York, NY.

Credit Cards (pp. 261–263), Greg Tunks, Houston, TX.

Dairy Collectibles (pp. 264–268), Mary Brougham, M. T. Dairy Bottles, Manchester, ME.

Decoys (pp. 269–273), James D. Julia Auctions, Fairfield, ME.

Disneyana (pp. 274–278), Richard Friz, author of *The Official Price Guide to Collectible Toys,* 4th ed., published by House of Collectibles, New York, NY.

Dollhouses (pp. 279–287), Christie's East, New York, NY.

Dolls (pp. 288–298), Christie's East, New York, NY; Phillips, New York, NY; Butterfield & Butterfield, San Francisco, CA.

Eyeglasses (pp. 299–301), Stein's Antiques, Fayetteville, NC.

Firearms (pp. 302–309), Christie's East, New York, NY.

Fishing Tackle (pp. 310–313), National Fishing Lure Collectors' Club, Portage, MI.

Flasks (pp. 314–317), Christie's East, New York, NY; Frank H. Boos Gallery, Bloomfield, MI.

Furniture (pp. 324–338), Christie's East, New York, NY; Phillips, New York, NY; Frank H. Boos Gallery, Bloomfield, MI.

Glassware (pp. 339–354), Christie's East, New York, NY; Butterfield & Butterfield, San Francisco, CA.

Holiday Memorabilia (pp. 355–361), Phillips, New York, NY.

Inkwells and Inkstands (pp. 362–364), Vincent D. McGraw, Society of Inkwell Collectors, Minneapolis, MN.

Insulators (pp. 365–366), Carol MacDougall, Cleveland, OH.

Ivory (pp. 367–368), Frank H. Boos Gallery, Bloomfield, MI.

Jewelry (pp. 369–372), Frank H. Boos Gallery, Bloomfield, MI; Phillips, New York, NY; Arthur Guy Kaplan, author of *The Official Price Guide to Antique Jewelry,* 5th ed., published by House of Collectibles, New York, NY.

Kitchenware (pp. 373–377), Marilyn Kelley, Cleveland, TN.

Knives (pp. 378–381), James F. Parker, author of *The Official Price Guide to Collector Knives,* 9th ed., published by House of Collectibles, New York, NY.

Labels (pp. 382–391), David Cerebro, Cerebro Lithographs, Lancaster, PA.

Lamps and Lighting Fixtures (pp. 392–401), Christie's East, New York, NY; Phillips, New York, NY; Butterfield & Butterfield, San Francisco, CA.

Limited Editions (pp. 402–409), Christie's East, New York, NY; Frank H. Boos Gallery, Bloomfield, MI; Gene Ehlert, author of *The Official Price Guide to Collector Plates,* 5th ed., published by House of Collectibles, New York, NY.

Marbles (pp. 417–421), Marbles Collectors' Society of America, Trumbull, CT.

Metalware (pp. 429–444), Christie's East, New York, NY; Christie's, New York, NY; Frank H. Boos Gallery, Bloomfield, MI; Butterfield & Butterfield, San Francisco, CA.

Movie Collectibles (pp. 445–451), Collectors' Bookstore, Hollywood, CA; Jack B. Good Autographs, Ft. Lauderdale, FL.

Newspapers (pp. 452–458), Old Newspaper and Map Mail Auction, Bethesda, MD.

Ocean Liner Collectibles (pp. 459–465), Charles Ira Sachs, Oceanic Navigational Society, Universal City, CA; Ken Schultz, Hoboken NJ.

Oriental Collectibles (pp. 466–473), Phillips, New York, NY; Butterfield & Butterfield, San Francisco, CA; Frank H. Boos Gallery, Bloomfield, MI; Joan F. Van Patten, past president of the International Nippon Collectors' Club, Rexford, NY.

Paper Collectibles (pp. 474–478), Barry L. Neeb, Berlin, MD; Phillips, New York, NY.

Paper Money (pp. 483–498), Herbert Kwart, Contributing editor, *Private Coin Collector* and *Currency Market Review,* Ridgecrest, CA.

Paperweights (pp. 499–501), Frank H. Boos Gallery, Bloomfield, MI.

Pens and Pencils (pp. 502–507), Pen Fancier's Club, Dunedin, FL.

Photography (pp. 508–512), Phillips, New York, NY.

Pipes (pp. 513–519), Chuck Thompson, Houston, TX.

Political Memorabilia (pp. 520–526), Richard Friz, author of *The Official Price Guide to Political Memorabilia,* 1st ed., published by House of Collectibles, New York, NY.

Radios (pp. 537–540), Gary B. Schneider, North Royalton, OH; Christie's East, New York, NY; Phillips, New York, NY.

Railroad Memorabilia (pp. 541–546), Barry L. Neeb, Berlin, MD; Butterfield & Butterfield, San Francisco, CA.

Records (pp. 547–556), Jerry Osborne, author of *The Official Price Guide to Records,* 8th ed., published by House of Collectibles, New York, NY, with reference to Joel Whitburn's *Record Research.* (For further information, write Record Research, Inc., P.O. Box 200, Menomonee Falls, WI.)

Scouting Memorabilia (pp. 568–572), Richard E. Shields, Jr., president of *The Carolina Trader,* Charlotte, NC.

Scrimshaw (pp. 573–575), Phillips, New York, NY.

Scripophily (pp. 576–579), Buttonwood Galleries, Throggs Neck Station, NY.

Sewing Collectibles (pp. 580–583), Joyce Clement, author of *The Official Price Guide to Sewing Collectibles,* 1st ed., published by House of Collectibles, New York, NY.

Sports Collectibles (pp. 589–636), Phillips, New York, NY; Dr. James Beckett, author of *The Official Price Guide to Baseball Cards,* 8th ed., and *The Official Price Guide to Football Cards,* 7th ed., published by House of Collectibles, New York, NY.

Steins (pp. 637–639), Jack G. Lowenstein, Stein Collectors' International, Kingston, NJ.

Stoves (pp. 640–642), Clifford Boram, Midwest Antique Stoves, Inc., Monticello, IN.

Teddy Bears (pp. 643–645), Christie's East, New York, NY.

Telephones (pp. 646–648), Tom Vaugn, Antique Telephone Collectors' Association, Fairfield, TX.

Textiles (pp. 649–661), Christie's East, New York, NY; Frank H. Boos Gallery, Bloomfield, MI.

Toys and Games (pp. 662–672), Phillips, New York, NY; Richard Friz, author of *The Official Price Guide to Collectible Toys,* 4th ed., published by House of Collectibles, New York, NY.

Typewriters (pp. 673–675), Paul Lippman, Antique Typewriters, Hoboken, NJ.

Watches (pp. 676–686), Phillips, New York, NY.

The 1980s—Collectibles for the Future (pp. 693–709), Charles J. Jordan, author of *What to Save from the '80s,* published by Ballantine Books, New York, NY; *Comic Books* section, Robert Overstreet, author of *The Official Overstreet Comic Book Price Guide,* 18th ed., published by House of Collectibles, New York, NY.

Index

The HOUSE OF COLLECTIBLES Series

☐ Please send me the following price guides—
☐ I would like the most current edition of the books listed below.

THE OFFICIAL PRICE GUIDES TO:

☐ 199-3	**American Silver & Silver Plate** 5th Ed.	$11.95
☐ 513-1	**Antique Clocks** 3rd Ed.	10.95
☐ 283-3	**Antique & Modern Dolls** 3rd Ed.	10.95
☐ 287-6	**Antique & Modern Firearms** 6th Ed.	11.95
☐ 738-X	**Antiques & Collectibles** 8th Ed.	10.95
☐ 289-2	**Antique Jewelry** 5th Ed.	11.95
☐ 539-5	**Beer Cans & Collectibles** 4th Ed.	7.95
☐ 521-2	**Bottles Old & New** 10th Ed.	10.95
☐ 532-8	**Carnival Glass** 2nd Ed.	10.95
☐ 295-7	**Collectible Cameras** 2nd Ed.	10.95
☐ 548-4	**Collectibles of the '50s & '60s** 1st Ed.	9.95
☐ 740-1	**Collectible Toys** 4th Ed.	10.95
☐ 531-X	**Collector Cars** 7th Ed.	12.95
☐ 538-7	**Collector Handguns** 4th Ed.	14.95
☐ 748-7	**Collector Knives** 9th Ed.	12.95
☐ 361-9	**Collector Plates** 5th Ed.	11.95
☐ 296-5	**Collector Prints** 7th Ed.	12.95
☐ 001-6	**Depression Glass** 2nd Ed.	9.95
☐ 589-1	**Fine Art** 1st Ed.	19.95
☐ 311-2	**Glassware** 3rd Ed.	10.95
☐ 243-4	**Hummel Figurines & Plates** 6th Ed.	10.95
☐ 523-9	**Kitchen Collectibles** 2nd Ed.	10.95
☐ 291-4	**Military Collectibles** 5th Ed.	11.95
☐ 525-5	**Music Collectibles** 6th Ed.	11.95
☐ 313-9	**Old Books & Autographs** 7th Ed.	11.95
☐ 298-1	**Oriental Collectibles** 3rd Ed.	11.95
☐ 746-0	**Overstreet Comic Book** 17th Ed.	11.95
☐ 522-0	**Paperbacks & Magazines** 1st Ed.	10.95
☐ 297-3	**Paper Collectibles** 5th Ed.	10.95
☐ 744-4	**Political Memorabilia** 1st Ed.	10.95
☐ 529-8	**Pottery & Porcelain** 6th Ed.	11.95
☐ 524-7	**Radio, TV & Movie Memorabilia** 3rd Ed.	11.95
☐ 288-4	**Records** 7th Ed.	10.95
☐ 247-2	**Royal Doulton** 5th Ed.	11.95
☐ 280-9	**Science Fiction & Fantasy Collectibles** 2nd Ed.	10.95
☐ 747-9	**Sewing Collectibles** 1st Ed.	8.95
☐ 358-9	**Star Trek/Star Wars Collectibles** 2nd Ed.	8.95
☐ 086-5	**Watches** 8th Ed.	12.95
☐ 248-5	**Wicker** 3rd Ed.	10.95

THE OFFICIAL:

☐ 445-3	**Collector's Journal** 1st Ed.	4.95
☐ 549-2	**Directory to U.S. Flea Markets** 1st Ed.	4.95
☐ 365-1	**Encyclopedia of Antiques** 1st Ed.	9.95
☐ 369-4	**Guide to Buying and Selling Antiques** 1st Ed.	9.95
☐ 414-3	**Identification Guide to Early American Furniture** 1st Ed.	9.95
☐ 413-5	**Identification Guide to Glassware** 1st Ed.	9.95
☐ 448-8	**Identification Guide to Gunmarks** 2nd Ed.	9.95
☐ 412-7	**Identification Guide to Pottery & Porcelain** 1st Ed.	$9.95
☐ 415-1	**Identification Guide to Victorian Furniture** 1st Ed.	9.95

THE OFFICIAL (SMALL SIZE) PRICE GUIDES TO:

☐ 309-0	**Antiques & Flea Markets** 4th Ed.	4.95
☐ 269-8	**Antique Jewelry** 3rd Ed.	4.95
☐ 085-7	**Baseball Cards** 8th Ed.	4.95
☐ 647-2	**Bottles** 3rd Ed.	4.95
☐ 544-1	**Cars & Trucks** 3rd Ed.	5.95
☐ 519-0	**Collectible Americana** 2nd Ed.	4.95
☐ 294-9	**Collectible Records** 3rd Ed.	4.95
☐ 306-6	**Dolls** 4th Ed.	4.95
☐ 359-7	**Football Cards** 7th Ed.	4.95
☐ 540-9	**Glassware** 3rd Ed.	4.95
☐ 526-3	**Hummels** 4th Ed.	4.95
☐ 279-5	**Military Collectibles** 3rd Ed.	4.95
☐ 745-2	**Overstreet Comic Book Companion** 1st Ed.	4.95
☐ 278-7	**Pocket Knives** 3rd Ed.	4.95
☐ 527-1	**Scouting Collectibles** 4th Ed.	4.95
☐ 494-1	**Star Trek/Star Wars Collectibles** 3rd Ed.	3.95
☐ 307-4	**Toys** 4th Ed.	4.95

THE OFFICIAL BLACKBOOK PRICE GUIDES OF:

☐ 743-6	**U.S. Coins** 26th Ed.	3.95
☐ 742-8	**U.S. Paper Money** 20th Ed.	3.95
☐ 741-X	**U.S. Postage Stamps** 10th Ed.	3.95

THE OFFICIAL INVESTORS GUIDE TO BUYING & SELLING:

☐ 534-4	**Gold, Silver & Diamonds** 2nd Ed.	12.95
☐ 535-2	**Gold Coins** 2nd Ed.	12.95
☐ 536-0	**Silver Coins** 2nd Ed.	12.95
☐ 537-9	**Silver Dollars** 2nd Ed.	12.95

THE OFFICIAL NUMISMATIC GUIDE SERIES:

☐ 254-X	**The Official Guide to Detecting Counterfeit Money** 2nd Ed.	7.95
☐ 257-4	**The Official Guide to Mint Errors** 4th Ed.	7.95

SPECIAL INTEREST SERIES:

☐ 506-9	**From Hearth to Cookstove** 3rd Ed.	17.95
☐ 530-1	**Lucky Number Lottery Guide** 1st Ed.	4.95
☐ 504-2	**On Method Acting** 8th Printing	6.95

	TOTAL	

SEE REVERSE SIDE FOR ORDERING INSTRUCTIONS